MILLIONS FOR DEFENSE

MILLIONS
for
DEFENSE

The Subscription Warships of 1798

Frederick C. Leiner

NAVAL INSTITUTE PRESS
ANNAPOLIS, MARYLAND

Naval Institute Press
291 Wood Road
Annapolis, MD 21402

Library of Congress Cataloging-in-Publication Data
Leiner, Frederick C., 1958–
    Millions for defense : the subscription warships of 1798 / Frederick C. Leiner.
       p.   cm.
    Includes bibliographical references and index.
    ISBN 1-55750-508-X (alk. paper)
    1. United States. Navy—History—18th century. 2. Warships—United
States—History—18th century. 3. United States—History—1797–1801.
4. United States—History, Naval—18th century. I. Title.
VA56.L45 1999
359'.00973'09033—dc21   99-15206

Printed in the United States of America on acid-free paper ∞
06 05 04 03 02 01 00 99   9 8 7 6 5 4 3 2
First printing

Chapter 5 is based on an article by Frederick C. Leiner, "The Baltimore Merchants'
Warships: *Maryland* and *Patapsco* in the Quasi-War with France," *Maryland Histor-
ical Magazine* 88 (1993): 260–85. Used by permission of the Maryland Historical
Society.

Chapter 9 is based on an article by W. M. P. Dunne, "The South Carolina Frigate:
A History of the U.S. Ship *John Adams*," *American Neptune* 47 (1989): 22–32. Used
by permission of the Estate of W. M. P. Dunne and the Peabody Essex Museum of
Salem, Massachusetts.

Contents

Acknowledgments

In 1986, I wrote an article published in *The American Neptune* about the subscription warships. A few months later, I received a telephone call from W. M. P. Dunne, a maritime historian and sometime yacht designer who was a stranger to me. Although I soon discovered that Bill Dunne could be a tough critic, he liked the article. In the following year, Bill wrote an article about the subscription frigate *John Adams* (which forms the basis of chapter 9 in this book). Over the ensuing months and years, Bill and I exchanged calls, letters, and draft articles, and became friends. Bill had discovered American naval history in his fifties, and it became his passion. He loved uncovering information from the most arcane sources, and enjoyed boldly crafting his arguments. In 1994, we approached the Naval Institute Press to write a book about the subscription warships. We hardly had begun to organize our thoughts when Bill became sick, and he died before we wrote any new material. I decided to carry on with the book. I can only hope that Bill would have been proud of the final product.

I have been helped by a number of colleagues and friends. Christopher McKee, Rosenthal Professor of History and Librarian of Grinnell College, shared his research on a number of the naval officers mentioned in this book. Donald A. Petrie and Geoffrey Footner critically reviewed draft chapters and provided needed advice. The staffs of the National Archives; the Historical Society of Pennsylvania; the Peabody Essex Museum of Salem, Massachusetts; and the Enoch Pratt Free Library in Baltimore found books or photocopied critical papers, journals, logs, and prize case files. My secretary at Tydings & Rosenberg LLP, Valerie Dailey, typed almost every word of this book, and some passages she stoically typed two or three times. My parents, Robert W. Leiner and Mary Ann Leiner, have, as always, been a source of strength and support. I could not have written a word, of course, without the understanding of my wife, Jill, who bore the burden when I wandered off to research or write. My greatest critics may turn out to be my sons, Ben and Josh, who may pick up this book when they are old enough, but who, for now, just want to know why I am so interested in sailing ships.

MILLIONS FOR DEFENSE

Introduction

In the summer of 1798, the United States teetered toward open war with France, America's erstwhile revolutionary ally, egged on by the publication of humiliating demands for bribes by French diplomats labeled X, Y, and Z, and by galling seizures of merchant ships outside American harbors and in far-off seas. In the midst of the diplomatic crisis, private American citizens in Newburyport, Massachusetts, met to discuss what action they could take to help the country, and opened a subscription to fund a 20-gun warship for the United States Navy. Their example set off a reaction down the coast as each city learned of the Newburyport subscription, creating a navy frenzy in which ten port towns pledged subscriptions for, and actually began to build, warships, even though the United States had no secretary of the navy nor any fleet to speak of. This book is about the idea of subscribing for warships, the men who did so, and the ships they built.

What possible relevance does a shipbuilding program begun in 1798 by men in cockaded hats and silk stockings have to the postmodern world? How can ships built from live oak, with hemp rigging, pine masts, brass cannon, and canvas sails be anything more than antiquarian in a world of Stealth bombers, lasers, cellular phones, and the Internet? What makes those people, and what they did, of any concern?

There are several answers. First, the warships that the American ports rallied to build in 1798 were perhaps the epitome of how Federalist America saw itself and what was best of that age. A half-century after the subscription warships, John Ruskin was asked to provide a preface to a portfolio of J. M. W. Turner's maritime paintings. Ruskin wrote that future ages would look back and conclude that his century had done one thing, and only one thing, superbly, and that was "They Built Ships of the Line." Ruskin explained:

> Take it all in all a Ship of the Line is the most honorable thing that man, as a gregarious animal, has ever produced. By himself, unhelped, he can do better than ships of the line; he can make poems and pictures, and other such concentrations of what is best in him. But as a being living in flocks, and hammering out, with alternate strokes and mutual agreement . . . the ship of the line is his first work. Into it he has put as much of his human patience, common sense, forethought, experimental philosophy, self-control, habits of order and obedience, thoroughly wrought handi-work, defiance of brute elements, careless courage, careful patriotism and calm expectation of the judgment of God as can be put into a space 300 feet long by 80 broad. And I am grateful to have lived in an age when I could see the thing so done.[1]

The subscription warships were not ships of the line, the largest and most powerful battleships of that day; the United States was not to launch ships of the line until 1815. Otherwise, Ruskin's words ring true. The private American citizens who conceived of these ships put up the money, arranged for the designs, selected the timber and materials, laid the keels and planked up the hulls, selected the officers, and sent the ships off to war. Into each ship they put their experience, belief in their country, and their confidence in the future. The subscription warships were a compelling expression of that society's projection of itself, like the building of cathedrals in the Middle Ages or, perhaps, the funding of a city's orchestra today.

The subscription warships also are relevant for reasons of political economy. The balance struck by the then-new Constitution between the public sphere and the private does not envision private citizens building the nation's navy. As the democratic systems of the West now weigh "privatization"—use of or return to entrepreneurial activity to do public work—the 1798 "subscription ships" were built by concerned citizenry weighing the meaning of "citizen" in a republic that had won its freedom only a few years before. These men acted before there was any bureaucracy or governmental infrastructure to do public tasks. But the 1798 crash shipbuilding program is a microcosm of the timeless American debate of the balance between private and public tasks, about the nature of government and the nature of the citizen. While most of the subscribers were Federalists, and thus believed in a creed that leading citizens had a moral obligation to display civic virtue, the subscription ships program was not a particularly partisan activity. After Americans subscribed money for a half-dozen ships, the United States Congress enacted a statute, signed into law by President John Adams on 30 June 1798, that provided interest-bearing "stock" to the private subscribers, the first time the United States resorted to issuing what in this century are called "bonds" to build warships in a national emergency.

Yet, if accepted modern economic theory is correct, those patriots in wigs and breeches never should have built warships. Under the "public goods" hypothesis, government should provide goods—in this case, warships—when individuals acting privately cannot provide the appropriate level of expenditures and where it is impossible to "meter" the costs born by some against the benefits received by all. Warships, ironically, are the paradigm of "public goods." Each port that contributed a vessel—Newburyport, Salem, Boston, Providence, New York, Philadelphia, Baltimore, Charleston, and (together) Norfolk and Richmond—had little incentive to act first, and then an increasing disincentive to act because each had only a small fraction of the people, ships, and cargo affected by French maritime attacks. In addition, once completed and handed over to the federal government to prosecute the Quasi-War against the French navy and privateers, the benefits from a given city's ship would not accrue to that city alone but to America generally. Despite modern economic theory, Americans voluntarily contributed warships for the national good, highly suggestive of an earlier concept of citizenship.

While political theory and economic incentives are a part of the story of subscription warships, it is mostly a story of now-forgotten ships and barely remembered Americans. The subscribers largely consisted of merchant-capitalists in the booming port towns along the Atlantic coast. The Appendix provides the known subscription lists. Yet in the discussions of each ship, profiles of some of these men suggest that they were not all of a predictable stamp. To be sure, the old merchant families of

Boston, New York, and Philadelphia dominated the subscription lists. Suggestive of how the United States was to develop, however, Thomas FitzSimons, an Irish immigrant and Catholic, led the Philadelphia subscription committee, and Moses Myers, a Jewish merchant, contributed one of his ships as the Norfolk and Richmond subscription warship.

The stories of the individual ships go far beyond the typical naval history. While the frigate *Boston* fought a knockdown, scrambling fight against a French corvette, *Le Berceau,* the *Boston* also serves as a potent example of the risks of the maritime prize "game." The building of the frigate *Philadelphia* reveals simultaneously both the hesitation toward and the ultimate embrace of advances in naval architecture wrought by Joshua Humphreys. The *Essex,* built by popular subscription in Salem, sailed around the Cape of Good Hope into the Indian Ocean to protect America's budding trade with Java, demonstrating a strategic vision of American destiny. Some ships, such as the little-known *New York,* reflect shabby mismanagement; while others reflect politics, preference, and greed. The subscription warships, then, are a story of patriotism, of "hammering out," of politics and greed and entrepreneurial spirit. In touching on all of these topics, this book attempts to show another aspect of the early republic, and that what began as a small vignette of Federalist America in the summer of 1798 reverberates down to the America of today.

neutrality in the French Revolutionary Wars despite American gratitude for France's decisive intervention in America's own revolution, and despite popular support for the fraternal republic casting off the yoke of its monarchy. Neutrality allowed American merchant ships to trade with all the belligerents. With the largest neutral carrying trade and with huge crops of grain for export, profits were staggering. So too were losses, because Britain with its powerful navy could not accept the principle of "free ships, free goods" while fighting for her existence against the French Revolutionary juggernaut. In 1795, Washington needed all his moral standing to persuade a polarized Senate to ratify the Jay Treaty, which ameliorated some of the diplomatic, territorial, and trade issues festering between the former colonies and the mother country. British warships still brazenly stopped American merchant ships on the high seas, looking for contraband and impressing seamen into their warships. Some of the seamen British Royal Navy officers removed were Americans by birth, some were Americans by naturalization (a concept Britain rejected), and most held certificates of their American nationality, called "protections," issued by collectors of customs in American ports to seafarers. Yet the British high-handedness was nothing new, and sometimes could be averted or reversed by appeals or diplomatic remonstrances. But the Jay Treaty allowed France to vent its displeasure, or to have a pretext to argue, that America preferred England over France. A French decree—promulgated in July 1796 but first made known to the United States when the French minister, Pierre Adet, published it in the Philadelphia newspapers on 31 October 1796—established that France would treat neutral shipping as to searches and capture as the neutrals allowed their ships to be treated by England. No American understood quite what the decree meant as a matter of construction. As a matter of practice, however, France had declared open season on America's carrying trade to Europe, the Mediterranean, and the West Indies. Backed by the decree's authority, French privateers, private armed ships licensed with letters of marque, swarmed out of French colonial ports to plunder American trade. Even Jefferson, averse to military force and Francophile as he was, admitted that "the French have behaved atrociously towards neutral nations, and us particularly; and though we might not be disposed to charge them with all the enormities committed in their name in the West Indies, yet they are to be blamed for not doing more to prevent them."[6]

America's international presence was only through its merchant ships flying the Stars and Stripes because the United States had no navy whatsoever. The last ship of the Continental navy of the Revolution, the frigate *Alliance*, had been sold in 1785, a victim of a Congress that, under the Articles of Confederation, lacked both the money to provide for essential services and the wherewithal to get more, since it had no power to lay taxes and depended on the states for contributions. James Madison observed in Federalist Paper No. 41 that "[t]he palpable necessity of the power to provide and maintain a navy has protected that part of the Constitution against a spirit of censure which has spared few other parts." While Madison acknowledged that a navy had utility as "batteries most capable of repelling foreign enterprises," what he liked mainly was that a navy was not a standing army, i.e., it "can never be turned by a perfidious government against our liberties."[7]

Alexander Hamilton in Federalist Paper No. 11 recognized both the strategic necessity of a navy and what Federalists regarded as the wholesome symbiotic relationship between maritime commerce and the navy. "[F]or influencing the conduct of European nations towards us," Hamilton wrote, the establishment of a federal navy would be a central concern of government under the new Constitution. While a navy need "not vie with those of the great maritime powers," it should be of "respectable weight if thrown into the scale" of the warring European nations, particularly for operations in the West Indies. Hamilton warned that without the Union, there would be no navy, and without a navy "our commerce would be a prey to the wanton intermeddlings of all nations at war with each other, who having nothing to fear from us, would with little scruple or remorse supply their wants by depredations on our property as often as it fell in their way. The rights of neutrality will only be respected when they are defended by an adequate power. A nation, despicable by its weakness, forfeits even the privilege of being neutral." The federal union could produce a navy, and Hamilton predicted that each institution of the country would flourish in direct proportion to its support of naval force. "To this great national object, a NAVY," the Southern states would furnish durable timber and naval stores, the mid-Atlantic states would supply the ironwork, and the New England states would produce the seamen. Simply put, maritime trade needed a navy, and the nation could build one.[8]

Yet when the new government was established in 1789, it had no money for a navy and more pressing tasks at hand than to even consider starting to construct ships. In 1793, however, Portugal switched sides in the French Revolutionary Wars and removed its warships from the Straits of Gibraltar. Out flowed Algerine pirate ships into the Atlantic like wine uncorked from a bottle. The rapacious corsairs found American merchant shipping easy pickings. They seized Yankee ships and property and consigned American seamen to dungeons or slave labor. Toward the end of 1793, President Washington recommended to Congress the propriety of a naval force; on 27 March 1794, he signed into law a statute authorizing six frigates, large three-masted cruisers rated to carry thirty-six or forty-four cannon on their broadsides. In 1796, however, all work on the six frigates stopped when word reached Philadelphia that Algiers had agreed to release the American hostages in exchange for ransom and a "gift" of an American-built 32-gun frigate. The 1794 statute provided that construction should stop with peace. Washington, however, urged Congress to authorize all six frigates to be finished. After tumultuous debate, Congress agreed that the three frigates most advanced on the building ways— the *United States,* a 44-gun frigate, in Philadelphia; the *Constitution,* also a 44, in Boston; and the *Constellation,* a 36, in Baltimore—could be completed, and President Washington signed that law on 20 April 1796.[9]

Without a navy, America had to buy peace with the Algerines and, as Hamilton foresaw, America's commerce was "prey to the wanton intermeddlings of all nations at war with each other," namely Britain and France. Upon his inauguration as president in March 1797, John Adams justly viewed the foreign relations of the United States as his greatest concern. In 1797, Adams was sixty-one years old, a short, fat, balding man, sensitive to slights, temperamental, and unsocial. A central figure from the Revolution and the first vice president, Adams was a man of wide learning, great rectitude, and absolute integrity. In the Revolution, none stood more defiant of Britain or more zealous for independence. His economic ideas were conventional for the times, with the usual fear of public debt, but Adams was an economic nationalist and generally supported the merchants' entrepreneurialism. As president, Adams had no loyal coterie in Congress. He disdained parties as factions, relying on the patriots of 1776 and on men of independence and property to vote for the good of the nation. While filled with moral courage and guided by principle, he was also irritable, opinionated, defiantly proud of his independence, and always concerned with duty. He liked England but disliked the English; he distrusted France; and, although a man of great passions, his only permanent attachments extended to his family and to the United States. Benjamin Franklin's famous deflation of him, that Adams "means well for his Country, is always an honest Man, often a wise one, but sometimes, and in some things, absolutely out of his senses," was tinctured by the back-stabbing between the two men as diplomats in Paris during the Revolution. Late in his life, Jefferson confided to Madison that, whatever the political differences that divided him from his old friend, "[t]his . . . I will say for Mr. Adams, that he supported the Declaration [of Independence] with zeal and ability, fighting fearlessly for every word of it."[10]

Even before his first day as president, a foreign crisis shadowed Adams's administration. As a sign of its displeasure with the United States, France refused to receive the special American envoy, Charles Cotesworth Pinckney, whom President Washington had sent to try to repair relations. The French authorities vaguely threatened that, not having accepted his credentials, they might find Pinckney subject to arrest. Pinckney withdrew to Amsterdam to await instructions from the new president. Pierre Adet, the French minister in Philadelphia, had the audacity to write public letters urging Americans to elect the perceived Francophile, Jefferson, and vaguely suggested that, if Adams and the Federalists won, there would be war. Immediately after the 1796 election, Adet announced to Secretary of State Timothy Pickering that he, Adet, had been recalled to France without a replacement. Worse yet, a new French decree annulled the principle of "free ships, free goods" enunciated in America's treaty of alliance with France in 1778 and, instead, officially allowed French ships to seize as contraband British goods found on neutral vessels. Only those vessels carrying a *role d'equipage* (a roster of passengers and cargo) in a form approved by France were immune from seizure and condemnation as prizes. In all but name, France had declared a maritime war on the United States. American newspapers contained accounts, day after day, of American merchant vessels seized and plundered by French privateers, or taken into ports to be condemned by local French tribunals, particularly in the West Indies. Sometimes, the privateering descended into piracy, with looting and murder, and Americans noted with alarm that the French government did nothing to curb these aggressions. Writing to his son, John Quincy Adams, the new president observed,

> My entrance into office is marked by a misunderstanding with France, which I shall endeavor to reconcile, provided that no violation of faith, no stain upon honor, is exacted. But if infidelity, dishonor, or too much humiliation is demanded, France shall do as she pleases, and take her own course. America is not SCARED.[11]

In Adams, the United States had a new president who called the navy his "hobby-horse," unlike the Republicans who depreciated all military force, and unlike Federalists like Hamilton who preferred the army as a vehicle of social cohesion. Yet Adams's understanding of his role as chief executive did not include a role as a political whip; he had little personal following in Congress, his cabinet secretaries were all Washington administration holdovers and mostly second rate, and he abjured the very notion of party. When it became clear in early 1797 that Adams was elected over him, Jefferson wrote to Madison that "I do not believe Mr. Adams wishes war with France; nor do I believe he will truckle to England as servilely as has been done." But what Jefferson and Madison could not fathom was why, if Adams wished to avoid war, he pressed Congress to build up a navy.[12]

Adams urged Congress to finish the frigates authorized in 1794, to build sloops of war (three-masted ships with lighter and fewer cannon than frigates) to provide convoys for unarmed merchantmen, to reorganize the militia, to build seacoast fortifications, and to allow merchant vessels to carry cannon to protect themselves from illegal attacks. After a trying, roiling debate, Congress approved an Act Providing a Naval Armament on 1 July 1797. That act funded the equipping and manning of the *Constitution, United States,* and *Constellation,* and provided some money for harbor forts, but nothing more. The House decisively voted down building more warships or allowing merchant vessels trading to the Caribbean to arm, despite Secretary of State Pickering's report that over the previous eleven months, French privateers had captured three hundred American vessels.[13]

Yet Adams, no less than the Republicans, wanted peace. From the first day of his presidency, he resolved on making an overture to France, although he feared the humiliation of having another diplomatic mission turned away. General Pinckney, the solid, patrician South Carolinian forced to retreat to Amsterdam, was a Federalist but not extreme in his views, indeed known to be sympathetic to the French Revolution; the dignity of the United States required him to be part of the mission. Adams wanted a prominent Republican to go also, sounding out both Vice President Jefferson and James Madison, both of whom declined. Adams settled on an old friend, Elbridge Gerry of Massachusetts. Gerry, a member of the Continental Congress in 1776 and a delegate to the Constitutional Convention, was a slight, quirky, unpredictable man, so theoretical in his republicanism that he refused to support any peacetime army or even taxes to pay for government; and he had quit Congress in 1793 when he thought it had become too factional. Gerry was wary of federal power and fearful that a failure to appease France would plunge the United States into war. The third member of the American team of envoys, selected after Patrick Henry declined because of health, was a forty-three-year-old Richmond lawyer named John Marshall. Born on the Virginia frontier, Marshall, along with his father and brothers, had left their farm at the start of the Revolutionary War to fight the British. Like many Revolutionary War veterans—Marshall was an officer in Daniel Morgan's light infantry, suffered through the winters at Valley Forge, and came to Washington's notice—Marshall became a staunch nationalist and was a rising Federalist leader in the South. Tall, athletic, loose-jointed, Marshall was sociable and easy in his manner, fond of spirits and quoits. His only real enemy was his cousin, Jefferson. Adams described Marshall to Gerry as "a plain man, very sensible, cautious, guarded, and learned in the law of nations." The three American envoys did not know each other but President Adams believed that "manoeuvres practised to excite jealousies among you . . . should press you closer together." Adams hoped that "an accomodation may take place; but our national faith, and the honor of our government, cannot be sacrificed." He warned his friend Gerry that "[y]ou will be surrounded with projectors and swindlers. You will not be deceived by them."[14]

The instructions to the envoys were reasonable and accommodating. The Americans were going to Paris to reestablish rapport, and they were neither to blame France for the threats and attacks on trade nor to acknowledge that their own government was in any way at fault. While the Americans were to press for compensation for damages to American shipping, they were given leeway as to terms and timing and, ultimately, could abandon reparations if a treaty could not be made including compensation. The envoys were enjoined not to agree to restrict American trade, and not to vitiate the Jay Treaty, but were to work out the precise ship papers that the French privateers would respect. The Adams administration even allowed them to abandon the "free ships, free goods" principle to get a treaty. Last, they could not commit the United States to making any loans to France.[15]

The three American diplomats—Pinckney, Gerry, and Marshall—gathered in Amsterdam in September and traveled to Paris at the end of the month. Thereafter, there was no news in the United States about the progress of the negotiations. Week after week passed without word, and with the question of peace or war seemingly held in the balance, American political leaders grew nervous. Four successive letters from Jefferson to Madison demonstrate the fixation on the silence from Paris. On 25 January 1798, Jefferson wrote that "[e]ither the Envoys have not written to the government, or their communications are hushed up. This last is suspected, because so many [ship] arrivals have happened from Bordeaux and Havre. . . . I am entirely suspended as to what is expected." Two weeks later, on 8 February 1798, the vice president wrote that "we hear nothing. Yet it seems reasonably believed that the executive has heard, and that it is something which would not promote their views of arming." Another week went by without news, and on 15 February 1798, Jefferson noted that "[w]e have still not a word from our Envoys. This long silence (if they have been silent) proves things are not going on very roughly." A fourth letter in this series came a week later. "We still hear nothing from our Envoys," Jefferson reported. "Whether the executive hear, we know not. But if war were to be apprehended, it is impossible our Envoys should not find means of putting us on our guard . . . No news, therefore, is good news."[16]

On 4 March 1798, Secretary of State Pickering received a bundle of letters from the three envoys, all encoded. The next morning, President Adams sent to Congress the last of the letters, dated 8 January 1798, which made clear that the French government had not officially received Pinckney, Gerry, and Marshall, and that their mission was an utter failure. Adams again asked Congress to ready the nation for war. Two weeks later, the president, having read privately the dispatches and knowing what had happened in Paris, reiterated the need to provide a naval defense and to lift the prohibition against allowing merchant ships to arm. Jefferson, still convinced of French goodwill, thought the president's message "insane." The message created what he called "[e]xultation" among the Republicans, who gleefully foresaw Adams's defense program being voted down.[17]

Thinking that Adams was bluffing, the Republicans forced a vote to lay the actual letters from the envoys, along with the instructions to them, before Congress. Rarely has so partisan a measure backfired so completely. On 3 April 1798, the president sent the whole mass of documents to Congress, obscuring only the actual names of certain French intermediaries, "projectors and swindlers" acting for Charles-Maurice de Talleyrand-Périgord, the French foreign minister, with the code letters, X, Y, and Z. The documents told a sordid story.

In October 1797, the three American diplomats first met Talleyrand's agents, Jean Hottinger and Pierre Bellamy, to discuss peace terms. The French go-betweens proposed that the United States government assume its citizens' private claims against France; that the United States provide a huge loan to France on favorable terms; that the envoys disavow or apologize for President Adams's speech to a joint session of Congress on 16 May 1797 in which the president had denounced French efforts to divide the American people from their government, "attempts [which] ought to be repelled with a decision which shall convince France and the world that we are not a degraded people," and had suggested building warships as a precaution against French aggression; and that the envoys pay £50,000 as a douceur to Talleyrand personally. Baron d'Osmond, Talleyrand's secretary, told the Americans that, to be received officially by the French Directory, they would have to provide an explanation (i.e., an apology) for Adams's "offensive" speech. The envoys refused this request as an insult to both the president and their country; the speech need not be explained. Talleyrand sent his toadies back to sound out the American envoys individually. They chose to approach Pinckney on 18 October 1797. Hottinger, later called "X" by Adams, told Pinckney that an accommodation with France would depend on a loan of 32 million Dutch florins (over £1 million), as well as a *pot-de-vin* for his minister. Pinckney, a proper, upstanding gentleman imbued with the civic virtue characteristic of Federalists, scarcely could believe his ears. He asked Hottinger to repeat the terms to Marshall and Gerry, who immediately refused to consider them. The next day, Bellamy ("Y") and Lucien Hauteval ("Z") pressed the Americans, and again they were refused. For his part, Talleyrand, an able diplomat with few principles except his own advancement, could not believe the naive Americans, even though Talleyrand had spent two years in the United States in the 1790s as an émigré from the Reign of Terror and had met many of the leading American politicians. European diplomats had passed douceurs to him before; it was the currency of diplomatic business in Paris. A week later, Hottinger and Bellamy began hectoring the envoys for money. They mixed their demands for bribes with threats. Bellamy told Gerry that they should "consider whether by so small a sacrifice [a loan] they would establish a peace with France, or whether they would risk the consequences; that if nothing could be done by the envoys, arrangements could be made forthwith to ravage the coasts of the United States by frigates from Santo Domingo; that small States which had offended France were suffering by it. . .; and that the present period was the most favorable, if we wished to adopt any measures for pacification." And X, Y, and Z became adamant about bribe money. Finally, Pinckney, apoplectic with anger and disgust, exclaimed

"No, no, not a sixpence," an outburst later transmogrified into the toast, "Millions for defense but not a penny for tribute." Although the envoys lingered a few months to see if France's position would change, it did not. Bellamy continued to malign them, even suggesting that if they returned to America to expose the unreasonableness of the French demands, they would not be believed, and France would work with her friends in America to blame them for the rupture. Marshall and Pinckney packed their bags and sailed for home in April and May 1798 while Gerry, still desperate to save the peace, stayed in Paris until ordered home by Secretary of State Pickering.[18]

The publication of the dispatches from Paris caused an explosion of indignation among the American people. Abigail Adams wrote to her son, John Quincy Adams, that the effects of publication have "made the blind to see and the deaf to hear. It has been like an Electrical Shock . . ." Before their publication, public meetings had sent petitions to Congress not to take any active measures against France. With the publication of the XYZ documents—and the Federalists in Congress made sure that ten thousand copies were printed for distribution throughout the Union—Americans saw that President Adams had tried for an honorable peace but that his efforts had been rebuffed. For the one time in his four-year term, Adams became a popular hero. Throughout the country, people gathered, decried the French cupidity, and rallied to the administration, sending in long addresses of support to the president. Adams wrote them all back—Dartmouth, Williams, Harvard, Dickinson, and Princeton students; the citizens of towns throughout the Union, from Boston to Richmond and as far west as Cincinnati; grand juries; state legislatures; militia units; even the Agricultural Society of Beaver Creek & Hanging Rock of Kershaw County, South Carolina. Federalist gentlemen took to wearing black cockades in their hats, to distinguish themselves from Republicans sporting the red, white, and blue of the French tricolor. Riots broke out between black-cockaded and tricolor-cockaded youths and, in President Adams's words, "even Governor Mifflin himself thought it his duty to order a patrol of horse and foot to preserve the peace." Philadelphia had been a hotbed of pro-French feeling and on one frenzied day, "Market Street was as full as men could stand by one another," threatening the president's safety "when I, myself, judged it prudent and necessary to order chests of arms from the war-office to be brought through by-lanes and back-doors, determined to defend my house at the expense of my life . . ." But the American people did rally to Adams. He began to be cheered in public. Mrs. Adams saw a marked change when the president attended the theatre, which, she observed, "has been call'd the pulse of the people, if so the pulse of ours precedes *a fever.* It has been customary to play and sing French songs and Airs; Çi era ['Ça ira'] and other songs have been countenanced at all the Theatres untill since the Dispatches from France have been made publick. The first attempt afterwards was hist and the [P]residents March called for. The musicians not regarding the case, were driven off." A new song, "Adams and Liberty" was greeted so warmly that "the last time of singing it (for it was four times encord) the whole Audience rose and joined in the chorus . . ."[19]

In the space of only a few days, the temper of the people had changed from vacillation and the desire for peace to determination and a super-charged patriotism. On 8 April 1798, Representative Samuel Sewall, a Federalist from Marblehead, Massachusetts, reintroduced Adams's defense program. Over the next few months, the administration pushed for a pro-visional army in case of French invasion, arming the merchant ships, fin-ishing the 1794 frigates, harbor fortifications, suspending the 1778 treaty of alliance with France, organizing the United States Marine Corps, and creating a Department of the Navy. Few of these measures passed Con-gress by large majorities. And Congress was slow in approving laws that readied the nation for war. On 27 April 1798, Congress passed a law allow-ing the president to buy or rent twelve merchant vessels and convert them into warships. On 4 May 1798, Congress authorized the president to spend $800,000 for cannon, small arms, and ammunition, and another $100,000 to buy or lease foundries for casting cannon. Mrs. Adams, despite her euphoria over the tone of the people, despaired at the Repub-lican Congressional "opposition with Gallatin at their Head go on striv-ing to obstruct every energitic measure and there will be some timid geniuses who fear everything . . ."[20]

In forming an army, a measure that Adams faced reluctantly— "whenever I must come to that extremity"—he turned to George Wash-ington for advice and as a potent symbol of national unity. In the sum-mer of 1798, the French army appeared capable of any exercise: their commanders were gamblers, ready to play high stakes. That very spring, Napoleon Bonaparte led a large army on hundreds of transport ships onto the shores of Egypt. Only eighteen months before, French generals Lazare Hoche and Emmanuel de Grouchy had embarked twenty thou-sand troops at Brest to invade Ireland at the time of the Irish rebellion. And the French had sizable troops in their colonies in the West Indies.

There were fears of a French landing somewhere in the South, perhaps tied into a slave insurrection. The possibility of invasion was discussed openly. Henry Knox, a Revolutionary War general and the former secretary of war, warned of ten thousand black troops under French command landing in the South. In an article reprinted in a New York newspaper, a correspondent wrote, "The fear of actual invasion is treated by some as a bugbear; by others as a thing to be expected. A few frigates, and a few thousand soldiers, chiefly negroes, may possibly come from Guadaloupe, to hoist the standard of liberty, and to raise the blacks in Carolina. . . ." To add to the concerns about French invasion and slave revolt, there was the example before all of them of the bloody and successful slave insurrection in Saint-Domingue and the charismatic Toussaint L'Overture leading a black republic. In a few months, fears of actual invasion would seem chimerical—but that was after Horatio Nelson smashed the French fleet at the battle of the Nile on 1 August 1798. By that time, as Adams wrote at the end of October 1798, "there is no more prospect of seeing a French army here, than there is in Heaven." But anything and everything seemed possible in the war crisis of the spring and summer of 1798. To pay the great costs of forming regiments and equipping an army, the Adams administration was forced to lay new taxes on houses and slaves. To repress domestic dissent and to provide a united front to the world, the Federalists in Congress pushed through alien and sedition laws that later would undermine the popular enthusiasm that Adams's unblemished patriotism had wrought.[21]

At the beginning of the crisis in the spring of 1798, however, the popular support for strong measures of defense outpaced the government in Philadelphia. The leading citizens in towns across America formed committees of safety, and collected arms. At the ports, gun batteries were sited to protect the harbors, and plans were drawn up to build forts to withstand French raiders. Old militia companies were mustered, drilled, and paraded, and newspapers in every city screamed out advertisements for volunteers to join newly named units under local commanders. The desire to defend the country bubbled up everywhere, North and South, and among all classes, including the merchants.

2 "A Navy Spring Up Like the Gourd of Jonah"

While the militia was turning out, the merchants of Newburyport, Massachusetts, having lost dozens of vessels to French privateers,[1] decided that they themselves would build a warship for the federal navy. Precisely whose idea it was is unknown. But leading Newburyport merchants met on 23 May 1798, and they resolved to open a subscription to build a 20-gun warship in ninety days to be loaned to the United States. Two days later, the local paper reported the news without fanfare, in two sentences in the local news column.[2]

Within a week, a committee was appointed to direct the project, the details were set, and, almost as an afterthought, the local congressman was contacted. The Newburyport committee numbered nine men, all of whom were merchant-capitalists, and all of whom were Federalists. The committee consisted of William Bartlet, William Coombs, Dudley A. Tyng, Moses Brown, William P. Johnson, Nicholas Johnson, William Farris, Ebenezer Stocker, and Samuel A. Otis, Jr. All ranked among Newburyport's wealthiest citizens. Several had sailed in or held shares in privateers during the Revolution, so the idea of privately built and privately armed vessels was not alien to their thinking. Moreover, in an era of strictly limited government, these very men had cooperated before on local "public" projects; they organized the Merrimack Bank in 1795, the Newburyport Woolen Manufactory in 1793, the Newburyport Turnpike, and the Merrimack River bridge.[3] It is true that these other ventures were for profit, and warships donated to the navy were not like privateers, since the subscribers would not get any return from prizes taken by a public ship. But the Newburyport merchants had an answer to that.

On 1 June 1798, the Newburyport committee wrote their congressman, Bailey Bartlett.[4] They announced their project to build a 355-ton ship, armed with 20 six-pounder cannon, in ninety days. For this they would "not accept of any further or other compensation from the government than an interest of six per cent per annum on the net cost of the ship and equipments, and a final reimbursement, at the convenience of the government, of the said net cost." The "best calculations" of the cost, "if the utmost attention to economy and despatch can effect any thing," would be $30,000. All they desired of Congressman Bartlett was that "so far as the same shall appear necessary," he would "promote a provision whereby they may be enabled to carry their designs into execution." Yet hoping that their example would "lead to proportionate exertions in larger and wealthier towns," the Newburyport committee suggested that "any provision which may be thought proper and applicable to the case might be general." Nor did the committee shrink from elaborating upon the perceived advantages of their scheme: the federal government, deluged by "so many calls for money," might "procure the means of defence without actual advances, perhaps with more promptitude and undoubtedly with considerably less expense than in the common mode of contracts."[5]

Privately subscribing to build warships may not have been radically new for men accustomed to combining private resources for public improvements. Indeed, the whole idea of exchanging stock for contributions may have owed something to foreign example. In December 1795, British Prime Minister William Pitt had to adopt the then-revolutionary procedure of applying directly to the people for the Loyalty Loan (issued at £112 10s. per £100 of stock bearing a 5 percent interest rate), which was fully subscribed in sixteen hours. Even more recently, in January 1798, with their nation £19 million in debt, the British Parliament had turned to voluntary contributions to pay for defense expenditures. Again, the whole country responded, from £100,000 from the Duke of Bedford to ten shillings from every sailor on the HMS *Argonaut*. Reportedly, £2.5 million were contributed. A generation earlier, in the 1760s, the French minister of marine, the Duke of Choiseul, desperate to reform the French navy, had appealed to the public for contributions. As a result of his appeal, no less than fifteen ships of the line were built by the subscription of Paris guilds of merchants; the Estates of Burgundy, Languedoc, and Artois; and cities including Bordeaux and Marseilles. In addition, a huge popular subscription brought in thirteen million livres.[6] While there is no reference in the documents to prove that the French or English examples inspired Newburyport or ultimately played a role in shaping the legislation, the English and French experiences were too generally known to Americans to believe that they had no effect.

And even if not drawn from the French or English precedents, the notion of financing warships with stock was an idea in the air. Alexander Hamilton, out of government office but enormously influential in Federalist circles and with the president's cabinet, wrote his successor as secretary of the treasury, Oliver Wolcott, Jr., on 5 June 1798, with "a sketch of some ideas which have run through my mind." While Hamilton conceded that "perhaps none of them [are] new," he forwarded a list of nine points on military preparations "as the evidence of my Opinion." His fifth point urged a naval expansion with six ships of the line, twelve frigates, and smaller vessels, and Hamilton noted the possibility that the ships of the line and frigates "may be purchased from G. Britain to be paid for in *Stock*."[7]

Even if the idea of subscribing to build warships was not revolutionary, there were obstacles, at least in theory, to raising money for warships, obstacles that modern economists call the public goods problem. Generally, modern economic theorists have seen government intervention in the economy necessary where individuals cannot produce goods or procure services efficiently. Government should intervene where "externalities" prevent the private production of the good, in other words, where costs are borne directly by one individual or group but the benefits are shared by all, and those who do *not* contribute "free ride" on the benefits—the recognition of which acts as a disincentive for producing the goods in the first place. Having baldly stated the economic axioms, it seems obvious to add that "battleships" are typically cited as the prime example of public goods. Nobel laureate Paul Samuelson has written,

> [N]ational defense, regarded as a commodity, differs completely from the case of a private commodity like bread. Ten loaves of bread can be divided up in many ways among individuals in a group; but national defense has to be provided *more or less automatically for all.* Many individuals will appreciate

it, . . . but even among them, some would be willing to give up more bread, if necessary, for a given level of defense than others would . . .

Could market laissez-faire, with no political voting and no coercion, give the group the national defense desired by the majority? Evidently not. If I knew I was going to benefit from the defense you had paid for, why should I come into the marketplace and exercise a dollar demand for it? Patriotism would of course motivate me, but it would show itself in the way my neighbors and I vote . . . rather than in our day-to-day private purchasing.[8]

What is so striking about Newburyport citizens financing a 20-gun warship for the United States is that *if* they were not profiting on the 6 percent stock-loan, they were acting in the face of the public goods hypothesis. In the first place, although a bustling port, Newburyport had little incentive to act first since it had only a fraction of the people, wealth, and ships affected by the French depredations. In addition, once completed and handed over to the federal government, "their" ship's benefits would not accrue to Newburyport directly but to all Americans or all American merchants generally.[9]

Yet Newburyport acted. And what is more, Newburyport did not act alone. The *Newburyport Herald and Country Gazette* of 25 May 1798 contained a two-sentence piece on the town's subscription ship project.[10] The next day, the Boston *Columbian Centinel* carried a dispatch from Newburyport that read in its entirety:

The patriotic citizens of this town, determined to show their attachment to their own government, and to vindicate its commercial rights, have opened a subscription for the purpose of building a 20 gun ship; and loaning her to government. The sum proposed for building her is 20,000 dollars. MOSES BROWN, Esq. patriotically subscribed 1500 dollars.

An example this, worthy [of] prompt imitation.[11]

Philadelphia's *Aurora & General Advertiser* reprinted the Newburyport article on 1 June;[12] *The Spectator* of New York copied the *Columbian Centinel* piece verbatim on 2 June;[13] faroff Charleston, South Carolina, reported the news two weeks later.[14] Other papers reported that the Newburyport subscription was filled within a week of its opening.[15]

Besides the editorial support of the *Columbian Centinel,* there were more direct admonitions. After reporting on 9 June that the Newburyport merchants had filled their subscription and that contracts had been let, William Cobbett, the prickly English publisher of *Porcupine's Gazette* in Philadelphia,[16] wrote, "This is excellent. It proves that the true spirit of patriotism is gone forward, to the Northward at least—What our rich merchants are about here I know not. They have a good deal to lose; and they may take my word for it, that if they will not give a *little*, they will *lose all*."[17] But the self-styled Porcupine (Cobbett) was preaching to the converted. In that same paper, the next column over, appeared the following advertisement:

> **The Merchants and Traders** of this City, are requested to meet at the Coffee-House on Monday the 11th instant, at 12 o'clock, on business important to the Commerce of the State.[18]

The subscription ship program developed in two areas: in Congress, an enabling act was passed, and in the cities, subscription lists were signed. Historians generally have implied that the law engendered private action.[19] Instead, the reverse was true; the statute merely reflected what American citizens were doing on their own.

The legislative history of what would become the Act of 30 June 1798 is extremely spare. On 6 June 1798, the Senate heard the first reading of a bill that merely authorized the president to accept "any armed vessel built within the United States, and voluntarily offered to him for the use of the United States, to be employed in public service." On the 7th, the bill was read a second time but postponed. The next day, it was committed. When the bill emerged from committee on the 13th, a second section was added providing that the president might accept such vessels "on such terms as he may deem beneficial to the public interest," but the maximum number of ships accepted could be twelve, none "of a less force than twenty guns, nine pounders."[20] The bill, as amended, was read for a third time and passed 16-7 on 14 June.[21] Vice President Jefferson, no friend of naval expansion, reported on the progress of the bill to his friend Madison. Jefferson observed that "neither the terms as to interest or paiment of the principal, nor the maximum of size are limited, but a proposition to limit was rejected. Some treated the apprehension that large ships might be obtained as chimerical, while others wished they might be all of the line, and at least 3, 4, or half a dozen 74s. This bill is in fact to open *a loan* in the form of ships."[22]

The background of the Senate bill cannot be known with certainty. Philadelphia knew of the Newburyport ship plan by 1 June when the *Aurora* carried the story. Perhaps Federalist Senator Benjamin Goodhue of Massachusetts, who played a leading role on the naval committee, wrote the bill. The letter of the Newburyport committee to Bartlett proposing the 6 percent stock-loan was dated 1 June and could scarcely have arrived in Philadelphia, the nation's capital, before 5 or 6 June. Had Bartlett approached Goodhue with the loan plan, the Federalists, not the opposition Republicans, might have committed the bill to rewrite it as per the changed circumstances.[23]

In diverse parts of the United States, thousands of dollars were being raised by citizens without government sanction or direction. The Senate bill did not pass before subscriptions in Newburyport, Philadelphia, and New York were well underway, and the Senate bill was not printed in newspapers until Baltimore had begun its list.[24] The House did not take up the bill before Norfolk, Richmond, and Petersburg, Virginia, had also entered the subscription frenzy.

In an era when a skilled ship carpenter earned a dollar and a half per day in wages and a common laborer a mere dollar,[25] the sums raised practically overnight to build warships for the navy were extraordinary. Yet not only was there no legislative approval but also there was no Executive Department role. There could be little executive supervision without an executive, but the first secretary of the navy, Benjamin Stoddert, only entered into his duties at 139 Walnut Street, Philadelphia, on 19 June 1798.[26] Stoddert, a forty-seven-year-old merchant from Georgetown (then in Maryland), had been a merchant who owned and managed ships from his Potomac landing. As an officer in the Pennsylvania line during the Revolution, Stoddert had been wounded in the battle of Brandywine. He then served for two years as the secretary to the Continental Board of War. When he arrived in Philadelphia to take up the navy post in June 1798, he dined with President and Mrs. Adams. She wrote of him: "Mr. Stoddard is said by those who know him to be an amiable man, and for a Southern Man, a man of activity & industry. He will have one advantage over a Northern Man that he will not be sacrificed and dissected anatomized & parilized by his Southern brethren. . . . " In fact, Stoddert would prove an able and active organizer of the navy, and a loyal supporter of President Adams, but he played no role in the initial surge of popular enthusiasm for building ships by subscription for the navy. Over the next few weeks, as Stoddert took control of the national effort to build and equip a navy, he would stoke the subscription efforts in some cities, offer to send designs and supplies, and make suggestions. Nevertheless, six months after his appointment, when Stoddert was well ensconced, the citizens still controlled the shipbuilding. Stoddert reported to Congress in December 1798 that he had not figured into the naval estimates for the budget the costs "of equipping the Vessels building for the Public by the Citizens. Some of these Vessels will probably be entirely equipped by the Citizens,—others only partially. . . . In some cases, the Citizens will furnish the Military Stores—in others, they will require aid from the Public, even to rig the Vessels."[27]

The most astounding feature, however, was not the huge sums raised by citizen initiative, nor even the lack of political coordination. It was instead the undertaking itself: the decisions by private citizens to build warships for a navy that sent its first vessel, the USS *Ganges*, a converted merchant ship, to sea only at the end of May 1798.[28] That the United States Navy would be a success was not some ineluctable truth in the summer of 1798. The navy's three large frigates, the *Constitution, United States,* and *Constellation,* had never yet been to sea.[29] There was no bipartisan political support for a navy, and the Continental Navy of the Revolutionary War provided a checkered example on which to build a new navy.[30] Yet the mercantile towns had the audacity to build warships to take on the French navy, which, before Nelson trounced them at the Nile, seemed as powerful or as ominous as the British navy itself. These American merchants were not faint of heart. In his New York newspaper, Noah Webster[31] opined that the warships the people were building,

> when combined, will constitute a force of some magnitude; and altho in the estimation of insolent European powers they may be regarded with a sneer, they will, nevertheless, be managed with the energy of hardy FREEMEN, who know the *motives* of their duty, and who possess a spirit unaccustomed to being cowed or conquered.[32]

By the time the House of Representatives took up the Senate bill to accept up to twelve warships from the people, five subscriptions were being filled in seven towns. In the House, Albert Gallatin, the Swiss-born Republican leader from Pennsylvania,[33] had already succeeded in stemming Federalist military preparations, earning him the enmity of the First Lady. Abigail Adams wrote of Gallatin that, "If it were not for that specious, subtle, spare Cassius, that imported foreigner, the House of Reps would proceed with energy and act with decision."[34] Yet to the subscription ship bill, Gallatin's real concern was to specify statutorily the terms of the loan, the point that had most concerned Jefferson. He therefore moved to add a clause to the bill specifying a 6 percent interest rate. The Federalists agreed to such a proviso and to language allowing some subscription ships to mount fewer than twenty guns. As amended, the bill was approved without recorded vote on 25 June.[35] The Republicans were satisfied that even at 6 percent interest, no one would subscribe to make money: as Gallatin put it, such certificates "would not sell for 20 s[hillings] in the pound."[36] The Senate accepted the House amendments,[37] and President Adams signed the bill into law on 30 June 1798. The 6 percent Navy Stock of 1798 was a general obligation of the United States, not security for the return of the ships, which became government property. The stock had no specified date of maturity; the certificates were redeemable by the government at any time.[38]

With the legislation in the offing and all the money being raised, Abigail Adams had reason to exult to her son, John Quincy Adams, "Newburyport has set an example, by voteing & raising money to build a 20 gun ship and loaning it to Government. . . . [T]he sea ports will all follow the example and we shall have a Navy spring up like the Gourd of Jonah. . . ."[39]

3 The Newburyport Example

Newburyport lies at the mouth of the Merrimack River, forty miles north of Boston. After a visit in 1800, Timothy Dwight, the Congregationalist theologian and Yale College president, wrote that "[t]he houses, taken collectively, make a better appearance than those of any other town in New-England. . . . Indeed, an air of wealth, taste and elegance, is spread over this beautiful spot." Newburyport owed its wealth and elegance to the sea. For a century before Talleyrand and Messrs. X, Y, and Z became household names, or letters, for Americans, Newburyport had built ships to trade along the coast and overseas. By the 1790s, six shipyards fronted the Merrimack in Newburyport, and others sprouted upriver to Haverhill. In 1790, Newburyport merchants owned 108 vessels totaling 11,870 tons. By 1793, local merchants boasted more than eighteen thousand tons of registered vessels, three-quarters of which cleared for Caribbean ports. The local shipyards were supported by an infrastructure of ropewalks, blockmakers, and foundries. Although one of America's major ports, as late as 1800 Newburyport numbered only 5,937 inhabitants.[1]

Newburyport's trade to the West Indies and northern Europe made it a wealthier, and more sophisticated, place than its size suggested. But as the risks and rewards of merchant voyages increased in the 1790s, Newburyport merchants sought different outlets for their capital, and were a step ahead of the country in doing so. In 1792, the "Proprietors of the Locks and Canals on Merrimack River" organized a corporation—at that time, a suspected entity in American law, smacking of monarchism, requiring a special enactment from the state legislature—that cut a canal around the Pawtucket Falls. The next year, 1793, a generation before the textile mills of Lawrence or Lowell, the Newburyport Woolen Manufactory was projected, and thirty-one merchants petitioned the General Court for a corporate charter. The factory was built, and production began in mid-1794. In 1795, the Newburyport merchants organized the first local bank, the Merrimack Bank, with a corporate charter and $150,000 capital.[2]

All these entrepreneurial ventures centered on the idea of sharing risk of loss and pooling capital through syndications. The Newburyport merchants knew all about syndications from outfitting, owning, or commanding privateers twenty years earlier, during the Revolution. While the government licensed privateers by granting "letters of marque and reprisal," and regulated how privateers could set about their business, private citizens put up the money to buy, arm, and equip the ships for privateering. Privateer ships ranged from the smallest coasting sloop with a single cannon to ship-rigged 20-gunners. Privateers had one goal, to make money. To do so, privateers first had to capture an enemy merchant ship, hopefully without inflicting too much damage, and then to sail the captured ship into a port of their own nation or of a co-belligerent for a court proceeding legitimizing the capture as a good prize. Once a valid prize, title vested in the captor, and the vessel and its cargo were sold at public auction. After deducting court costs, auctioneers' fees, wharfage expenses, and the like, the proceeds were shared between the privateer's owners and the crew. Privateering was a risky venture: outfitting the ships was expensive, the enemy's merchant ships might be escorted by warships or put up a stout defense in their own right, and the admiralty court proceedings sometimes ensnared the privateers. The men involved in the privateering business understood the sense of sharing the costs and risks of loss.[3]

The Newburyport men in 1798 who thought of building a warship for the federal government in exchange for stock were steeped in syndications from both civic projects and from Revolutionary War privateering. William Bartlet (1747–1841), the wealthiest Newburyport citizen, owned a wharf and a fleet of merchant ships, and was a principal shareholder in the Woolen Manufactory, the Bank, and a host of civic projects. William

Coombs (1736–1814), a merchant and the long-serving president of the Newburyport Marine Society, had served as an artillery captain during the Revolution before owning a half-interest in a privateer, and acting as the bond or surety for two others. Coombs was an investor in the Woolen Manufactory and the Bank as well. Dudley Tyng, whom President Washington had selected to be the collector of the port in 1795, administered customs, navigation, and clearances. Moses Brown (1742–1827), a chaisemaker before the Revolution, became the town's second wealthiest man after the war as a merchant and shipowner. William Johnson (1745–1802) and his brother Nicholas were well-to-do merchants, and while Nicholas had commanded one privateer in the Revolution, William had commanded no less than three. William Farris (1753–1837), an Irish immigrant, commanded two privateers during the war and, afterward, became the mercantile and banking partner of Ebenezer Stocker. Stocker, a shipmaster and merchant, organized the Merrimack Bank. During the Revolution, he had commanded two privateers, a 4-gun brigantine and a 12-gun ship. And serving as a patron to the Newburyport subscription ship was not Stocker's only contribution to his country in the summer of 1798; Stocker wrote to the president, offering to raise a company of infantry styled the "Newbury Port Federal Volunteers" to defend the beaches against a possible French invasion, an offer John Adams accepted. The last Newburyport committeeman, Samuel A. Otis, Jr. (1768–1814), the brother of Federalist luminary Harrison Gray Otis of Boston, was too young to have served in the war.[4]

The nine Newburyport merchant-capitalists not only provided a model by which the cash-strapped new republic could finance a navy but also suggested the way the federal government could tap into the merchants' experience and expertise to build warships. In truth, the federal government had few options. As Secretary of the Navy Benjamin Stoddert wrote to a Portsmouth, New Hampshire, merchant, "while the practice continues of building our Ships at a number of places, the public Interest will be best promoted, by putting the entire direction into the hands of intelligent Merchants of great respectability of character" so that "the whole power, and of course the whole responsibility" could be focused.[5] But this was the power and responsibility the merchants wanted. As the very men who owned ships, they knew to whom to turn to design "their" warship. On 4 June 1798, Ebenezer Stocker, on behalf of "the Committee for building a 20 Gun Ship," wrote to William Hackett of Salisbury, Massachusetts, asking him to cross over to Newburyport to consult the committee about the draft and dimensions of the Newburyport ship.[6]

Hackett, fifty-nine years old in 1798, had spent forty-seven years in shipbuilding. At age twelve, he had apprenticed in the family shipyard in Salisbury, across the Merrimack from Newburyport. With his cousin, James Hackett, William Hackett turned out fine warships and privateers for the Continental cause, including the frigate *Alliance.* Many years later, John Adams recounted a conversation over dinner he had had with the French navy intendant at Lorient, Monsieur Thevenard, in June 1779, in which Adams suggested that American shipwrights were not on a par with those of Europe:

> "The frigate in which you came here," said Mr. Thevenard (the Alliance, Captain Landais) "is equal to any in Europe. I have examined her, and I assure you there is not in the King's service, nor in the English navy, a frigate more perfect and complete in materials or workmanship." "It gives me great pleasure, Sir, to hear your opinion. I know we had or might have materials, but I had not flattered myself that we had artists equal to those in Europe." Mr. Thevenard repeated with emphasis, "You may depend on it, there is not in Europe a more perfect piece of naval architecture than your Alliance . . ."

After the Revolution, the Hackett yard produced merchant vessels. Among his designs was the 800-ton merchantman *Massachusetts,* launched at Quincy in 1789 for trading voyages with China. The *Massachusetts,* as large as a frigate and, indeed, pierced for thirty-six cannon, was considered a triumph. Captain Job Prince wrote Hackett of the rival European shipmasters in Canton that "tho there eyes were open to spy defects and there tongues ready to find fault, they confessed they could not." Nevertheless, the *Massachusetts* reputedly had been built with unseasoned white oak that was already decayed so much that the *Massachusetts* herself was sold after arriving in China. Regardless, Hackett was a leading New England ship designer, whom Howard Chapelle calls "one of the greatest American naval architects of the sailing ship era." Though something of a traditionalist, William Hackett was not a safe choice in one respect. In retaining him, the Newburyport committee gambled that he would not succumb to another bout of temporary insanity, which had buffeted him in the 1790s and which, in 1806, would lead to a judicial declaration that Hackett was mentally incompetent. The plans of the Newburyport ship, which soon came to be called the *Merrimack,* are lost, but given William Hackett's involvement and reputation, it seems clear that he designed the ship.[7]

But the $30,000 pledged at the end of May was insufficient to construct a ship of war, and within two weeks of the opening of the subscription, the Newburyport committee assessed each subscriber an additional 25 percent—in other words, forced each subscriber to volunteer another quarter on every promised dollar within one more week. It was critical to have the money committed because by 4 June 1798, many of the ship's contracts had been executed, and Newburyport committed itself to launching its warship in ninety days. Ultimately, the people of Newburyport subscribed $41,158.639, although the total cost of the ship, rigged and equipped, came to $72,648.73.[8]

On 13 June 1798, representatives of the Newburyport committee—Bartlet, Coombs, Nicholas Johnson, Stocker, and Abraham Wainwright—signed a contract with William Cross and Thomas M. Clark to build the subscription ship. The contract specified a ninety-two-foot keel, a thirty-foot beam, and a depth of hold to the gun deck of a mere fifteen feet, perhaps a recognition that the entrance to the Newburyport harbor lay over a bar with only seven feet of water on it at low tide. The contract provided that the ship would carry 20 six-pounder cannon and that she would be launched on 30 September 1798. In consideration, the Newburyport committee promised to pay Cross and Clark $22.50 per ton for the carpenters' work, "one third down, one third when [the] ship is shut in under the wale[s], [and the] remaining one third when the hull of the ship is completed and delivered afloat in Newburyport."[9]

On 9 July 1798, the keel of Newburyport's ship was laid in Cross's shipyard at the foot of what is now Federal Street.[10] But the town had not let Independence Day pass without celebrating their warship. That morning, a group of young men with a band playing patriotic songs assembled into parade formation on State Street. They spotted Capt. Moses Brown walking through town—not Moses Brown the chaisemaker-turned-shipowner on the committee, but a master mariner of the same name and age. The youths cheered Captain Brown and asked him to lead their parade. Down they marched to the Federal shipyard where a "large number" of ship carpenters were already at work preparing the site for the keel-laying. Captain Brown gave a brief, patriotic speech extolling the workmen "employed in the laudable business of building a ship" so that the sons of the Revolutionary generation could defend the sovereignty and independence won by their fathers. The marchers gave three cheers to the carpenters. The procession then marched up and down Newburyport streets, stopping in turn at the house of each subscriber to acknowledge and applaud each.[11]

Whether Captain Brown contributed to the design of the ship or to the subscription is not known, but he was the very man to command her. William Hackett may have been a brilliant naval architect and Cross and Clark able builders, but the Newburyport committee needed a reliable and experienced captain to superintend the effort, outfit the ship properly, and sail her off to war. The United States in the summer of 1798 had less than a handful of warships in commission, a new Navy Department with a just-appointed secretary, Benjamin Stoddert, in charge, and no professional officer corps. But Moses Brown had more than forty years of experience as a shipmaster in peace and command of privateers in war.

Born in January 1742 in Salisbury, Massachusetts, Brown first went to sea at age fifteen. By the late 1750s, Brown had sailed to the Caribbean on trading voyages. At age eighteen, as mate of the schooner *Phoebe,* hired by the Royal Navy to transport part of a Scottish regiment to the West Indies, Brown came under fire from two French privateers. Although the *Phoebe* escaped, Brown received a gunshot wound in the arm that forced his hospitalization. On another voyage to the Caribbean, in 1766, Brown contracted smallpox and was given up for dead. His body was actually sewn into a sheet for burial at sea, but at the last second, someone saw that Brown wasn't actually dead and stopped the proceedings. Miraculously, Brown survived. By 1767, Brown had become a shipmaster, although he was not always successful: in 1773, Brown's ship sank from under him, leaving him and his crew adrift in the Caribbean for seven days until a Philadelphia ship rescued them. In 1775, Brown determined to try his mercantile prowess in Europe.

Brown sailed a brig to Cadiz, loaded with pipe staves. He sold the cargo, bought flour, and sailed to Matro where he landed the flour and took on ballast to return to Cadiz. There, loading with salt, Brown sailed the brig to Falmouth, England, arriving in October 1775, six months after Lexington and Concord, although he carried on trading unmolested. Selling the salt, Brown bought pilchards and set off for Venice on 18 November 1775. He arrived there in January 1776 and spent ten weeks seeing the sights, "it being carnival time and no business done." While docked at Venice, Brown learned that British law allowed for the seizure of all American property found on the high seas. Brown made a sham sale of his brig, chartered her to load with currants at Zante (now Zakynthos) and Cephalonia to London, and boldly sailed up the Thames to London in July 1776. With no alarm but obvious audacity he wrote, "After delivering my freight I sold my brig for eight hundred pounds and spent two months in seeing the fashions of London." Nevertheless, he knew his string of luck would soon run out, and took passage on a vessel to St. Eustatius, and then to Philadelphia, and then by cart and carriage back to Newburyport. Brown had been absent from his family for two years, one month, and three days.

Brown's first cruise from Newburyport during the Revolution ended on its second day in April 1777; the brig *Hannah* was taken and Brown was tossed into a British prison ship in Rhode Island for three months. That experience turned Moses Brown into a privateersman. Over the winter of 1777 to 1778, Brown supervised the conversion of a merchant vessel, the ship *General Arnold*, into an 18-gun privateer. The early cruises of the *General Arnold* are unrecorded. On the third cruise of the *General Arnold*, in February 1779, Brown took several prizes but seemed "destined to receive little but hard knocks with little remuneration." The *General Arnold* fought a two-hour battle with an English privateer, the *Gregson*, that left the Englishman scurrying for repairs, and then fought a second English privateer, the *Nancy*, in a hour-long scramble that left the *General Arnold*'s rigging and masts shattered and the 350-ton *Nancy* sunk.

Two weeks later, a British frigate captured the *General Arnold* and Brown again was tossed into a prison ship. After being exchanged, Brown returned to strictly mercantile voyages, to Amsterdam and to Saint-Domingue, albeit in armed ships like the 12-gun *Intrepid*. After the war, Brown commanded vessels trading to Ireland, the West Indies, Senegal, London, and Surinam. By 1798, Moses Brown, at age fifty-six, had been a seaman for forty years with probably sixty voyages and a local reputation as a privateer captain who did not shirk a fight.

Although a patriot in the Revolution, Moses Brown was an old-fashioned man in his habits, appearance, and speech. Brown's letters use "Ye" instead of "the," already an antique usage. Despite the trends in naval fashion, he continued to wear a wig. He was also out of fashion in his belief in temperance in a navy that consumed grog by the tumbler, and in his aversion to flogging. And although it seems quixotic today, Brown's concern for the health of his crew led him to take seemingly advanced measures to prevent yellow fever in Caribbean ports by fumigating and cleansing his ship with vinegar and lime juice.[12]

On 9 July 1798, William Bartlet proposed to Navy Secretary Stoddert that Moses Brown be appointed a captain in the burgeoning United States Navy. Newburyport again set the pattern: over the next year, as each city that subscribed to build a warship started to put the ship together, the merchants running the project would suggest a captain and sometimes the other officers. Bartlet recommended Brown as the captain and continued with recommendations for every commissioned and warrant officer, from sailing master to boatswain to gunner, fourteen positions in all. The Adams administration deferred to their choices. A system of patronage, unquestionably, but the local merchants knew the local shipmasters and seafaring men, could overlook politics if they wanted, and were unlikely to choose untested or even mediocre men to command or officer "their" contribution to the federal navy. Stoddert, pleased at Newburyport's "celerity" in laying down the ship, and impressed by the "very honorable Testimony" Bartlet provided in support of Brown, agreed to suggest a commission for him to President Adams. Although Stoddert passed along to the Newburyport merchants the "high sense" the president "entertains of their Patriotic exertions" in building a ship, Stoddert waited to submit Moses Brown's name until 1 September 1798. His delay allowed a batch of new captains to be commissioned with greater seniority commensurate with the larger ships they would command. Stoddert acknowledged that captains like Moses Brown "may be equally meritorious but are not so well known" as the men designated to command the frigates. Stoddert finally sent Brown his commission on 4 October 1798, listing Brown as the twentieth, and then-most-junior, captain in the navy.[13]

Still, the knowledge that Moses Brown would be commissioned as the captain gave the Newburyport merchants great satisfaction, and Brown's authoritative presence undoubtedly speeded construction. A Boston newspaper in early September reported that the "Newburyport patriotic 20 gun ship, which some imagine will be called the *Merrimack,* is completdly timbered, and planked above her bends. Her lower deck is laid, and the workmen are now butt bolting her." The newspaper called the *Merrimack* an "elegant specimen of American ingenuity" although in what respects Hackett introduced new features in her is not known. The one extant ship portrait is in profile and reveals a foremast far forward, a huge main topmast staysail, and a small mizzenmast carrying a mizzen sail and topsail but no topgallant.[14] By mid-September, the local newspaper predicted that the *Merrimack* would be launched in one month as the carpenters had "planked [her] up and the gun deck is laid." The work had progressed at breakneck speed and, somewhat tepidly, the newspaper thought the ship "as well done as . . . any ship ever built in so short a time."[15]

On 12 October 1798, according to the local newspaper,

> Our beautiful patriotic ship, majestically descended from her native land, to the embrace of the watery God . . . She is called the Merrimack, and will mount 20 nines and 8 sixes, is finely coppered, and the best judges say, she will not suffer by a comparison with the finest vessel of her size ever built. . . .
>
> A vast concourse of people attended to be witness to the interesting scene. A federal salute from the artillery pieces announced to distant friends the happy issue of the launch. . . .
>
> The keel of this ship was laid on the 9th July, since which there have been 74 working days; and I dare presume to say, that . . . she will be ready for sea in 14 days. . . .[16]

After the launch, the town celebrated with a "Music on Launching Day" concert, in which a company of Boston musicians introduced a new piece, "The New Federal Song—Hail patriots all." After the concert, well-heeled Newburyporters gavotted at a ball.[17]

Captain Brown received his commission from Secretary Stoddert along with his first orders, dated 4 October. Stoddert instructed Brown to recruit the *Merrimack*'s crew. While the Marine Corps commandant, Maj. William Burrows, supplied the "Serjeant, Corporal, Music & 21 Privates" for the marine detachment under Newburyport-nominated Lt. David Stickney, Brown needed to enlist a total of 105 sailors for a one-year term: sixty-five able seamen, and forty ordinary seamen and boys. Stoddert urged Brown to "Get as good a Crew" as possible and immediately contradicted himself, informing Brown that, as it was "our best policy to create Seamen," Brown should recruit as many boys as possible. All hands were to be "sound and healthy," all were to be true volunteers, but "No Negroes, or Mulattoes are to be admitted" nor anyone "of a suspicious character." If a volunteer insisted on an advance of pay, Brown could extend up to two months' wages but only if a surety properly bonded that the volunteer would not desert. The *Merrimack*'s officers would receive a $2 bounty for each seaman they enlisted while on recruiting forays, plus every expense—transportation, ribbons for the hats of the volunteers, and (rum) punch.[18] Among the *Merrimack*'s midshipmen, Brown had the satisfaction of seeing one of his sons, Joseph Brown, receive a coveted warrant.

By the end of December, the *Merrimack*'s crew was aboard but the *Merrimack*'s captain was "much Surprised to finde So few on Board on Examination that Ever Saw a gun fired in Anger but when we Reflect on So Long a peace tis no wonder." Captain Brown tried to dampen expectations, recognizing his friends in Newburyport had "Raise[d] there minds So high on this Ship," although, if he had time, he could turn his volunteers into a disciplined unit. Brown found no room to store the ship's provisions. Hogsheads of bread were stored everywhere, fourteen on deck, "ye hold full & all ye Sides of the tween decks." Brown invited his first lieutenant, Michael Titcomb, Jr., to berth with him in the captain's cabin so that the lieutenant's quarters could be temporarily made a bread locker. Brown also had muted criticism for both the *Merrimack*'s design and for the mounting of her guns. Brown noted "Twas well" that he had insisted that the *Merrimack*'s aft guns be cast six inches longer "for the Ship flairs So much aft they only gest go without ye Side port." Also troubling were the gun carriages, which were all too low to depress the guns' elevation; "if a Small fellow gits to windward & comes on board I shall be puzzled to hitt him."[19]

Secretary Stoddert ordered Brown to take the *Merrimack* to Prince Rupert Bay in the island of Dominica to join Capt. John Barry's newly created Windward Islands squadron. The *Merrimack*'s mission was to "intercept the Armed Vessels of the Enemy, & to give most protection to our own Commercial Vessels" trading in the area from St. Kitts southward to Barbados, Tobago, Cayenne, and Curaçao. Capt. Thomas Truxtun had a small squadron in the Leeward Islands between St. Kitts and Puerto Rico; Capt. Thomas Tingey had two ships guarding the Windward Passage between Cuba and Saint-Domingue; and Capt. Stephen Decatur, Sr., had one or two ships off Havana. But Stoddert dispatched America's principal naval force—the frigates *Constitution* and *United States*, each of 44 guns; the 32-gun ship *George Washington;* and the *Merrimack;* with the promise of four or five more ships, as soon as they could sail—to Barry's command. "[A]bove all," the secretary wrote to Barry, "your Efforts must be directed to relieve our Commerce, from the piccaroons, and pirates, continually issuing from the Island of Guadaloupe."[20]

On 9 December 1798, the *Merrimack* set her sails and, taking advantage of the "Spring Tides" of the full moon, passed over the Newburyport bar, arriving at Boston the same day.[21] Brown needed three weeks in Boston to get the *Merrimack* ready for sea. Finally, at one o'clock on 2 January 1799, the *Merrimack* hoisted her anchors and made sail. By four o'clock, the Boston lighthouse was fast receding from sight, four leagues west by south.[22]

The *Merrimack* sailed on a gray, frigid afternoon. Snow showered the ship; and the crew, barely organized into watches and divisions, had to go aloft to keep ice from forming on the newly set rigging and yards. By nightfall, the *Merrimack* was hurtling over a heavy sea, and few of the officers and men were spared from a sleepless, cold, wet night. Yet by daylight, the *Merrimack* had sailed one hundred miles, and by 6 January 1799, the *Merrimack* approached the warmth of the Gulf Stream. As the ship headed further south, the rapid change in temperature and humidity, welcome as it may have been to the men, created vast dangers. All of the *Merrimack*'s standing and running rigging was hemp rope, and what was taut in freezing Boston became slack in warmer waters, rendering little lateral support for the masts, and risking the mast rolling out in a rough sea. Captains who were not demanding seamen, like James Sever in the *Congress,* almost lost their ships and lives to the warm air loosening the winter-set rigging. But a taut old tarpaulin like Moses Brown would not run such risks. On 6 January, Midshipman Brown's journal records "all hands employ'd setting up the rigging," a wearying task the crew repeated five days later, with the ship roughly eight hundred miles further south.[23]

The *Merrimack* plowed southwards through rough seas and squalls. Her lookouts spotted two ships, and Brown chased each: an English merchantman, the *Carteret,* nine days out from Tortola, bound to Falmouth, England; and the English brig *Three Friends,* bound to Barbados. Brown let them go on their way. As the *Merrimack* entered the Caribbean, where she might spot a privateer or French navy ship, Brown remembered the lack of combat experience among his sailors. Under topsails on a pleasant afternoon on 16 January, Brown put his crew "through the manouvres of a Sham Action," followed by two days of exercising the great guns in broadsides at imaginary enemies.[24] The *Merrimack* arrived off Dominica on 19 January but did not find the Windward Islands squadron at hand. For a week, Brown cruised around, looking for American warships or for the enemy; he took the *Merrimack* inshore so close to a French artillery battery on Marie Galante off Guadeloupe that the *Merrimack* took two hits, although no real damage was done. On 27 January, the *Merrimack* "came too" in Prince Rupert Bay, Dominica, where she rendezvoused with Barry's three frigates.[25]

The purpose of ships like the *Merrimack* in a *guerre de course* was, as Navy Secretary Stoddert recognized, to escort American cargo ships trading in the Islands to safer waters and to search out and capture or destroy the French privateers that feasted on American merchantmen. Every few weeks, a convoy formed in the Islands that, with one or two naval escorts, would creep from island to island gathering more and more America-bound vessels. There was little glory to be won in convoying and no prize money, but preventing losses meant winning the war. Moses Brown, a veteran of other wars, knew how trying it was to keep dozens of merchant vessels organized and sailing together, with their various sailing abilities and insubordinate masters. "You may think there is an honor in this business," Brown wrote about convoy duty, "but there is more trouble to keep them together." One or two warships could hardly play sheepdog to thirty or forty merchantmen by day, relying on simple flag hoists backed by warning cannon shots; at night, with nothing other than colored lanterns or flares, escort captains relied on the herd instinct or the power of prayer. The tactics of escort vessels in the sailing era were simple—stay to windward of the convoy so that any threat would be downwind (and thus could be interdicted). Alternately, warships might take station ahead and astern of the convoy (no matter what the wind direction) to set the appropriate speed for all and to ensure that no laggards fell behind. As more U.S. naval vessels arrived, the slower warships (or the less favored captains) received convoy duty. The secretary of the navy suggested consigning the sluggards for escorting, allowing the faster warships to patrol offensively, by which they "may render more effectual protection to our Commerce, by capturing the Vessels which annoy it."[26]

After watering and taking on ballast for four days, the *Merrimack* sortied from Prince Rupert Bay on 1 February 1799 with the three frigates and seven merchantmen bound for American ports. After two hours, the *Merrimack* parted in search of privateers since the merchant vessels were to stop in Martinique to await more arrivals. For ten days, the *Merrimack* crisscrossed around the islands, pursuing unknown sails but losing the chases to darkness or finding that they were American or British. On 13 February, the *Merrimack* arrived off the St. Pierre roadstead in Martinique, and at 8 A.M. signaled for the merchant vessels to form convoy. For five hours, the *Merrimack* "lay off and on," waiting for the merchantmen to form up; nineteen ships departed Martinique for Dominica, the next stop, although the nineteen were joined by two more from Fort Royal. At 11 A.M. on 14 February, with the *Merrimack* poised to enter Prince Rupert Bay, her lookouts spotted two unknown sails bearing down on the rear of the convoy. Brown turned to intercept them but found as they closed that his signals were answered correctly. By noon, the *Merrimack*'s hail revealed the strangers to be a 20-gun British ship and an armed transport. The *Merrimack* set a course back to Prince Rupert Bay but, according to Midshipman Brown, "finding the fleet so far to leeward & mostly dull sailers [we] Bore away for Montseratt." As his father explained to Commodore Barry, "You would have met with me at Prince Ruperts Bay had not my Convoy got so far to Leeward in comeing from Martinico, that they could not beat up, notwithstanding my perticuler orders to keep close in with Land." Brown mentioned his encounter with the British warships, and then poured out his exasperation about escort duty: "Our Countrymen want Convoy but pay no attention to keep with it, and such Tubs as some of them are under my Convoy I never saw, & they are sure to spread each Night, as far as it is possible to see them."[27]

It was now the *Merrimack*'s job to take the convoy island to island, picking up any American merchantmen that wanted to join. At Montserrat on the 15th, Lieutenant Titcomb went ashore to find a schooner ready for sea, and three other ships sailed into the fleet and opted for the escort. Each received the signal book and a place in the formation, but Captain Brown had to signal the lead merchantmen to shorten sail so that the whole group could stay together. At Nevis, Titcomb found no Americans ready, so the *Merrimack* bore away for neighboring St. Kitts, where the convoy anchored on the morning of the 16th in Basseterre Roads' ten fathoms of water. The Americans found to their delight Truxtun's frigate *Constellation* in port with her prize, the French frigate *Insurgente*. Twenty more American merchant vessels, escorted by the warship *Montezuma*, arrived on the 17th to join the fleet, and at 11 A.M. on the 18th, the *Merrimack* made sail, shepherding forty-two merchantmen bound for America.[28]

The next two days provided one scare after another. The 18th was a beautiful balmy day and the *Merrimack* "made sail as occasion required." At 6 P.M., with Saba bearing north by west, five leagues off, the *Merrimack* led her convoy, the "fleet Close under our Stern." At 4:30 A.M., however, *Merrimack*'s lookouts somehow spotted a strange sail. The stranger did not respond to lantern signals and the *Merrimack* fired three shots to bring her to. At 6 A.M., a boarding party from the *Merrimack* determined that the stranger was an English privateer and let her go. An hour later, the *Merrimack* found another unknown sail to leeward and bore down in chase. This second vessel, obviously armed, broke out British colors but, as it was a standard ruse to fly false flags until immediately before an action, the Union Jack did not cause Brown to turn away. Indeed, when the stranger did not respond to the *Merrimack*'s flag hoists, Brown's suspicions rose, and he again beat to quarters. For the second time that morning, the *Merrimack* opened fire to bring a strange sail to. But this ship replied by firing her guns both to leeward and to windward (the latter traditionally a signal of readiness to fight). At 10 A.M., the *Merrimack* came within hailing distance and learned that the stranger was the 24-gun HMS *Perdrix* on a cruise.[29]

Moses Brown's nerves frayed even more that afternoon, the 19th, as the convoy neared St. Thomas. At four o'clock, the *Merrimack* discovered a 10-gun lugger in the middle of the convoy; an armed boarding party found her to be English. But the seeming lack of concern by the merchantmen about unidentified armed ships penetrating the convoy left Brown boiling. At 8 A.M. the next day, Brown saw a brig belonging to the convoy "who paid no attention to our signals." Brown turned his nine-pounders on the negligent brig and ordered three shots fired at her. That gesture caught the attention of the violator, and Brown sent his second lieutenant, Samuel Chase, over to give her master a tongue-lashing. By noon, the convoy anchored, unscathed, in St. Thomas's bay.[30]

At 6 A.M. on the 22nd, the *Merrimack* got underway and greeted the sunrise with a seventeen-gun salute in honor of Washington's birthday, answered in turn by other Americans in St. Thomas's anchorage. By eight o'clock, the forty-three-ship convoy made sail. Over the next few days, the *Merrimack* kept her flock close together and chased various sails, none of which turned out to be French. At noon on the 28th, Brown ordered the signal hoisted 'Make the best of your way home,' and with that, hauled *Merrimack*'s wind and turned her back. In one of the first convoys of the war, the *Merrimack* had brought all the merchantmen through.[31]

The next several weeks, the *Merrimack* cruised desultorily and restocked firewood and fresh water at Prince Rupert Bay. For a week, she cruised as a squadron with the *United States, Constitution,* and *Eagle,* poking into the French harbor at Point-à-Pitre, Guadeloupe, but seeing no action. Before dawn on 26 March, with La Désirade bearing nine leagues southeast, the *Merrimack*'s lookouts spotted a ship to leeward and a brig to windward. Despite weather Midshipman Brown described as "fresh gales & Squally," Captain Brown chose to pursue the brig. After more than twelve hours, the *Merrimack* was close enough and "gave her two Shott," which forced the chase to heave to. By 6 P.M., the *Merrimack* came alongside the *Harmony,* a Baltimore brig that a French privateer schooner had captured and manned with a prize crew. Captain Brown mustered a prize crew from the *Merrimack,* a midshipman and six sailors, to take the *Harmony* into Martinique (which Britain had conquered and controlled). The *Harmony*'s recapture meant salvage money for the officers and crew of the *Merrimack,* and after the fruitless pursuits of the previous two months, the idea of splitting cash must have been a charming thought to all hands. Ultimately, the *Harmony*'s owners paid $2,625.18 in salvage.[32]

For the next month, the *Merrimack* returned to cruising, mostly between Martinique and La Désirade, looking in vain for French privateers. On 15 April 1799, Commodore Barry ordered the *Merrimack* to sail to Martinique, to bring back three merchantmen to help form another convoy, and the *Merrimack* returned past Dominica, Montserrat, St. Kitts, and St. Thomas. Off St. Thomas, the *Merrimack* found the *Constitution* escorting a sixteen-ship convoy. Barry ordered the *Merrimack* to bring up the rear, which required the *Merrimack* to prompt the wayward merchant vessels to stay in formation, and the *Merrimack* was forced to tow one particularly sluggish sloop. Five days' sail north of St. Thomas, the *Merrimack* let go her tow rope and left the convoy so that she could sail to Boston. At 5 A.M. on 11 May, the *Merrimack* rounded Cape Cod, and by 9 P.M., amidst "Squalls of Snow & rain & very cold for the season," the Newburyport ship came to in Nantasket Roads in seven fathoms of water. There is no indication why Barry ordered the *Merrimack* home but the secretary of the navy knew that Barry "intended to leave the Islands about the Middle of April" and hoped he had done so. In his report to the Navy Department, Barry observed that the *Merrimack* could only carry two months' provisions and stated "she is not so fine a Vessel as was expected."[33]

Secretary Stoddert wanted the *Merrimack* to sail immediately back to the Caribbean, on a mission of national importance: to inform Truxtun that one of his ships had to be sent to Kingston, Jamaica, to carry money back to Philadelphia, "a measure which Mr. Wolcott [the secretary of the treasury] represents as essential, to relieve the great distress for want of Specie, in this & in other Commercial places." Stoddert followed those orders with more critical orders the next week, the president's decision to keep all vessels of the Windward Islands squadron concentrated off Guadeloupe. Stoddert directed Brown to intercept every U.S. Navy vessel he could find and inform each captain to stay in the Islands "no matter what other orders any particular Vessel may have received" from Barry or Truxtun. So imperative did Stoddert regard the need to keep American warships on station that he ordered Brown to give each captain a written copy of his instructions, and ordered Brown to transmit to him a register of each captain who received the orders with the date. The *Merrimack,* then, was Stoddert's messenger for strategic naval and financial matters. But by the time Stoddert's orders reached Brown in Boston, the president himself had stymied Stoddert's plans.[34]

On Thursday, 30 May 1799, John Adams invited two captains whose ships lay at Boston, Moses Brown of the *Merrimack* and Daniel McNeill of the *Portsmouth,* to dinner that afternoon at the president's house in Braintree. Adams, of course, was a great champion of the navy. Six months earlier, during the naval buildup of the summer of 1798, Adams answered an address by the Boston Marine Society by proclaiming "Floating Batteries and wooden walls have been my favorite system of warfare and Defence for this Country, for three and twenty years." Adams kept himself informed of ship movements and personally helped select officers for the new navy. Merchants from all the ports deluged the president, as well as Stoddert, for convoys, and before the president at the end of May was a request from Boston shipowners for protection for their ships bound to the Caribbean. Adams knew that Brown planned to sail with the *Merrimack* within a few days, as soon as the *Merrimack* reballasted and completed watering. After dinner, exercising his prerogative as commander in chief, the president wrote out his own orders, referring to the petition from the merchants and instructing the captain of the *Merrimack* "to take under convoy any merchant vessel that may be ready to sail when you shall put to sea." The *Merrimack* did not weigh anchor until the afternoon of 6 June, disappointing Stoddert, who groused about the "great importance" in the *Merrimack* performing its mission by the 10th or 12th, which Brown "must have known from his Instructions." Ironically, when the *Merrimack* left Boston, Midshipman Brown in his journal does not record any merchant ship under convoy.[35]

The second cruise of the *Merrimack* began like the first, chasing down sails, and speaking to or boarding ships from all over the world: the ship *Lavina,* 42 days from Falmouth, England, to Philadelphia, on the morning of the 11th; the brig *Anna Catharina,* from St. Barts to Hamburg on the 15th; the brig *Forsoket,* 17 days out from St. Barts to Gothenburg, the next day; the sloop *Hannah,* out 22 days from their own Newburyport, to Martinique, on the 21st; and the ship *Alexander,* out 134 days from Canton, bound to Boston, on the 24th. All of the ships the *Merrimack* ran down were either American or neutrals. But on 28 June 1799 came the action that all American captains craved.

At 2 P.M., the *Merrimack* saw a sail under the tricolor flag of France. Brown ordered the *Merrimack* to chase, and despite "fresh breezes" the Newburyport ship pulled slowly closer. As the afternoon wore on, the French ship jettisoned eight cannon, casks of gunpowder, and a ship's boat in a desperate effort to lighten ship and gain an extra knot or two of speed. As the *Merrimack* came within cannon range, her long nine-pounder bow chaser banged out twenty-three shots. At 5:30, the *Merrimack* surged up abreast of the enemy, the French navy schooner *Magicienne*, rated for twelve guns, and "gave her part of a Broadside which obliged them to hall down their colours." The French crew, 63 officers and men, were ferried across the water as prisoners. Brown put his sailing master, a midshipman, and eight men aboard the *Magicienne* as a prize crew, and escorted the prize into St. Kitts. In one of the war's strangest twists of fate, the *Magicienne* reputedly had been built in Baltimore; had been a French privateer called the *Croyable* when Stephen Decatur, Sr., in the *Delaware* had captured her on 7 July 1798 as the U.S. Navy's first victory and first prize of the war; had been taken into the U.S. Navy as the *Retaliation;* but, as the first command of William Bainbridge, had been recaptured on 20 November 1798 by the French frigates *Volontaire* and *Insurgente* and brought back into the French navy as the *Magicienne*. When Brown brought her into St. Kitts, the acting squadron commander, Thomas Tingey, took her back into the U.S. Navy (again calling her the *Retaliation*) and used her to escort a convoy to Philadelphia. There, the *Magicienne* played her last trick; recognizing her as a dull sailer, the Navy Department sold the *Retaliation* at auction. But because the *Magicienne* had been a French navy vessel at the time of her capture, the *Merrimack*'s officers and crew received "head money" and "gun money" for their effort, $40 per Frenchman and $50 per cannon aboard, or $2,820. Even so, Secretary Stoddert drove the valuation down by paying only for the six guns left on board when the prize crew took over, not for the eight thrown overboard.[36]

For the next three months, the *Merrimack* cruised around and about the islands. For much of July, the *Merrimack* sailed in a little squadron with the brig *Norfolk*, under William Bainbridge, and the 24-gun ship *Ganges*, commanded by Thomas Tingey. As senior captain, Tingey liked ordering Brown and Bainbridge about, and wrote the secretary of the navy long, officious letters about his squadron's operations. For twelve days (6–19 July), the *Merrimack* tacked around Guadeloupe "without effecting any thing (except the chase of one small privateer, which however got too near the land 'ere the *Merrimack* could come up fully with him)." In fact, the *Merrimack* barely missed catching the privateer schooner, but could only manage two shots at her before she escaped into shallow water. Tingey then sent his squadron to Martinique to allow the *Norfolk* to step a new foremast, and dispatched the *Merrimack* to escort several merchant vessels straggling behind a convoy from Martinique to St. Kitts. The *Merrimack* brought five or six merchantmen safely to St. Thomas before doubling back to St. Kitts. Off the western end of that island on 5 August, Tingey spoke to the *Merrimack*, reporting that the *Ganges* had spotted a French letter of marque schooner, the *Buonaparte*, ready to sail from St. Barts. Brown cracked on all sail and found his quarry.

At 8 P.M. on 6 August 1799, the *Merrimack*'s lookouts picked up the *Buonaparte* about twelve miles northeast of Nevis, and caught her an hour later, after three cannon shots convinced the French that resistance was futile. The *Buonaparte* carried eight guns and thirty-four men, but as she carried a letter of marque she also was loaded with beef, pork, and dry goods, which Brown estimated would fetch about $20,000 at auction.[37] The *Merrimack* brought her prize safely into St. Kitts the next morning, where a British vice-admiralty court stood open to the libel and condemnation procedure that would convert the *Buonaparte* into cash. But if Moses Brown thought that pocketing the three-twentieths share of the proceeds due to a captain would be as easy as capturing the *Buonaparte*, he was sadly mistaken. For one thing, Tingey, who complained that "I seem'd destin'd to such continuance of ill-luck that I've hardly expectation of meeting success," congratulated himself in a letter to Stoddert that "I had been fortunate in the direction given Capt. Brown, relative to the situation he should place himself in, to intercept the *Buonaparte* . . ." The upshot, of course, was that Tingey put in a claim for one of Brown's three-twentieths of the proceeds, apparently due to his status as acting squadron commander. Brown contested Tingey's claim. More important, the *Buonaparte* carried Swedish (neutral) cargo, and the Swedish minister to the United States, Richard Soderstrom, pestered the secretaries of state and of the navy with letters demanding compensation. Ultimately, Brown had to refund about $1,600 to the Swedish diplomat because Soderstrom put documentary proof in front of Stoddert that Swedes actually owned the goods.[38] Worse still, at Brown's request, the U.S. Navy agent at St. Kitts, David Clarkson, provided bills of exchange for the proceeds of the auction of the *Buonaparte* and her cargo, and the market discounted the bills so steeply that Stoddert thought there would not be enough to pay off the Swedish creditors. Stoddert was beside himself, exclaiming "But why should these bills have been sold on credit? Were they not Government Bills? and could any doubt exist as to their punctual payment? The sale however being an act of your own . . . you must abide the consequences."[39] The document trail peters out without a clear answer as to the result.

All of this, of course, could not be divined in August 1799 when the *Merrimack* brought the *Buonaparte* into St. Kitts. On 11 August, the *Merrimack* rejoined Tingey's little squadron of the *Ganges* and the *Pickering* (in place of the *Norfolk*, sent off to escort a convoy) off Barbuda where Tingey reported that "nothing material" occurred "except for a few fruitless chaces." One of the fruitless chases was on the 15th, when the three Americans discovered a sail six miles east of Antigua that turned out to be the fifty-seven-ton schooner *John* from Gloucester. The *John* had just been seized by the French privateer *Revellieu*, and the *Revellieu* was in fact still in sight, trying to steal away. The Americans spotted the *Revellieu*, and while the slower-sailing *Pickering* took care of the *John*, the *Ganges* and *Merrimack* made sail in hot pursuit of the privateer. The *Revellieu* raced desperately for Guadeloupe, and the chase continued for eight hours under full sail. Captain Tingey narrated that his ship, the *Ganges*, "had pass'd the *Merrimack*, gain'd within half or at most 3/4 of a mile of the privateer, & a mile & half, or very little more from the shore of Guadaloupe, when the wind becoming light, she gain'd to the windward of us, disappear'd under the land & the chace given up." Yet it was the *Merrimack* that had closed within range and fired four shots at the *Revellieu* before breaking off pursuit, albeit the *Merrimack* gave up when she stood four miles off Guadeloupe. In his self-congratulatory, officious way, Tingey paid a backhanded tribute to the speed of the Hackett-designed Newburyport ship: Tingey boasted that the *Ganges* "has out-saild every ship & vessel of the United States, that we have been in company with; *when in chace under a press of canvas;* even the *Merrimack*, we have twice past in full chace."[40]

The *Merrimack* rendezvoused with a ten-ship convoy off St. Kitts on 18 August and took it clear of the Islands without mishap.[41] Upon her return, the *Merrimack* sailed "in company" with the *Ganges* for much of the next few weeks. Finally, on 18 September, Tingey passed along to Brown the navy secretary's orders dispatching the *Merrimack* to Vera Cruz to intercept any privateers that the Spanish authorities allowed to refit. Since Stoddert understood that, as a merchant mariner, Brown had sailed in those waters, it made sense to send the *Merrimack*, by way of the southern coasts of Saint-Domingue and Cuba, to "scour the Coast" between the Yucatan and Vera Cruz. On 15 November, however, he was to stop his scouring and sail the *Merrimack* to Boston.[42] The *Merrimack* first put into St. Kitts, and spent several days loading food and twenty-two casks of water before departing on her long, elliptical cruise to Mexico on 21 September.[43] At 11 A.M. on her second day out, while in sight of Puerto Rico, the *Merri-*

mack saw a sail and Brown ordered "all sail set in chase." After two hours, the *Merrimack* came up to an English schooner, the *Charming Nancy,* Abraham Honey, master, that a French privateer had captured eleven days earlier. Instead, Brown took out the Frenchmen and put a *Merrimack* midshipman and five sailors aboard as a prize crew, sent along "some water, Beef & Spare rigging," and ordered the *Charming Nancy* to New York.[44] Scarcely had the *Charming Nancy* cast off when the *Merrimack*'s lookouts spotted two more sails and, after a three-hour pursuit, retook the sloop *Elizabeth,* which the French had captured en route from New York to Curaçao.[45]

Over the next few days, as the *Merrimack* sailed along the south coast of Saint-Domingue and then Cuba, she chased a number of ships. Some turned out to be American, like the brig *Hope,* sailing to Richmond (although she needed a gun fired to stop and verify her nationality to the *Merrimack*); some turned out to be English or Spanish warships; one turned out to be a French schooner but so tiny that Brown let her go; other sails the *Merrimack* lost in the dark.[46] Off Grand Cayman Island, bumboats came alongside and Captain Brown purchased turtles for his soup; at sunrise a few days later, his crew caught fifty groupers for *their* dinners.[47]

Finally, on 20 October, the *Merrimack* came to anchor in thirty feet of water in the Vera Cruz Roads. While Captain Brown went ashore to pay his respects to the local authorities and see if any French privateers were about, the *Merrimack* moored with both bower anchors. Then the crew replenished fresh water, bringing fifty-two casks aboard in one day, and thirteen more aboard over the next two days.[48] Apparently, the *Merrimack*'s cruise to Vera Cruz was unnecessary in that no French privateers were in port or likely to arrive. Instead, Brown prepared his ship for sea, awaiting only a wind.

When the wind came, however, it was gale force and from the wrong direction. Brown tried to navigate the *Merrimack* out, anyway, and weighed his anchors. But he could not bring his ship under control. The *Merrimack* drifted and threatened to run aground. In desperation, a hawser was heaved to a Spanish frigate moored nearby. The line held and the *Merrimack* rather ignominiously hung on her, riding out the storm. The next morning, 26 October 1799, when the *Merrimack* successfully made sail and beat out of Vera Cruz, her thirteen-gun salute to the Spanish flag was more grateful than honorific.[49]

The *Merrimack*'s three-week journey to Havana was uneventful except for some severe storms, although Midshipman Brown twice recorded that, in "moderate & pleasant weather," his father, the captain, hove to "to fish."[50] The *Merrimack* spent three days in Havana, taking on fifty casks of fresh water, sixteen barrels of beef and pork, and a pipe of brandy for her voyage to Boston. The *Merrimack* began the last leg of her second war cruise on 24 November. Four days out from Cuba, a leak was discovered somewhere down the forepeak, but with "Brisk gales . . . with a rough sea," and a hold that had been stowed carelessly, no one could figure out exactly where the sea was coming in. Worse, coal stowed in the bilges, apparently as ballast, interfered with the pumps. Brown ordered all hands to bailing while a party of sailors dumped the coal overboard so that the seawater could sluice down to the pumps. The next morning, the *Merrimack*'s carpenter found the leak but could not fix it. But, between the bailing and the pumps, the ship was out of danger. For ballast, Brown ordered his eight quarterdeck guns into the hold. At noon on 8 December, the *Merrimack* sighted Cape Ann and at five o'clock came to off Gloucester. She arrived at Boston on 10 December and moored at Hartt's shipyard, where Secretary Stoddert's orders to pay off the crew and immediately refit the *Merrimack* awaited Captain Brown.[51]

The Navy Department deluged Brown with paperwork because, a year before, Brown had advanced $4,000 to sailors to fill out his crew without submitting vouchers. There was also the vexing litigation about the *Merrimack*'s prizes, and replacements to be found for the many *Merrimack* officers who resigned from the service, including his journal-keeping son, Midshipman Joseph Brown. But Stoddert allowed Moses Brown a leave of absence as soon as he could leave the ship "with propriety" and until the *Merrimack* would be ready to sail. The refitting of the *Merrimack* apparently was left in the capable hands of Stephen Higginson, the Boston navy agent.[52]

On 28 January 1800, Stoddert ordered Brown to take the *Merrimack* back to St. Kitts where he would "fall in with our Squadron on that Station" under Commodore Truxtun. Perhaps recalling the *Merrimack*'s tarrying in Boston seven months before, waiting to convoy merchant ships that never materialized, Stoddert added in a postscript that Brown should escort any vessels bound to the St. Kitts vicinity "but wait for none that are not ready." The *Merrimack* sailed on 9 February.[53] Many of her movements thereafter are scarcely documented.

She departed Basseterre, St. Kitts, on 8 March and, in the words of one of her officers, "cruised for many days from E to W and from N to S and chased several vessels, which proved to be friends." The *Merrimack* also brought a twenty-five-ship convoy out of the Islands, breaking away on 16 March. On 4 April, the *Merrimack* recaptured the brig *Anna,* "deeply loaded with live stock, provisions, etc. which had been taken a few days before by a French privateer," which entitled all those aboard the *Merrimack* to share £205, or one-eighth its appraised salvage value.[54]

In mid-April, the *Merrimack* escorted a nine-ship convoy from St. Barts. Brown still had not mastered the combination of bluster and cajolery needed to keep a flock of merchantmen together. Several of the ships straggled and, this time, a jackal-like privateer, the *Hasard,* lay in wait. On the second day out, the 6-gun *Hasard* captured the *Hope,* bound for Georgetown, South Carolina, although Blandineau, the French commander, let her go as a Swedish-flagged vessel. On the third day out, the *Hasard* snatched up the *Chance,* bound for Norfolk, as well as the sloop *Union,* bound for Newburyport. How Moses Brown let one-third of his convoy fall out in three days is unclear. Perhaps savvy privateer captains like Blandineau had altered their tactics based on intelligence about U.S. Navy convoy tactics. There is evidence that the French knew the makeup of these later convoys and when they were supposed to break up: off Saba at the end of May, the *Merrimack* spoke to the schooner *Lively* of Boston, and offered to escort her to St. Thomas to join a homeward-bound convoy protected by the U.S. naval brig *Scammel.* The French privateer *Courageux* later captured the *Lively,* whose master reported that Bousson, the French commander, "had so good information of the Americans, that without the least hesitation he asked me how long since I left the fleet, and whether the *Scammel* was going to America with them. He knew the time the fleet sailed and the name of the convoy."[55] Perhaps Blandineau in the *Hasard* had received help from other privateers, luring the *Merrimack* away from the convoy.

On 6 June 1800, off Puerto Rico, the *Merrimack* recaptured the brig *Ceres* that the *Hasard* had seized on 18 May, and Brown ordered a midshipman to muster five sailors and bring the *Ceres* to Philadelphia for salvage proceedings.[56] The *Merrimack* has left no record as to her activities for the next three months, but she lay moored at St. Kitts in mid-September 1800 with the light frigate *John Adams* and the sloop of war *Patapsco* when a man named William Robinson arrived with a plea to help Americans under siege on the island of Curaçao.

The French invasion of the Dutch island of Curaçao played out like a comic opera, so elephantine that *American* newspapers reported it months before the first shot. On 20 August 1800, the *Federal Gazette &*

Baltimore Daily Advertiser printed an extract of a letter from Henry Geddes, captain of the Baltimore-built subscription ship *Patapsco,* in which Geddes reported learning that a French expedition had sailed for Curaçao and his fear that "a great deal of American property [would] be lost." Three days later, the same Baltimore paper printed a letter from Curaçao, in which the writer announced that 1,500 French soldiers and sailors had landed across the Willemstad, Curaçao, harbor from the Dutch fort—hardly a *coup de main* in the Napoleonic fashion. The French commander demanded money and that the Dutch government capitulate, but the Dutch governor refused and called the militia out, after which the French army was "very quiet." Curiously, despite Geddes's knowledge, the U.S. naval squadron at St. Kitts did not react.[57]

On 5 September, however, the French commander published an order suggesting that American citizens and property were subject to confiscation, and made military demonstrations that rattled the Dutch burghers. Benjamin Phillips, the U.S. consul at Curaçao, chartered a small schooner, aptly named the *Escape,* and sent his friend William Robinson out in it carrying Phillips's written plea for help. The *Escape* reached St. Kitts eight days later, on the 14th, where Robinson found the *John Adams, Merrimack,* and *Patapsco* in the harbor. The American captains met in a council of war. Cross, the senior officer, declined to take the *John Adams*—the most powerful ship and only frigate—off station. But Cross "cheerfully gave his consent" to Brown and Geddes. The *Merrimack* and *Patapsco* sailed the next morning, and appeared off Curaçao on the 22nd. While the U.S. warships were en route, the Dutch had capitulated to a British frigate, the *Nereid,* hoping for protection, but the British refused to sail into the confined waters of Willemstad's harbor, justly fearing artillery batteries the French erected to command the water approach. Still, the French general, Jannet, had not attacked. Nevertheless, Phillips and Robinson, who reconnoitered the situation on the night of the 22nd, believed the French were about to launch an amphibious assault across the St. Ana Bay, a channel separating the Dutch in Willemstad from the French positions in an area called the Othrabanda, and that American merchant seamen helping the Dutchmen would be slaughtered.

Robinson went on board the *Merrimack,* Brown being senior to Geddes, to ask that one of the American warships enter the St. Ana Bay to blast the French and interdict any assault. The *Patapsco,* rated for 20 guns, was smaller than the 24-gun *Merrimack,* or at least Brown thought so.[58] He ordered Geddes into the bay, although Brown dispatched all twenty of the *Merrimack*'s marines to bolster the *Patapsco*'s detachment. The marines, already renown for marksmanship, were used in the sailing navy as sharpshooters. The *Patapsco* stood into the bay, and as her great guns blasted at the French batteries, the forty marines peppered the houses and embankment of the Othrabanda with lead. The French cannon were silenced. The next morning, the 24th, fifty sailors and marines from the *Patapsco*, and the twenty *Merrimack* marines, landed in Willemstad to help the Dutch-American line. The expected French attack never came, however, and the French evacuated from Curaçao, as the *Merrimack* discovered when she stood in toward shore at first light on the 25th.[59]

The British claimed victory, took control of the island, and asked the *Merrimack* and *Patapsco* to sail out to intercept a supposed second French invasion force. When the U.S. warships departed, English privateers seized all the American shipping in Willemstad for carrying "contraband." For these indignities, Commodore Truxtun condemned Geddes, not Brown, although Brown was the senior officer and Brown, not Geddes, brought the bad news back to St. Kitts.[60] Perhaps Truxtun, a man who reveled in the thought of prize money, felt mollified by the *Merrimack*'s capture of the 14-gun privateer brig *Phénix* on the sortie from Curaçao.[61] Truxtun ordered the *Merrimack* to cruise off Marie Galante to intercept privateers but he ordered Geddes and the *Patapsco* to escort a convoy back to America.[62] Within days, the *Merrimack* chased and captured another 14-gun privateer brig, the *Brillant,* which, sent into admiralty court at Williamsburg, Virginia, netted the *Merrimack* $1,634.80 (with $195.83 going to Truxtun as squadron commander).[63]

By the time the U.S. district court passed its decree, however, the *Merrimack* was back in Boston. On 4 January 1801, Truxtun ordered Brown to sail from St. Kitts to St. Barts to pick up any homeward-bound American ships, and then to St. Thomas, and then to see them safe to the "Northward of Bermuda." The one-year enlistments of the *Merrimack*'s crew were expiring, and Moses Brown was in poor health, prompting Truxtun, who could be a warm friend to men he respected, to close his letter wishing Brown an easy passage and a return to health.[64] Secretary Stoddert also was solicitous, ordering Brown to pay off his crew but allowing him a "leave of absence for such time as may be necessary for the recovery of your health, or until called on."[65]

The call never came. The United States had negotiated a settlement with France, and peace meant that the navy would be pared down drastically. Less than one month after taking office, Jefferson's administration directed that the *Merrimack,* with her "sails, rigging tackle apparel & furniture," be sold at public auction after fifteen days notice in the newspapers of Boston, Salem, Providence, and Newport.[66] The navy sold off the *Merrimack* for $21,154.59. Renamed the *Monticello,* and fitted out as a merchantman, she was wrecked soon after on the sands of Cape Cod.[67]

Two days after ordering the sale of the *Merrimack,* the new administration dismissed Moses Brown from the service. He was past fifty-nine and old enough to be the grandfather of the sailors and officers serving under him. As tried a seaman as he was, Moses Brown was a citizen-captain, not a man around whom the navy might build a professional officer corps. While a successful privateer hunter in the naval war against France, Moses Brown may have been too little of a disciplinarian for the smaller peacetime professional navy. Acting Secretary of the Navy Samuel Smith had the good graces to suggest that President Jefferson himself had a "Just Sense of the Services rendered by you to your Country," making the decision to retire him "a painful duty." The navy gave Brown and the other retired captains four months severance pay.[68] Brown recognized the world as an unforgiving place and threw himself, as he put it, "once more on the wide world for employment to earn bread for myself and family." Into his sixties, he captained Newburyport merchantmen trading to the West Indies. On the homeward leg of a voyage to Guadeloupe, on New Year's Day, 1804, off Long Island, Brown suffered a stroke. He asked to be carried on deck to look on America, and was turned in a circle to view the entire horizon. Carried below, he died within the hour. Although Martha's Vineyard was in sight, Moses Brown was buried at sea, an appropriate end for a man who had devoted his life to it.[69]

President John Adams; painting by G. P. A. Healey, ca. 1864
Library of Congress

Moses Brown, captain of the *Merrimack;* painting attributed to
Benjamin Blythe, ca. 1780 *Courtesy of the Newburyport Maritime Society,
Newburyport, Massachusetts; photograph by Patricia Bashford*

William Hackett, designer of the *Merrimack* and *Essex ;* artist unknown
Courtesy of the Peabody Essex Museum, Salem, Massachusetts

USS *Merrimack;* painting attributed to William Drown, ca. 1798

Photograph courtesy of the Peabody Essex Museum, Salem, Massachusetts; original painting courtesy of the Newburyport Maritime Society, Newburyport, Massachusetts

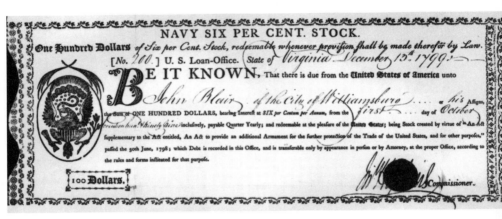

Navy Six Per Cent Stock Certificate

Records of the Bureau of the Public Debt, National Archives

Robert Haswell, first lieutenant of the *Boston;* painting attributed to
James Sharples. *Courtesy of the Massachusetts Historical Society*

USS *Boston;* printed originally in *Recueil de Navires de Guerre et Marchands
de Diverses Nations* (Paris, 1812)

"Preparation for WAR to defend Commerce. The Swedish Church *Southwark with the building of the FRIGATE PHILADELPHIA,*" engraving by W. Birch & Son, 1800 *Library of Congress*

John Brown, a merchant from Providence, ca. 1794; miniature by
Edward Malbone ©*Collection of the New-York Historical Society*

USS *George Washington;* painting by Thomas Chambers, ca. 1838
Courtesy of the Rhode Island Historical Society, Providence, Rhode Island

Moses Myers, a merchant from Norfolk, ca. 1803; painting by Gilbert Stuart
Courtesy of the Moses Myers House/Scott Wolff, Chrysler Museum of Art, Norfolk, Virginia

Elias Hasket Derby, a merchant from Salem; painting by James Frothingham
Courtesy of the Peabody Essex Museum, Salem, Massachusetts

Edward Preble, captain of the *Essex*
Library of Congress

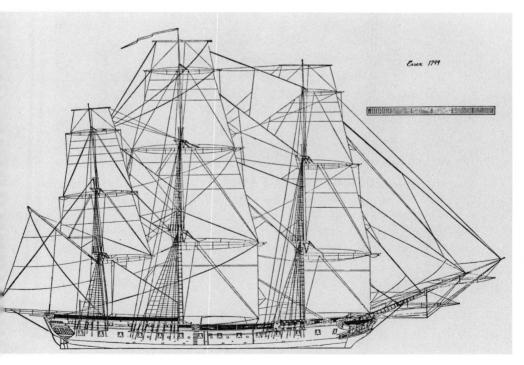

Sail plan of the USS *Essex;* drawing by Howard I. Chapelle

Liverpool pitcher depicting the launch of the *Patapsco* in Baltimore
Courtesy of the Herbert and James Barnett families of Baltimore, Maryland

4 *The Philadelphia's Story*

The first city to respond to the Newburyport subscription-loan example was Philadelphia.

In 1798, Philadelphia was the capital of the United States, America's largest city with almost 70,000 people, and a leading port. To a young English visitor, Philadelphia was "certainly a very fine town" of "well built [houses] of good brick," but "extremely dull" and with a layout so regular as to be "disagreeable." Unlike most American towns, Philadelphia boasted cobblestoned streets, brick sidewalks, and elms and poplars planted for shade. Moreau de St. Méry, an escapee from the excesses of the French Revolution, counted 662 street lamps in Philadelphia and praised the night watchmen who deterred crime and shouted out the weather hourly. But the weather was intolerable, "frigid in winter and stifling in summer," so suffocating that Moreau blamed the heat for "dysentery, slow and putrid fevers, and other dangerous sicknesses." In fact, virulent attacks of yellow fever killed thousands of people every summer, and caused the federal government and perhaps one-third of the population to evacuate the city. Moreau depreciated the Quakers, attributing to them "the melancholy customs of this city, which has less society than most places." Yet Philadelphia contained not only the public buildings housing the government but also two theatres, circuses, a museum, a public library, a philosophical society, a university, and many philanthropic and artisanal societies.[1]

Yet Americans generally, and Philadelphians particularly, stood accused even in the 1790s of the original capitalist sin—they were "a nation of Merchants: always alive to their interests; & therefore almost wholly engrossed with the thoughts of it . . ." The merchants' "interests" were arrayed along the docks of Philadelphia. Dozens of wharves jutted out into the Delaware River. Great obstacles confronted merchant-shipowners. The river was filled with shoals and prone to silting up; the river froze for as much as three months each winter; and Philadelphia lies more than one hundred miles from the ocean. Nevertheless, entrepreneurial spirit made Philadelphia a great port. Philadelphia ships reputedly began American trade with both India and South America, and by 1798, twenty Philadelphia vessels had sailed to Canton. To support such trade, Philadelphia counted fourteen shipyards between Kensington and Southwark, and the 1800 City Directory lists seventeen ship chandlers, twenty riggers, and no fewer than forty-three sailmakers. As in Newburyport, the Philadelphia merchants knew all about syndications. The Bank of North America, organized in 1782 and rechartered in 1787, was situated in Philadelphia and, at its creation, was the only chartered bank in the world run exclusively for profit for its shareholders. In 1792, the Insurance Company of North America was founded, and two years later incorporated, primarily to provide marine casualty insurance. In 1791, the Philadelphia & Lancaster Turnpike Co. had offered shares in a private enterprise to build the first hard-surfaced road between two American towns, a sixty-mile road completed in 1794.[2]

On 1 June 1798, the Philadelphia *Aurora & General Advertiser* first printed the report of the subscription-loan undertaking at Newburyport. Within five days, Benjamin Goodhue, a Federalist from Massachusetts, introduced the Senate bill authorizing stock. While the Senate weighed the legislation, Philadelphia merchants convened at the City Tavern[3] on Monday, 11 June, where they agreed to subscribe monies for two 20-gun ships to loan to the federal government. They raised $23,000 immediately and set up a five-man committee of merchants to collect additional pledges.[4] The committee consisted of Joseph Anthony,[5] David H. Conyngham,[6] Daniel Smith,[7] James Crawford, and Joseph Smith.[8] By noon the next day, subscribers had pledged $50,000; after two days, $64,000; and on Thursday, the 14th, the day the Senate passed the enabling bill, the

Philadelphia list topped $70,000.[9] By then, the committee recast itself to include the most prominent private citizens of Philadelphia.

The chairman was Thomas FitzSimons (1741–1811), an Irishman by birth whose family emigrated to America in the mid-1750s. FitzSimons rose to great wealth as a merchant in partnership with his brother-in-law, George Meade (grandfather of the Union general in the Civil War). During the Revolution, FitzSimons commanded a company of Philadelphia militia in Col. John Cadwalader's battalion during the winter of 1776–77 in Washington's army, although his unit missed combat at the battles of Trenton and Princeton. With his active military service over, FitzSimons was appointed to the Pennsylvania Council of Safety and to the Navy Board, overseeing the Pennsylvania state navy and the defense of the river approach to Philadelphia. The first Catholic elected to any government position in Pennsylvania, FitzSimons escorted General Washington to a Catholic mass in May 1778 at a Philadelphia church; Washington noted in his diary, "led by curiosity and good company attended the Romish Church." After the war, FitzSimons was elected to the Constitutional Convention in 1787, where he championed a powerful federal government, and then was elected to Congress for three terms as a Federalist from Philadelphia. As a representative, FitzSimons advocated protective tariffs to encourage American manufacturing, and served on the House select committee that drafted the 1794 bill to authorize construction of the navy's six original frigates. In private life, FitzSimons was also a leading financier, helping to establish the Bank of North America and the Insurance Company of North America. After his congressional defeat, FitzSimons never again held elective office. Yet he remained a powerful force in Philadelphia as a financier, as a philanthropist, as president of the Philadelphia Chamber of Commerce, and as an adviser on naval matters to the Washington and Adams administrations. A devout Catholic, FitzSimons combined entrepreneurial skills with a generous, loyal personality.[10]

Assisting FitzSimons on the committee was Thomas M. Willing (1731–1821), a millionaire, former (colonial) mayor of Philadelphia, and incumbent president of the Bank of the United States.[11] A younger member, William Jones (1760–1831), had been a Revolutionary War soldier and privateersman, a shipmaster out of Charleston, and, in 1798, a Philadelphia merchant and head of the city board of health. Unlike the rest of the committee, Jones was a Republican; he later served one term in Congress, and during the War of 1812, President James Madison prevailed upon him to be secretary of the navy. Jones's selection to the frigate committee suggests the sense of unity or national purpose sweeping the nation in the crisis atmosphere during the summer of 1798. Ideology took a backseat; the Federalist-dominated committee wanted the affable Jones to appeal to "right-minded" Republicans who recognized that the nation needed their money and talents.[12] The committee members, taken together, were leaders of Philadelphia's mercantile community, and politically connected.[13] After only five business days, the Philadelphia subscription approached $80,000, helped by a pledge of $5,000 from William Bingham, United States senator from Pennsylvania, who happened to be Willing's son-in-law. Ultimately, about $101,000 was raised in Philadelphia.[14]

The city of Philadelphia had raised $100,000 in less than one week, and then no more subscribers came forward, suggesting that the committee's goal had been reached, and the loan-subscription effort then shut down. The goal of $100,000 made sense given the Philadelphia merchants' idea that they were going to build two small warships, each of twenty guns, for the federal government. Two hundred years later, the $100,000 raised in Philadelphia may seem paltry. In 1798, however, a skilled ship carpenter received $1.50 a day when he could find work; the gross receipts of the United States government were $7.9 million. That the Philadelphia merchants rallied to augment the navy was not lost on the nation; at a Fourth of July celebration in 1798 at the Oaks, near Dover, Delaware, the light infantry company of the 5th Delaware Regiment paraded with their colors of an eagle and snake emblazoned with the motto "Don't tread on me." After a patriotic dinner, the light infantry gave a round of celebratory toasts, followed by cheers and "regular platoon firings;" No. 10 was to "The American Merchants—may their patriotic and disinterested conduct, receive the gratitude, as it commands the respect, of every class of their fellow-citizens." Patriotic to be sure, but hardly disinterested. The merchants' capital assets—their ships—were at risk on the seas, and the merchants' livelihood therefore threatened. Moreover, in the building of a large warship, many of these same merchants might receive contracts, a result William Cobbett in *Porcupine's Gazette* thought only just.[15]

By the middle of July, at Benjamin Stoddert's prompting, the committee changed the plan from building two 20-gun ships to one 44-gun frigate. The navy's assistant constructor, Josiah Fox, provided the design. The keel of the new frigate was laid in July 1798 on the very stocks in Joshua Humphreys's shipyard in Southwark on which the navy's first frigate, the *United States,* was built and from which she was launched in October 1797. Just days after the keel-laying, Fox received orders to Norfolk to build the Navy's frigate there, soon to be called the *Chesapeake.* In his stead, the Philadelphia committee chose Samuel Humphreys, Nathaniel Hutton, and John Delavue to oversee construction of their ship.[16]

The designer of the merchants' frigate, Josiah Fox, was a recent immigrant to America. Born in 1763 to a Quaker family in Falmouth, England, Fox received professional training as an apprentice to the master constructor in the naval dockyard at Plymouth in the 1780s. Fox developed draftsman skills not readily found in America. In the late 1780s, Fox toured English shipyards and went to the Continent to study foreign methods at Archangel, Cadiz, and at the famous Arsenal of Venice. He came to the United States in 1793 to examine American woods. Fox's extended family in America introduced him to Secretary of War Henry Knox, who came away impressed by Fox's technical prowess. Since the United States had no navy before 1797, nor a navy department before June 1798, the War Department looked after the federal government's maritime concerns. By the middle of 1794, however, Knox hired a prominent Philadelphia shipbuilder named Joshua Humphreys to be naval constructor and design the new frigates the United States had decided to build. Knox hired Fox to assist Humphreys, although for bureaucratic reasons, Fox's job title was War Department clerk.[17]

Joshua Humphreys was born in Haverford, Pennsylvania, in 1751. In January 1774, with a partner named John Wharton, Humphreys bought out a shipyard at Southwark in Philadelphia, and began building ships. At the start of the Revolution, Humphreys & Wharton turned to constructing warships, launching the 32-gun frigate *Randolph* before the British army's occupation of Philadelphia ended that effort. After the Revolution, Joshua Humphreys consolidated a reputation as a leading shipbuilder. While Humphreys, unlike Fox, had never been to sea or made the tour of Europe, he had applied himself in a prototypical American way to self-study of naval architectural treatises. When the federal government moved to Philadelphia and began to think of reestablishing the navy that had been sold off after the Revolution, Humphreys was interested, available, and an experienced ship designer. The War Department consulted Humphreys, as well as Revolutionary War sea officers and other shipbuilders—John Foster Williams of Boston; John Wharton, Humphreys' former partner; William Penrose, another Philadelphia builder; and John Hackett of Newburyport—when the Washington administration decided to build ships to deal forcefully with the festering nuisance of the Barbary pirates on the North Africa coast. But Humphreys and the others understood that the warships the new nation was to build were not merely to fight Tripolitans or Algerines, but would provide the nucleus of a naval force in any confrontation with European naval powers. Humphreys advocated vessels to "overmatch" those of an enemy, with great length and a deep draft so that they could be weatherly and outrun any ship they could not outfight. "Frigates will be the first object," Humphreys wrote, "and none ought to be built less than 150 feet keel, to carry thirty twenty-four-pounders on the gun-deck. Ships of this construction have everything in their favor; their great length gives them the advantage of sailing, which is an object of the first magnitude. They are superior to any European frigate, and if others be in company, our frigates can always lead ahead and never be obliged to go into action but on their own terms, except in a calm . . ."[18]

From the beginning, a faction of naval architects, shipbuilders, and Revolutionary War sea officers doubted Humphreys's design, and Josiah Fox by all accounts was one of the main skeptics. Secretary Knox accepted Humphreys's conception, however, and although the six frigates authorized by Congress were reduced to three, Humphreys saw to it that these frigates—the *United States,* 44 guns, building at Humphreys's yard in Philadelphia; the *Constitution,* 44 guns, building in Boston; and the *Constellation,* 36 guns, building in Baltimore—were of enormous scale and made with the finest materials. As C. S. Forester aptly pointed out, the Humphreys frigates were the pocket battleships of their day. But they also provided an early and egregious example of a military cost overrun, and when they were launched in 1797, no one was quite sure if they would work.[19]

The sailing-navy historian Howard Chapelle speculates that the Philadelphia frigate committee asked Josiah Fox to design the "local Frigate," rather than "their fellow townsman, Joshua Humphreys," because in July 1798, Secretary Stoddert kept Humphreys, the chief constructor, busy with repairs, surveying possible merchant vessels to take into the navy, and in designing a prototype 74-gun ship of the line. According to this hypothesis, Fox's known ability and experience preparing draughts for the original group of frigates made him the natural fallback choice.[20] Chapelle's theory does not ring true. In July 1798, Stoddert charged Humphreys to take "immediate Steps" to prepare a captured French privateer, *Croyable,* for service as the U.S. schooner *Retaliation.*[21]

Humphreys also spent a day looking at a merchant brig owned by Clement Hothar, concluding that she was "not a strong well built Vessel."[22] For part of August, Humphreys surveyed the USS *Ganges*, a merchant-man recently taken into the navy.[23] As to the 74-gun ships, Humphreys' design work apparently began eight months later, in the spring of 1799.[24] But the theory that Humphreys was "too busy" does not explain why the frigate committee rejected the existing (Humphreys) design of the 44-gun *United States* for their "local" frigate in the first place. And if Joshua Humphreys was too busy to draw up the plans for Philadelphia's sub-scription frigate, Chapelle's theory does not explain why the Philadel-phia merchants did not turn to any of a number of candidates, such as Penrose (with whom they had personal ties and who had designed mer-chant ships for these very merchants) or Joshua Humphreys' son, Samuel Humphreys. After all, the 23-year old Samuel Humphreys drew the lines for New York's subscription frigate only a few weeks later, and for the New York merchants, the Humphreys name and reputation would have less influence than in Philadelphia.

The Navy Department's correspondence provides another hypothe-sis. On 26 June 1798, Stoddert, who had been installed as navy secretary for exactly one week, wrote to Thomas FitzSimons. Stoddert seemed obliv-ious to the capital city's enthusiastic support for a subscription warship despite his physical presence in Philadelphia at the same moment the merchants pledged their monies and despite the articles in the Philadel-phia newspapers. Stoddert wrote that it would be "highly desireable" that the "Patriotic Merchants and Citizens" of Philadelphia should furnish a frigate of at least 32, but preferably 36, or even 44, guns. Yet Stoddert con-cluded, "Our Three Frigates, already built [the *United States, Constitution,* and *Constellation*] are of a Size, one third at least larger than Frigates of the same number of Guns in Europe. An English Frigate of 38 guns will not measure so much as 900 Tons. Our 36 Guns Frigates measures near 1200. I doubt whether a Ship of 900 Tons could not be found equal to 44 Guns." Again and again Stoddert harped on the unnecessary size of the American frigates. To Representative Samuel Sewall, Stoddert rhetori-cally posed the question "to be determined whether, a Ship carrying the same Number of Guns, is better for being so much larger, than the size adopted by the British Nation." To Jeremiah Yellott, the navy agent in Bal-timore, Stoddert wrote a few days later, "The Frigates heretofore built have been on a scale too large. . . ."[25] Joshua Humphreys had been the prophet and exponent of those out-of-size frigates, and he had not retreated from his view. Only the month before, Humphreys had written Oliver Wolcott, the secretary of the treasury, that since the United States could not possibly match European navies in numbers, it would be "highly improper to follow their dimentions or construction for our Vessels . . . Therefore some plan must be adopted for providing Classes of ships Superior to theirs."[26] It would hardly do to give the same man the commission for what Stoddert hoped would be a smaller design. Fox, with his British Admiralty training, had strongly criticized the Humphreys designs as producing unwieldy, cumbersome vessels, although Fox had helped prepare the revisions of Humphreys's original draughts under Humphreys's direction.[27] With Stoddert dubious as to the virtues of size in frigates, it was logical for him to recommend Josiah Fox to the locals.

Ironically, despite his professional opposition to the oversize Humphreys design, Fox produced plans for Philadelphia's subscription frigate to be 1,240 tons, more than one-third larger than the size in which Stoddert hoped a new 44-gun frigate could be built. Ultimately, the Philadelphia frigate's rate was reduced to a 36, and British frigates mounting 36 guns were more than four hundred tons smaller than Fox's design. Fox, then, certainly felt no compulsion to follow English methods blindly. Like the standard Deptford or Chatham dockyard English frigate of the day, the Fox design envisioned a main gun battery of eighteen-pounders, rejecting Humphreys's fixation on twenty-four-pounders, but his ship was far bigger than the typical English model, with a 157-foot keel, a 39-foot moulded beam, and a 13 1/2-foot depth of hold. The Fox ship, initially called the *City of Philadelphia,* but then universally abridged to the *Philadelphia,* differed from the Humphreys designs, with their long entries from the bow and sheer lines. Fox's design resembled the blunter English archetype in that she had a more bulbous cross section near the keel, and therefore a more rounded bottom. Like the Humphreys frigates, however, the *Philadelphia* had a spar deck. Adopting the critical Humphreys innovation, Fox designed "diagonal riders" into the ship, a form of internal bracing with heavy timbers that transferred the weight of the upper decks downward to the rigidity of the keel to prevent "hogging," the gradual sagging of the keel at each end. The installation of the diagonal riders in the *Philadelphia* suggests that Humphreys and Fox were not so antagonistic professionally that the one could not recognize advances by the other. Fox also accepted the American preference for live-oak timber for structural hull pieces such as futtocks and knees, rejecting the English prejudice against live oak. To save weight and cost, however, the upper frames and parts of the hull utilized red cedar, another wood from the South, but less dense and easier to use than live oak. With his design for the *Philadelphia,* Fox tried to synthesize more traditional hull shapes, albeit elongated, with "engineering" innovations; although never copied, the *Philadelphia* ultimately proved a beautiful vessel.[28]

Thomas FitzSimons's position as chairman of the frigate committee made him controller, contracting agent, and grand purveyor of materials. Unlike the smaller warships built for the navy during the 1798 war crisis, the *Philadelphia* was meant to be a permanent addition to the navy, and therefore needed the best timber and materials. On the face of things, timber seemed to be no problem. As the keel was being laid down in July 1798, the exuberant William Cobbett, editor of *Porcupine's Gazette,* wrote that the *Philadelphia* would be built "very speedily" because the committee "purchased of government the metirials which were left on hand, after finishing the *United States.*" Although Cobbett overstated the situation in writing that "sufficient timber is ready for the whole of the work, except for the stern post and transom,"[29] the Philadelphia committee had made a deal with Benjamin Stoddert that they could use all of the government's wood remaining from building the *United States* but, in exchange, they would underwrite the cutting of additional live oak. Stoddert ordered Joshua Humphreys to inventory the stocks, and Humphreys determined that a great deal of live oak was at hand.[30]

American forests, if not virginal in 1798, still had the best wood in the world for ships. In 1794, Tench Coxe, the commissioner of the revenue in the Department of the Treasury and a political economist,[31] had observed: "Shipbuilding is a business in which the port of Philadelphia exceeds most parts of the world. Mast, spars, timber and plank, not only from our own State and the other states on the Delaware, are constantly for sale in our market; but the mulberry of the Chesapeake and the evergreen or live oak, and red cedar of the Carolinas and Georgia, are so abundantly imported that nine tenths of our vessels are built of them."[32] Samuel Humphreys, one of the three constructors of the *Philadelphia,* provided FitzSimons with an indent after his 53 3/4-day search for keel-raising timbers in the Delaware woods near New Castle and up Alloways Creek across the Delaware River in New Jersey on three forays between July and December 1798. He later spent a few days in June 1799 in the New Jersey forests looking for timber suitable for knees. But as Tench Coxe had noted, the most durable, dense, and disease-resistant wood was live oak, available from the sea islands and coastal areas of Georgia and South Carolina.

Live oak, *Quercus virginiana,* is a "semi-evergreen" that grows to seventy feet in height and may have a crown that spans 150 feet. Today, Americans discover these majestic trees in the parks of colonial plantations in the tidewater South, picturesquely draped with Spanish moss. But live oak's density and naturally curved branches suited American ship-builders because, without cross-grain cutting, live oak could be shaped for the most critical structural pieces that had to withstand the greatest stresses—the futtocks, knees, knightheads, stem, and sternpost. Even before the Revolution, Philadelphia shipbuilders, including Joshua Humphreys, used live oak. The best designers and seagoing officers of the day believed that a live-oak-built ship might last for fifty years. Getting a supply of live oak was one of FitzSimons's priorities.[33]

The Philadelphia committee literally needed to send an expedition to find, cut, and ship the balance of the live-oak timber. A live-oaking expedition was no small undertaking. Axmen need to be recruited, paid, and provisioned. Trees needed to be found, marked, and cut. The massive, rough-cut timbers needed to be pulled to the water, often where no roads existed, so that coastal vessels could load the timber and transport the wood to Philadelphia. Once the timbers were at the Philadelphia ship-yards, skilled ship carpenters could shave and shape them to their final dimensions. The whole process would take months, but if the *Philadelphia* were ever to sail in this war, the committee had no time to lose. On 17 July 1798, FitzSimons entered into a contract with John T. Morgan, formerly a Boston shipwright, who had spent most of 1794 and 1795 in Georgia felling live oak for the *Constitution, Constellation,* and *United States.* Morgan's earlier expedition had been nightmarish, with men dying of fever in malarial swamps, no logistical support, almost unimaginable difficulties in cutting and hauling, and some shipments lost at sea. Nevertheless, Morgan agreed to go back for live oak for the *Philadelphia.* According to the contract, Morgan promised to deliver two lots of live-oak timber, one to Philadelphia and the other to New York (for the frigate building by public subscription there), in November and December 1798. In that simpler era, FitzSimons and Morgan needed only three pages to hammer out the deal; Morgan covenanted that all the live oak would be "sound & good" and "as near to the shape according to the moulds as such Timber is usually obtained," and the committee promised to pay 75 cents per cubic yard of delivered wood. The third page of the contract listed the number of pieces of live oak needed, their respective uses (and therefore shapes), lengths, and thicknesses. The navy's audits of FitzSimons's accounts reflect payments ultimately to Morgan of $741.42 for "992 ¼ cu. ft. live oak" and $1,000 for "contract for timber."[34]

The committee needed more than wood for their ship. Although Philadelphia had the infrastructure needed to build ships—ropewalks, joiners, docks, ship carpenters, and the like—late nineteenth century America had few manufacturing establishments. Goods were handcrafted by artisans. For certain equipment, most notably cannon, copper, and canvas for sails, the committee could not turn to a military-industrial complex, although Secretary Stoddert hoped that the crash naval ship-building program would create one.[35] There were few American foundries that could cast reliable cannon at the start of the Quasi-War. Six of the initial eight cannon destined for the *United States* burst on the first day's test firing; five out of six exploded on the second day; overall, only twelve passed as acceptable out of the forty-four tested.[36] Similarly, there was a lack of copper. By the time of the American Revolution, the British navy had introduced into general use the practice of sheathing the bottom of its warships with a thin sheet of copper. "Coppering" staved off the action of *Teredo navalis,* a sea worm that bored into the wooden hulls of all ships and gradually reduced the hull to a leaky sieve, and prevented the encrustation of the hull with barnacles and seaweed that ruined speed. Paul Revere had discovered a process to turn scrap copper into "malleable" copper suitable for copper sheathing and for molding copper bolts and spikes, but there was precious little scrap copper to be found and only a limited supply of malleable copper that the small American shops could roll out. Joshua Humphreys highlighted the disparity between supply and demand when he wrote to the Navy Department in December 1798 that a ship with twenty feet less keel than the *Philadelphia* would require 12,000 feet of thirty-two-ounce sheathing; 276,000 copper nails; 8,155 feet of copper bolts (from 1 inch to 1⅞ inches in size); and more than 14,250 eight- and nine-inch copper spikes. Besides exploding cannon and little copper, yet another problem was canvas duck for sails; as skilled as American sailmakers were, the best canvas came from Europe.[37]

FitzSimons bought as much copper domestically as he could for the *Philadelphia:* 742 copper spikes from Philadelphia fabricators, Peter and Thomas McIlvaham; copper bolts from Paul Beck of Philadelphia; and more than $10,000 worth of copper bolts and spikes from a New York shop, J. Mark & Co.—although $740 worth of bolts were returned to J. Mark & Co., and $1,305 was on account to the McIlvahams as shoddy product. But for copper sheathing for the *Philadelphia*'s bottom, and for the best duck for her sails, FitzSimons turned to English suppliers. On 30 September 1798, FitzSimons sent his own note, drawn on Ketland & Co., London, for £750, as well as Thomas Willing's note for £1250, drawn on Baring Brothers (to whom Willing was related through the marriage of his granddaughter), to fund purchases of copper and sailcloth through J. Strachan and Mackenzie & Co. Ultimately, the Philadelphia committee sent £3769-18-7 (or $16,755.23) to Britain for materials. Strachan and Mackenzie shipped the copper and sailcloth aboard the *Sally* in November 1798, five months before a steep rise in price prompted the British Parliament to pass a law prohibiting the export of copper. The committee's records show that FitzSimons paid Captain Lockyear of the *Sally* $390 for freight and, despite the national defense purposes of the purchases, FitzSimons handed over another $276.85 for import duties to George Latimer, the U.S. collector of customs at Philadelphia. On the other hand, the *Philadelphia* received her cannon and military stores without charge to the committee; the Navy Department provided the *Philadelphia*'s armament out of government stocks. One year into the war, American foundries were beginning to produce cannon that, if not "mass production," sufficed in numbers and quality to arm the fleet.[38]

Building the *Philadelphia* drew in hundreds of people and dozens of trades, from patrician merchants to illiterate dockyard workers, when the real work began in the spring of 1799. Joshua Humphreys furnished not only his shipyard but also crafted the frigate's spars. David Patterson shaped and stepped the masts. John Thurston sold the frigate committee almost $9,400 worth of hemp and John Leamny $5,100 more, which Henry Mitchell wove into cordage for $9,800. Ludlow & Co.'s skilled laborers sheathed the *Philadelphia*'s bottom, and William and John Clifton's ironworkers bored and pounded the copper fastenings. FitzSimons oversaw the payment of more than $40,000 in wages to shipyard workers, which, given wage rates, meant that the committee theoretically put the equivalent of fifty men to work for five hundred days. In addition to the skilled trades, the ship was not without an artistic touch; the great Philadelphia shipcarver, William Rush, carved a Hercules figurehead for the prow of the *Philadelphia,* a work described as "a very handsome piece of sculpture," although some philosophical eyebrows were raised over the Roman fasces, clasped in Hercules's left hand, which was intended to represent the American union.[39]

The ship carpenters had the most difficult job. So hard is live oak that the carpenters' axes and adzes reportedly required sharpening hourly.

Shaping the rough-cut timbers to the moulds required sweat, skill, and patience, and ship carpenters classically were lubricated with generous doses of rum. FitzSimons's accounts show that in the first week of August 1799—three months before the *Philadelphia* was launched—thirty ship carpenters worked on the ship, and the workweek was six days. From June through September 1799, FitzSimons bought no fewer than 110 gallons of rum each month. FitzSimons's liquor supply, even allowing for the occasional celebratory tankard as some merchant-subscriber came down the waterfront to watch the progress on the *Philadelphia,* meant that each worker downed a pint of the demon rum every day. Spread over the course of the day, and mixed with one or two parts water and a little molasses as "grog," this must have kept the shipyard gangs in a perpetual haze. One percent of the approximately $192,000 spent on the frigate was sunk into alcohol.[40]

Week by week, the frigate took shape. Finally, on 28 November 1799, "this elegant ship" was launched safely into the Delaware, "accompanied by the acclamations of thousands of spectators, who lined the shore." The warships moored nearby, the *Ganges, Richmond,* and *Augusta,* fired out salutes to greet the new arrival.[41]

The *Philadelphia*'s launching did not end FitzSimons's involvement with the frigate. In a peculiarly modern-sounding twist, the navy's accountant, Thomas Turner, could not make heads or tails out of FitzSimons's books and records. Indeed, FitzSimons's bookkeeping practices included arithmetic errors, payments made without invoices or receipts, and expenditures funded through himself. The Navy Department spent years probing, questioning, and trying to decipher the expenditures of the committee. In 1806, Turner's audit revealed that of the $192,534.07 spent by the committee on the *Philadelphia,* the navy would not recognize $18,453.21 because the expenditures were unsupported. Finally, a Reconciling Statement dated 30 June 1808, ten years after FitzSimons became the chairman and more than four years after the *Philadelphia* ceased to exist, seems to have balanced the navy's books with FitzSimons's lists of advances, but only after FitzSimons personally paid $2,324.38 to cover the most evident gaps. That the frigate committee's accounts were so haphazard seems a strange failing for a man who helped finance the Revolution and set up some of the new nation's first banks and insurance companies. Even more tragic was FitzSimons's ensuing bankruptcy, brought about by his unswerving loyalty and generosity to fellow Revolutionary War financier Robert Morris.[42]

For the *Philadelphia*'s commander, the merchants committee chose
Stephen Decatur, Sr. Before the Revolution, while still in his early twen-
ties, Decatur had been the master of a merchant sloop. During the Revolutionary War, Decatur served as a privateersman and achieved some
success in a succession of Philadelphia-syndicated ships. In the 1780s and
1790s, Decatur commanded and had an ownership interest in two ships,
the *Pennsylvania* and the *Aerial,* belonging to the Gurney & Smith merchant firm, in which he conducted many successful trading voyages
across the Atlantic. As the war scare erupted in 1798, the War Department chose him to be the first new captain since President Washington
had selected the first six in 1794 to superintend the frigates.[43] After
supervising the conversion of the *Hamburgh Packet* into the sloop of war
Delaware of 20 guns in May and June 1798, Decatur sailed out of the
Delaware Bay on 6 July, and curled around Cape May to follow the New
Jersey coastline northwards looking for French privateers. The next afternoon, 7 July 1798, off Little Egg Harbor, New Jersey, the *Delaware* hailed
a merchant ship called the *Alexander Hamilton,* whose captain reported
that, that very morning, a French privateer schooner had sacked his ship
of seven cases of wine, thirty dollars, "one large Bayonne Ham," some
razors, sweetmeats, and ladies' shoes. The *Alexander Hamilton*'s master
suggested a course on which the *Delaware* might find the privateer. The
Delaware soon came upon a group of schooners. Decatur played the old
ruse of pretending to be a hapless merchantman and, of course, she
looked the part, having been a merchantman only a few weeks earlier.
Decatur made a show of trying to sail away from the schooners, hoping
that the privateer would rise to the bait. The old tricks work the best—a
lightly armed privateer, the *Croyable,* sheered away from the other
schooners and followed the *Delaware* out to sea. When the French priva-
teersmen realized their mistake, the *Croyable* changed tack and headed
back for U.S. territorial waters, ironically thinking that the *Delaware* must
be an English warship and might not violate the neutral Americans'
three-mile limit. The *Delaware* followed the *Croyable,* banging away at her
with a nine-pounder chase gun, until the *Croyable* hauled down the tricolor and surrendered. Despite having just seized a Philadelphia ship,
the *Liberty,* bound for Liverpool, when the French commander came
aboard the *Delaware* he sputtered that he was unaware that the two
republics were at war. Decatur replied that France had been warring on
America for a long time, and Americans were now taking matters into
their own hands. The French captain murmured his embarrassment at

having surrendered and said he wished that he had fought the *Croyable* until she sank; he received little solace from Decatur, who told him that he, too, wished the French had fought it out. The *Delaware's* capture of the *Croyable* was the first American naval victory, and made Decatur a hero. Stoddert ordered Decatur back to sea, to cruise off Havana "for the protection of our trade to that place." Decatur performed the trade protection mission to the accolades of the American merchants resident in Havana, and to the secretary's satisfaction as well. Upon his return to Philadelphia, the merchants' frigate was his reward.[44] And Decatur, a Philadelphian well connected to the merchants, wanted the *Philadelphia,* bypassing command of the storied *Constellation* when Thomas Truxtun temporarily resigned and when the president himself thought Decatur the best captain available. President Adams, "sincerely sorry for the resignation of Captain Truxtun," wrote Stoddert that it could not be helped but, in the "[m]eantime I am very desirous that Captain Decatur should take the *Constellation*. If, however, he prefers the merchants' frigate, as you call her, I will not urge him from his bias." Decatur stayed the captain-designate of the building *Philadelphia* and stayed in the president's good graces as well.[45]

Perhaps Decatur thought the *Philadelphia* would be the better ship. Perhaps he looked forward to the special patronage opportunities accorded the merchants to name officers. Decatur knew all the leading merchants and there were those relationships to cultivate. Decatur was an entrepreneur as well, in partnership with a man named William Lane, to manufacture gunpowder for the army and navy.[46] The influence he might bring to bear in naming midshipmen might help cement friendships. And there was his own family to consider. Decatur's eldest son, Stephen, Jr., was already a midshipman aboard the *United States;* he brought his second son, James Decatur, aboard the *Philadelphia* as a midshipman, along with his son-in-law, James McKnight, who received a United States Marine Corps commission as captain and command of the marines aboard the *Philadelphia*. Presumably Decatur ensured that midshipmen warrants went to sons of friends and mentors—to the secretary of state's son, Timothy Pickering, Jr., and to a Biddle, a Wharton, and a Penrose, among others.[47]

The *Philadelphia* was completed, fitted out, and ready for sea in April 1800.[48] Stoddert sent orders to Decatur in February 1800 to recruit 120 able seamen and 172 ordinary seamen and boys, "None but sound & healthy men." Recruiting rendezvous were sent as far as New York to get prime seamen, and Stoddert ordered the Marine Corps commandant to detach fifty marines for the frigate.[49] Although initially Secretary Stoddert thought of sending the *Philadelphia* to the Mediterranean to establish an American naval presence in those waters,[50] by the spring of 1800, it was clear that the *Philadelphia* was essential for the Guadeloupe station. The other large American frigates were returning to U.S. ports with their year-long enlistments expiring, and Stoddert held as an article of faith that one of the larger frigates was indispensable were any major French navy ships to materialize. Indeed, with Truxtun himself returning to the United States, Decatur in the *Philadelphia* was to command the entire eleven-ship squadron, based at St. Kitts.[51] Before the frigate sailed, Decatur invited President Adams, Secretary Stoddert, and indeed, most of the federal government to dinner aboard the *Philadelphia*. Decatur put his crew through "naval exhibitions" for his guests. With gun salutes, manning the side for the president and the other dignitaries, a huge dinner, and drinking that led to rounds of song, all "entered into the spirit of the party." Despite the strained relations between Adams and Pickering, Representative Benjamin Griswold of Connecticut observed the "whole executive branch of the Government with the President at the head laughed until they wept."[52]

As the *Philadelphia* headed slowly down the Delaware, Decatur mused on the breadth of his command. Off of New Castle, Delaware, he wrote the secretary of state, informing him that Timothy, Jr., was in fine fettle and, given the newspaper rumor that the Adams administration was about to appoint five admirals, "beg[ged] the favor of your friendly interference in my behalf." Despite Decatur's attempts to ingratiate himself with politicians who counted, Decatur was ignorant of political realities: relations between Pickering and John Adams were bitter, indeed openly hostile, and only two weeks after Decatur posted his letter, the President fired Pickering as secretary of state. Decatur was never to become an admiral. The United States Navy was not to have its first admiral until the Civil War.[53]

Commodore Decatur's frigate reached the West Indies in May 1800 and began a campaign of undoing the damage wrought by French privateers. On 23 May, the *Philadelphia* recaptured the Philadelphia schooner *Betsey* off Guadeloupe, prize to the French privateer *L'Union*. On 15 July, *Philadelphia* came up in sight of the *Connecticut* when she took the French letter-of-marque ketch *Le Chou Chou*, armed with four swivel guns, entitling the *Philadelphia* to share in the prize.[54] On the 25th, the

Philadelphia recaptured the American brig *Diligence,* originally hailing from
Charleston. Marine Capt. James McKnight, Decatur's son-in-law, reported
to the commandant on 1 August: "We have made two recaptures, & one
capture of a French letter of Marquee valued at Twenty Thousand Dollars
[sic];" then in a postscript that would please Secretary Stoddert, added
"[w]e have been but 3 days in port[;] our last Cruize was for 56 days." The
Philadelphia clearly was a speedster. Even as she cleared Cape Henlopen on
her first cruise, reports filtered back to the newspapers that the *Philadelphia* "sails remarkably fast." McKnight, perhaps no authority as a marine,
wrote in the same terms. A letter writer aboard wrote that "[o]ur ship sails
better than any of those on the windward station excepting the *President,*
Commodore Truxtun, with which we have not yet had a trial."[55]

The redoubtable Truxtun arrived in early autumn in his new flagship,
the 44-gun *President,* to reassume command of the squadron. In a navy
already marked by sensitivity to seniority and honor, Stoddert and Truxtun assured Decatur that no slight was intended by Decatur's displace-
ment, and Truxtun assured Decatur that the *Philadelphia* would cruise
where prizes were likely to be found. Truxtun was prescient. Decatur
began reeling in prizes: the *Philadelphia* recaptured the English sloop
Eliza, originally from Alexandria, on 26 November; recaptured the New
London schooner *Sally* on the 27th; and took the 6-gun French privateer
schooner *La Levrette* at 4:30 A.M. on 3 December, escorting her into St. Kitts
six days later. Back to sea, the *Philadelphia*'s lookouts spotted two ships
sailing close ashore off Dominica on Christmas morning. When the
Philadelphia pursued, the two vessels refused to be drawn out into deeper
water. No matter; Decatur ordered Midshipman Clement Biddle to man
the frigate's barge with an armed crew that set sail after one of the two
vessels, later found to be the schooner *Peggy* from Hartford. Biddle's
bargemen quickly overcame the French prize crew after firing a gun, and
retook the *Peggy.* The very next day, the *Philadelphia* recaptured the brig
Dove and the sloop *Lucy,* both out of New London and both prizes to the
privateer *Patriot,* and sent both to Martinique and the British vice-admiralty
court. On the 27th, it was the turn of the schooner *Ann and Susan* from
New York to be recaptured with a cargo of flour and forty oxen, prize to
the *Flambeau;* and on 29 December, the *Philadelphia* seized the captured
brig *Sir John Wentworth* of Halifax, and sent her off to Martinique for a salvage determination. The frigate's prize agent, Francis Gurney of Gurney
& Smith in Philadelphia, must have been busy collecting salvage monies
from the navy agents on St. Kitts and Martinique for many months. The

recall of the navy's ships with the conclusion of peace with France coincided with the end of the one-year enlistments of the crew; Decatur brought the *Philadelphia* home and the frigate entered the Delaware on 27 March 1801.[56]

The undeclared naval war with France was resolved, but the Navy Department had immediate plans for the *Philadelphia.* The Jefferson administration, however unfriendly to the navy, decided to send a squadron to the Mediterranean to deal decisively with the Barbary despots. The navy instructed Joshua Humphreys to examine the *Philadelphia* and make whatever repairs might be necessary "with the utmost dispatch" for a year-long cruise; the *Philadelphia* was to be in a squadron under Commodore Truxtun that assembled at Hampton Roads on 1 May and sailed ten days later. In the shrunken peacetime navy, the department showed the standing of Decatur in the service by retaining three of the *Philadelphia*'s lieutenants and many of its midshipmen, including James Decatur, young Pickering, Joseph Wharton, and Clement Biddle. Yet Decatur himself begged off the command, apparently telling the acting secretary of the navy that, with a year away from home already, his family and private business interests required his attention. Within a week, Decatur changed his mind, but it was too late; the navy installed Samuel Barron as the *Philadelphia*'s captain and would not create havoc in its officer corps by catering to the whims of a captain. Stephen Decatur served a few more months in the navy, and then was politely dismissed. He spent his last years manufacturing gunpowder, tending his estate, and reveling in the achievements of his naval officer sons, James Decatur and Stephen Decatur, Jr.[57]

Samuel Barron took the *Philadelphia* into the Mediterranean on a desultory year-long cruise in which the frigate's primary role was to watch two Tripolitan ships of war in Gibraltar. The *Philadelphia* arrived back in Philadelphia in April 1802, was laid up "in ordinary" (the sailing age's equivalent of "mothballing") for a year, and then was called back into service and given to William Bainbridge for another deployment to the Mediterranean.[58]

On 31 October 1803, after giving up the chase of a Tripolitan ship that had led him close ashore near the town of Tripoli, Bainbridge ran the *Philadelphia* onto some submerged rocks. Bainbridge desperately tried to free the frigate. As he recounted, he

> laid all sails aback, loosed top Gallt. Sails and set a heavy press of Canvass on the Ship, blowing fresh to get her off, cast Three Anchors away from the Bows, started the Water in the hold, hove overboard the Guns except

some abaft, to defend the ship against the Gun Boats . . . made the last resort of lightning her forward by Cutting away the Fore Mast, which carried the Main Top Gallt. mast with it, but labour & enterprize was in Vain; for our fate was direfully fixed.

After withstanding the Tripolitan gunboats' cannonade for four hours, Bainbridge concluded he had no alternative but to haul down the Stars and Stripes. He and the 306 Americans on board were taken into captivity; the *Philadelphia*, thought to be wrecked on the rocks, refloated forty hours later in a rising sea, and was towed into Tripoli harbor where she might be repaired and used against American naval forces. Bainbridge recognized the loss of the ship was a "calamity;" upon learning of the disaster three weeks later, Edward Preble, the commander of the Mediterranean squadron, confided in his diary that the *Philadelphia*'s capture ranked as "most serious and alarming" to the United States.[59]

The *Philadelphia*'s existence in the hands of the enemy threatened to wreak havoc on American forces and imperil American foreign relations. Preble believed that, at almost any cost, the *Philadelphia* needed to be destroyed. Preble selected Stephen Decatur, Jr., from among his junior officers to command a desperate mission to burn the *Philadelphia*. Preble's choice of Decatur was inspired; although Preble hardly knew the young lieutenant personally, Decatur already was a charismatic leader. And the choice was laden with unintended irony—the man ordered to destroy the frigate was the son of the man who had superintended her construction and who had commanded her in triumph.

On the night of 16 February 1804, Decatur with a picked force of volunteers entered Tripoli harbor aboard the ketch *Intrepid*. He laid the ketch alongside the *Philadelphia*, which was moored within a half gunshot of the batteries of the Bashaw's castle and amidst Tripolitan gunboats and warships. Decatur gave the command to board. The American sailors swarmed aboard the frigate, and set fires in the storerooms, gun deck, cockpit, and along the berth deck. With flames leaping from the hatches, Decatur's boarders jumped to safety, and as they departed the harbor, the *Philadelphia* in Decatur's words, "drifted in under the Castle where she was consumed" in a spectacular ball of fire. While Bainbridge's loss of the *Philadelphia* was a calamity, the burning of the *Philadelphia* set an example of audacity and bravery for the United States Navy for generations to come.[60]

5 Baltimore's "Charming Little Ships"

The launching of the citizen-built sloop of war *Maryland* on 3 June 1799, from William Price's shipyard in Fells Point, "drew together an immense concourse of spectators, who filled the adjacent wharves, and occupied a number of vessels, which were moored in the channel for that purpose." At six o'clock, the 114-foot-long *Maryland* slid down her ways and splashed into the water. Armed merchant ships in the harbor—and most merchant ships mounted cannon against the threat of French privateers in the state of Quasi-War between the two republics—the *Charming Betsy*, the *Isabella*, the *Industrious Mary*, the *David Stewart*, the *Olive*—all fired off "Federal salutes." Other cannon fired salvoes from the wharves and from the defensive entrenchments at Whetstone Point, just beginning to be called Fort McHenry. Not since the navy launched the frigate *Constellation* nearly two years before had Baltimore beheld such a scene:

> The steady and majestic movement of the ship, the immense crowd of spectators which occupied the surrounding wharves and eminences, the continued roar of cannon, and repeated huzzas, which seemed to rend the circumambient air, formed a *tout ensemble* . . . In the evening, several splendid entertainments were given on

board different vessels in the harbor, and the Select Company were munificently entertained, with a number of other citizens, at Mr. Price's house.[1]

The spectacle at Fells Point had its sequel less than three weeks later. On 20 June 1799, the citizens of Baltimore launched a second sloop of war into the harbor, this one from the Fells Point shipyard of Lewis de Rochbrune. Called the *Chesapeake* (but renamed the *Patapsco* after the Navy recalled that a frigate building at Norfolk was to have the bay's name), she too slid down the ways from Fells Point into the harbor "amidst the loud acclamations of a large concourse of spectators, the discharge of cannon from the new brig *John Brickwood,* and a ship at the fort, seconded by vollies from the volunteers and marines on board." De Rochbrune repaid the "patriotic gentlemen" who subscribed to and built the *Patapsco,* the *Federal Gazette* newspaper observed with obvious pride, with "a vessel judged to be as complete as any of her size in the American or any other navy." The carving on her prow depicted a bearded Neptune; the *Federal Gazette* closed its account of the launch with the wish that "the thunder from his *ports* be a *death tribute* to the apostate Talleyrand and all his adherents."[2]

Baltimore in the 1790s was a vibrant port town. A future King of France, visiting in March 1797, mused on Baltimore's resemblance to Marseilles, its new but plain houses, and its prosperity based on the export of flour from western Maryland. Another émigré noble, Moreau de St. Méry, had visited Baltimore in 1794 and noted its wide, paved streets (some of which were lit at night), its constant commercial hum, and its three thousand houses, "the greater part brick and elegantly built." The city, which in the 1790 census numbered a mere 13,758 (including 1,255 slaves), grew to 31,514 in 1800.[3] Although within eighteen miles, there were fifty "capital merchant" mills, a gunpowder mill, two paper mills, several furnaces, and two forges, the city owed its boom to shipbuilding, maritime trade, and the attendant service businesses, insurance and banking. The merchant-capitalists who were the city's business elite were sophisticated assessors of risk and profit: Baltimore contained two banks, a factoring office, and a marine insurance office.[4] The merchants developed the international contacts for trade; discounted commercial paper; ordered and owned merchant vessels; directed exports and imports; and invested in real estate, banks, and more shipping.

But by the beginning of 1798, the merchants' entrepreneurial world faced ruin at the hands of French privateers. Robert Oliver, one of the leading Baltimore merchants, wrote to his London agent that upon the safe return to Baltimore of his ship, the *Harmony,* "All our risks are now nearly determined and we don't intend to adventure any more until we see how we stand with the French." The same day, writing to a contact in Virginia, Oliver advised that the "situation with France is a little short of war. Wheat & Flour [prices] must fall & we advise you to lay by until you see how matters are likely to turn. You must not . . . run risks for the sake of doing business. The times are alarming & the People here seem disposed to do little or no business until a Change takes place."[5]

The change, however, was not salutary. On 4 April 1798, newspapers published the dispatches of the American envoys in Paris: French intermediaries, diplomatically labeled X, Y, and Z, refused the American envoys access to Talleyrand without a douceur of £50,000. The popular response was unmistakable throughout the country. A gathering of five hundred young men of Baltimore sent an address to the president, expressing their confidence in him, their dismay that France received American overtures for peace with "abject contempt," and their pledge to vindicate the country's rights if war came. Old militia companies mustered and volunteer units organized and drilled in public spaces under colorful names like the "Maryland Sans Culottes" and the "Fells Point Light Dragoons." The threat from France seemed almost palpable: Mark Pringle, a Baltimore merchant, refused to insure a Philadelphia merchant's cargo, "as it appears there are two French Privateers cruising off the Capes of the Delaware." Robert Oliver could not find any American vessel willing to run the gauntlet of French privateers and the British navy's blockade of Cadiz, and a merchant vessel to Algeciras and Malaga could not be insured for less than 50 percent of its value.[6]

Amidst the confusion and uncertainty, the fears of privateers and the advertisements for militia, the 2 June 1798 issue of the *Federal Gazette & Baltimore Daily Advertiser* contained a four-sentence article reprinted from Boston's *Columbian Centinel,* dated a week earlier. It noted that "patriotic citizens" of Newburyport had "opened a subscription for the purpose of building a 20 gun ship" that would be loaned to the government. The article ended prophetically, "An example this, worthy [of] prompt imitation." A week later the Baltimore newspaper noted that Newburyport citizens filled their $20,000 subscription and let the contract for building the ship; and then the *Federal Gazette* reprinted the entire letter from the Newburyport citizens to their congressman, Bailey Bartlett, suggesting that their example lead to "proportionate exertions in larger and wealthier towns," with subscriptions exchanged for 6 percent government stock.[7]

Baltimore now had a blueprint for action. On 15 June the *Federal Gazette* printed a notice:

> The Merchants and Traders of the city of Baltimore are requested to meet at the Exchange, To-morrow, at 12 o'clock, for the purpose of subscribing to purchase or build a Ship of War, for the use of the Government of the United States.[8]

Meet they did. One of the city's two magistrates, Thorowgood Smith, took the chair.[9] The meeting resolved to build two ships of war for the federal government and set as an immediate goal the sum of $30,000, but those present pledged $40,300 on the spot. The merchants selected a five-man committee consisting of Robert Oliver, David Stewart, George Sears, John Stricker, and James Barry to raise more funds.[10] The money poured in: from $40,300 the first day, 16 June; to $65,000 by 19 June; to $76,100 by 20 June; to $84,200 by 22 June; to $92,000 by 23 June; and in the end, over $100,000.[11]

On 16 June the merchants reconvened and selected a committee to superintend the construction of a Baltimore subscription ship. The merchants retained Oliver, Stewart, and Sears from the fundraising committee, and added Jeremiah Yellott,[12] Robert Gilmor,[13] William Patterson,[14] Thomas Cole,[15] Archibald Campbell,[16] and Mark Pringle[17] to form a building committee.

Of the subscribers (and amounts in dollars) to the Baltimore sloops of war, only a fragmentary list survives:[18]

William McCreary[19]	500	
Dr. Moore Falls[20]	2300	
Margaret Sprigg[21]	1500	
John E. Howard[22] &		
John Swan[23]	4700	Society of Cincinnati in Maryland
John McDowell	400	
Benjamin Harwood[24]	5300	
Dr. Moore Falls	500	

In addition, the newspapers noted that John O'Donnell contributed $4,000.[25] The total of the eight known contributors, $19,200, is only about one-fifth of the approximately $100,000 raised overall. Of course, the great merchants of Baltimore who sat on the committees and oversaw the construction contributed substantially. As the *Federal Gazette & Baltimore Daily Advertiser* put it, "The mercantile part of our community, truly sensible of the great national advantages of a free trade, and alarmed at the piratical depradations constantly made on American property, could no longer remain idle spectators of so disgraceful a scene; they have stepped forth with a ready and liberal spirit, that does honor to their principles—*nearly one hundred thousand dollars* are already subscribed for building and equipping ships of war." But the local newspapers display a republican modesty about who contributed, and how much, and even the personal papers and letters of Mark Pringle and Robert Oliver reveal nothing. Clearly, most of the contributors were merchants, with shared mercantile, banking, and militia ties. These men were the grandees of Baltimore. Many were Federalist politically: David Stewart, Thorowgood Smith, Robert Gilmor, Archibald Campbell, Mark Pringle, James Barry, Robert Oliver, John Swan, George Sears, and Jeremiah Yellott signed a public letter in support of James Winchester, the Federalist candidate for Congress in the 1798 election against Gen. Samuel Smith, the incumbent Republican.[26] The identical set of men (except Sears) composed the board of the marine insurance office. Three of the committeemen, Stewart, Stricker, and Thorowgood Smith, sat on the board of the Bank of Baltimore; and six others—Patterson, Campbell, Oliver, Yellott, Gilmor, and O'Donnell—were officers or directors of the Bank of Maryland. In the militia the Federalist cast broke down: Swan was a brigadier general, O'Donnell a lieutenant colonel, and Gilmor a brigade-major, but Samuel Smith, the Republican congressman, was the major general in overall command and Stricker, also a Republican, was a colonel. Despite the notation of Swan's and Howard's contribution as "Society of Cincinnati" (the organization of Washington's ex-officers that was coincident with Federalist Party organization), the known committee members and subscribers do not otherwise appear represented in that group.[27] But the Federalist complexion of subscribers should not be overstated. Colonel Stricker, Mr. McCreary, and Mrs. Sprigg, all prominent Republicans, were contributors, and after the initial meeting at the Exchange, a Baltimore gentleman wrote a New York friend, "So far for the *doubtful city* of Baltimore. I admit a most extraordinary change has taken place amongst us, many who were reckoned in the first rank of Jacobins [i.e., Republicans] are among the highest subscribers."[28]

In any case, the Baltimore merchants had a subscription of about $100,000 and a committee of experienced merchants set to superintend the building of a warship for the Federal government. But what actually were they to build?

Beginning with the 16 June meeting, the subscribers always envisioned two ships. Benjamin Stoddert, a Georgetown merchant who became the first secretary of the navy on 19 June, tried to persuade the Baltimoreans to build one larger ship, a frigate, instead. After noting to the navy agent at Baltimore, Jeremiah Yellott, that the money subscribed by the merchants would be reimbursed with 6 percent stock, he referred to the thousand-ton frigate building by the Philadelphia merchants and hoped "one at least as large can be built at Baltimore, where the Spirit of the Merchants and Citizens has been so patriotically displayed." The Baltimore merchants remained steadfast. Stoddert tried again, writing David Stewart that if they insisted on "small ships in Baltimore, I must acquiesce— Tho I fear we shall have ample occasion for the largest size Ships." The enabling act provided that the department might accept five frigates, and Stoddert counted on Baltimore to furnish one. On the same day he wrote Stewart, Stoddert tried his hand again with Yellott, entreating that his "Native State, not less Federal, & not less in earnest to defend the rights of the Country, than any in the Union, will afford one of these [frigates];" the navy secretary believed Yellott could alter the committee's stand, but "despair[ed] of getting the Ship & soon if you do not concur."[29] The Baltimore merchants did not budge from two ships. Perhaps they recognized that ferreting out French privateers from Caribbean coves required handier, smaller ships. The navy secretary wanted larger, more powerful ships to engage French warships and to create the nucleus for a permanent navy. Although Baltimore's reluctance to build a frigate dismayed Stoddert, in the end he got his five frigates.

When Archibald Campbell wrote the Navy Department for drawings and plans on which to build the Baltimore vessels, Stoddert gave the merchants wide discretion. He requested that each Baltimore vessel be "rated" to carry eighteen cannon so as not to offend the statutory authorization. As to plans, Stoddert replied breezily,

> As to a draft, and every thing relating to these Vessels, the subject is as well understood at Baltimore as here. It is desirable, that they should be fine Sailors, so as to suffer nothing to escape them, & to be taken by nothing. This can be done at Baltimore, if any where.[30]

The merchants turned to two local shipwrights, William Price and Lewis de Rochbrune. William Price's shipyard was on Pitt Street (now Fell Street) in Fells Point. Originally from Hampton, Virginia, where he began building pilot schooners, Price was one of the leading Baltimore shipbuilders from 1794 to 1833. He was also the largest slave owner in the city of Baltimore, using more than twenty slaves in his yard. After building the subscription warship soon to be called the *Maryland,* Price became the navy's major Baltimore shipwright, building the schooners *Experiment* (1799) and *Vixen* (1803), the sloop of war *Hornet* (1805), and Gunboat No. 5 (1805). Renowned locally by 1798 as a builder of pilot-boat schooners, which were later called Baltimore clippers, Price held advanced building ideas.[31] De Rochbrune's yard on Thames Street, east of Caroline Street, in Fells Point, existed from 1796 to 1803. Little is known about de Rochbrune. Born in about 1764 on Kent Island on Maryland's Eastern Shore, it is not known when or how de Rochbrune became a shipwright. It may well be that he and Price assisted in building the *Constellation* in Baltimore in the mid-1790s.[32] De Rochbrune launched the sixty-eight-foot, 160-ton brig *Swallow* with "Indian head, quarter galleries" for Mark Pringle in April 1798, as well as the sixty-five-foot, 159-ton schooner *Nancy* in June 1798 for Louis Noailles, the Marquis de Lafayette's émigré brother-in-law, then living in Philadelphia.[33]

By 24 July 1798, Price and de Rochbrune had contracts to build four-hundred-ton ships. The two shipwrights laid keels and began building the sloops of war immediately. With the permission of the secretary of the navy, the committee helped themselves to naval stores, timber, and other materials—at cost—from David Stodder's yard on Harris Creek, where the *Constellation* had been built. The merchants could not find or manufacture locally the three tons of copper sheathing and the three tons of copper bolts and eight-inch copper spikes necessary to build the vessels, and the Navy Department promised to furnish them. Stoddert put the materials of Stodder's yard at the committee's disposal but hoped they would leave the live-oak timber for frigates. Stoddert asked whether the committee meant to procure the ship's cannon or have them manufactured; he certainly did not know the design of the ships, reiterating the need for them to be rated 18s, as opposed to 20s or 24s, and hoped that the Baltimore vessels would be strong enough to mount nine-pounder or twelve-pounder guns. The merchants operated independently from the department's direction: Robert Oliver wrote Stoddert that "Our vessels"—the two Baltimore ships—"will be larger than you mention" but would conform to the enabling Act of 30 June and carry nine-pounder or twelve-pounder cannon. The committee intended "to expend the whole of the Money subscribed" which they hoped would cover the ships, completed, with their guns.[34]

Only scraps of documentary evidence exist concerning the two Balti-more subscription warships' dimensions, and their plans are lost. When the navy sold the *Maryland* in December 1801, she measured 114 feet in length; 30 feet, 4 inches in beam; and 464 ^{4}/$_{95}$ tons.[35] The *Patapsco*, by con-trast, was smaller, measuring 418 ^{4}/$_{95}$ tons.[36] While who drew up the *Mary-land* and *Patapsco* plans is not known definitively, they almost certainly were designed in Baltimore.[37]

The secretary of the navy kept President Adams, summering in Quincy, abreast of the national naval construction boom. Stoddert wrote at the end of July that two of the 18-gun sloops of war authorized by statute "are building by the Merchants of Baltimore," and would be at sea in three months. Robert Oliver wrote the navy secretary a month later, "Our car-penters go on rapidly and I expect we will have two complete Ships Launched in December." The merchants were not sure if their subscrip-tions would suffice to pay for the cannon and reminded the overwhelmed Stoddert that the two sloops of war lacked them, offering to find cannon or contract for them. Oliver suggested that at least one of the ship's captains be appointed to superintend the rigging and outfitting of the ships.[38]

As for armament, Stoddert at first left the merchants to find cannon for the vessels. Samuel Hughes, owner of the Principio Furnace near Havre de Grace, Maryland, offered to contract for the guns at $370 per pair, but Charles Ridgely, whose Northampton Furnace metal Oliver con-sidered "the best in this country," wanted only $350 per pair, although he did not have a model and refused to bore his cannon. Oliver and Yel-lott thought Ridgely's "as good as Mr. Hughes cast solid," but were will-ing to contract with either. In the end, the secretary sent most of the can-non from Philadelphia. Yellott, the navy agent, laid out $2602.18 for "18 pieces 9 lb. cannon" for which he was later reimbursed by the government, signifying that the merchants' money had indeed run out, after supply-ing only one vessel's guns.[39]

The other concern was finding appropriate captains. Stoddert informed the committee that "When the Citizens furnish Vessels for the public, it is the wish of the President to consult them—Indeed to pay very great respect to their recommendation, in the choice of Officers." Would-be officers del-uged the merchants committee. Even George Washington lent his support to one candidate as "a good Navigator, and . . . sober." Although Robert Oliver suggested as a captain a "Scotchman of the name Conyngham" who had experience "last war" in the British navy and aboard a British priva-teer, Oliver also bluntly informed Secretary Stoddert that the Baltimore merchants committee had "no other object in recommending any person but the good of the service and that you do not confer any obligations by appointing in consequence of our recommendations."[40]

Stoddert waited until the merchants launched the *Maryland* to name John Rodgers as her commander. Rodgers, only twenty-six in 1799, was a darkly handsome man with long sideburns who hailed from Havre de Grace, Maryland. His experience included many years as a mate and captain on merchant ships out of Baltimore, including capture by the French while in command of Samuel Smith's ship *Hope*. In the early months of the Quasi-War, Rodgers served as first lieutenant to Truxtun aboard the *Constellation,* and was widely considered Truxtun's protege. The fact that Rodgers's brother-in-law was William Pinkney, a Maryland Federalist state legislator and sometime diplomat, probably helped secure him the command of a Maryland-built ship. Stoddert promoted Rodgers to captain in May 1799 and ordered him on 13 June to take command of the *Maryland* and to make her ready for sea.[41]

For the *Patapsco,* Stoddert selected an older man, Henry Geddes, who had "long been an Applicant for a command in the Navy" and who came recommended by Senator James Bayard, Federalist from Delaware. Geddes, an Irishman by birth, commanded the Pennsylvania state navy ship *Congress* in the Revolution, capturing the British sloop of war *Savage.* In the 1790s, Geddes commanded the State Department's brig *Sophia,* ferrying dispatches to and from Algiers. While other captains received encomiums from Stoddert, in recommending Geddes to the president, the navy secretary tepidly allowed that he "appears to be a man of understanding." Adams replied that Stoddert might fill in Geddes's name in a blank commission, "if you persist in your opinion concerning him. The gentlemen who recommend him, are respectable & I know nothing to excite a question" about Geddes.[42]

Rodgers complained about the delays in getting the *Maryland* ready for sea. The "mechanicks employed on the ship have not been as Expeditious as I expected," he wrote, and the blacksmith, blockmakers, and sailmaker all needed more time. Moreover, a recruiting effort at Mr. Harrison's tavern in Fells Point in early August was not entirely successful. Gaps in the crew remained until September, which Rodgers blamed on the "scarcity of seamen, the great Number of Merchantmen fiting out, and the extravagant wages given by them." Rodgers eventually got his men; with his commissioned and warrant officers, and complement of marines, 160 men packed into the *Maryland.*[43]

As the *Maryland* readied for sea, critics harped on the *Maryland*'s sharp-built design. In January 1799 Captain Truxtun sent a long letter to his friend, Captain Yellott, responding to the design of the Baltimore subscription ships. As the building had begun, Truxtun refused comment "below the Whales," but strongly concurred with "a light Spar Deck being put on them." Truxtun urged that "these sharp built Vessels" not be over-armed, which would make them "laboursome and crank" sailers and give them a low freeboard—or as Truxtun put it, "too deep in the water." Over-arming, in short, "injures their Sailing" and "makes them wet, uncomfortable, and difficult to fight." He suggested they mount 24 six-pounder cannon. Instead, the *Maryland* carried 20 nine-pounders and 6 six-pounders. Captain Rodgers, inspecting his new command, reported to the secretary of the navy that the *Maryland* carried her battery too low, prompting Stoddert, in a near-panic, to write Captain Yellott to "do all in your power at this late hour to prevent this defect in the two ships at Baltimore." But it was too late to alter the design. James Buchanan, the merchant partner of Gen. Samuel Smith, thought the *Maryland* "a Charming Little Ship, Exceedingly well fitted w[it]h The best Materials," but listed two faults. The first, which Buchanan conceded was "certainly not esteem'd So by The Builder," Price, was the *Maryland*'s flush deck: a spar deck covered the *Maryland*'s cannon. But the other problem was "irremediable:" "Swimming too low in The Water. & Her Gun-Ports being too near The Waters Edge," which made them "*Crank* or *Tender*, & even Dangerous Ships, either in a Gale of Wind—or in Battle if any Sea is Going."[44]

It is interesting to contrast these descriptions of the *Maryland* with the archetypical Baltimore pilot-boat schooner. In the 1790s, Price's yard produced many pilot-boat schooners, characterized by long and extremely raked masts, little rigging, a low freeboard, a great rake to stem and stern posts, and a flush deck.[45] Although neither the *Maryland* nor the *Patapsco* were pilot-boat schooners—their "ship" rig (i.e., square rig), three masts, and comparatively great size set them apart—Truxtun's design critique and Buchanan's description of the *Maryland* suggest that she incorporated some of the advanced features Baltimore shipwrights were crafting into topsail schooners. The *Maryland* was a "sharp built" ship, implying an acute angle of entry into the water at the bow; she sat low in the water, with little freeboard; and she had a flush deck, with a gun deck below, as if the *Maryland* were a miniature frigate.

On 21 August 1799, the *Maryland* got under way for the first time, sailing down the Patapsco to anchor below Ft. McHenry. She glided down the bay at the end of August, anchoring in Hampton Roads on 2 September. On 15 September, the *Maryland* weighed anchor to head out into the Atlantic; ten days before her departure, a newspaper noted— correctly—that she was "destined . . . on a cruise off Surinam."[46] In a letter Rodgers sent back to Norfolk with the pilot, he reported that it took five days to clear Cape Henry owing to headwinds "blowing with unabated obstinacy from the SE and ESE until the morning of the 19th." Rodgers called the *Maryland* "a handsome little ship" but reiterated that "like a number of our small Ships she Carrys her Guns to[o] low, the Gun Deck at present being only 18 Inches above the Surface of the water and the Sills of the ports Barely three feet ten Inches [above the waterline] the consequences of which you know too well."[47]

Stoddert ordered the *Maryland* to proceed to Surinam. With more and more American warships launched and sent out to suppress privateering in the West Indies, Adams and Stoddert feared that the French would exploit American naval weakness off the coast of South America. Adams asked Stoddert "to crowd as much force as possible to Cayenne & Surinam as the French will probably make their principal exertions there."[48] Stoddert enjoined Rodgers "to give all possible Security to our trade by Capturing Enemy Vessels wherever to be found on the high seas and by occasionally convoying our own, tho the most protection is afforded to the whole trade by capturing the Vessels which annoy it." To the young captain, Secretary Stoddert offered his own good wishes for success and the president's belief in Rodgers's "activity Zeal & Bravery."[49]

Accustomed to the bare-knuckle discipline of the merchant marine and the autocratic Truxtun, Rodgers, at twenty-six, held his first command in the navy. He ran a taut ship. As Buchanan reported, "[t]he order on Board was *Great, & Probably* too much *all a mode L'Truxton*—& Too distant, For Officer to Officer—& more than I ever Saw in any Ship of War before, of any *Rate,* or any Nation!"[50] Indeed, Rodgers adopted Commodore Truxtun's scheme of organization and rigorous discipline. Like Truxtun, Rodgers insisted on proper subordination and instant obedience. Just as Truxtun urged his officers to steer between "too great a disposition to punish" and "improper familiarity" that was ruinous to hierarchy, so Rodgers did aboard the *Maryland*. The captain of a man-of-war was a near-absolute ruler, and in a ship packed with men Rodgers made clear from the beginning both his own authority and the need for system. On 29 August, Rodgers posted the gun drill and forty-four paragraphs of standing orders that encompassed everything from etiquette ("The weather side of the quarter deck is reserved for the walk of the Captain"), to cleanliness ("The head and seats therein are to be washed every morning"), to maintaining the ship ("Every morning the Boatswain or his mates are to overhaul the rigging fore and aft, and from each mast head including Jibboom, bowsprit, gaff, etc. and to report what may be seen out of order or wanting repair"), to exercising the men at the guns.[51]

Rodgers sailed the *Maryland* to Surinam, which the British had recently taken from the Dutch, in twenty-six days. One *Maryland* officer boasted that in eighteen years at sea he had never served "in so fast a sailer." Rodgers anchored the ship eight or nine miles below the mouth of the Suriname River, "being unacquainted with the Navigation," and sent a lieutenant into Paramaribo with the navy secretary's orders for Capt. Daniel McNeill, senior officer on the station. McNeill being away on a cruise, Rodgers left the orders—to bottle up any French warships in Cayenne, although the Surinam squadron of three ships was to patrol from Cayenne to Curaçao—with the American consul, Turell Tufts. Secretary Stoddert made clear that the vessels in the Surinam squadron "are never to leave [the area] unless compelled by superior force" or to bring home their sailors after their one-year enlistments expired.[52]

The *Maryland* thus began a series of desultory cruises. Rodgers craved the opportunity for ship-to-ship action. Instead, he saw nothing but open ocean. At the end of his first, month-long cruise, he reported to Secretary Stoddert:

> During the whole of our cruize we have not seen anything Wearing the french flag Except the Port at Cayenne, altho I believe we have seen over and over again every Remarkable Rock and Tree Between Surinam and that place, and from the particular situation of the french at present, I can see their privateers have all left those Seas, having no place on this Coast, to send their Prizes since the British have been in possession of Surinam, and [it] is Impossible to get them into Cayenne, Owing to a continual Strong Current Setting to Leeward. In our cruise we were at Anchor five days at the Devils Island, during which time no vessel could have passed into or out of Cayenne, without our knowledge.[53]

A *Maryland* officer wrote home that the *Maryland* returned to Surinam to water on 21 November, after "a cruise of four weeks to windward, without any success." The *Maryland* met no French privateers but probed into Cayenne "so near in as to distinctly see the tri colored flag flying at the fort." Later on the cruise the *Maryland* raced the *Insurgente*, narrowly losing to her in a two-day contest; but the *Maryland* then raced McNeill in the *Portsmouth,* distancing her so much that the *Maryland* might have "run her nearly out of sight in 24 hours." Of course, every captain and officer thought that his own ship was the fastest and best. Capt. Alexander Murray of the *Insurgente* reported to Secretary Stoddert that he cruised with Rodgers "for a day or two to try his sailing . . . and I found I could beat him every way notwithstanding my bottom is in very bad order the copper being off . . ." The lieutenant of marines in the *Maryland,* Joseph Neale, wrote the commandant that "our Ship is thought to be the fastest" in the American fleet. While Neale conceded that the *Insurgente,* in "a short tryal Sailing . . . out Sailed us a verry little indeed," Neale noted that the *Maryland* at the time "was not in propper trim." Neale reported that all his marines, and the crew generally, were healthy and in good spirits, if "bad off for cloth[in]g," and that they anticipated a squadron action, with the *Maryland, Portsmouth,* and light frigate *John Adams* squaring off against three French frigates that reportedly had arrived off South America.[54]

While the *Maryland* refilled its water casks in Surinam, the *Patapsco* remained at her mooring in Baltimore. Geddes, for all his purported desire for a command, showed little energy: Stoddert enclosed his commission in a letter on 24 September 1799, and asked him to get to Baltimore as soon "as your convenience will admit." Geddes did not move, and it took two direct orders from the secretary of the navy and a month's time for Captain Geddes to take command. Fortunately for Geddes, the *Patapsco* inherited most of her crew from the *Montezuma,* a merchantman taken into the navy but then sold in Baltimore as deficient. Forty-five able seamen, forty-one ordinary seamen and boys, and four of the ship's warrant officers—ninety of the one hundred forty in the *Patapsco*'s company— were ex-*Montezuma*'s.[55]

For the *Patapsco*'s complement of twenty-one marines, there was the one-man recruiting service of a Sergeant Corcorran. In a piece entitled "*To the* BRAVE," and anticipating Madison Avenue marketing by a century, Corcorran assured Baltimoreans

> inclined to serve their country, in the *Marine Corps,* that on board the governmental ships of war, the men are *plentifully* provided with *good meat, drink* and *comfortable lodging;* and that the marines, with whom he has *conversed* and *served* appear to him quite satisfied and happy in their situation and prospects—and as but FEW MEN are now wanting, such as apply to him may depend on a HARDY [sic] WELCOME, KIND TREATMENT and GOOD ENCOURAGEMENT.[56]

With the ninety men of the *Montezuma* forming the rest of the *Patapsco*'s crew, Stoddert was not about to brook delays in the sailing of the *Patapsco*. On 11 November, he wrote to Geddes that the *Patapsco* could not remain at Baltimore after the 17th and pointedly mentioned that "no exertion on your part will be omitted to prepare you for sailing by the time mentioned." Geddes' orders followed three days later. The *Patapsco* was to embark Brig. Gen. James Wilkinson, ranking officer of the United States Army, and carry him "to the mouth of the Mississippi, and if it can be done, without danger and too much detention," drop him off at the Spanish city of New Orleans. From there the *Patapsco* was to sail to Cape Francais and join the American squadron off Saint-Domingue. The *Patapsco* finally sailed in mid-November.[57]

The *Patapsco* took two months to arrive at the Mississippi's mouth, only to be immediately driven into the Gulf of Mexico by a gale. She clawed her way back to the bar of the Mississippi eight days later. On 3 February 1800, General Wilkinson and his staff went ashore, where Spanish emissaries received them and conveyed the general and his entourage the 110 miles up the river to New Orleans. Geddes refused to cross the bar, fearing he would run the *Patapsco* aground, since the bar only allowed ships with a draft of less than thirteen feet.[58]

Retracing her route to Havana, the *Patapsco* then rendezvoused with merchant ships bound for American ports and convoyed eighteen vessels up the coast. In mid-March Geddes put the *Patapsco* into New Castle, Delaware, and reported his ship in need of caulking, his crew sickly, and merchants' specie on board entitling him to a half percent commission. While the *Patapsco*'s layover in New Castle suggests that Geddes wanted to be near his hearth in Delaware, the secretary promised him fresh provisions for his men and "a parcel of Carpenters" from Philadelphia to plug the *Patapsco*'s seams. The Navy needed every ship in the West Indies. Three weeks later, Stoddert ordered the *Patapsco* to convoy a provision ship, the *Florida*, to St. Kitts, and then to join the American squadron off Guadeloupe.[59]

Meanwhile, John Rodgers and the *Maryland* sailed into headwinds and looked upon empty seas off the coast of South America. In late November 1799, the *Maryland* left Surinam to cruise to the windward. The ship got nowhere. As Rodgers confessed in a letter written the day after Christmas, "I have found it very difficult to get to Windward, owing to an intollerable Strong Current Setting to Leward, and the Squally disagreeable Weather, Such as I have never met with in these Latitudes before." Finally, he returned to Surinam and anchored off the river, writing the American consul that "after a five weeks cruize" (it was nearer to eight) he was "without any success . . . I found it impossible to get to Windward. . . ."[60]

Yet the *Maryland* was more or less driven away by the arrival of a French naval squadron. In November 1799, Rodgers informed Stoddert of a rumor that three French frigates were on the South American coast with troops to relieve Cayenne; and in early February, the American consul, Tufts, reported that a French frigate, two brigs, and two corvettes arrived there. Tufts warned that "if the present protection is not withdrawn or increased to Higher force—we shall loose the *Maryland*—and the trade also." In reality, the French force amounted to the 36-gun frigate *La Sirene* and the corvettes *La Bergere* and *l'Arethuse*.[61] The *Maryland* would have had a difficult battle with either of the smaller ships; to fight a combination, or the frigate, would have been disastrous. No help was at hand. Since December 1799, when the British authorities ordered the *Portsmouth* to depart after a touchy diplomatic incident, the *Maryland* was the only United States naval vessel on the station.[62]

After the *Maryland*'s return to Surinam, Rodgers wrote to Tufts of his wish to extend to merchant vessels what protection he could, knowing "the Risk in passing the islands to be great," but noting his desire to sail no later than 24 January. Still at anchor on 27 January, he expressed "mortification" that he might meet a French frigate in a tête-à-tête. He later complained that the American merchants were "very dilatory" and "as many of them are so apt to be detained by trifles, I think you would do well to Hurry them." Tufts at last roused the merchant captains, and in early March the *Maryland* escorted a convoy of twelve merchant ships. The *Maryland* shepherded them through the Windward Islands to St. Kitts, where another ship assumed convoy duty, and by early May, Rodgers put the *Maryland* about and headed back to the Surinam station.[63]

By sailing back to the coast of South America, Rodgers took the *Maryland* away from the scene of action. Eight months earlier, Captain Murray in the *Insurgente* had briefly sailed the same waters with the *Maryland* but Murray had recognized that "it would be time lost my remaining on that station," and used the latitude Stoddert's orders gave him to cruise to the Windward Islands. Remaining off Surinam during the summer of 1800, the *Maryland* saw nothing but vast expanses of water although Rodgers relied on the secretary's command to "never" leave the station unless compelled by superior force. While expressing chagrin at having no enemy, Rodgers reminded the secretary that the *Maryland* had been ordered to the empty spaces of South American waters and, thus, the reality that the *Maryland* could do nothing to help the American cause was "no more I presume than you have had reason to expect." Rodgers, demonstrating a literalness and an officiousness that characterized his career, claimed that no American captain could do better, given "the British being in possession of Surinam totally prevents there being any french cruizers on its coast—owing to their having no place to send their prizes, and it is impossible to get them into Cayenne" owing to the strong currents. With few American merchant ships trading on the coast of South America there was little for the *Maryland* to defend and little for her to attack. Rodgers reported that some French ships operated out of Cayenne, but they cruised off Brazil and out into the Atlantic, and thus beyond the literal limit of Rodgers's station. Under the guise of a strict obedience to orders, Rodgers effectively conceded that he knew his orders were meaningless and suggested that he believed Stoddert would not want the *Maryland* where she was. Nevertheless, Rodgers stayed off of South America, fighting the currents. If there was no glory on his solitary patrol, he assured the secretary in obsequious tones that "no Ship ever cruized with more assiduity and unremitting attention."[64]

The *Maryland* did seize two merchant vessels, the brig *Gloria da Mar* in July 1800 and the ship-rigged *Aerial* in September. The *Gloria da Mar,* a Portuguese vessel that the *Maryland* recaptured from the French, sailed into St. Kitts harbor as part of the *Maryland*'s convoy. The British admiralty court decided that the American captors were not entitled to prize money—nor to take the brig away to the United States for a fresh adjudication—on the ground that the property of a friendly nation captured from an enemy reverted to the original owner. The British offered as consolation the payment of salvage. Truxtun sent all the communications and legal memoranda to the secretary of the navy "to prepare [Stoddert's] mind, to meet any complaint" against Rodgers, whom he still regarded as his protégé.[65]

Rodgers's vision of prize money entirely disappeared after he brought a convoy of more than fifty ships home. The *Maryland* seized her other would-be prize, the *Aerial,* commanded by a master aptly named Marriner, on 2 September. Rodgers claimed that Marriner, an American citizen, traded with French ports in the *Aerial* while flying neutral Swedish colors, and then made a bargain with an English privateer to capture the *Aerial,* to split the profits at the prize sale of the cargo, and to return the bill of ownership to Marriner. Rodgers hired a leading Baltimore lawyer,

Levi Hollingsworth, to file suit "libelling" the ship. The ensuing trial must have been a fiasco, as Rodgers attempted to testify—based on hearsay—to the *Aerial*'s illegal trading practices. The court did not admit Rodgers's hearsay, leading him to write forlornly to an English merchant in Montserrat to search local records for evidence to allow the suspended trial to resume. Apparently, the court never condemned the *Aerial*.[66]

To Rodgers's credit, the *Maryland*'s two convoys—twelve merchantmen in March 1800 and more than fifty in August and September—came through without a loss (leaving aside the *Gloria da Mar*). Rodgers left Surinam with seven vessels under convoy on 9 August, picked up five more from Berbice and Demerara (from which he sailed on 17 August), joined forces with another convoy escorted by the U.S. brig *Eagle* off Martinique, departed St. Kitts on 31 August with thirty-five American and several English merchantmen, and left St. Thomas on 10 September with fifty-two American and several English ships. Also a credit to Rodgers were his efforts to enforce United States law against the slave trade, particularly since Rodgers was (or was later) a slave owner himself. The Navy Department ordered captains who intercepted American slave ships to report the names of the ships, their tonnage, owners, and ports of destination and departure, with the number of slaves carried, and Rodgers did so. In January 1800, the *Maryland* stopped the schooner *Clarissa* of Boston, carrying eighty-one African slaves, which Rodgers reported. In July, the *Maryland* encountered the schooner *Ranger* of Charleston, with sixty-two slaves on board, in Surinam's territorial waters. Rodgers, conceiving his duty "to notice such violence," requested the colonial governor to turn the *Ranger* and its human cargo over to him for prosecution. Rodgers argued that the slave trade violated both countries' law. The governor, a man Rodgers described as having "all the address, Intrigue and artifice of a Frenchman," refused to surrender the *Ranger* on the pretext that the ship was unseaworthy. Rodgers, "highly incensed at him as a protector of the inhuman violators of the laws," could do nothing to prevent the Africans from being sold at the auction block.[67]

Upon the *Maryland*'s return to the Chesapeake Bay after almost exactly a year at sea, Stoddert ordered Rodgers to pay off the crew. The *Maryland*'s war record was truly unremarkable—two captures, both nullified, and two convoys escorted. Although the *Maryland* logged thousands of miles in the warm, vast waters of South America, her lookouts apparently never sighted a French cruiser nor did the *Maryland* ever fire her guns in anger.[68]

In the spring of 1800, Stoddert sent the *Patapsco* to the Guadeloupe squadron. In late May, Captain Geddes chased a schooner named the *Cecilia,* caught her in five hours, and discovered that she had no papers. He ordered a prize crew to take the *Cecilia* into St. Kitts for examination. The *Cecilia* never made it to court. A British privateer lugger seized the *Cecilia* by force, saying that the prizemaster's orders and warrant "would not do." The British sent their own prize crew aboard and sailed into Nevis. The collector of customs took possession of the *Cecilia* as a droit of the admiralty, and Geddes was accused of "impertinence" and threatened with arrest if he should disembark at St. Kitts.[69] The *Patapsco* later that summer captured the French letter-of-marque *La Dorade,* of six guns and forty-six men, which a prize crew sailed to Philadelphia. Civil authorities sold the ship and cargo for $3,251.50, excluding costs and commissions.[70]

At the end of July 1800, as we have seen, Geddes received intelligence while the *Patapsco* cruised off St. Thomas that an eight- or ten-ship French flotilla carrying seven hundred to a thousand troops was about to invade the Dutch colony of Curaçao. Although Geddes recognized that American merchant ships would be lost if the French captured the island, neither he nor any U.S. naval commander did anything.[71] Whether Geddes believed some other captain would take care of the problem, or thought the diplomatic and military problems of a neutral third party went beyond his orders, is unclear. But when the U.S. consul, Benjamin Phillips, summoned help from the American naval squadron off St. Kitts in mid-September, the *Patapsco* and *Merrimack* responded. On 14 September 1800, Phillips's emissary, William Robinson, reached Basseterre in the *Escape;* the next morning, after watering and taking on provisions, the two American warships set sail. On the 21st, the *Merrimack* and *Patapsco* arrived off Curaçao to discover that the island was "English"—the Dutch had surrendered the island to Britain in return for protection from the French. Yet the only British warship available to intervene, the 36-gun frigate *Nereid,* merely stood offshore. Her commander refused to take his ship into the 350-foot wide channel because the French had placed artillery batteries in the Outrabanda. Although the American captains doubted that their orders allowed them to intervene, the Dutch governor and American consul begged them to consider that, if something decisive were not done, the fort would surrender or be overwhelmed that very night and all the Americans slaughtered.[72]

That sufficed; the *Patapsco* would go into the channel to prevent a French crossing. At 5 o'clock in the afternoon on 22 September, the

Patapsco stood in for the channel. The French opened fire with a battery of five cannon at half pistol-shot range. French infantry tried to pick off the exposed men on the *Patapsco*'s decks with musket fire from the windows and rooftops of houses in the Outrabanda, but Sergeant Corcorran's twenty Baltimore-recruited marines, reinforced by the twenty marines out of the *Merrimack,* peppered the French snipers with shots from the *Patapsco*'s tops. Geddes backed his topsails, stopping the forward motion of the *Patapsco,* and ordered his port broadside to sweep the French gun batteries with grapeshot. At pointblank range the American gunners opened fire. Geddes kept the *Patapsco* off the Outrabanda, blasting the French position throughout the night. The *Patapsco,* much cut up in her hull and rigging, lost only two men wounded; an American officer aboard thought the French suffered 150 casualties.[73]

The next morning Geddes landed seventy men—the marines of the *Merrimack* and *Patapsco,* and thirty sailors off his ship—to reinforce the Dutch-American garrison in Fort Amsterdam on the eastern side of the harbor. The French evacuated Curaçao that same day. The *Nereid* sailed into Willemstad, and the British claimed victory and took possession. Consul Phillips applauded the "great promptitude & every disposition" on the American warships and gave the "praise & thanks of the Inhabitants in general, as well as the Americans in particular" for the *Patapsco*'s intervention.[74]

If the Americans had won the fight, the British duped them into losing the peace. The *Nereid*'s commander prevailed on the *Patapsco* and *Merrimack* to block another French invasion force supposedly on its way. Since it would take ten days for the fourteen American vessels in the harbor to be readied for sea, the American captains complied. The *Patapsco* and *Merrimack* went out, found nothing, and returned to Curaçao after ten days. There, much had changed. The British prohibited the American merchantmen from leaving with cargo, and sent out privateers to capture the "freed" American merchantmen. Geddes and Brown decided that their instructions did not allow them to intervene. Resigned to the situation, they sailed for St. Kitts on 11 October without any merchant vessels to protect.[75]

Soon afterward, Truxtun ordered the *Patapsco* to escort a convoy "safe to the Northward of Bermuda," where they might scatter to their ports of destination, then to sail to Norfolk.[76]

The naval war with France provided no further chances for distinction. At the end of September 1800 President Adams lifted the prohibition on U.S. trade with the islands and territories of France. The *Patapsco* came up the Delaware to Philadelphia in early December. Stoddert, who was by then aware of his lame-duck status in the outgoing Adams administration, and the incoming Republicans' disdain for a blue-water navy, immediately thought of selling the *Patapsco* as an easy step toward paring down the navy. At the end of March 1801, he ordered George Harrison, the navy agent in Philadelphia, to store the *Patapsco*'s guns and stores and to sell the ship and all her equipment at public auction. The sale brought in $24,680 to the Treasury. In April 1802 three Philadelphians, including Richard Dale, John Paul Jones's lieutenant during the Revolution and one of the senior captains of the new navy, registered as the *Patapsco*'s new owners.[77]

The *Maryland* had one last operational cruise. On 22 March 1801 she sailed for Le Havre carrying Congressman John Dawson, the American envoy with the draft peace treaty with France. Arriving on 9 May, the *Maryland* stayed in the harbor for two months, except when she rode out a gale in company with the British blockading squadron—after which Rodgers dined with the British admiral and told him about the masting and readiness of the French ships in port. Dawson wrote to Rodgers on 10 July that the *Maryland* should not await ratification of the treaty but should return home. Five days later, she departed with several private American gentlemen, public dispatches, and curiously, a present—a box containing a model of an Egyptian pyramid—sent to President Jefferson from Count Volney in Paris.[78]

The *Maryland* arrived in Baltimore in late August 1801. Immediately the navy put the *Maryland* in ordinary and paid off and discharged the crew. A month later Robert Smith, Jefferson's secretary of the navy, ordered the new navy agent at Baltimore, Col. John Stricker, to sell the ship after taking out her military stores. William Taylor of Baltimore bought the *Maryland* for $20,000; at some point afterwards, New York merchants William Bayard and Herman LeRoy purchased her and then she too disappeared from history.[79]

Both captains came close to fading into total obscurity as well. In October 1800, Truxtun destroyed Geddes's career by reprimanding the *Patapsco*'s late commander in a letter to Secretary Stoddert. Truxtun transmitted Geddes's account of the Curaçao affair, along with a newspaper clipping and correspondence from a witness on board one of the American merchantmen. Truxtun reported himself "much mortified at the management of the Curracoa business, & hurt at the Sneers and horse laughs at some here, at our Giving an Island to a nation, whoe's Officers instantly set traps to get hold of our property." Stoddert dismissed Geddes from the service. A year later, Stoddert's successor, Robert Smith, dismissed John Rodgers as a captain under the Naval Peace Establishment Act. Robert Smith not only was from Baltimore, the very port that Rodgers had sailed from as both a merchant mariner and captain of the *Maryland*, but also Robert Smith was the brother of Samuel Smith, whose vessels Rodgers had commanded in peacetime. Although Rodgers is said to have sworn never to wear his country's uniform again, he regained his rank in August 1802 and played a leading role in the Barbary Wars and was the Navy's senior seagoing captain in the War of 1812. As in his command of the *Maryland*, however, Rodgers never quite succeeded in the prize-money game, and never "quite succeed[ed] in coming to grips with his adversary."[80]

6 The Boston and the Perils of Taking Prizes

Everything about the launch of the frigate *Boston* on 20 May 1799, from Boston's North End, suggested a splendid future. At half past eleven that morning, workmen knocked away the spur shores and afterblock. The *Boston* slid down the ways from the Hartt shipyard without incident, to the booming of cannon from Captain Gardner's artillery company on Jeffrey & Russell's wharf and from festooned merchant vessels in the harbor. The president of the United States, John Adams, who had driven over from Quincy, looked on with thousands of spectators. As the president had approached the site, escorted by civilian and military dignitaries, the crowd applauded, a band played patriotic tunes, and Captain Gardner's guns fired a salute. In shipwright Edmund Hartt, the *Boston* had the same craftsman who had built the *Constitution:* the *Constitution* had taken four years to build, but the wartime emergency was such that the *Boston* entered the water only nine months after her keel was laid. As the newspapers noted, the *Boston* was "the first Copperbottomed ship built in America, whose bolts and spikes (drawn from Malleable Copper) had been manufactured in the United States." As soon as she was afloat, the *Boston* was warped to Hancock's wharf to be completed, to have her masts and rigging set up, and to be readied for war.[1]

However neat Hartt's handiwork, warships do not come into being without planning and money, and the *Boston* was no different. A year before, in May and June 1798, the local newspapers had printed the same dispatches from Newburyport that had electrified Philadelphia, Baltimore, and the Virginia towns: private citizens were combining their funds to build ships to loan to the federal government.[2] The subscription frenzy swept into Boston: a notice in the *Columbian Centinel* invited gentlemen to affix their signatures to a subscription list to be opened that afternoon, 27 June 1798, to build a warship in Boston for the federal government. Thirty-four men met in the "Chamber over Taylor's Insurance-Office" on State Street and immediately pledged $75,000.[3] By the next evening, the subscription amounted to $102,750, and when the list reached $115,250 after only two days the arch-Federalist *Columbian Centinel* crowed that "Boston will outdo every city in the union in this demonstration of federal patriotism."[4] The newspaper proved to be prescient: 103 merchants and civic leaders pledged $136,000 to buy government stock to fund the building of a warship, more than any other city. The largest pledge in the entire country came from the great philanthropist, William Phillips,[5] who subscribed the astounding sum of $10,000. Thomas Handasyd Perkins,[6] a leader of Boston's trade with Canton, provided $3,000. Twenty-seven-year-old Josiah Quincy, about to embark on a career as Federalist leader, reform mayor of Boston, and president of Harvard[7] contributed, as did the leading Boston families like Higginson, Coolidge, Sargent, and Elliot.[8] Bostonians were "navy mad." Within the week, on 3 July 1798, the *Constitution* sailed out of Boston for the first time, and as she made sail, the "loud huzzas of a vast concourse" of onlookers saluted her.[9]

With $136,000 raised, the subscribers chose seven men to serve as a committee to select a design, let contracts, and oversee construction.[10] The first task, of course, was to find out what the national government wanted Boston to build, and the merchants committee sent off a letter to Philadelphia on 2 July. Navy Secretary Benjamin Stoddert, who had taken office only two weeks earlier, responded immediately. Stoddert hoped that Boston would "not be outdone" by New York and Philadelphia, which already had agreed to build large frigates rated to carry thirty-six or forty-four guns. Accordingly, Stoddert enclosed with a copy of the Act of June 30 dimensions for large frigates and promised a model as soon as he learned what Boston decided to build.[11] By the end of July, Stoddert knew that the Boston committee decided on a 24-gun ship, as he informed the president.[12] Given Stoddert's overwhelming responsibilities of creating a navy from scratch, the Boston committee was left practically to itself to bring its ship into being.

The Boston merchants turned to Edmund Hartt to design the ship. Hartt drew the plans without instruments but produced a handsome ship, 134 feet between perpendiculars, a 34½-foot molded beam, with an 11½-foot depth of hold.[13] A significant contribution to the *Boston,* and perhaps to the American metallurgical industry, came from Paul Revere. In the mid-1790s, Revere's foundry—already casting cannon for the navy—discovered "'after considerable labour expence . . . the method of melting Copper, making it Malable [sic], and drawing it into Bolts, Spikes &c. for Ship Building.'"[14] Revere did not fabricate copper per se but used a network of contacts throughout American ports to find scrap copper that he could melt down and rework into ship fittings. By January 1799, Revere's foundry had supplied to Hartt more than fifteen hundred pounds of spikes and four hundred pounds of bolts, made to Hartt's pattern, for the Boston frigate. In buying from a local entrepreneur, the Boston merchants sought to stimulate American manufacturing, on Stoddert's specific request. At least with Revere, the effort to create a domestic manufacturing base for the country's naval needs bore fruit; in January 1801, Revere announced the opening of the first copper-rolling mill, the major product of which was copper sheathing for United States Navy ships. Revere apparently subcontracted to Ward & Faxon of Roxbury, Massachusetts, the casting and boring of the frigate's light cannon, 12 six-pounders; the aging patriot attended only to prove the guns.[15]

The *Boston,* as the Boston committee named the ship with the president's concurrence, originally mounted 24 twelve-pounder cannon on her gun deck, with 2 twelve-pounders as bow chasers and 12 six-pounders on her elevated forecastle and quarterdeck. Stoddert merely wanted notification if the Boston committee expected the Navy Department to furnish any of the artillery and, if so, the "Wt. of mettle & the number—& when they must be at Boston." He asked if the merchants intended to "furnish the Anchors compleat, Rigging & two Suits of Sails" so that at the "exact point at which they mean to Stop, . . . I may make arrangements in time, for the rest." To the frigate committee Stoddert left everything, even nominating the commissioned and warrant officers for the ship. As Stoddert told them, President Adams wished the "Gentlemen who so particularly contributed to the expence of Building, should select the whole Officers for the Frigate."[16]

For captain, the committee chose Jonathan Chapman, already the commander of the 14-gun Revenue Service cutter *Pickering.* Chapman, who had served two years in the British navy, was the "man most agreeable to the Subscribers & the Committee . . .[and] would himself like to have her." Stoddert, and President Adams, obliged the subscribers. But when Chapman received his commission, he found that it was not dated from the moment he assumed command of the *Pickering* and that, consequently, twelve captains would be senior to him on the navy list. On 1 January 1799, he mailed his commission back to Philadelphia and Stoddert could not persuade him to become the thirteenth captain in the newly reestablished navy.[17] As Edmund Hartt and his ship carpenters planked up the *Boston*'s hull and knocked oakum into the spaces, the *Boston* had no superintending captain, indeed no captain at all, as week after week rolled by.

On 2 April 1799, John Coffin Jones, the chairman of the Boston frigate committee, wrote a one-page letter to a forty-five-year-old merchant captain, George Little, residing at his farm in Marshfield, Massachusetts. Noting that the president would endorse the committee's decision, and making the usual politenesses about Little's patriotism and abilities, Jones invited Little to "take the command." He was, as Jones wrote, the committee's unanimous (if second) choice. If Little wished to accept, he was to come up to Hartt's shipyard "immediately, that they may consult you relative to some of the interior arrangements of the Ship which is in great forwardness, having her bowsprit set."[18]

For a last-minute replacement, George Little seemed an inspired choice. One of the few authentic American naval heroes of the Revolutionary War, Little had served as Capt. John Foster Williams's first lieutenant of the Massachusetts state armed ship *Protector* in its June 1780 action against the British privateer *Admiral Duff* that ended with the enemy's ship blown to pieces. When the *Protector* was later captured, Little became a prisoner locked away in the Mill Prison outside of Plymouth, England. He bribed a guard, sailed a skiff over to France and, with the help of Benjamin Franklin, the American minister, returned to Massachusetts. Given command of the Massachusetts navy's armed sloop *Winthrop,* Little tried to turn back the British invasion of Penobscot Bay. After the war, Little tended a farm in Marshfield, raised six children, and captained Boston-owned merchant vessels on European trading voyages. The Boston merchants who appointed him captain of the *Boston* waxed enthusiastic about George Little, expecting him to become the "Nelson of the United States."[19]

Over the summer of 1799, Little readied the *Boston* for sea. Hartt's workmen set up the *Boston*'s rigging by the end of May, and on 11 June, the *Boston* "hauled off into the stream." Recruiting went slowly, with the *Constitution* also in Boston seeking sailors, and there were the interminable delays in getting a new ship prepared for war. Secretary Stoddert expressed impatience but President Adams calmly wrote back that the pairing of Little and the *Boston* was "one of the bravest men in one of the finest ships in the world."[20]

President Adams took a keen interest in the fledgling fleet and played a central role in the selection of the *Boston*'s officers. The President asked Little to accept Henry Jackson Knox, the son of the former secretary of war and Revolutionary War artillerist, as an "extra" lieutenant. President Adams endorsed Dr. Amos Winship's request to be appointed the *Boston*'s surgeon, recalling their 1779 voyage in the frigate *Alliance* in which Dr. Winship "appeared . . . of a humane disposition & attentive to the health of the people." The president even granted the request of two aspiring midshipmen, Joseph Williston and Habijah Savage, to call on him at Quincy, where he professed to be "so pleased with them that I shall make them midshipmen."[21]

Secretary Stoddert ordered the *Boston* to Saint-Domingue where, by late autumn, Commodore Silas Talbot would command a major squadron. Talbot's flag flew from the *Constitution* and the squadron contained one other frigate, Capt. Christopher Raymond Perry's 24-gun *General Greene*, as well as some smaller ships. As Stoddert relayed to Captain Little, the United States had negotiated with Toussaint L'Overture the opening of two ports, Cape Francais and Port Republicain, to American trade. "Our merchant vessels will be flocking in great numbers, to these Ports," and the French privateers undoubtedly would try "to annoy our Vessels." The *Boston*, cruising off the northern coast of Saint-Domingue, was to protect them and, like all the American naval commanders, Little was authorized to stop, seize, and send in for condemnation as prizes, armed French ships and American vessels trading to French-controlled ports.[22]

The *Boston* sailed out of Boston on 24 July 1799.[23] On her first cruise, the *Boston* exceeded "even the most sanguine expectations of Bostonians in sailing. We see nothing which we do not overtake," reported Little.[24] When Hartt's *Constitution* beat Hartt's *Boston* in one race, however, an officer aboard the *Constitution* noted that "with an Equal proportion of Canvass we found her [i.e., the *Boston*] far from Equability in sailing."[25] Gorham Parsons, a member of the Boston frigate committee, a staunch friend of Little and the *Boston*'s co-prize agent, wrote to Little that his friends hoped "Soon to be regail'd by Seeing one Column of the [*Columbian*] *Centinel* devoted to the libels filed" against the prize ships the *Boston* would send in for adjudication. Parsons reported "I tell them wait *one Southerly Wind* . . ."[26] There was not only newspaper fame at stake, but also real money. Little, as captain, and the *Boston*'s officers, sailors, marines, down to the youngest boy, all were entitled statutorily to a share of the proceeds of ships and cargoes declared by courts to be rightful prizes and sold at public auction.

The *Boston* reached Commodore Talbot's squadron off Saint-Domingue in August. After cruising with the squadron and watering in Cape Francais, the *Boston* was sent out along the northern coast of the island to sweep for French privateers. On 7 November 1799, the *Boston* stopped and captured a lugger, *Le Gourdie Le Pelican,* together with the 18-gun U.S. navy brig *Norfolk* under Master Commandant William Bainbridge. The captured ship was sailed to New York, condemned as a valid prize in the U.S. district court, and sold for $11,304.16, after expenses. Under the prize statute, one-half went to the federal treasury to capitalize the Navy Pension Fund, and the other half was divided proportionately between Bainbridge's *Norfolk* and Little's *Boston* based on the ratio of guns and men between the ships. Ultimately, George Little probably received about $500 from the sale of *Le Gourdie Le Pelican.*[27]

After rendezvousing with the squadron, the *Boston* cruised off the northern coast of the island in company with Captain Perry's *General Greene.* On 1 December 1799, the two American frigates spotted and chased two vessels. First was an American schooner, the *Weymouth,* originally bound from Cape Francais to Baltimore, which a French privateer had captured two weeks before. The *Boston* put a prizemaster and crew aboard and then made sail after a brig called the *Flying Fish* under (neutral) Danish colors. Sandwiched between two major combatants, the unarmed *Flying Fish* could not fight and, according to her master, 22-year-old Nicholas Hinson, with the wind blowing hard the *Flying Fish* could not shake out her close-reefed topsails to try to flee. The *Flying Fish* maintained her course. The warships slowly caused the gap.

Hinson, an experienced seaman despite his youth, certainly recognized the *Boston* because, three months before, the *Flying Fish* lay near the American frigate for four or five days at Cape Francais. Denmark, of course, was a neutral in the French-American maritime war. Nevertheless, Hinson tossed the *Flying Fish*'s logbook overboard. Hinson later insisted that he did so "before it was possible to ascertain what the ships were then in chase."[28] The helmsman, an American named William

Lacher James, contradicted him, later testifying that "when the *Boston* was coming up with us," Captain Hinson brought the *Flying Fish*'s log book and "a bundle of papers" on deck, tied them together, weighted them with a stone, and tossed the lot over the side.[29] By four o'clock in the afternoon, the *Boston* came within hailing distance. Hinson heard Captain Little bellow for the *Flying Fish* to "heave to" or be sunk, to "haul down [your] damned white washed colors" and then to "lower [your] boat down and come on board" the *Boston* for an interview.[30]

Hinson crossed over to the towering *Boston* with the balance of his ship's papers. His conversation with Captain Little went unrecorded but must have been brief and unsatisfactory. Captain Little kept the *Flying Fish*'s papers, sent Hinson back to his ship, and then ordered the *Boston*'s second lieutenant, Joseph Beale, to muster some sailors and seize the *Flying Fish*.[31]

Little and Perry now had two ships under their control, and two different legal problems. The *Weymouth*, with its restored American captain, crew, and cargo, wished to go about their business, but as a recaptured vessel, the American warships stood to recover the salvage value of the *Weymouth* after adjudication. Little ordered the *Weymouth* to sail to Boston under her navy prize crew; Perry "consented [that] she should be sent, only in compliance with Captain Little's earnest wishes, as he had not yet sent any thing in."[32] Of course, that statement was literally untrue—*Le Gourdie Le Pelican* was on her way to the prize court in New York—but it shows George Little's overwhelming concern for prize money, which was to bring down upon him all sorts of difficulties. With the *Weymouth*, the difficulties included a protest for the detention of the ship from her master, Thomas Burgess, and the need for the leaky *Weymouth* to put into Nassau in the Bahamas where her cargo was sold. Worse still, when the *Weymouth*'s insurer made demands upon the navy, there were inquiries from the secretary of the navy relating to their subrogation claim, how it was that the prize agents embezzled some of the proceeds, and why it was that Captain Little, "who it is presumed has recd. the Amount of the Sales," had not settled accounts with the Baltimore Insurance Company.[33] In the last correspondence found regarding the *Weymouth*, Secretary Stoddert, through the navy agent at Boston, insisted that the "honor of the Navy of the U.S. as well as your own reputation call for indemnity to the owners and vessel. & he wishes you at once to learn the true state of the business and to take some step to that effect."[34]

The *Flying Fish* created an even greater morass of legal problems, ones for which Little and Perry—or any other American naval officer—were completely unprepared. The *Flying Fish* flew neutral Danish "white washed" colors, carried 153,000 pounds of coffee, and was en route to St. Thomas, Danish territory. At first glance, the *Flying Fish*'s papers—a muster roll; a manifest; a bill of lading; a bill of sale of the brigantine from Cruyden & Co. to its present owner, one Samuel Goodman; and a "protest" against the brigantine's apparent former capture by a barge controlled by Benoit Joseph Rigaud, an insurrectionary against Toussaint—all seemed unexceptional. On the other hand, Hinson, the master, claimed to be a Dane, although he spoke a suspiciously "American" English;[35] the mate, David Needham, hailed from Danvers, Massachusetts, and therefore was unquestionably American;[36] Francois Barreme, the supercargo (i.e., the agent for the owner), was a Frenchman, with his French name and birth on Martinique, although he claimed to be a naturalized Swede;[37] Goodman, the owner, resided in St. Thomas and claimed to be a Dane by naturalization, although he was born in Berlin and carried a British passport;[38] and the *Flying Fish*'s crew was such a polyglot mix of Portuguese, Danes, Swedes, black Bermudians, and Americans that no one could answer definitively about the nationalities of the crew. Both the vessel and its coffee cargo, in sacks marked "SG," "NH," and "FB" (the initials of the owner, master, and supercargo, respectively), plausibly were owned by neutrals, as they belonged to alleged Danes and a supposed Swede but not to Americans. Yet it was exactly vessels like the *Flying Fish,* "covered" by Danish papers but perhaps "really American," that Secretary Stoddert wished American naval captains to interdict.

For ten days or so, the two American frigates and the captured *Flying Fish* sailed together as Little and Perry pondered what to do. Little wrote to the American consul at Cape Francais, Edward Stevens, for advice. He recounted the claims of Hinson and Barreme (whom Little called a "french merchant . . . who says he is also a burgher of St. Thomas") and the claimed attack by Rigaud's barges. But Little was not very credulous, noting that Danish law required two-thirds of the crew to be Danes, yet the *Flying Fish*'s crew were Americans, French, and Portuguese. Little asked Stevens "whether this Brig which is directly from Jeremie [a port in Saint-Domingue] will be condemned at the cape, if I send her there" and asked Stevens to send him his "candid opinion."[39]

Stevens replied that the Toussaint government had issued an *arrêt* making all neutral vessels trading with rebel-controlled ports subject to confiscation and condemnation as lawful prize. The *Flying Fish* therefore would be condemned "at the Cape as soon as the Fact of her coming from Jeremie is clearly ascertained. The most regular Papers, under such an Infraction of the Law, would not save her. But when the circumstances of her being without Register and Log Book is taken into consideration, her Condemnation is put beyond a Doubt." Moreover, Stevens cautioned Little not to send the *Flying Fish* to America for adjudication because Congress could "make no Laws to restrain the Commerce of other Nations with foreign Places; . . . our Courts of Admiralty can take no Cognizance of a foreign vessel for having carried on an illegal Trade with another Country" nor would a U.S. court pay any attention to her lack of regular papers. In short, if the *Flying Fish* were "sent in here she will be condemned, but if sent to America will be acquitted."[40] Stevens's thoughtful advice notwithstanding, Little did not send the *Flying Fish* into Cape Francais for local courts to decide. Within the previous week, Little had sent in a small schooner for condemnation but the Toussaint government refused to condemn the ship, given the lack of proof she was bound to Jeremie and sworn affidavits from her master, crew, and passengers in direct opposition. Frustrated by the failure of the Toussaint court to declare the schooner good prize, the navy agent at the Cape wrote Little, "do you intend to make a practice, of taking Vessels, and Sending them into this port for adjudication? If you do you will Stand a good chance of ever loosing by the Capture."[41] And perhaps Commodore Talbot advised differently; according to Captain Perry, he and Little awaited the commodore's arrival from the Môle St. Nicholas to receive his advice respecting the prize, and, in "all probability, [she] will be immediately sent to America."[42]

As they waited for Talbot, the bombshell dropped. Captain Little learned that Hinson had kept, and then jettisoned, a logbook, that the protest about the former capture among the papers was a fabrication, and that, even after the *Flying Fish*'s capture, Hinson asked his crew to lie in supporting the protest's "facts." Little summoned Hinson. To his sharp questions, Hinson replied that, at their initial interview on December 1, he had declared to Little that "I had not *then* a Log Book. And that I never affirm'd or pretended the Protest to be true."[43] Little's reaction to this dissembling, while not recorded, probably differed little from that of his first lieutenant, Robert Haswell. To Haswell, the *Flying Fish*'s perceived "press of sail" to try to outsail the American frigates initially, and then the discovery of a logbook thrown overboard and a false protest, suggested that the *Flying Fish* was not what it seemed. The American officers thought that either the vessel or some of its cargo probably had an American connection.[44] Talbot wanted the *Flying Fish* sent back to America; there were those friends of Little, who wished to be "regail'd" at the sight of *Boston* prizes; and even Consul Stevens had noted that "[w]ere this Brig under American Colours, being in Contravention of the Law, she would undoubtedly be liable to Confiscation."[45] On December 16, 1799, Little ordered Lt. Beale to sail the *Flying Fish* to Boston for condemnation.[46]

Although Little was not to know the final outcome for more than seven years, sending in the *Flying Fish* nearly ruined him. At trial in Boston, the U.S. attorney could not prove the captors' case and the judge ordered the brig and its cargo restored to its owners. On appeal, the circuit court held that Captain Little seized the ship "at his risque and peril if the property was neutral," and awarded damages to the injured Danes against Little personally. The Supreme Court, in an opinion by Chief Justice John Marshall, affirmed, laying down the rule that the commander of a U.S. Navy warship (or any officer of the federal government) is strictly liable in money damages for following the orders of his civilian superiors that misconstrue or go beyond the statutory authority when his execution of those orders injures any person or property. Captain Little faced the specter of being thrown into debtor's prison before Congress belatedly passed a private act for his relief; in 1807, the Danish owners received more than $10,500 in compensation. Ironically, the capture of the obscure *Flying Fish* may be George Little's lasting legacy, as the Supreme Court decision in *Little v. Barreme* is still "good law" almost two centuries later.[47]

But all that lay in the future. The *Boston* spent the last two weeks of 1799 cruising off and on Cape Francais with Commodore Talbot's *Constitution,* the *General Greene,* and the schooner *Experiment.* Talbot passed a rumor that a three-frigate French squadron was expected daily and ordered the *Boston* to sail within supporting distance. The French warships never materialized, but the American ships chased sail after sail— all American merchant vessels.[48] As the *Boston* and the *Constitution* sailed together, Captain Little had many opportunities to talk to Commodore Talbot, pacing the quarterdeck and in the privacy of the *Constitution's* cabin. Exactly what passed between the two captains is not known, but Little complained to Talbot that he had reserved for himself (i.e., for the *Constitution*) the cruising grounds most likely for capturing prizes to the detriment of the *Boston* (and Little). But the means for Talbot to make amends was at hand: fitting out at Cape Francais was an armed, 398-ton French merchantman, *Les Deux Anges* ["*Two Angels*"], crammed with coffee, tobacco, and sugar. On New Year's Day, 1800, Talbot and Little agreed "alone in the Cabin of the *Constitution*, that in case Either of them should capture the Said ship *Two Angels* (but more commonly called by them the Coffee Ship) the Captain & Crew of the other Ship Should be Equally Concerned as tho captured in Sight of Each other." The Talbot-Little "captains' pact" was a hedge, doubling the chance of gain, while halving the possible profit of each.[49]

Then came some critical intelligence from Captain Perry:

> while I lay in the Harbour of Cape Francais, in the month of January last, I obtained information that the French ship *Deux Anges* commonly called the Coffee Ship, then ready for Sea in said Harbour, would sail in a few days after the *Genl. Greene* left the Port, which was on the Twelfth day of January 1800—and that after laying a few days at the Island of Tortulas would go through either the Caicos Passage or Crooked Island Passage. This information I immediately sent by an officer to Capt. Talbot then laying off the Cape. . . .[50]

On 18 January 1800, Talbot ordered Captain Perry in the *General Greene* to cruise in the Turks Island passage and Captain Little in the *Boston* to cruise in the Caicos passage, while his *Constitution* patrolled the Crooked Island passage. Talbot hoped, as he wrote Perry, that once the American frigates disappeared over the horizon, the French merchant ship would emerge and become an easy American capture.[51]

Little, of course, was jubilant, and he did not hide his pact with Talbot. Prior to sailing for the Caicos passage, Captain Little spoke to Talbot's officers. The last time that Little was aboard *Constitution* prior to sailing, he walked the quarterdeck with Isaac Collins, a *Constitution* lieutenant. In their stroll, Little described the captains' agreement and the prospective sharing of prize money between the two ships. Dr. Peter St. Medard, the *Constitution*'s surgeon, later recalled that Captain Little patted his pocket containing Talbot's orders for emphasis during their conversation about the captains' prize-sharing pact. Dr. St. Medard added that Captain Little said his own officers were "perfectly agreeable" to the captains' arrangement. Noadiah Morris, Talbot's clerk, remembered the same basic facts, and Little's reiteration that if either the *Boston* or the *Constitution* captured the *Deux Anges* when the other was not in sight, they nonetheless would share in the prize equally.[52]

The three frigates then sailed from the Cape to their respective stations. As they departed, the *Constitution* spotted a schooner to the northeast and began to chase. In Captain Perry's words:

during [the] chase Capt. Little came on board the *Genl. Greene,* and I told him that I had born away several Times to induce the *Boston* to follow me as I wished to keep in sight of the *Constitution* that I might come in for a share of the Prize Should she prove one. His answer was, that he had no occasion to keep in sight of the *Constitution* for he and Commodore Talbot had entered into an agreement that the two ships should share in all Prize money equally. I replied to Capt. Little, then I have found you out. He made no answer but smiled. This was at the time . . . that we were with our respective ships to take our stations at the aforesaid Passages, and at the Turks Island Passage, which was my station. . . . It was however but a few days before we actually sailed for those stations. I mentioned this conversation with Capt. Little to my officers, and it gave general discontent, the agreement being much disapproved, as operating unfavourably & unfairly to the *Genl. Greene.*[53]

The source of the discontent in the *General Greene* is obvious. Talbot, having received intelligence from Perry that also suggested private gain, posted his three frigates in such a way as to all but eliminate Perry's chances to make the capture. In other words, Perry told Talbot the *Deux Anges* would sail by way of one of two routes; Talbot's *Constitution* patrolled one, and Little's *Boston* the other—so that they could make the capture and divide the spoils—while Perry's *General Greene* was sent into proverbial orbit.

As it turned out, the *Deux Anges* sailed by way of the Caicos Passage, where the *Boston* lay in wait. On 27 January 1800, the *Deux Anges,* with her 10 six-pounders and letter-of-marque commission came "running down upon" the *Boston,* as Little put it, apparently convinced that the American man-of-war was a huge fat merchantman. Instead, it was the tricolor flag on the *Deux Anges* that came down. As they hoped, the Americans discovered her to be filled with coffee and smaller quantities of cocoa, tobacco, and sugar. Captain Little ordered his first lieutenant, Robert Haswell, to sail the prize to Boston for adjudication.[54]

The prospect of big money proved too alluring to George Little. He never conceded that he had an agreement with Silas Talbot; he never volunteered to share the proceeds of the prize. Talbot's lawyers pursued his share in the federal courts, of course, from the trial court to the appeals court and even to the Supreme Court, but Talbot ended up with nothing. Little personally profited with about $3,675,[55] a lot of money in an era when a skilled artisan earned $1.50 per day.

Yet, on balance, Little's prize money tally during the naval war with France reflected near-disastrous captures like the *Flying Fish* and others like *L'Espoir* [*"Hope"*]. The *Boston* seized *L'Espoir* on 23 June 1800, and sent her prize into Boston for proceedings. Judge John Lowell, the same judge who had presided over the *Flying Fish* and the *Deux Anges* trials, acquitted the ship. In the *L'Espoir* case, Judge Lowell found that the captured brigantine was unarmed and that no American had an interest in the ship or her cargo. In ordering her restoration to her owners, Judge Lowell spared Captain Little from damages for the wrongful capture and detention given *L'Espoir*'s "false Papers calculated to deceive & the prevarication of the real & ostensible master."[56]

In fairness to Little, he could hardly anticipate how a judge thousands of miles away, with time to weigh testimony and reflect on the law of nations and the arguments of counsel, might interpret the statute and the secretary of the navy's orders. The captures might be "at his risque and peril," but Little was the commander on the spot with no proctor in admiralty to consult, no method to sound out his superiors—nothing but his common sense and a naval officer's respect for following orders energetically.

Moreover, George Little was no mere prizemonger. President Adams took an enormous personal interest in the ships, operations, and officers of the navy. Adams's first-hand view of Little as "one of the bravest men . . . in the world"—redolent of Napoleon's view of Marshal Ney as "the bravest of the brave"—is a title that should not be tossed aside lightly. George Little was a man of spirit, not easily cowed. On her passage out from Boston, the English frigate *Boston* spoke to the American *Boston,* and sent a lieutenant across to interview Little. The British officer asked whether the merchantmen Little had under convoy carried contraband goods; the British blithely assumed a right to inspect the American ships, but told Little that if he gave his word of honor as a gentleman that they did not carry contraband, the British would let them pass unmolested. Little replied "that he would give his word and honor that the fleet was bound to a free port, and was under his convoy, and as such he would protect them." The British did not press the issue further. Nor did Little shirk combat, but in the *Boston*'s first war cruise, there were no French warships at hand. Still, in the near-chaos of revolution on Saint-Domingue, there were pirates and murderous, loosely controlled armed insurrectionaries. The U.S. consul general reported that off the Point of Gonaives, in the western part of Saint-Domingue, were "a vast Number of Barges, manned by the Adherents of Rigaud," Toussaint's arch-nemesis, "who availing themselves of the unsettled state of Things, have thrown off all the Restraints of Law and Government, and plunder unarmed Merchantmen as they pass." Americans who encountered Rigaud's barges, like Simeon Toby, master of the schooner *Jane* out of New York, left harrowing accounts:

> Nov. 21 [,1799] at 6 A.M. saw two barges in shore, appearing to chase us; at 9 the wind died away, and we were brought too by two of Rigaud's barges, who plundered us of money . . . and took from us all of our provisions and cloth[e]s; also stabbed one Frenchman, John Besire, of Baltimore, a citizen of the United States in the breast; tied my arms, and was going to throw me overboard, then hung me up in the main shrouds until I was almost dead; afterwards took me down, and dragged me on the main deck, by the rope; and lashed me forward; beat the cook with the but[t] end of the musket.
>
> There being two vessels in sight, they left us and pulled for the *Polly;* she engaged them, fired about 9 guns, and then the barges made off. . . .[57]

Several months later, on 11 March 1800, the *Boston* sailed those same waters, off the Gonaive Islands. Rigaud's bargemen put out for what they took to be an unsuspecting American merchant vessel. As the *Boston's* lookouts spotted nine barges jammed with pirates making a beeline for their ship, Captain Little instantly ordered the *Boston's* cannon "housed" and run in from the gunports, which were closed, so as, in Captain Little's words, to "decoy them if possible. . . . [O]n approaching within shot [range] they found their mistake & turned to row away." But the *Boston* ran out her twelve-pounders and attacked the barges. For two hours, the *Boston* blasted away at the small craft, sinking three with their crews, the others escaping in the gathering darkness though "in a most shattered condition." Given the size and fragility of the twenty-oarred barges, the *Boston's* gunnery left something to be desired. Even Captain Little grumbled in his report that the "Powder & shot expended in firing at them, I fear, was of more value than their destruction."[58]

With the one-year enlistments of her sailors about to expire, the *Boston* returned to her home port in June 1800, discharging the men who chose not to reenlist and taking aboard many new officers. Captain Little called upon the president in nearby Quincy at least once, to get John Adams's approval of, and signature on, the *Boston's* new warrant officers' warrants. The *Boston* became a family ship: the captain had two of his sons aboard, George Little, Jr., a nineteen-year-old Harvard graduate who had read law, as schoolmaster and captain's clerk; and nine-year-old Edward Preble Little as an acting midshipman.[59] The captain's nephew, Stephen Clough, became second lieutenant.[60] The first lieutenant, Robert Haswell, rejoined the ship in Boston, where he had safely brought the prize *Deux Anges* six months earlier. The first lieutenant's younger brother, John Montressor Haswell, along with Robert's brother-in-law, Joseph Cordis, came aboard as midshipmen. President Adams was even lobbied to make the third brother, William Haswell, a lieutenant in the navy.[61] The president held up the *Boston* as the exemplar of a healthy, efficient ship—"Little has returned without the loss of a man by sickness, and with a ship in perfect health, only by keeping always at sea"[62]—and as a "school for officers"[63]—but the *Boston* was not a happy ship. For reasons now unclear, there was a vast turnover of enlisted men and officers, enough that the navy secretary expressed concern. Benjamin Stoddert wrote to Little that the navy agent in Boston, Stephen Higginson, informed him "that a number of your Officers purpose [*sic*] resigning" although Stoddert was pleased "to learn that it is not from disgust with the Ship or their Commander that so many of your Officers are about to leave you."[64]

Robert Haswell, the handsome and capable first lieutenant, seems to have had a correct, if not cordial, relationship with George Little. From the beginning of the war, Haswell had hoped for his own command, and he seemed to be on the cusp of receiving a captain's commission. Haswell was born in 1768. His parents remained loyal to the Crown at the onset of the Revolution, and the family emigrated to Halifax and then to Yorkshire in England. Young Robert served in the Royal Navy, probably as a midshipman, where he reportedly became "well versed in naval Tactics after the British manner." At some point in the 1780s, the three Haswell brothers, Robert, William, and John Montressor, migrated back to Boston. Robert at age 18 became the third mate of the *Columbia* on her first voyage to the Northwest Coast in September 1787. The *Columbia* spent ten months in the Nootka Sound before sailing on to Hawaii, China, and around Cape Horn back to Boston, the first vessel carrying the Stars and Stripes around the world. The circumnavigation took three years. Haswell made another around-the-world trading voyage in the *Columbia* (1790–93) and, as master, sailed the 280-ton *Hannah* to China (1793–96) and the 217-ton *John Jay* to Batavia (1796–98).

When war with France loomed in 1798, Haswell offered his services to the government, journeying to Philadelphia at his own expense. Hoping for a command, Haswell first turned down Capt. Samuel Nicholson's offer to be first lieutenant of the *Constitution* and then Capt. Daniel McNeill's offer to be the first lieutenant of the sloop of war *Portsmouth.* Haswell was a favorite of the Boston merchants, who had "a very good opinion of him as a man" and thought him "remarkably well qualified" for a command. Ultimately, they prevailed upon him to become the *Boston*'s first lieutenant. On her first war cruise, Captain Little made him the prizemaster of the *Deux Anges,* and Haswell had brought her safely to Boston. Reunited with the *Boston,* Haswell spent the summer of 1800 refitting the frigate for her second war cruise. A portrait of Robert Haswell painted at this time shows a young, round-faced man with arched eyebrows and unruly dark hair, suggesting athleticism or vigor and perhaps good-natured intelligence.[65]

The *Boston*'s second war cruise began at eight o'clock in the morning on 15 September 1800, when the frigate cast off her moorings and set sail for Guadeloupe, the roost of French privateers.[66] Immediately, the *Boston* ran into a gale. Second lieutenant Clough noted in his journal for 16 September that, with the storm mounting, the captain "thot best to go back to Nantasket road[. A]t 2 P.M. Bore away out all sails and run from abreast the Lighthouse on Cape Cod in to Nantasket road in three hours by our watches, a Distance of Eighteen Leagues . . ."[67] On 18 September, the *Boston* ventured out again, on a course roughly south-southeast, making about one hundred miles per day. Captain Little's journal records the routine of the frigate at sea: shaking out reefs and setting all sail as the wind allowed; taking in lighter sails as a squall approached; and, on 9 October, "all hands to Quarters Exercising Great Guns and small arms."[68]

On the morning of 12 October, when the *Boston* lay about six hundred miles northeast of Guadeloupe, her lookouts spotted two vessels sailing in company bearing south and about eight or nine miles distant. With variable winds coming from the east-northeast to southeast, the *Boston* gave chase. By 8 A.M., the *Boston* identified the chases as warships, one ship-rigged and the other a schooner. The schooner "Haul'd her wind to the Northward," and the ship "bore away before the wind" and set all sail. Unable to bring both to bay, the *Boston,* in George Little's words, "bore away after the Ship and Set Every Yard of Canvis in Chass of her." The *Boston* slowly gained ground on the fleeing warship but the hours crept by; if the quarry could keep away until sunset, perhaps she could avoid the *Boston* in the darkness. But there was no escape. At 4 P.M., Captain Little ordered the *Boston* cleared for action and at 4:30, the *Boston* opened fire from her bow gun. The stranger answered by hoisting the tricolor and, in the etiquette of fighting ships of the day, fired a gun to windward and shortened sail to indicate that she would run no more.

The *Boston*'s log continues:

> At 15 minutes Before 5 P.M. came up with the ship, hailed her and Ordered him to Strike his Collers to the United States flag. The captain replied that his Collers were too well made fast to haul down. The Action immediately commenced and lasted till 24 minutes past 5 P.M. The sails and riggin of boath ships being much shattered, it was impossible to work either ship in consequence of which we drifted too far apart for our Shot to do Execution. I then ordered all hands to be Employed repairing the riggin to commence the action again. At 9 P.M. the Action recommenced, which lasted till 20 minutes past 10 P.M., when her Fore and Main Masts were shot away. She then struck her Collers to the Boston. Not long after her Fore and Main Masts went over the Side, which I was sorry to Sea. . . .[69]

At some point well into the night, Captain Little learned that his prize was the French navy corvette *Le Berceau*, mounting 22 nine-pounders and 2 twelve-pounders, and commanded by Louis-Andre Senez. In the two-hour battle, the *Boston* lost four killed in action and three more men were mortally wounded, including the purser, Samuel Young, who had asked Captain Little before the battle to leave his safe combat post in the cockpit to serve as a gun captain. One of the first shots brought Young down. Among the *Boston*'s eight wounded was Midshipman John M. Haswell, shot through the wrist. The *Berceau*'s butcher bill was much worse—thirty-four men killed in action, including her first lieutenant and sailing master, and eighteen men wounded. Captain Little sent his nine-year-old son, acting Midshipman Edward P. Little, in the *Boston*'s boat along with his first lieutenant, Robert Haswell, to receive the *Berceau*'s surrender formally. Midshipman Little discovered, and recalled almost a half-century later, a strangely antiseptic scene: instead of blood in the scuppers and scenes of carnage, the surviving French crew had tossed the *Berceau*'s dead overboard and incoming waves had washed the decks clean. The *Boston*'s boats ferried American sailors over to clear the wreck and to bring 197 French prisoners aboard the *Boston*.[70]

The senior surviving French lieutenant, Louis-Marie Clement, as a prisoner in Boston with time on his hands and undoubtedly concerned for his reputation, wrote a report to the French Minister of the Navy and Colonies, Adm. Denis Decrès, that seems to narrate a different battle than that described by the Americans, even allowing for some Gascon bravado:

At half-past three o'clock the frigate hoisted the American flag and pennant and fired twice. We at once hoisted the French colors and pennant and answered by a single cannon shot. The frigate, at a quarter to four, being within speaking distance, asked us whence we came. A moment later she fired on us, and ranging along our port side within pistol shot, the battle began in a most spirited manner on both sides. The musketry was very sharp and well sustained, the only delays being to load the pieces. The battery was also served with the greatest activity, and the cry of 'Vive la Republique!' was often heard during the battle. At six o'clock our topgallant masts were seriously wounded, the shrouds were cut through, and the yards, sails, and lower masts were riddled with shot. At five minutes after six o'clock the frigate dropped astern, having her topsail ties cut and the yards on the caps. We boarded our fore and main tacks and came by the wind. The frigate from this moment ceased firing and we worked without ceasing at repairing damages.

At half-past eight o'clock the frigate again attacked us and we discharged a broadside. From that time the action was renewed with great ferocity at pistol shot. At half-past nine o'clock the captain, seeing a favorable opportunity of boarding the frigate, gave the order, and the crew only awaited the chance, and our vessel manoeuvred to favor the attempt. The frigate, however, took care not to allow herself to be boarded, and the action continued at pistol range up to eleven o'clock, when the frigate again hauled off to repair damages. We again set our courses, a short time after which our jibboom was carried away and the topmasts followed. At this time our shrouds and backstays were nearly all cut through, and the two spare topmasts had also been cut upon the gallows frame. We therefore found ourselves without the possibility of repairing, but we nevertheless made as much sail as we could. The frigate was also much damaged in her sails and rigging and she remained out of gunshot, but always in sight.

At five o'clock the next morning nobody had yet left his post and we expected any moment a third attack, when the frigate passed us to the starboard at a great distance and placed herself to leeward of us at half a league distance. In the course of the morning we saw that she was working at repairs. At half-past eleven o'clock our foremast, pierced with shot, fell to starboard, and a short time afterward the mainmast also fell. At two o'clock in the afternoon the frigate, which had now finished repairs, came up to us on the starboard side.[71]

The *Berceau* then surrendered.

The different accounts cannot be reconciled. In the terse American account, the battle was in two parts, of forty minutes and eighty minutes, separated by a 3½-hour lull. The French version has the action renewed again and again, lasting twelve hours overnight. Some aspects of the battle are clear, however. The *Boston-Berceau* battle was fought at a murderously close range. Although the American frigate mounted more and heavier cannon, Little chose to close with the French ship, suggesting that his largely new crew may not have been too handy with the *Boston*'s great guns. Given the three-to-two relative superiority of the *Boston*'s broadside to the *Berceau*'s, the *Berceau* could win only by luck, such as by shooting away the *Boston*'s masts, or by boarding. Clement's report states that the *Berceau* fired seven hundred cannonballs and no less than twenty-one hundred musket rounds ("coups de fusil"), but with surprisingly little human carnage. Despite all the cannonading at short range, the *Berceau*, following typical French naval doctrine, fired on the upward roll of their ship seeking to dismast the enemy. Had those tactics succeeded, the *Berceau* could either escape or engage at will. When those tactics failed, all that the *Berceau* had left was to try to grapple onto the *Boston* to board under a hail of small-arms fire.

While the French aimed high, so did the Americans. If a newspaper account published just after the *Boston*'s return to America can be believed, the *Boston*'s cannon spewed out fifteen hundred round shot, but nearly double that number of chain, double-headed shot, and grapeshot. The *Boston* sought to dismast the *Berceau* and changed to the canisters of grape upon seeing the *Berceau* attempt to board. George Little's motive in aiming high is not hard to divine. Captain Little, consumed by the idea of prize money, aimed at the *Berceau*'s masts so as not to sink a valuable property.

Both sides succeeded in devastating the other's masts and rigging. Captain Little acknowledged that the *Berceau* "fought a hard battle, attempted to board three times, and did not strike till all her masts were gone and the ship was unmanageable." The French admiralty concluded its report on the battle to Napoleon, the First Consul, that it was a "hard combat against immense superiority," which honored France and the naval officers who fought it. Little conceded that his own ship's sails and rigging were "much cut" and that the *Boston* required a new gang of shrouds and sails. Indeed, for three days after the battle, the *Boston*'s log records "all hands Employ'd Repairing the Riggin," with "Notting and Spliceing" and resetting shrouds and the running rigging. On the fourth day after the battle, the *Boston* bent new fore and main topsails, those set during the battle being "shot all to pieces," and sent the main topgallant mast down with "three shot through it." Still later, the *Boston* needed to rig a new main topmast, to bend new sails, and to fish the mainmast.[72]

Bringing the battered *Berceau* back to Boston challenged American seamanship even more. It took Lieutenant Haswell's prize crew two days to clear away the wreck on the *Berceau*'s decks, and the *Boston* linked up to the *Berceau* with its heaviest cable to begin to tow the dismasted, six-hundred-ton warship the two thousand miles across open ocean to Boston. After several days of light winds and pleasant weather, the breeze stiffened and the swells started to mount. On 17 and 18 October, storms hit the two warships with "sharp lightning and rain." In heavy seas on 19 October, the *Boston*'s carpenters fished the *Boston*'s old main topmast into the *Berceau* to make a jury mast, and amidst a "heavy Tumbling Sea" on 20 October, the *Boston*'s carpenters used two spars as shears to raise a jury foremast on the *Berceau*. It took another four days to rig yards on the *Berceau*'s jury masts. On 28 October, yet another storm hit, and the cable between the *Boston* and the *Berceau* parted in the heavy seas. The *Berceau* did not respond to three signal guns fired or to two lights hoisted aloft in the *Boston,* and Little considered the prize lost. On 30 October, the *Boston* discovered the *Berceau* still floating and took her in tow again, and the two warships finally arrived in Nantasket Roads outside of Boston on 14 November 1800.[73] Robert Haswell's navigation of the *Berceau* to Boston is one of the epic, if least known, feats of pure seamanship of the American sailing navy.

The *Berceau* was only the second major French warship captured by the United States Navy in the Quasi-War (the *Constellation*'s capture of the frigate *L'Insurgente* was the first) and she turned out to be the last. Indeed, just days before the *Boston* shepherded home the captured *Berceau,* Boston newspapers reported the first rumors of a peace treaty signed at Mortefontaine, France, that ended the maritime hostilities. But the Boston newspapers also grasped the magnitude of the capture. That the two-year-old U.S. Navy could capture any French navy warship was noteworthy. That the victorious ship was their own *Boston,* the frigate that they had conceived, financed, built, and officered, was magnificent. The *Berceau* had gained renown as a racer and Commodore Talbot termed her "a very good cruizer, well constructed." The French officers asserted that their ship was the best corvette ever built at Lorient. Built in 1793, the 120-foot-long *Berceau* had been a thorn in the side of American trade in the West Indies. In her last, twenty-five-day cruise from Cayenne, she had seized three American merchant vessels before running afoul of the *Boston*. A bit of doggerel captured Boston's acclaim:

> *Had the* Berceau *'tis said been a little more strong,*
> *She the* Boston *had matched to a tittle:*
> *And we've reason to think this conjecture not wrong,*
> *As she only was beat by a* Little.[74]

Captain Senez of the *Berceau* was not a prisoner, however, because in the chivalric code that governed the conduct of gentlemen and officers, Captain Little had granted Captain Senez his sword and parole twelve days after the battle, and had set him and his purser aboard a New London brig bound for Barbados. The 190-odd remaining French prisoners were disgorged into Fort Independence in Boston harbor. The surviving half-dozen French officers kept their swords and found room and board in Boston on the miserable dole of two dollars per week.

All in all, the victors could expect laurels for their glory and specie for their prize. For George Little, this meant the lion's share of money at the auction of the *Berceau* and, perhaps, recognition with Thomas Truxtun as one of the American navy's heroes. Robert Haswell might well have expected a captain's commission as the first lieutenant in a successful ship-to-ship action and in recognition of his towering seamanship in bringing the *Berceau* home. And, indeed, at first, their hopes seemed to be realized. Upon reading Little's report of the victory, Navy Secretary Stoddert wrote a short letter effusive with praise, noting that the "President desires me to offer to yourself, your officers & men his congratulations on your present success & his sincere wishes for your future glory."[75]

On 17 November 1800, the United States attorney in Boston filed the legal papers in the U.S. district court to condemn the *Berceau* as legal prize. Unlike the vexatious proceedings with the *Flying Fish* and the *Deux Anges,* the prize court proceedings against the *Berceau* went smoothly. After all, the *Berceau* was an enemy warship that had fought a pitched battle against the *Boston*. The French officers admitted in sworn answers to interrogatories all the facts necessary to make the prize valid. On 2 December 1800, Judge Lowell decreed the *Berceau* to be a valid prize, and on 7 January 1801, the *Berceau* and all her equipment were sold at auction. Stephen Higginson, the Boston navy agent, informed Stoddert that the *Berceau*'s copper was "worn out, her sails and rigging cut to pieces— her masts all gone, and she appears a wreck" but her hull remained strong. Secretary Stoddert, noting that British Admiralty practice was to acquire captured warships at low prices, directed Higginson to buy the *Berceau* at auction after bidding established a fair price. The navy bought the *Berceau* for $8,000. Her cannon, stores, ballast, provisions, and equipment (including forty-eight "hand granadoes" at 17 cents each) brought in about $9,000. Together with the $5,172.93 worth of gold and silver coins taken from the *Berceau* and deposited with the court by Captain Little, and subtracting costs and fees, the net prize money came to $20,687.40. Captain Little's own share came to $1,556.56.[76]

But the French officers' legal papers also contained disturbing allegations. They claimed that the officers and crew of the *Boston* pillaged their French prisoners of money, jewelry, and personal effects.

Prize crews' pillaging of the vanquished was standard European naval practice and the post-1789 French navy contained perhaps the most vicious freebooters.[77] But the United States Navy operated, or professed to operate, without the corruption of the Old World. Indeed, the French allegations were not that a few hands got carried away in the afterglow of victory or the bottle, but that two weeks after the battle, and then again in Boston harbor itself, Captain Little ordered systematic and calculated thievery. On 8 December 1800, Lieutenant Clement gave a report to the French consul at Boston, later transmitted to the French Ministry of Marine, in which he stated that Captain Little ordered his son, George Little, Jr., and Lieutenant Clough to search the officers' baggage, and then their persons, for money. As for the *Berceau* crew, Clement reported that the Americans undressed them, took watches, earrings, money, clothes, cut open their shoes, trousers, jacket linings, even soap bars looking for coins, and then chained them together, slave-ship–style, two by two, with one man on his front, and the other lying on his back. Clement reported that the captured Frenchmen had to buy their water ration, and that the Americans' rapaciousness was so great that they even opened the bandages of the French wounded to see whether the dressings contained coins. Clement stated that he wrote a letter of complaint to Captain Little, who threw the missive into the fire. Clement in his indignation did not see any irony in reporting that he "complained that some sailors were choked so hard that they lost their breath in order for them to surrender some gold coins believed to be hidden in their mouths." By way of answering his "respectful" complaints, Captain Little called his marine guard and had Clement "thrown from his cabin in the rudest manner."[78]

Clement also wrote Secretary Stoddert to complain about the alleged ill treatment. Stoddert could not believe Clement's claims because such conduct "would be unworthy of American Seamen." Stoddert, President Adams's outgoing navy secretary, apparently wished to let the matter go, but the Boston newspapers got wind of the charges. When the Federalist-leaning, pro-navy *Commercial Gazette* called the allegations of plundering "a base and pitiful lie," the querulous *Independent Chronicle* printed a letter from Clement and his brother officers attesting to the thievery and concluding "we were searched in places which modesty forbids to name."[79]

Although the Federalist *Columbian Centinel* fulminated against foreign slander and the stigmatizing of American sailors as pillagers, the French officers would not go gently into the night. The six surviving French officers swore out a statement before a Boston notary reiterating their charges that they and their men had twice been systematically and indecently searched, that the *Berceau*'s men had been shackled together, two by two, and been deprived of rations and water, and that Captain Little took away for his domestic service three black cabin boys against their will.[80]

With the new administration of President Jefferson, the navy had no chief for months. It was not until 16 June 1801, that the acting secretary of the navy, Henry Dearborn, ordered a court of inquiry convened. Three captains, Samuel Nicholson, Silas Talbot, and Daniel McNeill, assembled in the frigate *Constitution* beginning on 30 June 1801, to hear the charges against George Little. Sixteen witnesses testified. The French officers testified to the searches and pillaging in great detail and although no one could testify that Captain Little ordered it in advance, Clement testified that Little told him that he "would not leave a sailor enough money to play at cards." According to Lt. Louis Pouten, Captain Little's son took his watch and property and refused to return them, saying, "Papa would blame him if he did."

There was another side, however. Stephen Clough, second lieutenant of the *Boston,* testified that an impressed American sailor found among the *Berceau*'s crew, John Reed, had told him that the *Berceau* had on board money taken from two or three Portuguese prizes. Accordingly, Captain Little had ordered that everyone aboard the *Berceau* be searched, leaving $100 to each wardroom officer and $50 to each midshipman and surgeon's mate. Clough's searchers found money everywhere, and the *Berceau*'s crew, seeing the search unfolding, taunted the *Boston* crew by throwing coins overboard after asking if "we did not want it to buy Yankee drams." Clough insisted that the French sailors were only put in irons after a prisoners' uprising was discovered in the works.

Yet even American testimony was damning. Clough admitted as an after-thought that Captain Little kept one French boy as his own on the *Boston* and that another he saw at the captain's lodgings. James Bradford, surgeon's mate, testified matter-of-factly that, after the searches, Marine Lt. Jonathan Church gave him a silver buckle, Third Lt. Redmond Burr sported a silver watch, and George Little, Jr., wore silver buckles from the *Berceau* in his shoes.[81]

The French officers' charges embarrassed the navy and the new administration felt no loyalty to Little. Even as the court of inquiry sat—before any evidence at the Boston trial could have been known at Washington—Acting Secretary Dearborn removed Little from command of the *Boston,* appointing in his stead the mercurial, and possibly deranged, Daniel McNeill.[82] As the navy refit the *Boston* to transport the new American minister to France, Robert Livingston, across the Atlantic, the aristocratic Livingston, echoing what the newspaper-reading public may have been thinking, wrote Secretary of State James Madison with a certain hauteur: "By the bye, will it be quite proper to continue Little in command of a ship going to France (or indeed to any other place) after the charges made against him & supported by the officers of the *Burceau?*"[83]

And the evidence before the court of inquiry sufficed for the navy to order a court martial. Convening a court martial was in itself a major effort: under the Naval Peace Establishment Act of 1801, Congress reduced the navy to a mere nine captains, but the Act could not be put into effect with eight captains (and a master commandant) sitting in judgment on another captain. While the court consisted of at least one officer, Silas Talbot, seemingly predisposed against George Little because of their ongoing dispute related to the *Deux Anges* prize money, the court also included Edward Preble, who had served under George Little in the Revolutionary War and for whom one of Captain Little's sons was named. Neither man recused himself nor was either challenged. Although originally convened at the State House in Boston, the court unanimously agreed to move the proceedings to the cabin of the *Constitution,* lying in the harbor, "to avoid the confusion of inconvenience" of a public venue.

On 2 September, the court martial of George Little began with the judge advocate, George Blake (the United States attorney in Boston), reading the sworn declaration executed by the *Berceau* officers. Little moved the court for the assistance of counsel, which the court granted. When Blake then asked the court to swear in the *Berceau*'s officers as witnesses, Little's lawyer objected that it was "contrary to the policy of nations, that a prisoner of war be admitted to testify against his captor, unless the necessity of the case requires it." The court sustained the objection, and then sustained another objection, preventing Blake from admitting into the court martial proceedings the French officers' testimony from the court of inquiry.[84]

Blake still tried to make the case against Little, using witnesses only from the *Boston*. Masters mate Nathaniel Soley reported on searches, conducted by Lieutenant Clough and Marine Liuetenant Church, that found hidden coins in the clothes and underwear of the French sailors. Soley testified that one French sailor conceded that he had plundered the money from a Portuguese prize and that it was the "Fortune of war . . . to part with them." Soley testified as to the piles of coins, as well as buckles and rings, taken as booty and stacked on the *Boston*'s wardroom table. He insisted, however, that no clothing was taken and that each prisoner received his daily pound of beef and bread and three pints of water—the same fare as the American crew.

Captain Little's son and namesake was called to testify and produced two orders signed by his father. On 14 October 1800, two days after the battle, Captain Little ordered every one of his own sailors returning aboard to be searched for coins or property that they might have plundered. Later, on 26 October 1800, Captain Little ordered Clough and Church to "search such parts of the Ship [*Berceau*] as you may think probable money may be conceal'd in," ending "Look out or loose it." The younger Little admitted that he took part in the searches but insisted that only coins, a few watches and knives, and one pair of shoe buckles were taken. Of the three black boys, George Little, Jr., recalled seeing only one at his father's Marshfield farm, where he was content, well treated, and "appears to be attached to the family."

Midshipman John M. Haswell, whose arm had been nearly shot off in the *Berceau* fight, put in a discordant note. He testified that the captain's son ordered the prisoners to open their clothes to be searched and that two of the *Berceau*'s sailors "stripped themselves entirely naked except that their trousers hung down at their heels" while the boatswain and Soley took all of their money. Haswell stated that the stash amounted to much more than the younger Little testified and, significantly implicating his captain, that George Little came into the *Boston*'s wardroom to see the coins, jewelry, silver plate, and personal effects spread across the table.

Other *Boston* officers and warrant officers testified, Marine Lieutenant Church being "so confused ambiguous & contradictory," as the official record notes, that the court "interrupted and dismissed him as undeserving of further attention." Testimony lasted four days. In his defense, Captain Little called just one witness, James Howe, the ship's carpenter. His testimony was to establish that there was nothing indecent or cruel about the searches: "each prisoner was order'd to pass in review one by one, to cast loose their Jackets, & were then examined & their money taken from . . . Belts sew'd round their waists." Categorically, Howe testified that no one's shirt or trousers were taken off.

Captain Little did not testify in his own defense. But he was clearly active at the trial. His papers include, in his hand, a twenty-one-question cross-examination prepared for use of one of the *Boston*'s officers. If Captain Little drafted no question for which he did not already know how the witness would testify—a basic tenet of trial advocacy—he did a professional enough job. His questioning would have demonstrated that Captain Senez refused to take Clement back to France with him on parole; that Captain Little had refused to lock up Clement, despite the request of his officers; and that Clement acted "like a madman, or a man intoxicated with liquor." More to the point, Little's cross-examination showed that Captain Senez himself told the *Boston*'s officers that the *Berceau* contained "a very considerable sum of money" (perhaps from its American captures) and that it "would be concealed in different parts of the Ship and among the officers and men."[85]

Captain Little's lawyer began a long and florid closing argument against "charges so entirely unsupported." The charge of stripping French sailors was false; the Frenchmen had pulled down their own trousers as an insulting gesture, and "when every device was employed to conceal effects, when bandages were tied around their bodies, money sewed up in their clothing . . . what a picture is exhibited of the insolence and arrogance of these men who have raised such a clamour . . ." Little's lawyer contended that the other charges were also specious: the French received the same rations as the Americans, the officers retained their side arms and billeted with their American counterparts, and as to the expropriation of the black servant boys, "one boy only was recommended by the French Captain to Captain Little and taken as his servant" although he was free to leave. The invective of Clement and the other French officers, "repeated and circulated with industry," had made the matter a national concern. Yet the testimony showed that the only missing property was a "few paltry watches and gewgaws." At the same time, the proceedings had tarnished Captain Little's honor. He appealed to the nine captains sitting in judgment not to sacrifice George Little "to the rancour of men who with the same pleasure would see your epaulets torn from your shoulders and this ship brought a wreck. . . ."[86]

After the judge advocate summed up the evidence, the court retired. On the morning of 7 September 1801, the court reconvened. Finding the charges "malicious & ill-founded," the court unanimously "fully and honorably acquitted" George Little. President Jefferson's secretary of the navy, Robert Smith, a Baltimore lawyer, approved the sentence because Captain Little's orders were "perfectly correct" and because there was no evidence that he had profited personally. But Secretary Smith railed at "this mean and disgraceful pillage" of prisoners.[87] One month later, Smith discharged Captain Little from the navy, not even using the polite language and respectful tone employed with the other captains he released that day.[88]

With the reduction in the navy after the Quasi-War, Smith released Lieutenants Clough and Burr, Marine Lieutenant Church, and George Little, Jr. Of all the *Boston*'s officers, only Midshipman Haswell was retained in the peacetime navy. While he had served capably in the *Boston* and been wounded in battle, it seems that, given his court martial testimony, his selection represented Secretary Smith's message to the navy.[89] Captain Little had sought an appointment for George Little, Jr., as a purser in the shrunken peacetime navy, but in July 1801, Henry Dearborn nixed that idea because the Naval Peace Establishment Act forced him to dismiss many long-serving, deserving officers. What was doubly mortifying was that the same letter termed the double payments to George Little, Jr., as schoolmaster and captain's clerk in the *Boston,* "inadmissible" and required the captain to repay the smaller salary, despite Secretary Stoddert's earlier apparent acquiescence.[90]

Robert Haswell, the first lieutenant of the *Boston,* did not testify at the court martial. In command of the prize, Haswell may not have seen anything aboard the *Boston*. But there is almost certainly more to the story. In all their public statements, declarations, and testimony, the *Berceau*'s officers singled out Robert Haswell for his humanitarian conduct and exonerated him from their charges, which undoubtedly irked his accused captain. Moreover, a fragment of correspondence exists in George Little's papers, dated aboard the *Boston* on 18 July 1801—unidentified but certainly from an officer—in which the writer informed Little that he "can think as I please concerning" the accusations against Little.[91] No one besides Haswell would have had the maturity and confidence to take on his captain in that way. In addition, John M. Haswell, a mere midshipman, hardly would have testified as he did without the full support and knowledge of his older brother, the first lieutenant. Robert Haswell hoped for promotion, but with peace returning and a reduced navy in the offing, he saw his options limited. In February 1801, prior to Little's trials, Haswell requested promotion to captain or a furlough to take a merchant vessel to the East Indies, noting that "tho' Captain Little and myself have been on good terms with each other, yet many [things] have occurred to render it unpleasant for us to sail again." The navy allowed Haswell a furlough, and in August 1801 he sailed in command of the ship *Louisa* bound to Canton.[92] Robert Haswell was lost at sea in the *Louisa* and never knew that, had he returned, a court martial awaited him, apparently on charges brought by Captain Little. Among Little's surviving papers is an affidavit signed by James Howe, the *Boston*'s carpenter, dated 11 September 1801, just days after Little's own court martial. Howe swore that "during the heat of the action [with the *Berceau*] a Boy came from the Cock pit" where the ship's surgeon tended the wounded with a request from the dying purser, Samuel Young, to speak to Robert Haswell. According to Howe, Lieutenant Haswell went below decks to visit Young during the battle, absenting himself from his post for a half-hour, only reappearing on deck as the *Boston* fired her last broadside.[93] Haswell's disappearance saved the Navy another divisive trial.

Captain Little retired to his farm in Marshfield. He litigated his prize cases and died in 1809.[94] Louis-Marie Clement returned to France. He fought in various actions against the British navy, received the Legion of Honor, a title, and promotion to post-captain from Napoleon, and died in 1809 in an English prison of wounds that he had received in action while commanding the corvette *Silphe*. From a far-off battlefield, the Emperor remembered Clement's twenty-four-year-old widow with a small pension.[95]

Implementing the peace treaty with France, the United States agreed to return the *Berceau* to the French navy. During the spring and summer of 1801, while the navy tried George Little aboard the *Constitution*, the navy also purchased, repaired, remasted, and (with Paul Revere's manufacturing) recoppered the *Berceau* in Edmund Hartt's shipyard. The American taxpayers picked up the $32,839.54 tab.[96] Ironically, Clement and the other repatriated prisoners sailed their own corvette, now good as new, back to France in September 1801. Sent to Vice Admiral Linois's squadron in the Indian Ocean, the *Berceau* ravaged English trade; lying off Polo Bay in Sumatra, the *Berceau* sent in her boats to burn the English vessels at anchor and the English naval arsenal. Linois sent the *Berceau* back to Europe with dispatches, but after arriving in Spain, the *Berceau* was found to be in too poor shape to repair. In October 1805, the *Berceau* was sold out of the French navy for 21,000 piastres.[97]

The *Boston*, under Captain McNeill, carried Robert Livingston to France in the autumn of 1801, and then sailed into the Mediterranean to protect American trade against Tripoli. Although the *Boston* sank a Tripolitan gunboat in May 1802 and drove off two others, her Mediterranean deployment is remembered chiefly for McNeill's erratic behavior. At Malaga, Spain, McNeill sailed out of port, deliberately stranding three of his officers and their servants; at Toulon, McNeill ordered the *Boston* to stand to sea while entertaining three French visitors; at Messina, McNeill enticed an Italian military band to desert and join his ship; and McNeill simply ignored local quarantine requirements at every port the *Boston* entered. When word filtered back to Washington, Secretary Smith ordered the *Boston* to return home. After her arrival in the fall of 1802, the *Boston* remained in ordinary at the Washington Navy Yard, unrepaired and rotting away, month after month. A survey in February 1806 found the "after part of the frame from the stern to the Mizen Mast down to the Kelson entirely rotten," as were the "Beams generally through the Ship." While the "main body from the Mizen mast to the Breasthooks [was] some what sound," the gun deck showed "very much decay," and surveyors, who included Josiah Fox, concluded that the expenses to fix the ship "would amt. to the cost of a new Ship." Nothing was done.[98]

The hulk of the *Boston* somehow lingered. On 24 August 1814, however, as British troops closed in on Washington, sailors in the Navy Yard put the torch to the old frigate.[99]

7 *Politics of Procurement, Politics of Preferment*

The *George Washington* and the *Richmond*

Even before President Adams signed the Act of 30 June 1798, putting into law the subscription-loan scheme envisioned by the Newburyport merchants earlier that month, savvy shipowners in various ports tried to loan their ships to the navy. Some saw the stock offering as security if their ships were lost in battle or at sea while in government hands, and entitling the stockholders to interest payments until such time as the government returned the loaned ships. Other merchants, in offering their ships for wartime service, had no desire to get a storm-battered, battle-scarred ship returned; what they wanted was cash; in doing good for their country, they thought they might do well for themselves. As good capitalists, the American merchants recognized that with so much of their wealth invested in shipping, subject to loss to privateers hanging off the United States coast, transferring a ship to the navy for its market value in stock meant an extraordinary benefit. If, after the war was concluded, the navy wanted to sell the "loaned" ship, or perhaps return it at a depreciated price to the merchants who had loaned it, that was acceptable, too.

John Brown, a canny and wealthy merchant-capitalist from Providence, Rhode Island,[1] was the first to seize on the potential private benefits in loaning a ship under the new law. Brown approached the transaction obliquely. On 14 June 1798, he wrote to the secretary of the treasury, Oliver Wolcott (a letter not passed along to Secretary Stoddert until August); and sometime later, other "gentlemen" from Providence wrote to a leading Philadelphia merchant, Joseph Anthony, who they knew would lobby Stoddert. Anthony put the matter before Stoddert: the Providence merchants thought that the government had overlooked them, and they (Brown) had a fine ship, readily available, that the navy could convert into a warship. The navy secretary tried to rebuff the overture, informing Anthony that the "opinion prevailing" when Stoddert assumed office was that "New Ships had better be built;—and that the public had made bad bargains in their purchases [of merchantmen at the start of the crisis with France]. Hence my attention has been directed entirely to New Ships," and the congressional appropriations to buy ships outright already had been depleted. But Stoddert noted that under the Act of 30 June, three ships "still remain to be procured" and that the government looked to "the Merchants, in different places" to furnish them by "contributions," i.e., by buying stock. Graciously, Stoddert suggested that if Providence would build one of the ships remaining under the statute, he would lubricate the process with $10,000, the money remaining from the congressional appropriations, "towards assisting with the Business." A few weeks later, Wolcott sent Stoddert Brown's letter. The navy secretary responded directly to Brown, noting that had the law allowed, he would buy Brown's proffered ship with the "utmost pleasure," given Brown's assurances that she was an excellent vessel and ready immediately. But the public monies were gone, according to Stoddert, and he asked John Brown to use his influence to persuade Providence's merchants to purchase stock for a vessel. "Most of the Towns distinguished for Federalism, and public Spirit," Stoddert observed to Brown, had bought stock to fund a local vessel and Providence had not. Stoddert reminded Brown that 6 percent stock would issue for cash, and asked Providence for a copper-bolted, copper-sheathed vessel.[2]

But Brown, a savvy, dogged entrepreneur, was not to be dissuaded. Brown had in mind contributing a vessel, the *George Washington,* that was five years old, measured 624 tons, was built of cedar and live oak, coppered, rigged, "one of the best Sailers in America," and ready for service immediately. Brown pressed the navy secretary again. If the *George Washington* proved as sound, stout, and fast as advertised, Stoddert conceded that he might buy her as the final merchant vessel to be converted into a warship.

Stoddert ordered one of his senior captains, Silas Talbot, to Providence to "examine strictly, and critically this ship belonging to Mr. Brown," and report back. To Stoddert, Talbot must have seemed an inspired choice; as one of the most senior captains, as a Rhode Islander by birth, and as a former Federalist Congressman himself, Talbot knew John Brown yet had enough standing not to come under Brown's influence. Yet the reality was that Stoddert had selected a man that even President Adams knew "was not bred a seaman," and although the president admired Talbot, he recognized that Talbot was not "an officer of complete nautical skill." Thomas Truxtun, a rival, could not "bring myself to believe" that the inexperienced Talbot was a "proper Person" for a "Sea Officer, particularly in an infant Navy, where every Officer looks up for Instructions, and Information." If Talbot were "considered an Acquisition to the Service," Truxtun exclaimed, "there can be no Want of Captains for our Navy[;] the Army, and every City or Town in the U.S. will furnish a Plenty." In any case, Talbot was Stoddert's choice. Talbot rode up to Providence, puttered around the *George Washington,* and reported on her favorably although he never seems to have seen, or been aboard, the ship under sail. Stoddert's condition was met and he felt committed to the deal.[3]

Brown reeled in Stoddert. Once the navy indicated that it wanted his ship, Brown proposed that the Hope Furnace, one of his enterprises, supply the 24 nine-pounder cannon and 8 six-pounder cannon, a supply of cannonballs, and ballast at what Stoddert considered was an exorbitant price. To top everything, Brown insisted that the navy pay an extra $400 to him for its delay in deciding to buy the *George Washington.* Stoddert thought it "not worth disputing about Trifles, and if you insist on it, I must add the 400 Dollars," although why the secretary of the navy tamely submitted to such chiseling is puzzling. Stoddert, recognizing that John Brown was "a complete Master of the Art of bargain making," asked Talbot to "do the best you can with him, and let the public be Screwed as little as possible." Ultimately, the navy bought the *George Washington* for $10,400 in cash and $30,000 in 6 percent navy stock. While the navy regarded the *George Washington* as the last purchased vessel from the 1798 congressional authorization, obviously the deal closed primarily with stock. The best that can be said is that Stoddert used the subscription-loan scheme creatively to get another ship into the navy despite his reservation about bad bargains buying ships.[4]

There was no question that the *George Washington* initially was built sturdily; for Brown's merchant house, she had sailed to Canton and back on her first voyage. Otherwise, however, it soon became clear that Stoddert had been taken. Under Capt. Patrick Fletcher, the navy sent the *George Washington* in December 1798 to Commo. John Barry's newly formed Windward Islands squadron where she proved so ponderous that she was relegated to convoy escort duties. Even before the *George Washington* returned from her first cruise, word reached Stoddert that he had bought a "dull Sailer." In June 1799, Stoddert asked Fletcher for his "candid opinion of the Ship—and whether any alterations" could improve the *George Washington*'s speed. Even before Fletcher responded, Stoddert confided to the Boston navy agent that the *George Washington* was "so indifferent"— slower than even the notoriously slow *Herald*—as to be "worse than useless," and that the Navy "must get clear of them." For his part, Fletcher reported his command was "unfit for a cruizing Ship" although she "would answer well for a store Ship." Fletcher's point was not too subtle to be misunderstood, and Stoddert ordered the *George Washington* sold privately or at auction for $40,000. In November 1799, the navy agents at Newport, Rhode Island, found her copper sheathing of poor quality and "the thinnest kind used for any Vessel," and "so bad, that it is not fit she should proceed to sea." When Joshua Humphreys looked at the *George Washington,* he discovered decay in the lower futtocks and external planking. Stoddert agreed on lowering the asking price to $30,000. But no willing buyers appeared, and Stoddert, stuck with his purchase, ordered basic repairs. Ultimately, Stoddert ordered the *George Washington* to carry tribute (bribe money) to the dey of Algiers, essentially using her as an armed storage ship. The cruise, degrading in itself, turned into a humiliating spectacle; the dey ordered Capt. William Bainbridge, who had improvidently anchored the *George Washington* under the cannon of Algiers's fortress, to take the Algerine ambassador, complete with retinue and slaves (200 in all), plus a menagerie of domestic and wild animals (150 sheep, 25 head of cattle, lions, tigers, antelopes, and parrots included), to Constantinople under the dey's flag as the dey's tribute to the Sultan. A bad ship and a disgraced ship, the navy finally sold the *George Washington* out of service upon her return to America.[5]

Stoddert's purchase with stock of the *George Washington* was not only a bad bargain but it was also a suggestive precedent. The Crowninshield family of Salem, distinguished merchants and shipmasters, had the same idea as John Brown, although with a couple of twists. On 16 August 1798, the Crowninshields wrote to Secretary Stoddert announcing their patriotic "attachment to our Govt & Country at this serious crisis in our public affairs" and offered the navy not just one, but two, of the family's ships, the *America* and *Belisarius,* as a loan at depreciated cost. As historian Philip Chadwick Foster Smith points out, the Crowninshields in May 1798 already had offered to sell the *America* to the navy. The *America,* ironically, had once been a 28-gun French navy corvette called the *Blonde* and, while unquestionably suited for naval service, was a white elephant for George Crowninshield & Sons for she was too big to dock at any Salem wharf. In making the offer of the *America,* the Crowninshields wanted to do good for their country but were keenly interested in unloading a bad investment at cost. Which is not to say that the *America* would not have made an excellent warship; built in 1791, she was 750 tons, copper-sheathed, and wickedly fast—in 1801, she reached Mauritius from Salem in seventy-seven days. As the months passed, the Crowninshields watched, mortified, as other merchant houses sold their ships to the navy while they could not "move" their own. The Act of 30 June 1798 seemed to accord the Crowninshields another chance. While newspaper accounts reflected that "loans" for stock meant cash laid out, perhaps a "loan" encompassed the lending of the ship itself. Benjamin Stoddert obviously thought the statute malleable enough for the navy to use stock to buy ships; he used stock to buy the *George Washington* and, two months earlier, in July 1798, he had offered stock in payment for a Charleston ship that Stoddert initially thought would be the contribution from the "public Spirit of Charleston." The Crowninshields's interpretation was not far-fetched. To sweeten their offer, the Crowninshields offered to loan the *Belisarius,* Salem-built and renowned for speed. Unlike John Brown, the Crowninshields wanted to loan their ships and even envisioned getting them back "at any future day when these vessels may not be wanted for the service of our Govt we may be favored with the preference in the purchase." In their view, then, the navy stock compensated them for the use of the ships or was security if the ships were lost.[6]

Nevertheless, Secretary Stoddert promptly rejected the Crownin-shields' August 1798 offer, ostensibly because the "President can only procure by purchase, or accept on the condition of paying in 6 per cent Stock Vessels *now building or to be built.*" Stoddert's statement, coming just four days before he informed Captain Talbot that he had decided to buy the *George Washington* from John Brown (primarily with stock) if Talbot recommended the ship, seemed pure dissembling. Stoddert more legit-imately claimed, as he told Brown later, that Brown's ship was the "last I had authority to buy," but Stoddert at least owed the Crowninshields an honest explanation. The *George Washington* in August 1798 was certainly not "now building or to be built," nor was the Charleston ship. The Crowninshields, angered at their treatment, appealed directly to President Adams. Ben Crowninshield, a shipmaster, delivered to Quincy a letter from the family patriarch, George Crowninshield. Assuming that Secretary Stoddert's rejection was premised on the misconception that the Crowninshields wanted to sell the navy their two ships (Stoddert had categorized the Crowninshields' offer as an attempt "to dispose" of their ships), the Crowninshields reiterated that they intended the ships as a loan for which they would receive stock. President Adams refused to intervene or reverse his navy secretary's decision. For their part, the Crowninshield family later stayed conspicuously aloof from contributing to the Salem subscription that led to building the frigate *Essex,* the only leading Salem merchant family that refused to subscribe.[7]

The politics of procuring ships for stock continued with a small ship proposed for a loan by a group of Virginia towns. On 22 June 1798, just days after word arrived in the South of the Newburyport effort and the subscription campaigns spontaneously going forward in Philadelphia, New York, and Baltimore, Virginia newspapers noted:

> To evince to the world their determination to support the Government of their own choice, against the daring attempt making to render it tributary, a meeting of the people of Petersburg, is requested at J. R. Brewer's Tavern this Afternoon at 5 o'Clock, to consider the expediency of raising a sum of money by Subscription, which in conjunction with Richmond and Norfolk, may be sufficient to procure a *Vessel of Force,* to be loaned to the government, for the Public defense.[8]

It could not have been coincidental that the same evening citizens of Richmond and Manchester (then separate towns) met in the Eagle Tavern in Richmond for the same purpose. Before the night was over, more than $14,000 was raised in Richmond and over $10,000 in Petersburg, and each city had set up a coordinating committee.[9] Norfolk answered with a mass meeting in the town hall on 28 June that collected $10,000 and established another committee.[10]

John Marshall, the hero of the XYZ affair, back in Richmond to resume his private law practice, was the first listed subscriber in Richmond, pledging $500. Five names further down was another Richmond lawyer, Bushrod Washington, a nephew of George Washington, appointed to the Supreme Court in October 1798.[11] Other leading Virginians, men like

Edward Carrington and John Harvie, also pledged their funds.[12] In Norfolk, as in the rest of the country, most of the subscribers were merchants. Unlike John Brown in Providence or the Crowninshields in Salem, the Virginians tendered cash as their "loan," not a ship. But like them, the Norfolk merchants had a ship in mind, or rather a number of ships building for one of their leaders, Moses Myers, ready to become the Old Dominion's contribution ship. Myers, born in New York in 1752, was a partner in a merchant-trading firm with Samuel Myers before and during the Revolution. The Myers house had offices in Amsterdam and on the Dutch Caribbean island of St. Eustatius, a transshipment port for arms and munitions for the American patriots. But the firm went bankrupt in the post-Revolutionary War depression, and while Samuel Myers returned to Amsterdam to repay their creditors, Moses Myers found a new venue for the partners to begin again—Norfolk. Two things attracted Moses Myers to Virginia: Norfolk's late 1780s revival from its burning by Lord Dunmore in 1776, with the economic opportunities for entrepreneurs; and Virginia's adoption of the Bill for Establishing Religious Freedom in 1786, which allowed Jews like Myers full legal and civil rights. Moses Myers's future rose with his adopted city, although his partner, Samuel Myers, moved on to Petersburg. From a simple shopkeeper, Moses Myers progressed to owning coastal trading schooners, serving as a local agent for Stephen Girard of Philadelphia, investing in syndicated ships trading with the West Indies, and serving as superintendent of the Norfolk branch of the Bank of Richmond. Though one of the only Jews in Norfolk, the city nevertheless embraced him, electing him repeatedly to the Common Council. As a "gentleman," it was natural that Myers would be made a captain in the militia during the war crisis with France and, as a leading merchant, that he would serve on the Norfolk subscription committee and pledge $500 for a ship. Myers, a generous man, and portrayed by Moreau de St. Méry as a devoted family man, became a friend to cranky Federalists like Commodore Truxtun as well as to émigré penniless French nobles.[13]

Building along the Norfolk waterfront for Moses Myers in June 1798 was a brig nearing completion that he intended to call the *Augusta* after his second daughter (born in 1797).[14] No dimensions or plans exist for this ship; the only data that is known is that she was small (197 and $^{94}/_{95}$ tons) and that the Navy valued her purchase price as $27,896.87. At first, Secretary Stoddert thought that the Virginians meant to provide a 24-gun ship, which he rather undiplomatically noted on 31 July 1798 "could readily have been furnished from the Northward, but I am rather inclined to the acceptance of the one in your Quarter." Agents for the Norfolk committee wrote to Stoddert that, believing the nation needed a smaller ship quickly rather than a larger ship at an indeterminate date, any one of four Norfolk vessels nearing completion could be their contribution. Stoddert replied on 7 August that "Your Idea that Celerity . . . is of primary Importance coincides exactly with the views of Government." Stoddert's letter-writing style was to repeat to his correspondents the phrases and cadences of their letters; he responded to the Norfolk committee that "it will be more agreeable, that a Force, comparatively small, should speedily be in readiness Than that one more considerable should be obtained, at the expense of delay." As to the four ships placed at the navy's option, Stoddert decided that "Either of the Brigs . . . will be acceptable," and suggested the ultimate choice be left to Samuel Barron, who would receive a captain's commission and command the Virginia subscription ship. Stoddert pledged supplies, including scarce copper, although the outbreak of yellow fever in Philadelphia rendered his promise "very precarious." Samuel Barron picked the *Augusta,* which the Navy promptly renamed the *Richmond,* as the Virginia contribution ship.[15]

Ironically, within a year, the navy bought another brig from Moses Myers, also called the *Augusta* after the same daughter. This time, the navy kept the name, perhaps the only time in the navy's history that a commissioned warship was named for a two-year-old girl. Practically nothing is recorded about the *Augusta*'s specifications. Since both the *Richmond* and the *Augusta* were built for Myers, both were brigs, and they were built within a year at the same place, it is likely that the *Richmond* and *Augusta* were built on similar plans, perhaps by the same builder. Joshua Humphreys, who examined the *Augusta* for Stoddert, reported "she is like the Virginia built Vessels, very slight . . . Her waist is lined inside with inch board, and . . . filled in with Cork." Both brigs achieved reputations as fast sailers and perhaps the comments of an officer about *Augusta* covers the *Richmond,* that she sails "remarkably stiff, and sails uncommonly fast—with a very stiff breeze, and with single-reef'd topsails and topgallant sails over them, going by the wind, her lee ports were two feet clear of the water."[16]

In selecting Samuel Barron to command the *Richmond,* Stoddert chose a popular and well-connected local sea officer. Born in 1765, and raised at "Little England" plantation at Hampton, Virginia, with his younger brother James, also destined for a fateful naval career, Samuel Barron received a grammar school education in Petersburg and Williamsburg.

At age fourteen, he entered the Virginia state navy where he served under his father, the state navy's commodore, during the Revolutionary War. Before he was seventeen, Samuel Barron saw combat on the Chesapeake Bay and in land skirmishes near Newport News, once having a horse killed from under him. In the summer of 1781, Barron helped gather supplies for Washington's army descending on Yorktown, and he was on the field to witness the surrender of Cornwallis's army. Promoted to lieutenant and acting commander of the pilot-boat sloop *Patriot III,* Barron remained in the state navy until Virginia sold off its last vessel in 1788. Switching to the mercantile line, Barron commanded vessels out of Norfolk to Europe and the West Indies, including six years of service for Moses Myers. As early as 1794, with the congressional authorization of money for the first frigates, Myers supported Samuel Barron's drive to receive a commission. Barron, for whom Myers expressed "a particular friendship," was a "worthy man who is & has been some time in my Imploy." Myers recommended Barron as "a perfect Seaman an Industrious Active Sober man & in all respects a Gentleman," and offered to post security with the secretary of war, Henry Knox, for Barron's good conduct. Myers drew on his connections, asking Thomas FitzSimons's merchant partner, George Meade, to use his influence for Barron, too. In July 1798, Barron journeyed to Philadelphia to lobby personally for a commission, armed with an official letter of recommendation from the mayor and alderman of Norfolk; a letter from the Norfolk congressman, Col. Josiah Parker, to Stoddert; and a letter to President Adams signed by Myers and eleven other leading citizens of Norfolk. Myers orchestrated another letter supporting Barron, this from Robert Gilmore of Baltimore. Gilmore, conceding that he did not know Barron, wrote Stoddert that "my friend in Norfolk" reported that Barron was "universally esteemed" and perfectly qualified for a command, having proved his mettle over six years as a captain for Myers. Stoddert gladly complied with the wishes of Norfolk and made him captain of the "local" subscription ship.[17]

Barron supervised the completion of the *Richmond.* Stoddert ordered Barron in conjunction with Col. Parker, the Federalist congressman, to "nominate suitable characters for your Officers" by which Stoddert meant "men of Experience Courage and Integrity." Stoddert then directed Barron to recruit the ninety sailors for the *Richmond,* all of whom were to be true volunteers, "sound and healthy persons." A native Virginian like Barron needed little prompting that "suspicious characters," as well as "Negroes, or Mulattoes" were not to be enlisted.[18]

On 31 December 1798, the frigate *Constellation* under Capt. Thomas Truxtun "made the Signal for the United States' Brig *Richmond* of 16 Guns, Captain Barron, and four Merchant Vessels under Convoy to get underway" with a fine westerly breeze blowing the ships to sea. The *Richmond* was destined for Truxtun's squadron; her readiness to sail coincided with a marked shift of emphasis in the naval war with France. Instead of guarding the American coast, United States warships were being sent to fight in the Caribbean to deal with the French privateers at their source. As late as mid-October 1798, every American warship had been ordered to cruise off U.S. territorial waters except for one ship carrying dispatches to Halifax and a three-ship squadron that had sortied into the Caribbean and met with disaster. Truxtun commanded one of two American naval squadrons "employed in the West Indies, this Winter [1798–99], in protecting our commerce and punishing the deprodations on it." Truxtun, with the Leeward or St. Kitts squadron, was to patrol from St. Kitts to Puerto Rico, "paying attention to St. Martins and that Group of Islands, called the Virgin Gorda," and was authorized to "capture French armed Vessels wherever found on the high Sea, and to recapture our own Vessels taken by them." Stoddert cautioned Truxtun that "being at peace with all the rest of the World, and wishing to remain so, the Vessels and people of all other Nations, must experience from us civility, and Friendship; Our Laws will not even permit the Recapture of our Vessels, taken by the Vessels, of any of the Nations at War, except the French."[19]

On 12 January 1799, Truxtun's little squadron arrived off Antigua. Setting the pattern for the next four months, Truxtun immediately sent the *Richmond* to St. Thomas, convoying two merchant schooners, with orders to rejoin the *Constellation* at St. Kitts thereafter. Then it was back to Antigua, then off to Montserrat for the *Richmond,* to bring down to St. Kitts any American vessels so that the *Constellation* could convoy them safely out of the Caribbean. As Truxtun wrote to Capt. John Barry, the commodore of the so-called Windward Squadron, Secretary Stoddert had allowed Truxtun six warships and with them he would furnish regular convoys for vessels from Antigua, Montserrat, Nevis, St. Kitts and the islands as far as St. Thomas, just as Truxtun assumed Barry would do for shipping in his region.[20]

By the first week of February, Truxtun's ships had escorted three convoys north from St. Kitts with fifty vessels collected from the Leeward Islands. The scrambling back and forth "has been severe Service for our little Squadron," and Truxtun appealed to Stoddert for the six promised ships as he had only three. Two of the three, the *Richmond* and *Norfolk*, he ordered to collect ships from St. Barts and St. Martins, rendezvous at St. Kitts, and then escort a convoy northwards to latitude 20 ½° and presumed safety. No master or merchant was to be told, however, "how far you intend to convoy the Fleet, on any Account whatever." Truxtun relished the thought of battle and enjoined his commanders to use every means to capture French privateers, which he considered "armed" and thus good prize under his instructions "if they have even a Pair of Case Knives on Board." Unfortunately, the *Richmond* never had a tête-à-tête with a French cruiser despite her constant convoying.[21]

Still, Truxtun recognized Samuel Barron's seamanship in handling the little *Richmond* and his competency in running convoys. As a captain, Barron was quite senior for what was one of the smallest ships on the navy list, and Truxtun thought no officer that he had seen was more deserving of a bigger ship. Truxtun thought to transfer Samuel Barron to the 20-gun ship *Baltimore* about to join his squadron and to install James Barron, who already displayed outstanding seamanship as a lieutenant on Captain Barry's frigate, the *United States,* as captain of the *Richmond.* The "two Brothers," Truxtun thought, "will do well together." As it turned out, Samuel Barron received the *Baltimore* when she arrived in the Leeward Islands in March 1799, but command of the *Richmond* devolved to Lieutenant Josias Speake, the man who brought the *Baltimore* down from Norfolk.[22]

Speake probably was meant to be an interim commander. Before the war, he had been a master of Baltimore-based merchant ships. The well-connected merchants of that port persuaded Stoddert to name Speake a lieutenant in the navy at the time the *Adriana* of Baltimore was bought for the navy, armed with twenty cannon, and renamed the *Baltimore.* On her first cruise, the *Baltimore,* captained by Isaac Phillips, had been stopped by a British squadron outside of Havana and her navy crew searched for British subjects. Fifty-five of the *Baltimore*'s crew were shanghaied, although the British commander returned all but five. Phillips did not resist the humiliation, and resistance might well have provoked bloodshed, but what Secretary Stoddert later found unforgivable was Phillips's craven-ness in issuing orders cooperating with the British. Stoddert dismissed Phillips outright, although Phillips insisted he had left Speake in command on the *Baltimore* when he went to the British flagship to argue for his men, and that it was Speake who actively cooperated with the British. Nevertheless, Stoddert gave Speake the task of rebuilding the ship's morale and taking her to Truxtun's squadron.[23]

Truxtun assigned Speake, as the new commander of the *Richmond,* the duty of hunting French privateers. After Speake had the *Richmond*'s water casks filled at the Old Road, Basseterre, St. Kitts, and then convoyed a single schooner safe to latitude 20° north, Truxtun ordered the *Richmond,* together with another small ship, the revenue cutter *Virginia,* to cruise to the windward of St. Barts and St. Martins "in every direction about these Islands." Although the two-ship team was to call at Basseterre at least every other week, Truxtun enjoined Speake to "Be enterprizing, and send me in some French Cruisers, and Letters of Mark."[24]

Round about the islands the *Richmond* wheeled, joined by the cutters *Virginia* and *Eagle,* on three two-week cruises. Speake's enterprising nature got him into trouble as he stopped a Swedish (neutral) vessel, as well as a French ship flying a flag of truce, and sent them into St. Kitts. Truxtun, all aflame with indignation, reminded Speake in the "most preemptory, and positive Manner that you pay Respect to all Flags of Truce and neutral Vessels," and threatened Speake with "Measures by No Means . . . honorable to you" if he violated the law of nations again. But the choleric commodore was mollified a few days later when the *Richmond* brought in what Truxtun called "the little French armed schooner *Louis.*" Little she was, armed with a few light swivel guns and cutlasses, and she carried no letter of marque, but for all that *Louis* was judged a good prize.[25] On 17 May, the *Richmond* and *Eagle* came into St. Kitts with two American merchant vessels, the brig *Mahitable* and the ship *Nancy,* that they had recaptured from the French two days before. The *Richmond*'s successes received Stoddert's attention, who passed the information along to President Adams with the line that the *Richmond* was a "very fine sailor." Although some self-appointed experts apparently criticized the *Richmond* as not being designed big enough or fast enough, Stoddert called her one of "the most useful Vessels in our Service," small, nimble, and "strong enough for the French Cruzers."[26]

To intercept French privateers, the U.S. Navy turned from the reactive (escorting convoys) to the offensive, sending roving little flotillas wheeling around the islands or lying in wait outside the likely privateer bases. In mid-June, the *Richmond* sailed with the ship *Ganges* under Capt. Thomas Tingey from St. Barts towards Barbuda and "under the Lee of Antigua" in the wake of French privateers, but without success. The American ships then sailed directly for Guadeloupe, circumnavigating the island, hovering offshore. At night, they crept close in, about a mile offshore, so that at dawn they might surprise a privateer or its American prize and come between the French vessel and its haven. But on that mission, they were not able to cut off a privateer and, after a long, anxious chase, caught a vessel that proved to be English.[27]

At the end of June 1799, Speake brought the *Richmond* back to America. After taking on supplies at New York, Stoddert ordered Speake for coast guard duty, to sail the *Richmond* to St. Mary's River, Georgia, "being our Southern Extremity, cruising off and on the Coast" until Commodore Truxtun arrived. The *Richmond* put into Charleston, Savannah, and St. Mary's just enough for word to spread to any French intelligence agents that the *Richmond* was on guard. Summer cruising along the Southern coast was good duty and exhilarating sailing; the *Richmond*'s lieutenant of marines, Henry Williams, reported off Cape Henry that "we have seen & Spoke a Number of Vessels & are now in Chase of one, [with the ship heeling so much that] our Lee Guns under Water. But have taken no prize as yett." Lieutenant Williams thought the *Richmond* sailed well and found his fellow officers "agreeable," but the little *Richmond* was so cramped for space with her big navy crew that the marines drilled, kept watch, and slept on deck "in all weathers as no Room can be found below for them."[28]

In September 1799, Stoddert sent Speake to Norfolk to assist Josiah Fox in building the frigate later named the *Chesapeake*. In his stead, Stoddert ordered Lt. Commandant Cyrus Talbot to assume command of the *Richmond*. Cyrus Talbot was the oldest son of Capt. Silas Talbot. Through his father's connections to John Jay, secretary of foreign affairs of the post-Revolutionary War American government, who intervened with the French chargé d'affaires, Cyrus Talbot had spent one year as a midshipman aboard a French frigate in the last days of King Louis XVI's navy. In the 1790s, he served before the mast as an ordinary seaman on a merchant voyage from New York to St. Petersburg and, later, with a loan from his father, invested in a syndicate to own a vessel trading first with France, and then with Curaçao, on which he sailed as master. Cyrus Talbot, a hard-luck seaman, had delicate nerves; he sailed on a string of ill-starred voyages, wrecking one ship and twice being haled before foreign courts, and apparently had a nervous breakdown when a promised place as master was denied him. As Cyrus Talbot wrote to his father, "my late Voyages have been so unsuccessfull that I have almost made my mind up never again to Enter upon a Merchants Voyage as Long as the War Lasts in Europe." In addition to his father, his father's friends helped him gain a commission. John Hobart, the United States district judge for New York, wrote the president in support of the younger Talbot. Senator Foster of

Rhode Island actually took Cyrus Talbot around to meet the president and Secretary Stoddert, and when no appointment appeared in the offing, Hobart and Capt. Richard V. Morris volunteered to press Talbot's cause. In May 1799, Cyrus Talbot was twenty-six and had sufficient experience as well as the familial and political connections to support Stoddert's writing the president that "Captain Cyrus Talbott-son of Capt. Talbott, has had experience in the French service, and seems well qualified for Master and Commandant of a small Vessel building in Chesapeak Bay." As it turned out Stoddert appointed him a lieutenant commandant in June and offered him the *Richmond* the next month.[29]

Lieutenant Commandant Talbot picked up his command in Norfolk in early October 1799. His orders were the same as Speake's, to cruise up and down the coast until 15 November, when the *Richmond* was to be in Philadelphia. In truth, there was little to cruise for, the French privateers having long before retreated into the Caribbean. Lieutenant Williams of the marines wrote from the Chesapeake Bay after seventy-two days of patrolling the coast that "we were Unsuccessful not having mett one Frenchman." Williams had no complaint about the treatment meted out to the marines and, as far as it went, he liked the ship, which caught every one of the almost one hundred ships they had chased. But Williams wanted something bigger, a ship where the officers would not have to eat in shifts in the wardroom. Despite Williams's observations, in the two months Cyrus Talbot had the command, three of the seventeen marine privates aboard the *Richmond* deserted, as well as five sailors.[30]

The most notable event of Cyrus Talbot's two-month tenure was the loss of the *Richmond*'s rudder "by the stroke of a Sea in Wareing Ship, Shortly after a gale of wind." The *Richmond* lay in the Gulf Stream with the seas so rough that for four days the brig wallowed out of control. Talbot consulted his copy of David Steel's treatise and, through "Captain Packenham's method," was able to steer the brig into Charleston. While the *Richmond* underwent repairs at New York in mid-December 1799, Talbot relinquished command and returned home to Dighton, Massachusetts. He explained to his father that the departure was his own doing, that while the "Idea of a Separate Command" was "Extremely Flattering," he was convinced that he could gain the experience he needed only by serving as a lieutenant on one of the frigates. On a small ship like the *Richmond*, "one false and unintentional Slip" might ruin his reputation. Cyrus Talbot was perhaps the only serving U.S. navy officer to turn away a wartime command. Nevertheless, Secretary Stoddert treated him kindly, telling him that he would outrank every lieutenant, suggesting that he could pick the frigate in which he wanted to serve, and offering to introduce him to President Adams. When Stoddert "mentioned his extreme modesty to the President," Adams "justly considered it a proof of extraordinary merit," and rather than reduce Cyrus Talbot to lieutenant, on 1 February 1800 Secretary Stoddert promoted him to master commandant, backdated to 21 May 1799.[31]

With Cyrus Talbot's departure, Stoddert sent a master commandant's commission to Richard Law, Jr., a merchant ship captain from New London, Connecticut, who had long sought a command in the navy. Law had the appropriate pedigree, his father serving as the United States district judge from Connecticut; and an appropriate sponsor, in that his candidacy for a commission was supported by Capt. Elisha Hinman, the Continental navy commander of the frigate *Trumbull,* and by the chief justice of the Supreme Court, Oliver Ellsworth, who lobbied the president directly. Judge Law reminded the president that his son had served as a midshipman aboard the *Trumbull* for much of the war and "was on board at the time she had the Severe Action with the *Watt* [1 June 1780] and continued on board until she was afterwards taken, when he was made a Prisoner." Though young Law was then just a teenager, Judge Law reminded the president that his superior officers had recognized his merit.[32] Stoddert ordered Law to take command of the *Richmond* at New York in December, immediately after the one-year enlistments of the *Richmond*'s crew expired. When the newly minted master commandant was piped aboard his brig in the East River, he found a ship needing almost an entirely new crew. Stoddert expected the *Richmond* to be able to sail in early January 1800, to convoy a storeship to Commodore Talbot's squadron off Cape Francais. When the *Richmond* still lay dockside in early January, Stoddert admonished Law that the navy department expected to have learned the *Richmond* was ready for sea; he peremptorily demanded a crew enlisted, and the brig watered and provisioned, because Law's orders were on the way.[33]

Stoddert dispatched the *Richmond* with the storeship to Saint-Domingue with spare rigging and provisions for Talbot's ships, and the *Richmond* was then to join Talbot's command. The *Richmond* arrived on station on 17 February 1800 and after exchanging signals with Talbot in his flagship, the *Constitution,* Law came aboard to report to Talbot personally. The storeship brought down by the *Richmond* was the second sent to replenish the ships of that squadron, allowing the navy's ships to remain at sea as an effective force, and not subject the crews to exorbitant prices and diseases in tropical ports. In rolling seas, the underway replenishment took three days but was part of a process that kept the *Constitution* at sea for 347 of the 366 days Talbot flew his flag as commodore.[34] On 19 February 1800, Talbot ordered Law to sail the *Richmond* north through the Turks Island or Caicos Passage, then eastwards to the area between Puerto Rico and St. John's to intercept privateers that Talbot believed were tracking homeward-bound American convoys and falling upon stragglers. The *Richmond* sliced through the Caicos Passage and beat to windward. She found empty seas until daylight on 9 March, when her lookout spotted an armed schooner lying to off the *Richmond*'s weather beam. Having the wind, the suspect vessel bore away. To Law, the stranger had "the looks of a Cruiser." Like countless American captains in that war, Law ordered the *Richmond*'s cannon to be housed and his crew to lie down on deck, and he tried to handle the brig in a slovenly way to pass the *Richmond* off as a lubberly merchant vessel. In Law's words, the copper-bottomed schooner came

> Down to long gun shot [range], took in her Topsails, hauled by the Wind, fired a gun to Leeward and hoisted French Coulers . . . [The privateer] run down in our Wake so near that the man from his Mast head discovered our Men lying on Deck, on which he hauled his Wind and gave us a Broad Side and his musquitry. I immediately opened upon him with round & Double head [shot] in hopes to have Cut away some of his spars, but the sea being very rough could not effect it, and he held so much better Wind, and sailed so much faster than *Richmond* that by the time I fired 30 rounds he was out of gun shot . . .

The thirty musket balls that peppered the *Richmond*'s spars, sails, rigging, and boats caused no material damage. Law hoped that his own marines' "well directed fire" did something to the French crew, but the 14-gun schooner escaped. Shortly after the scrape with the privateer, Law told a marine officer that the marines "were the best men he had."[35]

Over the next few weeks, the *Richmond,* together with the frigate *Boston,* lay in the "Bite," the waters between the western forks of Saint-Domingue, an area infested with insurrectionaries against Toussaint L'Overture who sailed in small, murderous pirate barges. There is no record of *Richmond* firing on any enemy in the Bite. Law interpreted his orders widely enough to escort eight American merchant ships, including the brig *Pearl,* Captain Evelith, from St. Thomas into the Atlantic, the *Pearl* arriving safely in Norfolk in twelve days. Upon her return to Saint-Domingue, the *Richmond* recaptured the American schooner *Chance* and, a week later, with the *Connecticut* off Puerto Rico, recaptured the ship *Thomas Chalkey* of Philadelphia.[36]

As almost the smallest warship in the Navy, the *Richmond* was used as a jack-of-all-trades, sent to find privateers, convoy merchant ships, or deliver messages. Commodore Talbot, incensed that British ships opened his official mail, sent a strongly worded protest to the British fleet commander, Admiral Sir Hyde Parker, based at Jamaica, via the *Richmond*. In June 1800, Talbot sent the *Richmond* back into the Bite to destroy the pirate barges and to convoy merchant sails in alternate weeks from Cape St. Nicholas Môle and Port Republicain out of the Bite. Commodore Talbot struck his flag and sailed for America in the *Constitution* on 25 July 1800, having failed to recall the *Richmond*. Talbot's successor, Capt. Alexander Murray, normally a careful, methodical officer, sent for the *Richmond* a week later since "it appears there are no more pirates in the Bite to molest our Trade." Unbelievably, Murray's orders went undelivered, and it was only on 26 August that Murray sent another letter recalling the *Richmond*.[37]

The *Richmond* reached Cape Francais on 3 September. Murray promptly ordered the brig to the eastern end of Cuba "where it is supposed there are several Piratical Vessels that resort in that direction," but it was another fool's errand. After a month of cruising off Santiago and Baracoa and chasing only American merchant ships and British cruisers, Law had enough. An American merchant brig, the *Fox* of New York, sailing from Santiago, reported no privateers hailing from that port or hovering off it, and the "North side [of Cuba] seems equally useless for a Cruizer." Law suggested that as it was "entirely unnecessary for one of our Cruizers to be employed in this Quarter," he would take the *Richmond* to Cape St. Nicholas Môle to await further orders. There is no record of the *Richmond*'s activities thereafter until she arrived at New York at the end of February 1801.[38]

As the outgoing secretary of the navy, Stoddert ordered the *Richmond*'s crew to be discharged and paid off immediately and the brig to be moored safely with only enough men left to take care of the ship. Despite Alexander Murray's opinion that Law was a "clever active man," the last captain of the *Richmond* was dismissed with the standard four-months severance pay and the reported thanks of the new president, Thomas Jefferson. The other captains of the *Richmond* were offered places in the service: Samuel Barron finished the war as a frigate captain and was the seventh most senior captain retained under the Naval Peace Establishment Act of 1801, although his subsequent career fizzled; Josias Speake, dismissed as a lieutenant, accepted a position as a sailing master; and Cyrus Talbot was again offered independent command, this time of the schooner *Enterprize,* but as touchy as his father about rank, he would not accept a lieutenant's commission, and followed his father in resigning.[39] The little *Richmond* faded out of notice. Even before she arrived at New York, Stoddert had planned to sell the brig, along with almost every other small ship on the navy list, sixteen in all. The Jefferson administration made good on those plans, selling the *Richmond* for $6,250 at public auction. As a merchant brig, the *Richmond* apparently made one voyage to the West Indies and back, and there is some evidence that the *Richmond* was sold to foreign owners in Havana in February 1802.[40]

8 *Squandered Ship*

The Frigate *New York*

In the spring of 1798, after the publication of the XYZ documents created a national convulsion, embarrassment followed anger as armed French ships seized American merchant vessels in the very mouths of the port cities. New York harbor provided an easy target. In mid-May, a particularly brazen French privateer called the *Jean Bart,* of 14 guns, took a merchant ship, the *Rosseter,* from New York bound to Bristol and, the same day, seized the *Thomas,* inbound to Philadelphia from Liverpool, off the Narrows. Alexander Hamilton, in private law practice in New York with some of the wealthy merchants as his clients, is a fair gauge of the reaction. Hamilton wrote to the secretary of war, James McHenry, that "you will have heard . . . that a French Privateer has made captures at the mouth of our harbour. This is too much humiliation after all that has passed. Our merchants are very indignant. Our Government [is] very prostrate in the view of every man of energy."[1] Thus, once the idea of subscription ships percolated down from Newburyport—Noah Webster's newspaper reported the item on 2 June 1798 with the admonition "An example this, worthy [of] prompt imitation"—the New York merchants had an outlet for their "energy."[2]

By 13 June 1798, even before Congress passed the subscription ships bill, the merchants were circulating a subscription paper to buy for the navy "some stout ships who may guard our port from insult or danger, and occasionally brush away from our coasts those numerous pirates that every where infest them."[3] Great things were expected. Webster "rejoice[d] to see this display of liberality and firmness," and reckoned that "when citizens of such substantial wealth manifest such zeal and energy for the general good, . . . their efforts will be seconded by every man . . ."[4] Nevertheless, the New York subscription effort went quite slowly compared to the *rage navale* in Philadelphia, Baltimore, and elsewhere. On 19 June "numerous and respectable" merchants and underwriters met at the Tontine Coffee-House to organize the subscription effort. As in the other cities, a committee was organized to procure the loans and then to direct construction. John Murray[5] became chairman of the committee, on which George Barnewall,[6] William Bayard,[7] Isaac Clason, and John P. Mumford also served. Even so, only $29,000 was subscribed that day.[8] Four days later, $40,000 had been raised, $66,000 by noon on the 27th, and $70,000 by 4 July, but Noah Webster searched to explain the slow accretion of pledges. The *Spectator* praised the city "at length rousing into action. . . . Altho we are as yet considerably behind Philadelphia, and the spirited town of Baltimore; yet we advance Dutchmen like with a slow but sure pace." Given the greater population and "high spirits" of New Yorkers, Webster implored his readers "never suffer it to be told . . . that they were out done by Baltimore."[9]

If New Yorkers did not wait for the federal government to pass a law enabling the stock-loan, the new secretary of the navy, Benjamin Stoddert, did not wait for the "Dutchmen like" New Yorkers before bombarding them with plans, figures, and ideas of the ship they should build. On 27 June 1798, in a letter to the New York committee, Stoddert asked them to build a 44-gun frigate, or at least a 36-gun frigate, rather than the two 20-gun ships they had supposed the navy needed. Presuming that the New Yorkers would respect the "Views of Government" in building a frigate, he promised to forward on to them the dimensions, and then a model. Stoddert asked that "[i]n the mean Time, . . . Preparations for Beginning can be making" since "[t]he Vessel may be wanted before She can be finished."[10] On 30 June, Stoddert sent the New York committee Joshua Humphreys's principal dimensions for various sizes of frigates, with the promise that a draft would be prepared as soon as the New York committee informed him "of the Force & dimensions of the Ship" they decided to build.[11] Sometime in July 1798, the New York merchants decided on a 36-gun frigate, as the navy secretary reported to President Adams in summarizing the crash shipbuilding program in American ports.[12]

In mid-August 1798, the keel of the 36-gun frigate that the merchants decided to call the *New York* was laid in the yard of Peck and Carpenter on the East River.[13] Samuel Humphreys, the twenty-three-year-old son of Joshua Humphreys, designed the *New York* in July 1798. The original plans cannot be found. According to her design, the *New York* had a 120-foot keel "straight rabbitt," and her gun deck measured 144 feet, 2 inches between perpendiculars. On her gun deck, the *New York* was to carry 26 eighteen-pounders. The *New York* had a 37-foot molded breadth, and its carpenter tonnage "by the Old Mode" was 864 and $^{60}/_{95}$. Her depth of hold was 11 feet, 9 inches.[14]

As was the understanding with the other merchants building warships for the government, the New York committee was allowed to choose a captain for the *New York*, a choice President Adams was expected to rubber-stamp. The clear preference of the New Yorkers was Thomas Robinson, Sr., described in a letter to the president as "a Seaman, & master of his profession" who had commanded merchant vessels out of New York for more than fifteen years. Robinson had been impressed into the British navy toward the end of the Revolutionary War where he was "obliged to remain on board a British Ship of force;" the fact that his character and "propriety of his behavior" led to Robinson's appointment as a Royal Navy officer did not strike his supporters as either ironic or crippling to his candidacy. In fact, the president was assured of Robinson's "courage & ability" and of the "propriety of his political opinions." In September 1799, the New York committee instructed Robinson to superintend the frigate's construction.[15]

The *New York* was launched only on 24 April 1800, a full twenty months after her keel was laid, and despite Secretary Stoddert's efforts to have the subscription frigates afloat the previous summer. Little survives about the course of her construction. But the New York shipyards could not keep pace with the demands of the crash warship program. Within three weeks of one another in the summer of 1798, New York shipwrights had laid the keels of three frigates: the *Adams,* a 28-gun light frigate building in Jackson's yard; the *President,* the 44-gun sistership of the *Constitution,* building in Cheeseman's yard; and the *New York* herself.[16] Apparently, the New York shipyards did not have enough skilled ship carpenters to go around.[17] The *President* and *New York* were launched within days of each other, too, in almost identical ceremonies: uniformed militia companies paraded with drums and fifes and shot off musket volleys; the *Aspacia,* an Indiaman (as the ships that carried trade with India were known), and the *Governor Jay,* a revenue cutter, "brilliantly decorated with the colors of different nations" offshore, fired salutes; and thousands of citizens turned out to cheer.[18]

The launching of the *New York,* the last of the three frigates, was cause for celebration. The *President* was anchored just offshore, and awnings were rigged from her masts to cover the green in front of Belvidere House. At three o'clock, the master builders of the three frigates, their "various artificers employed in construction and equipping" the ships, and the naval officers posted to New York sat down to enjoy a celebratory dinner. The company basked, a newspaper reported, in the thought of "[t]hree ships of war, equal in strength and materials and perfection of workmanship to any," and then the company basked in the glow of sixteen toasts. The toasts at political dinners in the Federal period were always partisan, sometimes witty, sometimes mawkishly sentimental, and played a "vital part of eighteenth century political discourse."[19] Under the awnings of the *President,* the officers, builders, and workmen paid homage to President Adams, their "admiral," who "stands at the helm in 1800," and to the late General Washington. The assembled company drank to the fleet, its captains, and its brave tars, and to naval architecture as the "noblest combination of mechanic arts." Although the leading social historian of the sailing navy refers to the navy's "entirely Federalist" political predilection as "hoary myth," the banqueters then drank five toasts comparing various states' relative Federalist power with maintaining a fleet in proper formation: to New York, "may the hurricane of antifederalism never force her out of the line;" to the staunchly Federalist Connecticut, "the best sailer in the fleet;" to a dark vision of Jefferson's Virginia, "attempting to break the line, may she escape a mutiny from her crew of blacks." That the naval officers at New York would allow themselves to be associated with such partisan political jousts suggests that, in the turbulent last years of the Federalist party in power, a "national consensus of common identity and shared values" had yet to be formed. But, by the end of the revelry, the assembly returned to safer subjects, lifting their swaying glasses in No. 14 to "The mechanics of New York." By Number 16, they were reduced to toasting "The American fair—may they never cease to reward the brave," and by sunset the banquet closed amidst "cheerfulness and good humor."[20]

By the time the *New York* was completed, masted, and rigged, however, the Quasi-War with France was almost over. At the end of September 1800, President Adams issued a proclamation allowing commercial trade with the islands and territories of France to resume;[21] ten days later, the *New York* still lay in the East River, wanting fifty men to complete her crew.[22]

Manning the ship was not the only distraction, however. Captain Robinson, who had superintended the building of the *New York* for a year, was the most junior captain in the navy. Were he to continue in command, and take one of the navy's largest ships to sea, the rivalries and jealousies of more senior officers might damage the service. Or so Stoddert feared. Even when he had blessed Robinson's nomination as captain, he had informed the New York committee that giving the *New York* to the newest captain would cause "great inconvenience as well as great uneasiness among the other Captains" in that "Officers already in the Navy having acquired certain rights and getting more & more tenacious of them, it has become more difficult than heretofore to introduce new Captains expecially to Command the largest Ships." Stoddert suggested a deal: Robinson should superintend the building of the *New York* and he would be commissioned a captain but, in exchange, the *New York* would sail under a more senior captain, and Robinson would take a smaller ship. The return of the frigate *Adams* to New York after a ten-month cruise to the Leeward Islands allowed Stoddert to flip the officers of the two ships: Robinson and some of his lieutenants and midshipmen went to the *Adams* and, in exchange, the *New York* received some of the *Adams*'s officers, including her captain, Richard V. Morris, one of the Morrises of New York.[23]

In mid-October, 1800, Secretary Stoddert wrote to Thomas FitzSimons, informing him that the *New York* would be ordered to sail to the Delaware Capes, and cruise about Kiln Roads for two days, gathering up any merchant vessels from Philadelphia wishing a convoy to the Windward Islands. Exactly one week later, Stoddert planned for the *Adams* to sail from New York, following the same direction to call at the Capes of the Delaware, before it proceeded to Saint-Domingue. Stoddert asked FitzSimons to post the information about staging convoys on the Philadelphia Coffee House books.[24] Although Stoddert's orders followed in two days, the *New York* apparently was still off the Capes a week into November.[25]

On 6 December 1800, the *New York* arrived in Basseterre Roads, St. Kitts. Truxtun ordered Captain Morris to cruise to the windward of Guadeloupe, calling every fifteen days for instructions since Truxtun expected news from Stoddert about the signing of a peace treaty with France. The *New York*'s sortie was nearly calamitous; yellow fever swept through her crew and forty men had to be sent ashore to the hospital in Basseterre, although the infectious disease did not slow Truxtun from ordering her out again.[26]

The *New York*'s movements thereafter are unrecorded, although apparently the *New York* arrived back in the East River on 29 April 1801.[27] Although the *New York* had done next to nothing in the Quasi-War, having been completed too late, she was the navy's eighth largest ship and was retained by the Naval Peace Establishment Act of 1801. Although Captain Morris had done little in the Quasi-War either, he was retained as one of the thirteen captains, undoubtedly a recognition of the New Yorker's politics and powerful political connections. Morris was a Republican in a senior officer corps dominated by Federalists, and Thomas Jefferson had replaced John Adams as president. Morris was also the only New Yorker of the retained captains. More to the point, Morris was the youngest son of Lewis Morris, a signer of the Declaration of Independence; a nephew of Gouverneur Morris; and a brother of the congressman from Vermont who, by withholding his vote, allowed the state's electoral votes to go to Jefferson, making him president. On the other hand, Thomas Robinson, Sr., was politely dismissed as a captain, with four months pay as severance.[28]

By the end of May 1801, the *New York* had come up the Potomac River, and sailed up the Eastern Branch (now the Anacostia River) to be laid up in ordinary at the Washington Navy Yard. There, she was dismasted and given the rudimentary care that a skeleton crew and the rudimentary science of the day allowed, including seasonal unmoorings of the ship to swing the frigate in a half-circle, to allow the ship to wear evenly by exposing each side to the sun. But the *New York* inexorably began to waste away, which became clear when the *New York* was ordered back into active service in August 1802 to reinforce the squadron in the Mediterranean. The *New York*'s topmasts were declared unfit in a survey signed by the *New York*'s new first lieutenant, Stephen Decatur, in September 1802, after they had collapsed, causing one sailor's death in a spectacular fall from the main topgallant yard down to the main chains. Although the next month, the *New York* managed to sail across the Atlantic, she had to put in for repairs at Port Mahon. Surveys by Decatur found the "oakum worked out of the Seams the Decks Leaky and in want of Caulking" and the foremast "Badly Sprung in the Partners. . . ."[29]

The *New York's* second cruise was almost as barren as her first. She had been sent to the Mediterranean with money and gun carriages to pay off the Moslem potentates of Algiers and Morocco, if possible, or to fight them and Tripoli, if necessary. Though she was in the Mediterranean for one year, the *New York* never engaged any Tripolitan warships, although she once ran some coasting vessels ashore, where they were burned in a raid by a landing party under Lt. David Porter. For six months, the *New York* served as squadron flagship under her old captain, Richard Morris, but Morris, who had his wife aboard, seemed to enjoy port calls to Malta, Naples, Livorno, and Gibraltar more than active blockading or bombarding the Barbary cities. The *New York's* most perilous adventure came in April 1803, when a fire broke out in the gunner's storeroom, next to the magazine, that threatened to blow the ship to smithereens. As smoke billowed everywhere, the ship's first lieutenant, Isaac Chauncey, ordered the men to quarters. Commodore Morris lost his head and ordered the ships' boats to be hoisted out, in preparation for abandoning ship. Discipline fell apart, and Chauncey and Porter personally led some volunteers below to smother the fire with wet blankets and to organize a bucket line. The ship was saved; Chauncey's reputation for coolness was made but Morris was only confirmed as incompetent. The Navy recalled Morris from the Mediterranean and, a New York Morris or not, dismissed him from the service after a court of inquiry questioned his conduct. The *New York* was recalled in September 1803 and arrived back at the Washington Navy Yard in early December.[30]

President Jefferson, his entire cabinet, and many members of Congress visited the *New York* and *John Adams* at the Navy Yard on 12 December 1803. But the celebration of a ship festooned with flags, and sailors manning the yards and firing off salutes, could not conceal the Jefferson administration's distaste for fighting ships. The victim of an administration that prized gunboats and thought large warships both too expensive and provocative, the *New York* never set sail again. The *New York* lay at anchor in the Eastern Branch year after year, decaying into a waterlogged hulk. The lack of care for and degradation of the *New York,* as well as the *Boston, General Greene,* and other frigates, became a symbol of waste and mismanagement. Senator William Plumer, a New Hampshire Federalist, wrote in his journal on 26 November 1804, "Paid a visit to the Navy Yard—was surprised to find how fast our little navy is rotting in the mud of the Potomac." By 1809, the Navy Yard recognized that the *New York* was totally decayed, and was so beyond hope that no serious effort was made to repair her before the war of 1812. After the war of 1812 began, the Navy considered rebuilding the *New York* by private contract in Baltimore. A shipbuilder, unnamed in the correspondence, offered to rebuild the decrepit frigate either by the ton or on a per diem basis, and even had "a stern, stem & keel already engaged in case the old ones should prove rotten." In November 1812, the Navy dispatched five gunboats to escort the *New York* down the Potomac and up the Chesapeake Bay to Baltimore, but the old ship ultimately could not make even that voyage safely. On 22 February 1814, Secretary of the Navy William Jones reported to the Senate that the *New York*, along with two other ships that had faced a dozen years of neglect, were "rotten worthless hulks" that would cost more to rebuild than replace. Ironically, when Thomas Tingey, the commandant of the Washington Navy Yard, ordered his sailors to burn their ships when the British army seized the city in August 1814, the hulk of the *New York* escaped the flames, or perhaps she was too waterlogged to catch fire. The old ship, wrecked and moldering, was still at her moorings in 1830, when the navy tried to salvage her. After raising her, the Navy Board of Commissioners abandoned the project, letting the *New York* sink back into the Potomac mud, where perhaps timbers of her wooden hull linger today.[31]

9 Charleston's "Two-Sided" Frigate

In the spring of 1798, Charleston, like the other port cities, recognized that war with France was in the offing and took what steps it could to get ready. Workers completed Fort Mechanic (at what is now known as the Battery) and Fort Pinckney on Shute's Folly Island in the harbor. As spring turned to summer, the Charleston newspapers reprinted the Newburyport subscription effort and then the organizational meetings in Philadelphia, Baltimore, and Richmond.[1] On 21 July 1798, Secretary Stoddert wrote to James Simons of Charleston, enclosing a copy of the Act of 30 June, suggesting that Simons and his fellow Charlestonians might "Judge how much is expected from the Patriotism of our Citizens." Stoddert reported that four warships had already been subscribed for and hoped that "the Public Spirit of Charleston, should furnish one . . ." Stoddert suggested that an existing vessel, built by William Pritchard, could be purchased for the navy as Charleston's subscription contribution, provided that she was sheathed in copper and could mount sixteen guns.[2] But when the details of the Act of 30 June reached Charleston in late July, a meeting in Williams's Long Room authorized a subscription for a brand new 20-gun sloop of war. The Charleston subscribers organized themselves under the leadership of a committee consisting of William Crafts, Adam Gilchrist, Thomas Morris, David Alexander, Robert Hazlehurst, Adam Tunno, and James Miller.[3] Crafts wrote to Secretary Stoddert on 3 August that Charleston stood ready to provide a ship to the navy but, in a display of what Stoddert called the city's "ancient Spirit," offered their ship as a gift. Given the bar across the harbor, the largest vessel Charleston could furnish was a 24-gun light frigate. The navy secretary refused to accept the ship for free; as he explained, "As the whole number of Vessels to be paid for in Stock, have not yet been engaged, the President cannot think of taking greater advantage than necessary of the generous Spirit of the Citizens of Charleston." He accepted Charleston's warship on condition that the Charleston subscribers accept 6 percent navy stock. Stoddert enclosed dimensions and Josiah Fox's drafts of a 538-ton light frigate calculated to carry 24 twelve-pounder cannon on her gun deck and 28 guns overall.[4]

By 4 August, $100,000 had been raised and such leading citizens as Colonel William Washington, Thomas Pinckney, James Ladson, William Marshall, James Sinckler, Henry Laurens, William Allen Deas, John Bryan, John Gibbes, Joseph Jenkins, Nathaniel Russell, and William Price added their names to the committee.[5] On the 11th, the committee announced its decision to build the frigate instead of a sloop of war.[6] Although Charleston raised $100,000 in less than five days, and $114,000 overall,[7] the *City Gazette* contained a letter from "A CITIZEN" worried that "when contributions are the object to be obtained," some would abstain, claiming national defense was purely a federal responsibility. A CITIZEN urged his fellow South Carolinians to remember that the other cities had not been found wanting, that Beaufort, South Carolina, already had anted up $13,000 toward the Charleston subscription ship, and that the Southern coast lay open to French aggression:

> Although we are entitled to, and shall undoubtedly receive the protection of the general government, whether we loan a vessel of war or not; yet, I ask, if such a duty is necessary, on what part of the union does it lie most forcibly? Whose coast, shores and inlets are the most defenceless? Whose coasting trade is most liable to the depradations of the enemy?[8]

The Charleston committee requested permission to name their ship the *Adams* but Secretary Stoddert informed them that the president's name already had been taken by a frigate building at New York. Somewhat strangely, Stoddert thought it would be distinct enough "to have the Charleston Ship named the *John Adams*,"[9] leading to endless confusion ever since. The committee hired more than thirty shipwrights from the shipbuilding communities of northeastern Massachusetts to help in the construction, although slaves performed much of the manual labor.[10] Master Builder Paul Pritchard laid the keel of the *John Adams* on 10 November 1798.[11] The Navy Department, accepting the committee's suggestion, appointed Capt. George Cross to superintend the building of the *John Adams* and, ultimately, to command her. Cross had lobbied actively for her command.[12]

The *John Adams*'s futtocks were constructed of Carolina live oak and her top timbers were made from low-country cedar. Her keel and keelson were fashioned from Carolina pine and her masts and spars were of knot-free longleaf pine, also from local forests. The deck beams of the *John Adams* were shaped from yellow pine logs hewn along the Edisto River and the knees supporting them were formed from live oak. According to the construction foreman's memories twenty years later, the draft for the *John Adams* called for an eighty-six-foot keel, but the Carolina pine that the workmen scarfed together was so true and strong that the committee ordered her built five feet longer. Given the Charleston bar, the *John Adams* required a smallish depth of hold—twelve feet—and only a ten-inch deadrise.[13]

The frigate was built by hand, crafted by the simplest machines, blocks and tackle, and basic carpenters' tools. Given Charleston's climate, most of the construction occurred in the cooler months. Vessels were built out in the open, exposed to the weather, to season the framing and planking. Logs were stored in a pond at the shipyard to keep them sound and resilient until needed. The timbers were cut by sawyers, working one up and one down in a saw pit, and shaped by shipwrights using broadaxes and adzes. The ship's planking was fastened with wooden pegs called treenails that were pounded by mallets into holes bored with augers. *John Adams*'s keel pieces, frame futtocks, and top timbers were joined by bolts of iron.

> This Ship was contemplated to have been copper bolted, but no copper bolts could be had at that time, & the incapacity of only one Brass Founder here (at that time) to cast composition bolts, it was abandoned & the Ship was bolted with Iron throughout & her Plank put on with composition spikes & treenails.[14]

Ship carpenters used tons of oakum to caulk *John Adams*'s seams and fastened hundreds of sheets of copper below the waterline to protect her hull from the destructive attacks of shipworms and also to reduce the accumulation of barnacles and other marine growth. The *John Adams*'s figurehead, a bust of President Adams, was sculpted by William Rush of Philadelphia, America's leading shipcarver.[15] Local artisans completed the trail boards, quarter galleries, transom, and other carvings.

The *John Adams* was built with an asymmetrical hull. Perhaps this embarrassing anomaly owed to the committee's extemporaneous decision to extend her keel five feet longer than called for in Josiah Fox's design draft; perhaps it was because of the shortage of local skilled craftsmen, which reputedly forced the frames for each side of the ship to be cut in different yards and only assembled at Cochran's shipyard. But lopsided she was. Ten years after she was finished, Fox measured the *John Adams* at the Washington Navy Yard and found "[f]rom an unknown cause she is wider on the Larboard than Starboard Side, and always tends to list to Starboard, from which circumstance I am inclined to believe she will be considerably stiffer on the Starboard than the Larboard Tack."[16] Even if wags would call the *John Adams* the "two-sided" frigate, her launch made a magnificent spectacle.

"An immense number of spectators attended [the launching] in spite of the distance of over 3 miles from the city" (the yard was located on Shipyard Neck, the peninsula between the Cooper River and Shipyard Creek);[17] reportedly, the civic festival drew the largest crowd since President Washington came to Charleston on his Southern tour in May 1791. At eight o'clock in the morning on 3 June 1799, the launching of the *John Adams* began. At first, the frigate "moved with great velocity toward the water" down the ways to Shipyard Creek, but then she shuddered to a stop and settled into soft ground. Two days later, on 5 June 1799, they tried again and this time,

> the frigate *John Adams* was launched happily at 8 o'clock this morning, introduced into her element, with a rapid but beautiful movement. She hurried from off her ways before a number of shoes and blocks could be knocked away, and while a number of workmen, nine it is said, were still under her. . . . A profuse and elegant collation, enough for 500, was provided by the Committee of Subscribers as a social offering to their fellow citizens—Governor Edward Rutledge, Major General Charles Cotesworth Pinckney, Brigadier General William Washington, Colonel Read . . . attended . . . 16 toasts enumerated plus volunteers, including a band playing favorite federal tunes.[18]

Both the workmen and the heavily toasted partygoers survived unscathed. After the launch, the *John Adams* had to be fitted out. Riggers first stepped her lower masts and then set up the miles of cordage, stays, and shrouds, to support the masts. Then the riggers installed the network of running rigging necessary to control the sails. The merchant ship *South Carolina* brought the ship's main deck guns to Charleston from the Philadelphia Navy Yard.[19] As originally completed, the *John Adams* mounted 26 twelve-pounder cannon and 6 twenty-four-pounder carronades, short, light-weight, limited-range "smashers" developed from the Carron Iron Works in Scotland that could be fired more rapidly than the standard long guns. With a broadside firepower of 228 pounds, the *John Adams* was the most powerful sailing warship ever built in Charleston. She was also the first to mount carronades as part of her original armament.[20]

On 16 July 1799, Captain Cross brought the *John Adams* down the Cooper River to Charleston harbor to complete the frigate for sea. The new frigate was an impressive sight. Before she came to anchor off Prioleau's Wharf at the foot of Queen Street, cheering townsmen lining the shore and seamen on board the vessels in the harbor shouted "federal huzzahs" and the merchant craft lowered their colors in the new ship's honor.[21] The next day, Cross began the difficult task of recruiting the 220 able seamen, ordinary seamen, and boys to complete the ship's company. A recruiting rendezvous was established at the southeast corner of Governor's Bridge on East Bay (where the Charleston Market was later built on landfill). With one-year enlistments and parsimonious pay, it took months to sign on sailors, but Cross had a sufficient crew by autumn.[22] Meanwhile, topmasts were crossed and provisions lightered out from the merchants' wharves. Barrels of brined beef and pork were packed into the hold, water casks were filled, and the Navy shipped twenty thousand pounds of ship's bread from Norfolk in September.[23] By 23 October, everything was ready. The *John Adams* weighed her anchors but a strong easterly wind forced her to anchor near James Island. On passing Fort Mechanic, her cannon crashed out a grand salute to her creator city.[24] Somewhat anticlimactically, a week passed before the veering winds allowed the *John Adams* to sail down to Rebellion Roads, and it was not until 13 November that the *John Adams* crossed the bar into the Atlantic.[25] Captain Cross had the satisfaction to write that the *John Adams* was in "the 1st Class of sailers," an observation confirmed by the pilot who navigated the frigate out of the harbor, a Mr. Delano, who added that "she sails remarkably well."[26] Although a fast sailer, the heavy topside weight of the *John Adams* acting on her shallow draft, and lack of deadrise on the bottom of her hull, meant that the *John Adams* was subject to rolling her gunports under water in any strong breeze. The *John Adams*'s slight draft and high center of gravity, necessary to float her over the Charleston bar, meant she was not a "stiff" ship.[27]

By the time the *John Adams* put to sea, Secretary of the Navy Stoddert had established three naval squadrons: one off of Havana; the second between St. Kitts and Puerto Rico (rendezvousing off Saint-Domingue); and the third between St. Kitts and Barbados. It was the last squadron that drew Stoddert's particular attention. At the beginning of the Quasi-War a year earlier, Stoddert had written to President Adams that "the French have from 60 to 80 Privateers out of the little island of Guadeloupe. . . . It seems in vain to guard our Merchants vessels on our own Coasts, if we suffer them to be taken about the Islands, and tho' our means may not entirely prevent this, it seems certainly in our power to lessen the Evil, and to inflict some degree of Punishment in our turn."[28] On 1 October 1799, Stoddert directed Cross to cruise off Puerto Rico for one month and then to join the Leeward Islands squadron off Guadeloupe.[29] With the one-year enlistments of her crew set to expire in the autumn of 1800, the *John Adams* essentially would have one campaign "season" to help punish the French privateers.

After a minor contretemps with the Spanish governor of Puerto Rico caused by the detention and imprisonment of officers of the *John Adams* sent ashore to buy food,[30] the *John Adams* joined the Leeward Squadron in January 1800. Almost immediately, she recaptured the American brig *Dolphin*. Under the law, the captors were entitled to salvage value as a United States admiralty court would fix. Captain Cross sent the *Dolphin* into Charleston, where his prize agent and the agents for the owners agreed to set the value of the *Dolphin* and her cargo by appraisal and have the U.S. marshal auction so much of her cargo so as to pay Cross and his officers and crew their entitlement.[31] The *Dolphin* brought in $1,017.31 for distribution.[32]

On 3 April, after a four-hour chase, the *John Adams* caught and seized a privateer schooner, *La Jason,* a Virginia-built pilot schooner that the French had purchased to act as a privateer against British merchant vessels. *La Jason* threw six of her eight guns overboard in her flight and, even though the *La Jason* was new and coppered, the *John Adams* captured her fifty miles northeast of St. Lucia. Cross sent her into Charleston, where the prize court condemned her and she was auctioned for $3,500.[33] Tracking another French privateer called *Le President Tout* later that month, the *John Adams* recaptured the brig *Hannibal* on 22 April (seized the night before) and the brig *Atlantic* on 23 April (seized twenty hours earlier). If Cross never found the privateer, at least he undid her damage—and made some ready salvage money for himself.[34]

Off Guadeloupe on 13 June, the *John Adams* captured *La Decade*, another small privateer schooner, mounting 6 three-pounder cannon and carrying a crew of thirty-one men. *La Decade* was more of a leaky bucket than a nimble raider; her mainmast and chain-plates carried away in the chase and her sails were thin and could hardly hold the wind. When Cross brought her into St. Kitts, the American naval captains certified that *La Decade* was not seaworthy and certainly could not make it to an American port for prize adjudication. Instead, Cross had the ship libeled in the British vice-admiralty court at St. Kitts. The British judge obliged, although the leaky *La Decade* only sold for $518. When the proceeds were finally remitted to Charleston in April 1801, Captain Cross presumably received $36.90 for his efforts.[35]

The staple fare of the *John Adams*'s cruising was to convoy American merchantmen, laden with West Indian coffee and sugar, northwards to the open Atlantic, protecting them from the jackal-like privateers until they could scatter for their American destinations, and then to return with other American cargo vessels bound for West Indies ports. Few records survive of these forays, although Captain Cross apparently felt a strong duty towards convoy protection. When Curaçao fell to the French, the first word to reach the U.S. Navy came to St. Kitts in the person of William Robinson, the American consul's agent. Cross was the senior officer present, although the *Merrimack* and *Patapsco* also were in the port. On 14 September, when Robinson arrived at St. Kitts, he presented his papers to Cross and appealed for him to sail immediately to Curaçao's relief. According to Robinson, Captain Cross shared his view of "the necessity and singularity of the case, but expressed a delicacy at leaving his station at that time," although he "cheerfully" allowed the *Merrimack* and *Patapsco* to go. Robinson's statement is curious; all three warships' primary role was escort duty but if Robinson's report required action, the *John Adams,* a 28-gun frigate, was the most powerful ship and Cross the senior captain present. Cross was presented with a golden opportunity for independent action, which most officers craved, and he rightly should have led whatever force sent to Curaçao. Whether Cross was too fixed at his unimaginative convoying job or just not energetic enough to take decisive action, the *John Adams* played no role in one of the central and dramatic battles of the Quasi-War.[36]

Instead, *John Adams* stolidly pursued her escort role, although Commodore Truxtun also ordered her to cruise around St. Bart's to interdict any French privateers passing around that island.[37] On 20 November 1800, Truxtun ordered Cross to take a convoy to at least 32° north latitude "before you make the signal for each to take his own course," and then ordered him to sail the *John Adams* to Charleston.[38] The South Carolina frigate dropped her anchors in Charleston in mid-December and paid off her crew; Secretary Stoddert granted Captain Cross's request for a nine-month furlough, leaving a lieutenant and skeleton crew to make repairs including "a Gang of new Lower Rigging."[39] In her only Quasi-War cruise, *John Adams* had been away 397 days with only thirty-five days in harbor, and she had captured two French privateers and rescued eight merchant vessels that the French privateers had seized.[40]

Although the navy retained the *John Adams* as one of the thirteen warships in the "permanent navy" under the Naval Peace Establishment Act of 1801, she, like most vessels of the navy, was "laid up" at the Washington Navy Yard. There the *John Adams* would be, in the venomous and unmistakable words of the new president, Thomas Jefferson, "under the immediate eye of the department, and would require but one set of plunderers to take care of them."[41] But the outbreak of war against the Barbary pirates gave a reprieve to the *John Adams;* the Navy Department ordered the South Carolina frigate to the Mediterranean. Under a new captain, John Rodgers, the *John Adams* got underway on 22 October 1802.[42]

In the Tripolitan war, the *John Adams* bombarded the massive fortifications of Tripoli, captured the 28-gun cruiser *Meshouda* (the former American merchant ship *Betsy* of Boston, taken into the Bashaw's navy), and, with the schooner *Enterprize*, destroyed a 22-gun corvette that had been a tribute gift from the French republic.[43] After a brief return to America in 1804, the *John Adams* returned to the Mediterranean as the squadron's storeship until the war ended. In late 1805, the *John Adams* was placed in ordinary at the Washington Navy Yard. Two years later, Josiah Fox, *John Adams*'s original designer and the Navy's chief constructor, supervised her conversion from a light frigate to a flush-deck corvette. The *John Adams,* ordered back into commission in January 1809, played the unpopular role of enforcing the sequel to Jefferson's embargo, Madison's Non-Intercourse Act, by cruising off the United States coast looking for violators, until December 1811.[44]

The advent of the War of 1812 found the *John Adams* once again being rebuilt in the shipyards, this time at Boston, from a corvette to a "jackass" frigate (i.e., with a quarterdeck but no forecastle).[45] In July 1812, the *John Adams* sailed to New York where she remained, stymied by the British blockade, until early 1814. Only under a flag of truce could the *John Adams* clear the Narrows, carrying the U.S. peace commissioners, Henry Clay and Jonathan Russell, to Europe. Conveying Clay and Russell to Sweden, and from there taking them and John Quincy Adams, the third American negotiator, to Texel, Holland, was the *John Adams*'s only real contribution to the War of 1812.[46]

The *John Adams*'s career, however, was far from over. Although the *John Adams* did not take part in Stephen Decatur's lightning-like triumph over the Algerine pirates in 1815, the *John Adams* battled West Indies pirates in 1816 to 1817, showed the flag off of the newly independent South American nations in 1819, and caught slave ships while serving in the West African squadron. From 1829 to 1831, the *John Adams* was transformed yet again, this time at the Norfolk Navy Yard, into a second-class sloop of war. Retaining only her original main timbers, when the *John Adams* emerged again flush-decked, she bore little resemblance from the waterline up to the light frigate launched in Charleston thirty-two years earlier.[47]

In the 1830s, the *John Adams* was deployed in the Mediterranean, and from December 1837 to June 1840, circumnavigated the globe. After three years in the Brazil squadron, the *John Adams* was refurbished in time to see combat in the Mexican War. Part of what was then the largest American naval squadron in history, the *John Adams* blockaded Vera Cruz and Tampico, Mexican ports on the Gulf of Mexico. The next decade saw the *John Adams* chase slavers off Africa, and then saw her sail into the Pacific.[48]

When the *John Adams* was recalled from the Orient at the outbreak of the Civil War, it was for the honorable, dowager role as a sail-training ship for the U.S. Naval Academy, which had been removed from Annapolis to Newport, Rhode Island.[49] After all, the *John Adams* was not only an old ship but also a sailing ship at a time when steam engine technology had shown its dominance. Nevertheless, at the ripe old age of sixty-four, *John Adams* was ordered to war duty for the last time, arriving at Port Royal, South Carolina, on 21 August 1863 to join the Union's South Atlantic Blockading Squadron.[50] After remaining on that station for several months as a storeship, she joined the blockading fleet at Charleston. By the time the old ship arrived there in late December, Fort Sumter had been reduced to a pile of rubble and the federal guns on Morris Island were relentlessly pounding the beleaguered city.

The blockade of Charleston had gradually tightened until the city was effectively cut off from the sea. The ships of the Union squadron were divided between the inside of the bar and patrolling offshore. When she took up station off Morris Island, there were sixteen other Union vessels inside, and nine more outside the bar.[51] On 22 February 1864, the *John Adams* took on board forty survivors from the steam sloop of war *Housatonic,* sunk by the Confederate submarine *H. L. Hunley.*[52] The *John Adams,* launched in the days of men in powdered wigs and cockaded hats, had witnessed in her old age the first sinking by a submarine, with all that implied for the future.

The *John Adams* remained on duty inside the bar until February 1865, when the Confederates evacuated Charleston in the face of General Sherman's oncoming army. The former South Carolina frigate then sailed into her native harbor and proceeded up the Cooper River, where, in her original form, she had been built by the citizens of Charleston sixty-six years before. Upon her return to the Cooper River, however, there were no "federal huzzahs" from the grandsons and granddaughters of those citizens on the shore.[53]

The ancient warship was ordered to Boston Navy Yard in the summer of 1865 and decommissioned there in September. In October 1867, *John Adams* suffered the inglorious fate of so many glorious wooden warships when she was sold out of the U.S. Navy and sent to the breaker's yard.[54]

10 The Essex in the East Indies

By the end of 1799, Benjamin Stoddert could look back at his eighteen-month tenure as secretary of the navy with some satisfaction. During that year and a half, the navy purchased or built and placed into commission thirty ships, officered them with Revolutionary War veterans and promising younger men, and, after securing the United States's own coast, sent three squadrons into the Caribbean. Under Truxtun, Talbot, and Barry, the U.S. Navy established convoys to bring merchant vessels out of dangerous waters and fought or captured French privateers and warships. The navy's reach extended from Cayenne, where John Rodgers sailed the *Maryland* on her solitary mission; to Curaçao, where the *Patapsco* blasted her way into the harbor; and throughout the Islands. Although the West Indies was the focus of U.S. naval operations in the Quasi-War, Stoddert's strategic vision was broader.

Almost as soon as the navy had ships afloat, the merchants pressed for protection for their ships trading in distant seas. Adams and Stoddert received letter after letter calling upon the navy for escorts, and Stoddert invariably turned each down. A Baltimore merchant, James Barry, asked for a convoy to Europe in September 1798 only to be told "our force is yet too small." Two of the

New York merchants building the subscription frigate *New York* asked for convoys to, and in, the Mediterranean in January 1799, but again Stoddert demurred, replying that "by the Spring" he hoped that enough warships would be in commission "to afford such a force as you suggest." They never went. In the spring of 1799, Senator Goodhue of Massachusetts, the very man who introduced the subscription-loan bill in the Senate, wrote Stoddert on behalf of the Salem merchants for a convoy to and from the Baltic. Deferentially noting the importance of the Baltic trade and "feeling the utmost anxiety to make our litle Navy as useful as possible in the protection of all our Trade," Stoddert nevertheless replied that he could not spare ships for Elsinore because the whole force was needed in the West Indies. Only two weeks later, Congressman Samuel Sewall of Marblehead requested convoy protection for ships traveling to the port of Corunna, Spain, and Stoddert felt compelled to lay the question before the cabinet and to write President Adams with his thoughts. For the navy to convoy to "any part of Europe," Stoddert wrote, was "at least very questionable." The French were known to have privateers cruising off Corunna, and French warships or privateers might sortie out from Bordeaux, La Rochelle, or Bayonne to attack an American convoy to Spain. To provide effective protection, the navy would have to devote a substantial force as escorts. On the one hand, using his frigates and sloops of war on European convoys might "expose our Vessels to great hazards;" yet on the other hand, sending them across the Atlantic "might be to neglect other objects, which our force might accomplish" in the Caribbean. The "hazards" Stoddert feared was an ambush. As the navy secretary noted to Adams in defending his decision not to send the warships out to convoy, "A Convoy to be useful, must be known generally to the Merchants five or six weeks before it could sail. The French would probably hear of it, before it arrived in Europe, and might be prepared for it." In sum, Stoddert refused to send a meager force, announced, into French-controlled waters nor could he support any plan that would weaken the navy's effort in the Caribbean. Stoddert admitted to Sewall that, writ large, his strategic thinking meant France had the power "to shut us out from almost the whole of Europe."[1]

To the president, Stoddert confided that the cabinet fractured on a response to Sewall, each secretary having his own theory as to what could or should be done. Stoddert could not distinguish between granting protection to ships going to one port but not to another or, as he put it, "there is scarcely a considerable port in Europe, to which convoys are not wanted, and applied for." But then Secretary Stoddert let slip to President Adams a thought that occurred to him, an idea that might provide more "real protection" to the trade with Europe than a convoy "at a particular season [of] a few vessels." Why not, wrote Stoddert, send a frigate or even a squadron, during the hurricane season in the West Indies, hurdling across the Atlantic to sweep along the Spanish and French coasts from Cape Finisterre to Nantes, using surprise to strike unexpectedly at any French privateers cruising off the coast, and then departing as quickly as they came. Out of these musings grew a plan to send the navy's two most powerful frigates, the 44-gunners *United States* and *Constitution,* to sweep down from the English Channel through the Bay of Biscay down the Iberian coast and then back across the Atlantic. President Adams, who found the reasoning of Stoddert's answer to Sewall "so satisfactory," was "much pleased" at Stoddert's plan and suggested that the then-new frigate *Boston* join the strike force. But Stoddert ultimately had to cancel the mission when the *Constitution* returned from the Caribbean requiring extensive repairs and a new set of officers. Captain Alexander Murray in the frigate *Insurgent* thought to make the attempt when Stoddert gave him a roving commission, but the *Insurgent'*s nine-month cruise proved singularly uneventful. Stoddert's grand coup against French privateers out of France never materialized.[2]

As the war turned into its second winter, the strategic situation had become clear; the United States Navy commanded the Atlantic coast, and the Caribbean, if not an American "lake," was no longer the privateer haven of the summer of 1798. Yet the American navy was lilliputian compared to France's navy. America had no ships of the line and only two completed 44-gun frigates, and the entire United States Navy would have been crushed by any of the French navy's squadrons at Brest, Rochefort, Lorient, or Toulon. Stoddert dared not bring the war to France's Atlantic coast except for a surprise strike, and sending ships into the Mediterranean, where they would be far from reliable dockyard facilities and supplies, and could be sealed off at Gibraltar, was unthinkable.

One other operational theater existed, however, where American warships might intervene. On the "far side of the world," the Indian and Pacific Oceans, America had substantial trading interests under threat from French privateers based at Île-de-France (Mauritius) and Île Bourbon (Réunion). United States naval power might make a difference there. For one thing, metropolitan France was as distant from the southern seas as the United States, and French warships and privateers operating around the Cape of Good Hope were at the end of a long and precarious logistical string, subject to constant British attack. Moreover, the French navy rarely had more than a handful of warships in the Indian Ocean, and the British navy managed to burn, sink, or capture most of those ships over time. Above all, one or two U.S. Navy vessels could escort home American merchantmen from those waters, brushing aside any French privateers.

American merchant ships were not strangers to Canton, Java, or India. By 1799, American trade to East and South Asia had a fifteen-year lineage. In February 1784, almost before the last redcoats had evacuated Manhattan, the great New York financier Robert Morris had underwritten the voyage of the *Empress of China,* loaded with ginseng, hides, and cotton, for Canton, inaugurating American trade with China. Upon her return to the East River in May 1785, clearing a 25 percent profit on the syndicators' $120,000 investment, enterprising merchants turned to the new markets in the Pacific. Capt. Ebenezer West set sail in the *Grand Turk* for Elias Hasket Derby's house in Salem in December 1785, returning home in May 1787, after she became the first American vessel to trade at Bombay. In 1786, eight American vessels sailed for Asian ports, but by 1789, fifteen called at Canton alone. Hard on the heels of the opening of the China trade came American ships trading for peppers in Sumatra, coffee from Mocha, spices from Batavia (now Djakarta), and cottons from India. American trade with the Orient expanded so rapidly that, by 1800, ninety shipmasters from Salem had rounded the Cape of Good Hope.[3]

Even without the risk of Malay pirates or French privateers, the mere existence of substantial trade with the far side of the world in the 1790s was nothing short of miraculous. To make the outbound voyage took at least four months. The American sloops, brigs, and schooners that sailed halfway around the world and back rarely exceeded three hundred tons; indeed, the second American vessel to arrive at Canton was the eighty-ton sloop *Experiment,* which hailed from Albany, New York. Not only were many of the merchant vessels small enough to fit into an Olympic-size swimming pool that modern-day Americans might enjoy, but the Asian-bound merchant ships carried little or no navigational equipment. Although John Harrison had invented the marine chronometer a generation earlier, few American merchant vessels carried one. Nor were many American shipmasters able to perform the complex lunar observations necessary to find the longitude. Instead, American mariners relied on dead reckoning (i.e., not-so-educated guesswork) as to their likely positions, based on wildly inexact charts. Even the largest vessels, like the

William Hackett–designed *Massachusetts,* did not carry a chronometer and, consequently, lost three weeks time trying to find Java Head, having missed on the approach.[4]

If it was providential that small American trading vessels almost routinely sailed tens of thousands of miles on the open ocean without charts or chronometers or even set trading routes, the trade became a driving engine of American economic growth and a stimulus for entrepreneurship and expansion.[5] If Stoddert could offer no help from storms or navigational errors, he certainly could try to prevent French privateers from Île-de-France from reaping the fruits of American ingenuity and enterprise. The first place besides the Caribbean that Secretary Stoddert decided to send the navy to escort merchant vessels was to Java. And the first United States Navy ship there, the first warship flying the Stars and Stripes to weather the Cape of Good Hope, was the 32-gun frigate *Essex,* built by popular subscription of the citizens of Salem, Massachusetts, and readying for sea in the winter of 1799.

Salem's civic embarrassment produced the *Essex.* Even though Newburyport is just up the road, Salem initially seemed complaisant about what their neighbors took to be a war crisis. On 1 May 1798, Salem's militia was called out but few officers bothered to assemble and the men who mustered did not inspire confidence; the citizen-soldiers did not even go through the manual of arms, and an onlooker, Rev. William Bently, termed the display a "burlesque." While Newburyport's young men paraded with Capt. Moses Brown to the launching site of the *Merrimack* and Boston merchants pledged more than $115,000 for their subscription frigate, Bently confided in his diary on Independence Day, 1798, that Salem "has as yet taken no part in the Loans to Government for a Navy." Everyone in town knew, of course, of the Crowninshields' offer of the *Belisarius* and *America.* While a subscription list opened on 16 July 1798, little attention was paid or money pledged, only $16,000, "a sum so inadequate," according to Senator Goodhue, "that the matter has been asleep ever since." On 25 August 1798, Secretary of State Pickering wrote to Goodhue, inquiring about the Salem subscription, indicating by implication that Secretary Stoddert had declined the Crowninshields' offer definitively. Goodhue called on the two wealthiest men in town, Elias Hasket Derby[6] and William Gray,[7] and showed them Pickering's letter. Derby told Goodhue that, as he owned one-tenth of the capital in Salem, he would subscribe one-tenth of the town's loan. Derby's shipmaster sons, Richard Derby and E. H. Derby, Jr., interjected that Derby actually had twenty percent of Salem's trade and that he should subscribe accordingly, and from that embarrassing confession it was clear that Derby would be a major contributor. For his part, Gray agreed "that a Ship we must have" and that "if others did not subscribe a sufficient sum he would," it being understood that he would put up ninety cents for every dollar Derby subscribed. Senator Goodhue ruefully observed to Stoddert that Gray himself might fund a 20-gun ship "and not feel it."[8]

Despite the commitment of Salem's two millionaires, the town never displayed the wholehearted enthusiasm of the other ports. Reverend Bently noted that raising funds proceeded slowly: the organizers needed to go door-to-door to solicit subscribers; some pledges were for a mere ten dollars; and others asked to pay in work, "in which way," Bentley wrote caustically, "a Ship would be a dear acquisition." In the Salem *Gazette,* A SHOREMAN from Beverly satirized the subscription effort, proffering that Beverly could not offer "silver and gold" toward the subscription "but if government will take *good Grand Bank fish,* I have no doubt that 16,000 quintals might be obtained for their use at 6 per cent." In time, however, Salem's merchants stepped forward, Derby and Gray each subscribing $10,000, and the town $74,700 overall, although the main branch of the Crowninshield family refused to contribute a dollar.[9]

On 23 October 1798, the subscribers unanimously voted to build a 32-gun frigate, and as with every other port, set up a committee to superintend construction. The chairman of the five-man committee was William Gray. The first decision Gray made was to hire William Hackett to design the Salem ship. William Hackett, of course, was the same man who designed the *Merrimack,* which Newburyport had launched only ten days earlier. The Salem committee named Capt. Joseph Waters, a local shipmaster, as general agent, and appointed Enos Briggs the master builder. Over the winter of 1798 to 1799, Briggs advertised for "all true lovers of the Liberty of your Country" to come forward to assist "in building the frigate to oppose French insolence and piracy. Let every man in possession of a *White Oak Tree* . . . be foremost in hurrying down the timber to Salem. . . . Your largest and longest trees are wanted for the Keel, which all together will measure 146 feet in length, and hew 16 inches square," for which Briggs promised "READY CASH." The nearby towns of Danvers, Topsfield, Boxford, and Andover supplied most of the ship's white-oak timber.[10]

The noted sailing navy historian Howard Chapelle has written that Hackett designed the *Essex* "very much like a Continental [i.e., Revolutionary War] frigate in lines and general appearance." In planning the

Essex, Hackett may well have drawn on his earlier frigate designs, particularly the *Alliance* of 1778; historian Phillip Chadwick Foster Smith discovered, among the papers related to the *Essex,* Hackett's handwritten notations for the mast, yard, and hull dimensions of the *Alliance,* although the Revolutionary War frigate was seven feet longer and had a depth of hold three inches deeper than the *Essex.* It seems likely then that the *Essex* was a close copy of the earlier ship, although no plans remain of the *Alliance* to make a direct comparison. The *Essex*'s most prominent feature topside were detached forecastle and quarterdeck connected by gangways along each side.[11]

The keel of the Salem frigate was laid on 13 April 1799. Seventy years later, a man who had witnessed the building and launching of the frigate as a six-year-old boy recalled some verse he attributed to Enos Briggs:

> Next September is the time,
> When we'll launch her from the strand,
> And her cannon load and prime,
> With tribute due to Talleyrand.

The frigate was largely a local production. Much of her wood came from local forests. A Salem sailmaker, Buffum & Howard, made the sails from Russian duck woven at Daniel Rust's local shop. Three Salem ropewalks made the frigate's rigging, and when the heaviest cordage was finished in September 1799, it was carried from Thomas Briggs's ropewalk to the building site on the backs of two hundred men, accompanied by American flags and fifes and drums playing "Yankee Doodle." Common laborers made one dollar per day, joiners a quarter more, and ship carpenters received $1.50. Paul Revere of Boston fabricated the *Essex*'s copper sheathing and fastenings, and the ship's cannon also came from elsewhere; the twelve-pounders were shipped from Philadelphia, from either Lane & Salter or Henry Foxall & Co., and the six-pounders had been imported from England.[12]

The *Essex* was launched on 30 September 1799, within six months of the laying of her keel. Although Salem contained 9,500 people, reputedly a crowd of 12,000 came to witness the launch, including Paul Revere from Boston. In a spate of pique at the president, the man who championed "wooden walls" but who just had announced the sending of envoys to France to negotiate peace, the ultra-Federalists of Salem decided not to issue formal invitations to the ceremony so that they could snub John Adams privately. Petty and myopic as that gesture was, it epitomized the rifts in the Federalist Party that soon would drive the party into opposition and then oblivion. Even without the presence of the president, the launch of the *Essex* was a striking sight that no one in attendance ever forgot. Reverend Bently heard the morning gun fired and nothing remained to be done "but to prepare the tallow, drive the wedges, remove the blocks & let her go." The *Essex* slid down the ways into the water without any accident and to the hurrahs of the huge audience on shore. Afterward, the subscribers, builders, and contractors celebrated with rum punch and hot buttered rum, cider, slices of beef and cheese on crackers, with puddings for dessert.[13]

The Salem merchants initially chose Richard Derby, Jr., to command their frigate. Young Derby's father subscribed $1,500 for the ship and his uncle was Elias Hasket Derby, but few would decry his selection as nepotism. Derby, a Harvard graduate, was thirty-four years old and a veteran shipmaster. Although President Adams had appointed Derby a captain in February 1799, Derby immediately requested and received a furlough. Instead of superintending the construction of the *Essex*, Derby was at sea, and he missed the frigate's launching. In his stead, Stoddert appointed Edward Preble of Portland, Maine, to command the *Essex*.[14]

Preble, thirty-eight years old in 1799, was a consummate seaman. To his subordinates and sailors, he seemed dour, choleric, and a stern disciplinarian. To his social equals and those who showed promise, Preble was well spoken and popular. Educated at Governor Dummer Academy in Newbury, Preble left school as a teenager in 1779 to go to sea aboard the Massachusetts naval ship *Protector* under Capt. John Foster Williams. On his first cruise, the *Protector* fought a 36-gun British letter of marque, the *Admiral Duff*, which caught fire and blew up. Later in the Revolution, Preble served as a lieutenant to George Little in the *Winthrop* and boarded and captured an English brig lying in Penobscot Bay. After the war, Preble served as a shipmaster out of Boston. The Quasi-War allowed him to reenter naval service. Slated to be first lieutenant of the *Constitution*, Preble was famously described by Stephen Higginson, the navy agent at Boston, as "a smart active popular man, judicious & well qualified for his station, or for the first command." Reassigned to command the revenue cutter *Pickering*, which convoyed merchantmen out of the West Indies, Preble made a good impression on Stoddert who, in recommending his promotion to captain, wrote President Adams on 25 May 1799 that Preble "ought to have been a Captain from the beginning" of the war. To Higginson, Stoddert wrote that Preble would "make a figure in the Navy," and he sent Preble his captain's commission in June, hoping he would not resign as rumored to make a merchant voyage. Preble stayed in the navy, received command of the *Essex,* and met Stoddert's expectation of becoming an exemplary figure in the navy.[15]

Preble arrived in Salem on 6 November 1799 to find the *Essex* rigged, ballasted, and watered, but with only a solitary midshipman and twenty seamen aboard. In short order, Preble supervised the mounting of the *Essex*'s guns, 26 twelve-pounders on her gun deck and 10 sixes on her quarterdeck; engaged petty officers; and sent a lieutenant (the officers were named by the committee) and midshipmen to Boston, Cape Ann, and around Salem to recruit a crew. In his first set of orders to Preble, Secretary Stoddert stressed that the *Essex* be at Newport, Rhode Island, by 15 December to rendezvous with the 38-gun frigate *Congress* (under Capt. James Sever), and then convoy a number of ships bound for the East Indies "a certain distance on their voyage." Violent snowstorms delayed the *Essex,* and Preble was short on men, bread, coal, and medical supplies. Even the canisters and grapeshot were not on board. Ultimately, at 8 A.M. on 22 December 1799, the *Essex* unmoored, fired a salute, and left Salem harbor forever.[16]

In an attempt to outdo the pride of Salem, the Crowninshields sent the *Belisarius* to sea that morning, too. The *Belisarius* set more and more sail to catch the *Essex* but could not, as Captain Preble wrote when the *Essex* arrived at Newport:

> the *Essex,* with two reefs in each topsail and foresail sailed as fast as the *Belisaurias* with top and topgallant studding sails set. Capt. West's ship was so far astern that I could not so well judge of her sailing, but it appears to me this ship with the same sail set . . . would sail six miles to their four . . . The *Essex* is a good sea-boat, and sails remarkably fast. She went eleven miles per hour, with topgallant sail set and within six points of the wind.

Any vessel that could beat the *Belisarius* was a marvel, and Captain Walters relayed to William Hackett the news from Preble, which he trusted "will aford you a great Deall of pleasure as it does the Gentlemen of the Committee."[17]

Although Stoddert first thought that the *Essex* and *Congress* should convoy American vessels bound to the East Indies at least to the equator, President Adams intervened to direct the two frigates to go all the way to Batavia so that American naval power could provide "protection on the return voyage to a great number of vessels, and vast amount of property" sailing back to America in the spring of 1800. To dispatch two frigates halfway round the world made sense only if they actually had merchant ships to protect. The secretary of the navy himself sent notice to the merchants of Salem, New York, Newport, Philadelphia, Boston, and Baltimore of the pending departure of the *Essex* and *Congress* to Java. As an ex-merchant himself, Stoddert recognized that the few weeks' notice hardly sufficed for merchants whose ships were already at sea or committed to other routes or times. In the dead of a frigid New England winter, pelted by snow and hail, the Salem merchants told Preble that they would not send their ships in convoy "as they calculate the sea Risk to [Newport] equal to the risk of capture from this [Salem] to the Cape of Good Hope." Actuarially sound or not, the word spread among the leading merchants. Robert Oliver of Baltimore referred to the two frigates cruising to the East Indies in a letter to his London correspondent, musing whether the *Castor & Pollux,* a ship in which Oliver had a five-elevenths share, then lying in the port of Baltimore and carrying more than $100,000 in specie and goods bound to Livorno and Madras, might receive protection.[18]

The whole notion of an East India convoy soon seemed to be a farce. When the two frigates ultimately cast off from their moorings at Newport on 6 January 1800 to begin their cruise, only three merchant vessels had assembled at Newport to be convoyed. Despite the navy secretary's promises of outward-bound protection to all and sundry merchants, both Sever in the *Congress* and Preble in the *Essex* had no desire to tarry with the merchantmen very long. Sever told the merchant mariners that the frigates would stay with them "a few days," and Preble concurred that "the sooner we are clear of the merchant ships the better." Less than twenty-four hours after leaving Newport, the two navy captains jettisoned the slow-moving merchant vessels, Preble hailing the closest one to tell her master that the convoying had finished. The *Essex*'s sailing master, Rufus Low, noted in his journal that, on Sever's signal, "We bore away, the Commodore & Capt. Preble agreed to part with the two Ships & brig and proceed on our passage as they sail'd slow." In his report to Stoddert, Preble wrote that "The day after leaving Newport a snow storm came on, and we parted with the three merchant vessels," but the suggestion of cause and effect from the snow was pure subterfuge.[19]

Then the two-frigate force was reduced to one. After four or five cold days laced with snow and hail, the wind veered to the southward and brought a warm rain along with a heavy sea on the 11th. The rigging of the *Congress* went slack and Sever either could not or would not act quickly to take precautions. The masts of the *Congress* began to roll dangerously the next day, and the mainmast was sprung fifteen feet above the deck. To save the mast, Sever decided to chop down the main topmast, but while a lieutenant and five men climbed high to cut away the weight, the whole mainmast fell and, in domino effect, the mizzenmast fell seconds later. The *Congress* began to roll and pitch up and down in the heavy seas. The nightmarish scene continued as first the fore-topmast, then the bowsprit, and finally the foremast all gave way, leaving the once powerful frigate totally dismasted and wallowing at the mercy of the seas. Somehow, over the next few days, jury masts were lifted into place and rigged, and the *Congress* limped into Hampton Roads four weeks later.[20]

The *Essex* emerged from the same gale battered but essentially intact. The sudden warmth loosened the rigging that had been set up on the *Essex* in frigid Salem, just as it had loosened the *Congress*'s rigging, but Preble immediately recognized the danger. Preble ordered sails reefed or taken in and maneuvered the ship to reduce the wind's strain on the masts. As Preble recorded in his journal, "considering the bowsprit to be in danger, I bore away for a few minutes to take in the fore-topmast staysail to save the ship forward; at the same time hauled down the mizzen staysail, the wind blowing with great fury." The *Essex* lost contact with the *Congress* but Preble noted that "our rigging being so slack as to make it impossible to carry sail to keep up with her, without hazarding the loss of our masts." Despite the ship laboring in the large sea, Preble wore the *Essex* to run before the wind so that Preble could set up first the starboard, and then the larboard, lower rigging fore and aft. Cross seas crashed aboard, sending torrents of water down the hatchways; Lt. Richard Beale calmly observed the "decks [were] leaking in every part 6 inches." The *Essex* battled gales and "lofty seas" day after day. Although the *Essex* discovered her mainmast sprung on the 24th in yet another gale, the crew fished it securely; although the Salem-woven rigging was, in Preble's words, "infamously bad," the main shrouds and all the topmast stays having carried away in the repeated January storms, the *Essex*'s crew, led by their commander, met all the challenges.[21]

The *Essex*'s lookouts spotted land—Africa—on 9 March 1800. The *Essex* came to in Table Bay of Cape Town on 11 March in the midst of the British Navy's Indian Ocean squadron, under the stern of HMS *Adamant*, 50 guns, and on the port bow of HMS *Tremendous*, 74 guns. The British admiral, Sir Roger Curtis, as well as the governor of the Cape, Sir George Young, feted Preble and promised him dockyard services and supplies for the *Essex*. The American frigate stayed at her anchorage for seventeen days, filling water casks and taking on new stores. Preble fitted "a complete gang of new shrouds" and repaired or replaced shattered ironwork on the masts. In the whirl of visits between ships, the British captains openly gawked at the lines of the Hackett-designed frigate, and "all agreed in pronouncing her to be the most complete & beautiful Frigate they ever saw, and one of the Officers observ'd to the Capt. if you will build such handsome Frigates you must not think hard that so many Officers came on board to look at her." From the friendly British officers, Preble learned two important pieces of intelligence: that the only French frigate remaining in the Indian Ocean, *La Preneuse*, had been chased ashore and burned, meaning that the *Essex* faced no threat from an equal or superior enemy warship; and that French privateers had congregated around the Straits of Sunda, emboldened by an order of the governor of Île-de-France allowing all American property to be confiscated. The latter development, of course, merely corroborated what Secretary Stoddert in December had called the French government's "Privateering system—their regulations seem intended to cover the seas with strong privateers—It is not to be doubted, that they will know of the immense amount of American property bound to Batavia, nor that they will make efforts to intercept it particularly on its return." Preble was keen on hearing about the French privateers "to pick up some of them," and with the *Congress* not appearing at the Cape, Preble vowed "not [to] wait a moment for her, but make the best of my way" to Java. Stoddert, planning for such a contingency months before, had ordered either frigate to press on without the other.[22]

On 27 March 1800, the *Essex* beat out of Table Bay, her cannon salute of the Union Jack nobly answered by Admiral Curtis's flagship, the 64-gun *Lancaster*. The *Essex* sailed in company with the British sloop of war *Rattle Snake*. According to William Mumford, the *Essex*'s purser, "She got underway at the moment we did, for the express purpose of beating us, but to their great Mortification we ran her Hull down in about four Hours." Besides the occasional squall, the five-week cruise from Cape Town to Java was largely uneventful, allowing Preble to exercise his crew at the guns and, once again, to set up the rigging "below and aloft fore and aft." When the *Essex* arrived at the Straits of Sunda, she encountered two more British warships, the aptly named *Arrogant*, 74 guns, and the frigate *Orpheus*, 32 guns, which challenged the Salem frigate to what Purser Mumford called a "fair tryal" sailing. Mumford recounted that "we beat them above one half; we pass'd the *Arrogant* so close, that Capt. Osborne look[ed] at us out of his Quarter Gallery with a Degree of Astonishment & observed to Capt. Preble that she was the fastest sailing Vessel he ever met with." Lieutenant Beale heard Osborne hail that, since he had taken command, the *Essex* was the first ship to outsail him (if true, a remarkable comment by a captain of a ship of the line). Preble merely wrote that the *Essex* sailed "infinitely faster than either of them" and suggested that the *Essex* was America's fastest frigate.[23]

The *Essex* sighted Java on 4 May 1800. A landing party looking for fresh water was hastily recalled when a sail came in sight. After boarding a ship that flew Dutch colors, the American-built *Friends* of New York, Preble faced a legal quagmire. The *Friends* had been captured by a French privateer and duly libeled, condemned, and sold at Île-de-France. While her master was a Frenchman, she flew a neutral's flag and carried "Dutch" papers, although they were obviously irregular if not fraudulent. Preble decided to let her pass, motivated as much by the fact that she was in ballast (i.e., carried no cargo), and was too decayed to be worth much. The next day, the *Arrogant* and *Orpheus* "took" the same ship but, ultimately, they burned her.

As the *Essex* slowly sailed along the northern coast of Java towards Batavia, Preble still searched for water. On the 10th, he landed an officer to "procure refreshments" who "found the Natives" restless, "well Armed and inclined to be hostile," before he retreated to the safety of the frigate.[24] But there was discontent among the *Essex*'s crew, too, perhaps because of the hard, desultory voyage but more likely because of Preble's taste for flogging. An able seaman named William Ash spoke out against the oppressive discipline on board and called out to his mates to "rise" against the officers and "secure"—kill—them "as they did on board the *Hermione*," a reference to a British frigate on which the crew had hacked to pieces or tossed overboard the captain and loyal officers in September 1797 and sailed the ship into a Spanish port. Preble crushed the incipient mutiny, placing Ash in irons, hand and foot, where he stayed for months. But the Ash incident was not the first murmur of mutiny on the *Essex*. Five months earlier, another sailor had been shackled for "mutinous expressions" and threatening to set the frigate afire. Even after Preble's decisive handling of Ash, there was trouble aboard, a sense of unruliness and disquiet. On 17 July 1800, as the *Essex* was working her way back across the Indian Ocean, Capt. Joseph Sanford of the ship *Smallwood* returned to the *Essex* four sailors and a boy lent by Preble, calling them "troublesome," although

Lieutenant Beale characterized their conduct as "mutinous." While the boy was spared severe punishment, each of the sailors took a twelve-lash flogging and then was put in irons. But floggings were probably the cause, and certainly were not the cure, of the problems aboard the *Essex*. Christopher McKee, a historian, has concluded that Preble ordered the lash more often and more severely than most U.S. Navy captains. The Ash incident, with the suggestion of murdering Preble, manifested a lurking psychological demon—the rising of the men pushed by a rigid captain— that each serving officer feared. Preble may have been a fine seaman but he was a harsh, even brutal, disciplinarian.[25]

On 14 May 1800, the *Essex* arrived off Batavia. Her masthead spied a vast concourse of shipping at anchor in the roads. The *Essex* anchored the next day. After taking on provisions, Preble decided to retrace his route to cruise off the Straits of Sunda where any lurking privateers would likely be found. Before leaving Batavia, however, he wrote a letter to all the American shipmasters, tersely informing them that the *Essex* would sail for America on 10 June and would convoy "all the way home" any American ships ready to sail at that time. When the *Essex* sailed west in the face of vexing headwinds, the first sail her lookouts spotted was the merchant brig *Exchange,* a Salem ship. The master of the *Exchange* was Benjamin Webb, Jr., a stakeholder in the *Essex,* having subscribed $100 towards her construction, and the *Exchange* undoubtedly carried Salem friends and neighbors. The next day, farther west, the *Essex* encountered five more merchant vessels, all American—the ships *Fair American* and *Franklin* from Charleston, the brig *Lapwing* from New York, the brig *Lydia* from Boston, and the ship *Magin* from Philadelphia—and all bound to Batavia. On her two-week cruise, the *Essex* stopped thirteen American merchantmen overall, and the lesson was clear to Preble at least: all of the "richly loaded" ships "must have been captured had a single French Privateer of 16 guns been cruising in my stead." The convoy to Java may have been farcical but the need for a convoy on the return showed Stoddert's strategic insight. Preble found no privateers in the Straits. After watering the frigate, Preble turned the *Essex* back to Batavia where he arrived on 8 June. The American merchant vessels were not all ready to depart on the 10th. Trading and preparations for the homeward-bound voyage took another week or so but, at last, on 18 June 1800, the *Essex* unmoored and made sail with a dozen merchant vessels in company.[26]

The convoy was underway for less than two days when the crisis of the *Essex*'s cruise began to unfold. At 5 P.M. on 20 June 1800, a proa containing the captain, supercargo, and crew members from the ship *Alkno-mack* came alongside the *Essex*. The captain, Joel Vickers, came aboard and told Captain Preble that, off Java Head on 15 June, the *Alknomack* (then 135 days out from Baltimore) had spotted a strange sail and tried to flee. The suspicious stranger had chased and, loaded with armed men pre-pared to grapple and board, had caught the *Alknomack* at the entrance to the Straits, forcing Vickers to surrender. The stranger had turned out to be a large French privateer, the *Confiance,* mounting twenty cannon and commanded by a legendary privateer captain, Robert Surcouf. Sur-couf put a French prize crew aboard the *Alknomack* with orders to Île-de-France and a French admiralty court, and set Vickers and his people ashore at Anjer Point on the 18th, where the *Confiance* lay at anchor. Preble had a chance to bag the elusive Surcouf.[27]

Surcouf, only twenty-seven years old in 1800, came from one of France's historic privateering ports, St.-Malo. He first went to sea in a merchant brig at age thirteen and, in the last years of the ancien régime, served as a mate on traders and slavers. With the French Revolutionary wars and the British dominance at sea strangling French overseas trade, Surcouf turned to the one potentially profitable avenue remaining to shipmasters, privateering. Using the meager French dockyard facilities and the admi-ralty court at Île-de-France, Surcouf launched a series of solitary, brilliantly executed privateering expeditions across the breadth of the Indian Ocean. Surcouf was known for his chivalrous treatment of passengers cap-tured in the ships he seized—his gallantry towards women was particularly noteworthy—but also for the ferocity of his attacks on merchant ships that tried to resist. In late 1799 and early 1800 in the *Clarisse,* he made prizes of several English East Indiamen, as well as two American vessels, the *Louisa* and the *Mercury,* but the *Clarisse* then required an extensive refit. In April 1800, he sailed from Île-de-France in the *Confiance,* a beautiful, fast ship armed with 18 nine-pounders and 2 thirty-six-pounder cannon-ades, and crossed the Indian Ocean to the Straits of Sunda.[28]

Despite the looming presence of Surcouf, whom Preble described as "hovering about the Fleet," Preble at first seemed hesitant. At 8 A.M. on the 22nd, the *Essex* arrived at Anjer Roads with the convoy trailing behind. Nevertheless, Preble ordered the *Essex* to anchor and sent an offi-cer ashore "to procure refreshment." An hour later, the *Essex's* lookouts spotted a strange sail to the westward. Instead of giving chase immedi-ately, Preble first had to signal his officer to return. It was not until approximately 1 P.M., four hours after "the sail to the westward supposed to be the French privateer" was seen, that the *Essex* hove up her anchor and began to chase. Preble, ironically writing a Dutch official at Batavia that "I fear this French privateer will do much mischief if I do not catch her, but I am determined to have her" at the very moment when the *Essex*'s masthead hailed the quarterdeck that he had spotted the *Confiance*, lost precious time on the refreshment diversion. "Lose not an hour" was one of Nelson's adages, and the *Essex*'s pursuit of the *Confiance* bore him out. The wind, "light airs," dropped away to a calm, allowing the lighter *Confiance* to bring out sweeps and keep precious distance. Then the wind came back from virtually directly ahead. Able to sail closer to the wind, the *Confiance* gained ground on each tack. A little after six o'clock, Preble gave up with Surcouf nine miles off. The *Essex* bore up for the convoy at anchor at Anjer Roads lying unprotected.[29]

Surcouf had escaped but tried other tricks. The next day, the 23rd, a Dutch proa sailed suspiciously close to the convoy. Preble ordered her stopped. Under his cross-examination, the Dutch master admitted that Surcouf had paid him to reconnoiter the convoy and report back intelligence for the French privateer to determine how to attack. At 7 A.M. the next day, the *Essex*'s lookouts found a ship inshore under the Krakatoa volcano, creeping along towards the anchored American merchantmen. At noon, with a breeze coming up, the *Essex* weighed anchor and chased the intruder, the *Confiance*. Preble gave up pursuit at 5 P.M., although Lieutenant Beale put the time at 4:30 and the distance "so near as to see her waterline." The wind again was falling away to a calm and Preble again bore away to ensure the safety of the convoy. Greatly conflicted by his choice, Preble complained to the far-off navy secretary that "I had gained so much on her that nothing but falling calm and the assistance the Frenchman received from his numerous sweeps, saved him from capture; had there been only a moderate breeze I must have taken him." Surcouf had tried and failed again. He slipped away, and decided to ply British trading routes off Ceylon, where he captured several large East India Company ships. He amassed a huge fortune and was never caught.[30]

Despite alarms and the occasional pursuit of unknown sails, the *Essex* never came into contact with another French ship over the next five months and the ten thousand miles to New York. From the middle of the Indian Ocean on 6 August 1800, Preble wrote a lengthy report of the *Essex*'s activities since arriving in the East Indies, which he sent ahead with the brig *Lapwing*, whose master asked to leave the slow-moving convoy. Preble noted that the frigate's crew had been "remarkably healthy," but his statement was not really true, and tempted fate cruelly. Fletcher Pratt, an influential, popular historian whose rhetoric seldom was slowed by the facts, wrote that the *Essex*'s "crew [was] so healthy that he [Preble] returned with none dead and only nine men sick of the dreaded tropical fevers," in fact claiming that the healthiness of the *Essex*'s cruise was its most notable aspect.[31] Harold D. Langley, a methodical scholar, analyzing the *Essex*'s sick list and log, recognized that in the fetid summer climate of Java a dozen sailors were sick in June but concluded "The long voyage to the East Indies and back had cost only seven lives" of the three hundred on board.[32] In the leading scholarly narrative of the Quasi-War at sea, Michael Palmer also accepts Preble's suggestion that the cruise was "remarkably healthy," noting the "frigate's company [returned] in good health. Only 11 men had died out of a complement of 250 . . ."[33] In fact, according to Richard Beale, the first lieutenant, seven sailors died before Preble's letter, and seven more men died afterward, en route to America. Although Beale did not list the cause of death in most cases, three he did list—scurvy, dysentery, and a fever—all occurred after Preble's letter. At least one other sailor died whom Beale did not note. Given the fact that the *Essex* suffered no battle casualties and that no epidemic like yellow fever swept through the *Essex*'s crew, fifteen dead (at least 5 percent of the crew) hardly seems "remarkably healthy." The year-long cruise marked not only fifteen deaths but also a breakdown in the health of the captain; Edward Preble himself seems to have suffered from some disease, and he never fully recovered.[34]

The *Essex* began the homeward leg of the cruise on 1 July 1800, after four days at Mew Bay filling all the casks with fresh water, with fourteen merchant vessels under convoy. The return cruise was as much a test of Preble's patience and seamanship as the outward-bound voyage. For days at a stretch, the *Essex* took in tow the slowest vessel in the convoy, the brig *Delaware,* under Captain Dunphy, from Philadelphia. The *Essex,* as much in her element as a greyhound used for shepherding, continually made sail, then had to shorten sail, to let the sluggish convoy keep up. In the dead of night on 18 July, two of the faster merchant sailers surged ahead, and the *Essex* vainly tried to recall them by firing a blank charge. Only by firing a shot at the lead ship was Captain Preble able to dissuade them from sailing on. Every few days, Preble had to resort to firing cannon to maintain the convoy in a reasonably compact formation. On 26 July, Captain Webb of the *Exchange* requested medical help for all the sick men he had aboard, and Preble sent over a surgeon's mate with medicines, some seamen to help man the ship, and took the *Exchange* under tow; on the

28th, Preble gave bread over to the *Smallwood,* which had none left; on 31 July, Preble lent his carpenter and his mates to fix the damage when two of the merchantmen collided. The shipmasters of the faster vessels grew impatient at the sluggish pace. On 7 August 1800, Captain Clark of the *Lapwing* and Captain Stokeley of the *John Buckley* asked to leave the convoy, and Preble let them depart that afternoon. Two days later the captains of two of the Philadelphia ships, the *Dispatch* and the *Globe,* came aboard the *Essex* to deliver to Preble their signal books, for they too wished to make their way home independently. Ironically, all of the ships would be set loose almost immediately by a four-day gale with squalls and huge seas. Each ship battled the elements as best she could: the *Essex*'s main rigging went slack during torrential rain on 11 August; that evening the mainstaysail blew to shreds when the clew parted; by the night of the 13th, the sails and rigging were "failing in every part of the ship[,] the sails are bad and the rigging good for nothing[.] So ends third day dirty weather."[35]

The *Essex* rode out the storm and made essential repairs at sea. In case of separation, Preble's plans called for the convoy to reassemble at St. Helena in the South Atlantic. The *Essex* rounded the Cape and beat into St. Helena on 10 September. Slowly, the dispersed merchantmen reappeared—the *Globe* on the 11th; the *Juno* the next day; the *Nancy* and the *Lydia* on the 14th; and five more stragglers through the 25th, when the battered *Exchange* arrived. Two of the nine ships decided to sail on without the convoy; and Preble, always an impatient officer, decided to sail too. On 26 September, the *Essex* unmoored, gathered the seven merchant vessels that wished to continue in company, and the remnant started off. The balance of the cruise was uneventful. Two months later, on 28 November 1800, the *Essex* arrived at New York and anchored in the East River, her epic cruise to the East Indies completed.[36]

The *Essex*'s East Indies mission resulted in no ship-to-ship battles. Indeed, the *Essex* never fired her broadside at a French ship, and the one privateer she encountered proved maddeningly elusive. Because of the *Essex,* however, America's trade with Java returned home safely—a dozen ships laden with coffee, pepper, and spices arrived at Philadelphia, Boston, New York, and other ports. More importantly, the strategic sense of Stoddert was vindicated. Preble proved that American naval power could reach around the world; the U.S. Navy could operate in distant seas and protect American trade in far-flung parts of the globe. It was an important lesson, and one that the United States Navy has proved for two centuries. In one of his reports, Preble dwelt on the lack of a continuing naval presence off Java. It was "singularly unfortunate," Preble wrote, that after the *Essex* had cleared the Straits of Sunda of Surcouf and his privateering ilk, "now they can do as they please, as they have no force opposed to them." Preble predicted catastrophe for American trade and urged the "necessity of a constant protection of our trade in the Straits." Not surprisingly, Stoddert's ideas coincided exactly. Towards the end of the Quasi-War, the navy secretary ordered two warships, the *Connecticut* and the *Ganges,* to Batavia. The end of the naval war with France nullified Stoddert's plans, but not entirely. In the last days of President Adams's term, Congress enacted the Naval Peace Establishment Act, which created a thirteen-ship navy, of which six frigates were to be kept in active service. In the first week of the new administration, President Jefferson and his cabinet (including Stoddert as the caretaker navy secretary) considered where to deploy the naval force, contemplating "2 frigates to cruise in W. Indies, 2 in Miditerranean, 2 at Isle of Bourbon [Réunion]." These ambitious plans fell victim to an administration ill-disposed to naval force, but America's naval role on the other side of the world could not be sidetracked permanently.[37]

Before the war of 1812, various commanders of the *Essex* and Navy Yard commandants changed the frigate's masting and insisted on over-arming her, ruining the Salem frigate's vaunted speed. In the first months of the war, the Navy ordered a squadron consisting of the *Essex* under Capt. David Porter, the *Constitution,* and the sloop of war *Hornet* to the Indian Ocean to destroy British trade with the East Indies and India. Only the *Essex* rounded Cape Horn into the Pacific (becoming the first United States Navy ship to sail into the Pacific) where the American frigate decimated the British whaling fleet. For seven months, the 32-gun *Essex* controlled the eastern Pacific. After a year at sea, the *Essex* put into the Marquesas Islands for careening and repairs and her crew became involved with Polynesian native women and tribal warfare. Instead of sailing westward to the Straits of Sunda, the scene of her successful maiden cruise, the *Essex* returned to South American waters, where Porter tried to repeat the successful commerce-destroying mission of 1813. The *Essex* was trapped at Valparaíso, Chile, by a British force on the lookout for her. On 28 March 1814, Porter tried to break the blockade but the British frigate *Phoebe* and sloop of war *Cherub,* using their long guns, battered the *Essex* until Porter surrendered, with fifty-eight dead and thirty-one missing. It is hard to dispute the suggestion that had Porter stood for the East Indies, "there could have been no more catastrophic climax to the saga of the frigate *Essex*."[38]

Conclusion

Why the merchants of the various cities acted so vigorously to promote and subscribe to subscription ships is not readily apparent. Historian Howard Chapelle believes that the merchants subscribed as merchants, since as "the merchants who owned the ships were the chief sufferers from the seizures, . . . it seemed reasonable to Congress that they should make a special contribution."[1]

It is hard to credit Chapelle's statement. First, the merchants of Newburyport came up with the idea, not Congress, the sole role of which was to enact enabling legislation. More to the point, merchants were certainly the *immediate* sufferers from seizures, but since merchants insured their vessels and cargoes, the costs were passed along to consumers in the form of higher prices. As Representative Robert G. Harper observed to his South Carolina constituents,

> It has been said that . . . the saving in insurance, and captures, is a saving to the merchants alone; whereas the expence of a fleet is to be borne by the nation at large. But it is not true that the savings is to the merchants alone. To say it is to the consumers alone, would be much nearer the truth. The merchant will have his profits on his goods, whether they come high or low to him; and

this profit, together with the original price, the consumer must pay. If insurance rise[s] from seven per cent to fifteen per cent. the additional eight per cent. is laid on the price of the goods, and they come eight per cent higher to the consumer.[2]

Whether the merchants displayed virtue as subscribers, or were merely investors in government securities, is yet another issue: with a 6 percent return, it is not obvious that the merchant subscribers were making a "special contribution." The historian of the *Essex*, Philip Chadwick Foster Smith, has written that the subscribers *expected* to make a profit, that the subscriber "neither was nor was expected to be philanthropic."[3]

Yet the profit motive cannot be the real explanation. Albert Gallatin, a great opponent of military profiteering, commented that 6 percent stock certificates "would not sell for 20 s[hillings] in the pound" but the loss would be a "sacrifice to the public."[4] Navy Secretary Stoddert thought the subscribers faced "a certain loss" of 15 to 20 percent of the money advanced. The single contemporary dissenting view was that of the Philadelphia *Aurora*, which querulously observed, "The Massachusetts Mercury has taken with the usual effect a great deal of the *up-hill pains* to prove that—a *loan* at interest of *six per cent* is a *gift*, how are we loggerheads gifted."[5] While it is difficult to piece together to what extent subscribers of 6 percent stock were in fact investing at a loss, other, concurrent federal stock issues, such as the loan of 16 July 1798, provided an interest rate of 8 percent. Oliver Wolcott, the secretary of the treasury, took pains to assure President Adams that loans carrying an 8 percent interest rate did not reflect poorly on the credit of the nation or indicate a lack of patriotism. He noted perspicaciously that "When the subscriptions have been completed & the stock have found its natural level, we shall have a criteria for ascertaining the market rate of Interest in the United States. At that rate only, whatever it may be, will be just to expect future Loans. It is certain that the last loan [at eight percent] was not obtained on disadvantageous terms. . . ." If an 8 percent stock was favorable to the government, then the navy 6 percents were even more so; put another way, subscribers for the loan warships of 1798 probably lost a few cents for every dollar of stock.[6]

On the other hand, the merchants had great incentive to see that warships were built. Even with insurance, captures were so commonplace and the cost of insurance so high[7] that some vessels were just left in port. Thus, much of the merchants' capital was employed at no return, dismasted in a dozen harbors along the Atlantic coast. While merchants thus may have had little pecuniary interest in navy stock per se, their entire livelihood was dependent on the revival of trade. What they saw as the national interest—the creation of a navy—neatly coincided with their own.

If merchants as a class might have economic and patriotic motivations, certain individual merchants might try to "lie low," avoiding subscribing, realizing that other merchants would bear the loss from stock ownership while they all gained from a navy. What modern economists call the "freerider" problem was of great concern to subscription warship advocates. William Cobbett worried in *Porcupine's Gazette* that the Philadelphia frigate would be ascribed to merchants "in the lump, while, probably, very many of them will not subscribe a single sliver [sic]. It is not just that misers, drones, and democrats, should share in that praise."[8] In Charleston, "A CITIZEN" wrote to the *City Gazette* warning that with the money needed, "there will be found citizens, who under various pretexts shrink from the service, and in order, as they think, effectually to screen themselves from reproach, will even go so far as to oppose such measures with ingenuous argument."[9]

Undoubtedly there were merchants who did not subscribe, but there were social mechanisms that encouraged merchants to be stout patriots. For one thing, most merchants were Federalists. Secretary Stoddert recognized this and appealed to the politics of the merchants to fill out the authorization. In encouraging Providence to give a ship, Stoddert wrote, "most of the Towns distinguished for Federalism, and public Spirit, are making efforts to furnish the vessels still wanted."[10]

Moreover, merchants belonged to an intimate and close society. They belonged to business organizations like the New York or Philadelphia Chambers of Commerce, whose presidents, John Murray and Thomas FitzSimons, served on the subscription committees of their respective cities. They were linked to philanthropic and mutual insurance organizations like the Newburyport Marine Society, whose fifteen-year-president, William Coombs, also sat on that city's subscription committee. In Baltimore, there may have been shared ties among subscribers as militia commanders and members of the Society of Cincinnati.[11] Such an intricate web of social and civic ties must have made freeriders uncomfortably conspicuous.

While the intracity freerider problem may have been limited by social ties, it is not clear how the intercity "public goods" problem was overcome. Yet overcome it was: nine warships were subscribed to and built by eleven towns, although in theory each town had increasingly greater incentives to let the others or the federal government take care of the problem of naval protection. Of course, it may be true that *other* towns did not undertake a subscription ship because of the public goods problem. Perhaps New Haven or New London, Newport or Savannah, were so disinclined. Yet the greater fact is that Newburyport, leading off the movement, was not so affected, nor were towns like Charleston, which acted months later, after other towns and the United States itself had begun more warships.

Perhaps part of the answer to the public goods problem is parochialism: that each subscribing city believed its ship would guard its own harbor. It is true that New York merchants thought the *New York* "may guard our port from insult or danger, and occasionally brush away from our coasts those numerous pirates that every where infest them"[12] and that Charleston subscribers were well aware of their exposed position.[13] In fact, even after the ships had been presented to the navy, the local promoters retained influence: the Boston merchants advised the captain of the *Boston* where to sail to intercept French privateers, a direction that the secretary of the navy supported.[14]

Yet such answers go only so far. When Noah Webster wrote that the subscription ships would be "managed with the energy of hardy FREEMEN, who know the motives of their duty, and who possess a spirit unaccustomed to being cowed or conquered,"[15] he was not merely puffing patriotic. Instead, he was trying to strike a responsive chord with men who shared the rhetoric and memories of the Revolution. Many had fought in line regiments or in privateers and shared the prevailing mythos of the militia defending the hearth and homestead. The young men of 1776 and 1777 were, in 1798, the civic and mercantile leaders of the United States. In the Revolution, they came to their country's defense with their local officers, without a central government that could feed or support them. Twenty years later these men would not be slow to loan their money, even without central direction. They were not passive citizens in a large, established world power; they were active participants in a new, small republic that they had helped create. They thought that their formative experience in war and at the creation of the Union gave them responsibility and standing to act for their republic. In such a spirit, Newburyport began its subscription for the *Merrimack*. In effect, those merchants rang the tocsin for other cities in the same electric way that militia called out at Lexington and Concord in 1775 caused young men hundreds of miles away to assemble on village greens. In 1798, the merchants of Newburyport believed that their example would be followed, that other cities would see a duty to respond to even distant threats, and that the actions of private citizens might be an important, even decisive, influence on American naval and foreign policy.

They were right. In proposing an enabling act, the merchants of Newburyport had pointed to the treasury's financial straits and to the savings of time and money as the advantages of privately subscribed, privately built ships. All told, $711,700 of navy stock was issued[16] in a year when the total expenditure of the United States government was $7,607,000.[17] The subscription warships played a large role in the Quasi-War, convoying merchant ships, suppressing the French privateer menace, and occasionally fighting French ships.

One of the few Federalist criticisms of building warships by popular subscription was made by William Vans Murray, the United States minister to the Batavian Republic. Murray, a thoughtful, amusing man who had served in the Maryland legislature and three terms in the House of Representatives, was a firm friend of John Quincy Adams. On 17 August 1798, he wrote his fellow diplomat that he had only "scraps" of news from the United States but had heard that Baltimore in June had subscribed $90,000 to build warships. Murray footnoted his own letter that "I do not admire this mode of attempting to support government, unless in desparate cases and rebellion." While Murray did not explain himself, he presumably took the same tack as the president himself, who, a year earlier, told the House: "The consequences arising from the continual accumulation of public debts in other countries ought to admonish us to be careful to prevent their growth in our own. The national defence must be provided for, as well as the support of government; but both should be accomplished as much as possible by immediate taxes, and as little as possible by loans."[18]

Whether the subscription warships saved time and money is a more difficult question. One prominent historian suggests that they did not. According to Howard Chapelle, the "only drawback" to the subscription warships was delay, since "it required much time to raise funds for such a purpose in a community and to get the ships started. As a result, the frigates built by those ports financially able to handle such construction were slow in being completed. . . ."[19] This statement is certainly too sweeping. In every city except Salem, funds were raised in a matter of days or weeks. Boston, where the subscription was filled in July, launched the

Boston in ten months. Philadelphia, which raised $100,000 in June, launched the *Philadelphia* twenty-two months later. Although generalizations are problematic when only five frigates are involved, it seems that it was not how long it took to raise money, but rather the size of the ship and the local labor situation that determined how long it would take to build a ship. The *Philadelphia,* at 1,240 tons, and *New York,* at 1,130 tons, took much more time than the 700-ton *Boston,* the 850-ton *Essex,* or the 550-ton *John Adams.*[20] Furthermore, in New York, within days of laying down the keel of the subscription frigate *New York,* the keel of the 44-gun frigate *President* was laid down; the two keel layings were announced the same day, and another frigate was ordered later.[21] It is not surprising then that with a 600-ton merchant vessel also under construction, New York was said to have been drained of its ship carpenters.[22]

Cost and speed of construction can only be measured comparatively, yet it is impossible to compare without a basis. The frigates of 1794 took years to complete and ran over cost because of political backing-and-filling and supply problems. Government-built frigates in the wartime conditions of 1798 to 1799 competed with subscription frigates for workmen and materials, and cannot be isolated from them for comparison. No other American frigates were built until the United States had entered the War of 1812. To compare the speed and cost of construction of the subscription sloops of war with government-built ships is similarly difficult, since the vessels were built in different cities under different conditions to different designs.[23]

Almost all subscription warships passed into oblivion after 1800, although subscription ships made up a significant part of the American navy. The end of the naval war with France and the impending inauguration of Jefferson as president convinced the Federalists in Congress to preempt inevitable navy cuts by paring down the fleet to its best ships. The Naval Peace Establishment Act of 1801 retained thirteen frigates in the United States Navy, of which five—the *Boston, Essex, John Adams, New York,* and *Philadelphia*—were built by subscription. But almost all the subscription frigates were squandered.

The idea of privately subscribed warships fell prey to a new administration that abhorred public debt, disdained the merchants, and disliked the navy. When Jefferson became president in March 1801, the political and economic philosophy of government changed dramatically. As one economic historian notes, the "principal financial aim" of Jefferson and his secretary of the treasury, Gallatin, was "to eradicate an $82,000,000 debt which the Republicans regarded as an inherited 'moral canker' hanging on to the body politic of the young republic." By the middle of 1808, as Jefferson's second term was drawing to a close, 99 percent of the $711,700 of "Navy Six Per Cent Stock" had been redeemed. Thinkers like Jefferson put stock in commercial retaliation and public censure, not in naval force. President Jefferson initiated a gunboat navy, which cost less to maintain than the frigates, and which theoretically might protect American ports, but could not by its very nature defend merchant shipping. Gallatin, who thought a navy merely a perpetual bill of repairs, and not worth its costs, might have pushed for private subscriptions to help maintain the frigates. Such a scheme would have internalized the costs of protection on the merchants, who, in Republican eyes, solely benefited from a high-seas navy. Yet it would have meant carrying the public debt forward. No such idea was ever broached. Given the sale of the smaller subscription warships and the patent wasting of others, it would have been difficult anyway for Jefferson or Madison to turn to subscribers for warships. It is not surprising, then, that with the coming of the War of 1812, which disrupted the trade the war ostensibly was to protect, there was no rush by the merchants to subscribe to build warships. [24]

Nevertheless, subscription financing had provided ten warships to a new navy. To a joint session of Congress on 22 November 1800, President Adams spoke of the navy as a whole, but his comments are a fitting epitaph for the subscription ships: "called suddenly into existence by a great national exigency, [they have] raised us in our own esteem."[25] The way activist, public-spirited citizens thought to build warships, funded them, constructed them—created national policy by their own initiative—is revealing of an earlier America, and conversely shows the changing functions and expectations of government. The subscription warships have disappeared, and the merchants who built them are long forgotten. But when millions for defense were needed, those Americans were not found lacking.

Appendix
The Subscribers

An exact list of the people who subscribed for the "Navy Six Per Cent Stock" of 1798 probably cannot be reconstructed. But the subscribers are not completely lost to history. Apparently complete lists of subscribers exist for the *Boston* from Boston;[1] for the *Philadelphia* from Philadelphia;[2] for the *Richmond* from Richmond, Manchester, Petersburg, and Norfolk;[3] and for the *Essex* from Salem.[4] A fragment of the Baltimore list also exists.[5] Ultimately, the Federal government issued $711,700 in Navy Six Per Cent Stock, redeemable at the will of Congress, with interest paid quarterly.[6] Of that sum, John Brown of Providence, Rhode Island, received $30,000 in part payment for his ship, the *George Washington,* which the navy converted into a warship. Leaving that $30,000 aside, the United States issued $681,700 to citizen-subscribers throughout the nation. The following four lists total $345,192.90, accounting for about half of the total subscription, and suggest that well over one thousand Americans bought stock to loan warships to the United States Navy.

Subscribers to the *Boston*

"Subscribers to the fund for building the Frigate *Boston* for the United States Government in July 1798."

1.	Wm. Phillips	$10,000	37.	Head & Amory	1,000
2.	David Sears	3,000	38.	Benjamin Green	1,000
3.	Stephen Higginson	3,000	39.	Peter C. Brooks	1,000
4.	Eben Parsons	3,000	40.	David Greene	1,000
5.	John Codman	3,000	41.	Bradley & Fletcher	1,000
6.	J.Coolidge & Son	3,000	42.	James Scott	1,000
7.	Saml. Parkman	4,000	43.	Edward Tuckerman	1,000
8.	Theodore Lyman	3,000	44.	Boott & Pratt	3,000
9.	Jeffrey & Russell	2,000	45.	Danl. Dennison Rogers	1,000
10.	Mingo Mackay	1,000	46.	John Parker	2,000
11.	Wm. Parsons	2,000	47.	Charles Miller	1,000
12.	Wm. Smith	1,000	48.	Saml. Torrey	1,000
13.	Dr. John Warren	1,000	49.	Tuthill Hubbart	1,000
14.	Cornelius Durant	1,000	50.	Thomas & George Paine	1,000
15.	Jeremiah Alten	1,000	51.	Ebenezer Preble	1,000
16.	Jonathan Mason	1,000	52.	Benjamin Bussey	1,000
17.	Benjamin Joy	2,000	53.	Samuel Smith	1,000
18.	James & T. H. Perkins	3,000	54.	Rufus G. Amory	1,000
19.	Thomas Duckett, Jr.	3,000	55.	John Amory, Jr.	1,000
20.	Daniel Sargent, Jr.	1,000	56.	M. Hays	1,000
21.	Saml. G. Perkins	1,500	57.	John C. Jones	1,000
22.	Thomas G. Amory	1,500	58.	Henry Jackson	2,000
23.	Col. Marston Watson	1,000	59.	Benjamin Clarke	1,000
24.	John Lowell, Jr.	1,000	60.	Abiel Smith	2,000
25.	Nathan Frazier	2,000	61.	John Derby	1,000
26.	Stephen Higginson, Jr.	2,000	62.	John Gore	1,000
27.	Frederick Wm. Greyer, Jr.	1,500	63.	Dr. William Spooner	1,000
28.	William Stackpole	1,000	64.	Jones & Bass	1,000
29.	Gorham Parsons	1,000	65.	Elisha Sigourney & Sons	1,000
30.	John McLean	1,000	66.	John Gray	1,000
31.	Samuel Elliot	4,000	67.	Benjamin Cobb	1,000
32.	Arnold Welles	2,000	68.	William Powell	1,000
33.	James & Stephen Salisbury	3,000	69.	Gregory & Prichard	1,000
34.	Simon Elliot	1,000	70.	John Wells	1,000
35.	Stephen Gorham	1,000	71.	Edward Edes	1,000
36.	Thomas Walley	2,000	72.	Timothy Newell	1,000

73.	Brewer & Carter	1,000
74.	St. Andrews Lodge	1,000
75.	Nathaniel C. Lee	500
76.	Isaac P. Davis	500
77.	Timothy Williams	500
78.	Josiah Knapp	500
79.	Samuel P. Gardner	500
80.	Charles Sigourney	500
81.	Stephen Codman	500
82.	John Davis	500
83.	Benjamin Cobb, Jr.	500
84.	Thomas Dennie	500
85.	Joshua Davis, Jr.	500
86.	Benjamin Goddard	500
87.	Nathaniel Goddard	500
88.	Silvanius Gray	500
89.	Thomas Davis	750
90.	Arnold Welles, Jr.	750

91.	Thomas English	500
92.	Perrin May	500
93.	Nehemiah Parsons	500
94.	Dr. Isaac Rand	500
95.	Benjamin Sumner	400
96.	Edward Blake, Jr.	500
97.	Josiah Quincy	500
98.	Henry Hill	500
99.	Edward Davis & Son	500
100.	Thomas Bartlett	500
101.	Aaron Dexter	500
102.	John Hoffman	1,000
103.	Thomas Amory	1,000

Totals

Number of subscribers: 103

Gross amount of subscription: $136,300.00

Average subscribed: $1,323.30

Subscribers to the *Philadelphia*

"An Alphabetical list of Subscribers to the building and equipping of a Frigate to be loaned to the United States."

1.	Joseph & Josiah H. Anthony	$2,000
2.	John Ashley	1,000
3.	Thomas Allibone	1,000
4.	Thos. W. Armat	600
5.	Thomas Armat	200
6.	Edward Bird	500
7.	John Bleakly	500
8.	Thomas Brinton	200
9.	Charles Biddle	500
10.	Peter Blight	2,000
11.	Clement Biddle	200
12.	John Brown	200
13.	Joseph Brown	200
14.	Wm. & Abiah Brown	500
15.	Bethell & Cooper	600

16.	B. & J. Bohlen	500
17.	Jno. R. Brown	150
18.	Paul Beck, Jr.	500
19.	William Bingham	5,000
20.	Jacob Baker	500
21.	Benjamin Chew	500
22.	Thomas Cumpston	300
23.	Lewis Clapier	1,000
24.	Conyngham Nesbitt & Co.	1,000
25.	J. Cazenove	1,000
26.	James Crawford	1,000
27.	John Craig	500
28.	William Crammond	1,000
29.	Collins Wilkinson & Co.	1,000
30.	Thomas Cuthbert	500
31.	Joseph Clark	200

32.	Jacob Clark	100
33.	John Connelly	200
34.	Lewis Crousillet	400
35.	Thomas Clifford	300
36.	James S. Cox	200
37.	Thomas Dobson	50
38.	John Davis & Co.	300
39.	William Davy	500
40.	Andrew Douglass	500
41.	John Duffield	200
42.	George Davis	200
43.	Thomas Ewing	500
44.	George Emlin	500
45.	George Fox	500
46.	James C. Fisher	500
47.	Samuel M. Fox	1,000
48.	Kieren Fitzpatrick	500
49.	Thomas FitzSimons	—
50.	Thomas Greves	200
51.	John Guest	150
52.	Samuel Gatliff	500
53.	Gurney & Smith	1,000
54.	Samuel Howell	1,000
55.	Jos. Higbee	500
56.	Holmes & Rainey	500
57.	Isaac Hazlehurst & Son	1,000
58.	A. & G. Humphreys	1,000
59.	Robt. Henderson	500
60.	Jno. H. Huston	500
61.	Levi Hollingsworth & Son	200
62.	Henry Hutchins	100
63.	Wilson Hunt	200
64.	Parson Hunt	200
65.	Harvey & Davis	800
66.	Henry & Boggs	500
67.	Samuel Hays	400
68.	Jared Ingersoll	200
69.	Francis Ingraham	1,000
70.	Jones & Clarke	500
71.	Leonard Jacoby	200

72.	Charles & Wm. Jolly	100
73.	Stephen Kingston	500
	Thos. & Jno. Ketland	1,000[7]
74.	Knox & Henderson	500
75.	Frederick Kuhl	200
76.	Jacob S. Koch	1,000
77.	Wm. & Saml. Keith	600
78.	Willm. Knox & Co.	500
79.	Peter Kuhn	200
80.	Daniel King	200
81.	Sampson Levy	250
82.	John Leamy	1,000
83.	Geo. Latimer	500
84.	Mordecai Lewis	1,000
85.	James Lyle	500
86.	John Lisle	200
87.	Moses Levy	500
88.	Ludlam & Cousland	200
	Jno. Maybin	
	[rec'd with Jos. Anthony]	—
89.	Thos. McEwen & Co.	1,000
90.	Ben. R. Morgan	250
91.	Jasper Moylan	500
92.	James Milnor	100
93.	James & Wm. Miller	500
94.	Murgatroy & Sons	750
95.	John Miller, Jr.	500
96.	Montgomery & Newbold	500
97.	Arch. McCall	1,500
98.	Richard Milne	300
99.	Alex. J. Miller	100
100.	Jacob Morgan	500
101.	Morgan & Price	200
102.	M. H. Meschert	1,000
103.	Saml. Mecker	200
104.	John McCauley	100
105.	James McCrea	500
106.	Alex. Murray	300
107.	Thos. L. Moore	500
108.	Nicklin & Griffiths	1,000

109.	Notnagel & Co.	800	147.	Wm. Smith, Jr.	100
110.	John Nixon & Co.	1,000	148.	Jacob Sperry	200
111.	William Naylor	500	149.	Lawrence Seckle	200
112.	Peter Nairac	500	150.	John Savage	500
113.	James Oldden	500	151.	L. R. Tarrascon	300
114.	Petit & Bayard	500	152.	Jno. Travis	1,000
115.	Pragers & Co.	1,000	153.	Willm. Tilghman	500
116.	Geo. Plumsted	500	154.	Andrew Tybout	100
117.	Pratt & Kentsin	1,000	155.	Edw. Tilghman	1,000
118.	John Perott	800	156.	Henry Toland	300
119.	Samuel Price	200	157.	Danl. & Vincent Thuun	600
120.	William Poyntell	500	158.	John Taggert	200
121.	John Read, Jr.	200	159.	A. Vanbueren	500
122.	William Rawle	500	160.	Ambrose Vasse	1,500
123.	Michael Roberts	150	161.	Robt. Wharton	200
124.	John Ross	1,000	162.	Walker & Kennedy	500
125.	Mathew Randall	400	163.	Willm. Wright	200
126.	Wm. Read & Co.	500	164.	J. Wilson	200
127.	Ross & Simpson	800	165.	Saml. Wilcox	200
128.	Robt. Ralston	500	166.	Robt. Waln	1,000
129.	Richd. Rundle	1,000	167.	Simon Walker	1,000
130.	James Read	200	168.	Kearney Wharton	500
131.	Jacob Ridgway	200	169.	Willing & Francis	3,000
132.	Rundle & Leech	500	170.	J. G. Wachsmuth	2,000
133.	C. Rousset	300	171.	Jno. Waddington	500
134.	Edw. Shippen	500	172.	Rich. H. Wilcox	500
135.	Paul Siemen	1,000	173.	Wharton & Lewis	1,000
136.	James Strawbridge	500	174.	James Yard	1,000
137.	Robt. Smith & Co.	500		[additional names listed at end]	
138.	Joseph Sims	1,000	175.	Waddington & Harwood	800
139.	Summerl & Brown	500	176.	Snowden & North	400
140.	Jno. W. Swift	200	177.	Peter Brown	172.90
141.	Andrew Summers	500			
142.	Jno. & A. Singer	100			
143.	Jos. Swift	300			
144.	Jno. M. Souiller	500			
145.	Jno. Stille, Jr.	200			
146.	John Stille	200			

Totals

Number of subscribers: 177

Total subscription (per list):
$101,422.90[8]

Average subscribed (not including
FitzSimons's unknown): $576.27

Subscribers to the *Richmond*

1.	John Marshall	$500	39.	James McClurg	100
2.	John Harvie	200	40.	Joseph Marx	100
3.	William Heth	400	41.	Asher Marx	100
4.	John Hopkins	400	42.	William Radford	100
5.	Lewis Burwell	100	43.	James Henderson	100
6.	Bushrod Washington	200	44.	James Thompson	100
7.	Ebenezer MacNair	200	45.	James Currie	100
8.	Edward Carrington	200	46.	Robert Pollock	100
9.	John Brown	200	47.	Samuel Dyer	100
10.	John Wickham	200	48.	Charles Johnston	100
11.	Marcus Elcan	100	49.	Robert Rieves	100
12.	George Gray	200	50.	Samuel Calland	100
13.	William Wiseham	100	51.	William Marshall	100
14.	Alexander Brydie	500	52.	Andrew Leiper	100
15.	John Banks	500	53.	Adam Craig	100
16.	James Govan	500	54.	William Fenwick	100
17.	Thos. Gilliat	500	55.	George Yville & Co.	100
18.	George Pickett	500	56.	James Lyle	100
19.	James Brown	500	57.	James Lyle, Jr.	100
20.	Joseph Gallego	400	58.	Campbell & Wheeler	500
21.	Robert Gamble	500	59.	Robt & Walter Colquhoun	500
22.	Charles Copland	200	60.	Robert Moore	500
23.	Daniel Call	100	61.	Watson & E. Stott	500
24.	James Innes	100	62.	George Keith Taylor	100
25.	Macmurdo Fisher	400	63.	William Douglass	300
26.	William Berkeley	200	64.	William Haxhall	500
27.	Mitchell Gairdner	400	65.	Freeland & Gillies	500
28.	John Hook	300	66.	Robert Bolling	500
29.	William Austin	100	67.	Thomas Dent	500
30.	William Temple	100	68.	Donald McKenzie	300
31.	Robert Means	100	69.	John & Wm. Bell	300
32.	Samuel Myers	200	70.	William Sharp	300
33.	Thomas Hooper	100	71.	Buchanan Dunlop & Co.	500
34.	Augustine Davis	100	72.	Colquhuon Gatewood & Co.	500
35.	John Warden	100	73.	Gracie Anderson & Co.	500
36.	John Cringan	100	74.	Holliday & Stokes	500
37.	William MacKenzie	100	75.	John Grammer	200
38.	James Heron	100	76.	John Morrison	200

77. John McRae	200
78. John Osborne	500
79. Joseph Harding	100
80. Nathaniel Harris	200
81. John & Alex. Brown	200
82. John Grayson	500
83. James & Wm. Cummings	200
84. James Young	100
85. John Cowper & Co.	1,000
86. Gilbert Robertson	500
87. Warren Ashley	300
88. Macgill & Taylor	100
89. James Caton	100
90. James Dowdall	100
91. Phenias Dana	100
92. Lewis C. Durant & Co.	100
93. Otway Byrd	200
94. Alexander Cowan	100
95. John Lawrence	400
96. Francis Smith	100
97. Thomas Newton	1,000
98. Rose Owens	200
99. Thomas Willock	500
100. Richard Blow	100
101. Moses Myers	500
102. Byrd Beverley	100
103. Robert Farmer	200
104. Herman Redman	100
105. Giliat & Taylor	100
106. James Donaldson	100
107. Andrew Leckie & Co.	100
108. James Douglas	100
109. John Bramble	100
110. William Plume	500
111. John Brown	100
112. Randolph & Armstead	100
113. Campbell & Wheeler	200
114. Alexander Wilson	200
115. William Johnston	100
116. Harrison Allmond	100
117. John Nevison	200
118. Hugh McPhearson	100
119. William Dick	100
120. William Pennock	500
121. James Tucker	200
122. Conway Whittle	300
123. William Thompson	100
124. James Herron	100
125. George Loyall	100
126. Robert Taylor	100
127. Robert Gibson	100
128. William Cuthbert	100
129. James Taylor, Sr.	200
130. John Stratton	100
131. Will. & C. Rainock	100
132. Herman & Burke	100
133. John Kearns	100
134. James Boyce	200
135. Lattimore Holstead	100
136. Alexander Buchanan	800
137. Thomas Rutherford	300
138. William Galt	200
139. Robert Gordon & Co.	100
140. Charles Carter	800
141. Christopher Fry	100
142. Cary H. Hansford	100
143. Alexander Banks	100
144. Thomas Banks	100
145. George Pegram	100
146. William Moore	100
147. Thomas Gordon	100
148. Daniel Dodson	100
149. John W. Johnston	100
150. Holloway & Birchell	100
151. Edward Jeffers	100
152. William Galt	100
153. John McLeod	100
154. Cornelius Buck	100

155. Andrew Nicholson	100	
156. Edmonia Randolph	100	
157. Lucy Randolph	100	
158. Miles Bott	100	
159. William Randolph	200	
160. James Strange	100	
161. John Blair	100	
162. Robert Grenhow	300	

163. William Haxhall	100
164. Alexander Buchanan	100

Totals
Number of subscribers: 164
Gross amount of subscription: $32,300.00
Average subscribed: $195.76

Subscribers to the *Essex*

1.	Edward Allen, Jr.	1763–1845	Shipmaster	$500
2.	William Appleton	1764–1822	Cabinetmaker	50
3.	Samuel Archer	1768–1813	Hardware merchant	100
4.	Jacob Ashton	1744–1829	Merchant	1,000
5.	Thomas Bancroft	1766–1808	Clerk of the courts	100
6.	John Barr	1758–1832	Merchant	600
7.	Walter Price Bartlett	1743–1824	Auctioneer	100
8.	Nathaniel Batchelder	?–1810	Dry goods shopkeeper	50
9.	John Beckett	1746–1804	Boatbuilder-sparmaker	100
10.	Ebenezer Beckford	1737–1816	Merchant	2,000
11.	Enos Briggs	1746–1819	Shipbuilder	50
12.	Samuel Brooks	1758–1805	Dry goods merchant	50
13.	[Samuel] Buffum	1744–1818		
	& [John] Howard	1755–1848	Sailmakers	550
14.	Joseph Cabot	1770–1799	Merchant	500
15.	Benjamin Carpenter	1751–1823	Merchant	500
16.	Thomas Chipman	1756–1821	Shipmaster	100
17.	Clifford Crowninshield	1762–1809	Shipmaster-merchant	500
18.	Thomas C. Cushing	1764–1824	Editor, Salem *Gazette*	50
19.	John Daland	1768–1842	Mariner-storekeeper	100
20.	Elias Hasket Derby	1739–1799	Merchant	10,000
21.	Elias Hasket Derby, Jr.	1766–1826	Shipmaster	300
22.	Ezekiel Hersey Derby	1772–1852	Merchant	1,000
23.	John Derby	1741–1812	Merchant	1,000
24.	Richard Derby, Jr.	1765–1832	Shipmaster	1,500
25.	George Dodge	1750–1821	Merchant	1,000
26.	Israel Dodge	1740–1822	Merchant & distiller	500
27.	Ephraim Emmerton	1748–1824	Merchant	100
28.	Benjamin Felt	1770–1854	Pump & blockmaker	100
29.	Edmund Gale	1751–1831	Grog & victualling shopkeeper	10

30. Benjamin Goodhue	1748–1814	U.S. Senator	800
31. James Gould	1736–1810	Gun carriage maker	50
32. Samuel Gray	1760–1816	Merchant	2,000
33. William Gray, Jr.	1750–1825	Merchant	10,000
34. John Hathorne	1748–1834	Dry goods shopkeeper	200
35. Joseph Hiller	1748–1814	Collector of the Port	300
36. Benjamin Hodges	1754–1806	Merchant	500
37. Edward Augustus Holyoke	1728–1829	Physician	800
38. Daniel Jenks	1756–1834	Dry goods shopkeeper	500
39. John Jenks	1751–1817	Dry goods shopkeeper	1,550
40. Asa Killam	1752–1813	Lumber dealer	—
($20 transferred to Joseph Waters)			
41. Edward Killin	?	Shopkeeper	100
42. James King	1752–1831	Cashier, Essex Bank	500
43. Jonathan Lambert	1742–1804	Shipmaster	40
44. Peter Lander	1743–1834	Shipmaster-merchant	200
45. Lane & Son		Sailmakers	(In work)
46. Edward Symmes Lang	1775–1833	Apothecary	100
47. Abel Lawrence	1754–1822	Distiller	500
48. William Luscomb	1774–1820	House & ship painter	300
49. Samuel Daniels McIntire	1741–?	Carpenter	100
50. Richard Manning	1731–1811	Capitalist	1,000
51. Richard Manning, Jr.	1754–1813	Blacksmith-stablekeeper	200
52. William Marston	1751–1818	West India goods merchant	250
53. Jonathan Mason	1757–1808	Merchant	50
54. John Morong	?	Trader	50
55. Joseph Mosely	1760–1799	Shipmaster	100
56. John Murphy	1753?–1800?	Shipmaster	500
57. Jonathan Neal	1759–1837	Shipmaster	2,000
58. Joseph Newhall	1768–1827	Tinsmith	100
59. Ichabod Nichols	1749–1839	Merchant	1,000
60. John Norris	1751–1808	Merchant-distiller	5,000
61. William Orne	1751/2–1815	Merchant	5,000
62. Henry Osborn	1766–1820	Storekeeper	50
63. Isaac Osgood	?	Gentleman	500
64. John Osgood	1757–1826	Merchant	1,000
65. Joseph Osgood, Jr.	1772–1806	Shipmaster	—
($25 transferred to Joseph Waters)			
66. Page & Ropes		Ship chandlers	100
67. David Patten	1767–1805	Shipmaster	50

68. Joseph Peabody	1757–1844	Merchant	1,500
69. Asa Peirce	1761–1827	Tailor	50
70. Nathan Peirce	1749–1812	Merchant	250
71. Thomas Perkins	1758–1830	Merchant	500
72. Stephen Phillips	1766–1838	Shipmaster-merchant	1,000
73. John Pickering	1740–1811	Registrar of deeds	200
74. Benjamin Pickman	1740–1819	Merchant, town treasurer	1,650
75. Benjamin Pickman, Jr.	1763–1843	Merchant	1,500
76. William Prescott	1762–1844	Lawyer	1,000
77. Joshua Richardson	1750–1826	Merchant	500
78. Samuel Ropes, Jr.	1757–1841	Trader	50
79. Brackley Rose	1767–1823	Sugar baker	100
80. Thomas Sanders	1759?–1844?	Merchant	500
81. Elijah Sanderson	1751–1825	Cabinetmaker	100
82. Jacob Sanderson	1758–1810	Cabinetmaker	100
83. Moses Townsend	1760–1842	Shipmaster	100
84. John Treadwell	1738–1811	Shop owner	500
85. Edmund Upton	1769–1814	Shipmaster	300
86. Upton & Porter		Merchants	400
87. Samuel Very	1757?–1824?	Baker-merchant	100
88. Joseph Vincent	1735–1832	Ropemaker	200
89. [Aaron] Wait	1742–1830		
& [Jerathmiel] Peirce	1746/7–1827	Merchants	2,000
90. Jonathan Waldo	1754–1815	Trader-merchant	40
91. Joshua Ward	1752–1825	Merchant-distiller	750
92. William Ward	1761–1827	Shipmaster	500
93. Joseph Waters	1756–1833	Merchant	460
94. Benjamin Webb, Jr.	1759–1827	Shipmaster	100
95. Michael Webb	1762–1839	Grocer-merchant	—
($100 transferred to Stephen Webb)			
96. Stephen Webb	1756–1831	Shipmaster	600
97. Thomas Webb	1756–1825	Shipmaster	200
98. Timothy Wellman, Jr.	1768–1834	Shipmaster	100
99. Benjamin West, Jr.	1768–1825	Shipmaster	250
100. Nathaniel West	1756–1851	Merchant	1,500
101. Isaac Williams		Apothecary	50
(name in receipts only)			

Totals

Number of subscribers: 101

Gross amount of subscription: $75,150.00

Average subscribed: $744.06

$\mathcal{N}otes$

Introduction
1. Cited in Elting E. Morison, *From Know-How to Nowhere: The Development of Technology* (New York: New American Library, 1977 [orig. pub. 1974]), 139–40.

Chapter 1. On the Verge of War
1. Stanley Elkins and Eric McKitrick, *The Age of Federalism: The Early American Republic, 1788–1800* (New York: Oxford University Press, 1993), portrays this period masterfully. How the government initially was manned and administered is the subject of Leonard D. White, *The Federalists: A Study in Administrative History* (New York: Macmillan Co., 1967 [orig. pub. 1948]).
2. Portrayals of Hamilton are in Elkins and McKitrick, *Age of Federalism*, 94–114, and Forrest McDonald, *Alexander Hamilton: A Biography* (New York: W. W. Norton, 1979). Hamilton's financial program is dealt with in Elkins and McKitrick, *Age of Federalism*, 114–23, and McDonald, *Hamilton*, 143–88.
3. Douglass C. North, *The Economic Growth of the United States 1790–1860* (New York: W. W. Norton & Co., 1966 [orig. pub. 1961]), 46–53. Surprisingly, there is scant literature about the merchants as a socio-economic group. See Thomas C. Cochran, *Frontiers of Change: Early Industrialism in America* (New York: Oxford University Press, 1981), 20; Samuel Eliot Morison, *The Maritime History of Massachusetts 1783–1860* (Boston: Houghton Mifflin Co., 1941 [orig. pub. 1921]), 119–33.

4. Morison, *Maritime History*, 122–23, 125–29; Alexander Hamilton, James Madison, and John Jay, *The Federalist Papers* (Clinton Rossiter, ed.) No. 35 (New York: New American Library, Inc., 1961), 214–15.

5. As to the Republicans' philosophic views, see Elkins and McKitrick, *Age of Federalism*, 90–92 (concluding that "[d]ebt and the very idea of debt, merchants and the very idea of a mercantile way of life, were inseparable from the anglophobia of the Revolution"); *The Writings of Thomas Jefferson* (Andrew A. Lipscomb and Albert Ellery Bergh, eds.) 20 vols. (Washington, D.C.: Thomas Jefferson Memorial Association, 1903), 9:335–37, T. Jefferson to P. Mazzei, 24 April 1796 and ibid., 9:391–92, T. Jefferson to H. Gates, 30 May 1797; the Federalists' view of the political opposition is nicely captured in Marshall Smelser, "The Jacobin Phrenzy: Federalism and the Menace of Liberty, Equality, and Fraternity," *Review of Politics* 13 (1951), 457–82.

6. See generally Elkins and McKitrick, *Age of Federalism*, 388–449; Alexander DeConde, *The Quasi-War: The Politics and Diplomacy of the Undeclared War With France, 1797–1801* (New York: Charles Scribner's Sons, 1966), 9–10; Jefferson's "gloomy aspect" is in *Writings of Jefferson*, 9:351–52, T. Jefferson to J. Madison, 17 Dec. 1796. As to "protections," the certificates issued by collectors of customs, see Dudley Pope, *The Black Ship* (New York: Henry Holt & Co., 1998 [orig. pub. 1963]), 287–90; as to Jefferson's view of French "atrocious behavior," *Writings of Jefferson*, 10:104–10, T. Jefferson to E. Pendleton, 14 Feb. 1799. Jefferson believed that, instead of force, a "rational censure ought to be expressed on them" and insisted that the British "set the first example of violating neutral rights." Ibid.

7. As to Congress selling off the *Alliance*, see Nathan Miller, *Sea of Glory: A Naval History of the American Revolution* (Annapolis, Md.: Naval Institute Press, 1992 [orig. pub. 1974]), 521; Howard I. Chapelle, *The History of American Sailing Ships* (New York: Bonanza Books, 1935), 59. Madison's view is found in *The Federalist Papers*, No. 41, 260–61.

8. *The Federalist Papers*, No. 11, 86–89.

9. Marshall Smelser, *The Congress Founds the Navy 1787–1798* (Notre Dame: University of Notre Dame Press, 1959), 35–63, 72–87.

10. There are many biographies of Adams. See Page Smith, *John Adams*, 2 vols. (Garden City, N.Y.: Doubleday & Co., 1962); Peter Shaw, *The Character of John Adams* (New York: W. W. Norton & Co., 1977). Adams was not completely humorless, however. Jefferson reported (ruefully) the president's conversation with a man who had two sons, the elder aristocratic in outlook and the younger a democrat: "'Well,' said the President, 'a boy of fifteen who is not a democrat is good for nothing, and he is no better who is a democrat at twenty.'" *Writings of Jefferson*, 1:427, "Anas," Jan. 1799. As to Jefferson's late view of Adams as a fearless fighter for the Declaration, ibid., 15:46–64, T. Jefferson to J. Madison, 30 Aug. 1823.

11. Elkins and McKitrick, *Age of Federalism*, 537–39; DeConde, *Quasi-War*, 16–17; Stephen G. Kurtz, *The Presidency of John Adams: The Collapse of Federalism 1795–1800* (Philadelphia: University of Pennsylvania Press, 1957), 126–28; Ralph Adams Brown, *The Presidency of John Adams* (Lawrence: University Press of Kansas, 1975), 16–17; William Stinchcombe, *The XYZ Affair* (Westport, Conn.: Greenwood Press, 1980), 11–14; *The Life and Works of John Adams* (Charles Francis Adams, ed.) (Boston: Little Brown & Co., 1849–56), 8:537, J. Adams to J. Q. Adams, 31 March 1797.

12. *Works of John Adams*, 10:127, J. Adams to J. Lloyd, 21 Feb. 1815 (referring to the navy as his hobby-horse). As to Adams as a political organizer, see Brown, *Presidency of John Adams*, 30–31. Jefferson's temperate view of Adams is in *Writings of Jefferson*, 9:367–69, T. Jefferson to J. Madison, 22 Jan. 1797.

13. Smelser, *Congress Founds the Navy*, 107–118; DeConde, *Quasi-War*, 25–27, 31.

14. Elkins and McKitrick, *Age of Federalism*, 556-61 (profiles of three envoys); DeConde, *Quasi-War*, 28–30; *Works of John Adams*, 8:549, J. Adams to E. Gerry, 17 July 1797 (describing Marshall), and 8:547–48, J. Adams to E. Gerry, 8 July 1797 ("surrounded with projectors and swindlers").

15. Elkins and McKitrick, *Age of Federalism*, 562–63; Stinchcombe, *XYZ Affair*, 23.

16. *Writings of Jefferson*, 9:434–37, 9:437–39, 9:439–41, 9:444–46, T. Jefferson to J. Madison, 25 Jan., 8 Feb., 15 Feb., and 22 Feb. 1798.

17. Smelser, *Congress Founds the Navy*, 129–32; Brown, *Presidency of John Adams*, 49–50; DeConde, *Quasi-War*, 66–70; *Writings of Jefferson*, 10:9–11, T. Jefferson to J. Madison, 21 March 1798.

18. Elkins and McKitrick, *Age of Federalism*, 565–79; DeConde, *Quasi-War*, 46–59; Stinchcombe, *XYZ Affair*, 54–60, 112; Brown, *Presidency of John Adams*, 51–53; Jean Edward Smith, *John Marshall: Definer of a Nation* (New York: Henry Holt & Co., 1996), 192–223. The 11 July 1798 *Columbian Centinel* reported that: "The toast of the day is 'Millions for *defense*, but not a *cent* for *tribute:* no *tribute* but *blows;* and no declarations, but *manifestos.*'"

19. Adams Family Papers, Massachusetts Historical Society, roll 388, A. Adams to J. Q. Adams, 21 April 1798 ("Electrical Shock"); the addresses can be found in rolls 388 and 395 and *Works of John Adams*, 9:182–225; Brown, *Presidency of John Adams*, 54; Kurtz, *Presidency of John Adams*, 298–301. As to the threat to Adams, see *Works of John Adams*, 10:46–49, J. Adams to T. Jefferson, 30 June 1813. As to the change in the theatre crowd, see Adams Family Papers, roll 388, A. Adams to J. Q. Adams, 1 May 1798.

20. Smelser, *Congress Founds the Navy*, 139–48; Adams Family Papers, roll 388, A. Adams to J. Q. Adams, 26 May 1798.

21. *Works of John Adams*, 8:572–73, J. Adams to G. Washington, 22 June 1798 (Adams's reluctance as to the army, and asking Washington for his name and advice); ibid., 8:612–13, J. Adams to J. McHenry, 22 Oct. 1798 (prospect of seeing a French army). As to the French plans against Ireland, see Arthur Bryant, *The Years of Endurance, 1793–1802* (London: Collins, 1944), 165–71. There is, of course, a huge literature about the French invasion of Egypt, most recently in Alan Schom, *Napoleon Bonaparte* (New York: Harper Collins, 1997), 71–188. The article is from *The Spectator*, 30 June 1798, reprinted from the Dedham, Massachusetts newspaper *The Minerva*. There is, of course, an enormous literature on the Alien and Sedition Acts, all of which is irrelevant here.

Chapter 2. "A Navy Spring Up Like the Gourd of Jonah"

1. John J. Currier, *History of Newburyport, Mass. 1764–1905* (Newburyport: privately printed, 1906), 239–40, notes that in the late nineteenth century, after many of such claims were unprovable, the holders of claims against French reparations filed for $682,000 for the loss of seventy-nine vessels.

2. *Newburyport Herald and Country Gazette*, 25 May 1798.

3. Currier, *History of Newburyport,* 112 and Benjamin W. Labaree, *Patriots and Partisans: The Merchants of Newburyport 1764–1815* (Cambridge: Harvard University Press, 1962), 207–18.

4. Bailey Bartlett (1750–1830), a merchant from Haverhill, served two terms as a Federalist member of the House of Representatives (November 1797 to March 1801). *Biographical Dictionary of the American Congress 1774–1971* (Washington, D.C.: U.S. Government Printing Office, 1971), 559.

5. Currier, *History of Newburyport,* 111–12.

6. Bryant, *Years of Endurance,* 166, 217–18. See Act of 38 George III, chp. eight (30 Dec. 1797) in *Statutes at Large of England and of Great Britain* (London: Eyre and Strahan, 1811), 19:540; Roger G. Kennedy, *Orders From France: The Americans and the French in a Revolutionary World, 1780–1820* (New York: Alfred A. Knopf, 1989), 37–38; E. H. Jenkins, *A History of the French Navy* (London: Macdonald and Co., 1973), 142.

7. *The Papers of Alexander Hamilton,* ed. Harold G. Syrett (New York: Columbia University Press, 1974), 21:485–87, A. Hamilton to O. Wolcott, 5 June 1798 (emphasis in original).

8. Paul A. Samuelson, *Economics* (New York: McGraw-Hill Book Co., 10th ed. 1976), 157–60.

9. My analysis was suggested by Ronald H. Coase, "The Lighthouse in Economics," *Journal of Law and Economics* 17 (1974), 357–76. See also John D. Donahue, *The Privatization Decision* (New York: Basic Books, 1989).

10. *Newburyport Herald and Country Gazette,* 25 May 1798.

11. *Columbian Centinel,* 26 May 1798.

12. *Aurora & General Advertiser,* 11 June 1798.

13. *The Spectator,* 2 June 1798.

14. *The City Gazette and Daily Advertiser,* 16 June 1798.

15. See, for example, *Federal Gazette & Baltimore Daily Advertiser,* 9 June 1798; *Aurora & General Advertiser,* 9 June 1798. The *Norfolk Herald* went so far as to print the Newburyport committee's letter to Bartlett in its 21 June 1798 edition.

16. Cobbett (1763–1835), later a great English chronicler and radical, spent eight formative years in the United States. His arch-Federalist newspaper, notable for its "slashing, vigorous style," had a wide circulation of more than 3,000 daily. Cobbett egged on war with France, spurring military preparations, and "crying down those who raised a feeble voice for moderation." Mary Elizabeth Clark, "Peter Porcupine in America: The Career of William Cobbett, 1792–1800" (University of Pennsylvania Ph.D. dissertation, 1939), 126, 184.

17. *Porcupine's Gazette,* 9 June 1798.

18. Ibid.

19. John C. Miller, *The Federalist Era 1789–1801* (New York: Harper & Bros., 1960), 216, writes, "Congress enacted a law. . . . Under this law, subscriptions were opened in the principal seaports." Smelser, *Congress Founds the Navy,* 170, observes, "Even before final passage, subscription funds were being raised in the chief seaports." More egregious is Howard I. Chapelle, *The History of the American Sailing Navy* (New York: Bonanza Books, 1949), 157, who writes that the secretary of the navy "was able to induce citizens of Newburyport to build the 24-gun ship *Mer-*

rimack" with the law. The subscriptions were raised before the law; moreover, at that time, there was no secretary of the navy.

20. The Senate recorded votes only, not the discussion on the floor; the House debates were summarized or pruned down to the essentials. The readings of the bill are found in Library of Congress Photo-Duplication Service, 5th Congress, 1797–1799 Senate Bills (microfilm), 1966.

21. *Annals of Congress* (hereafter referred to as *Annals*), 5th Congress, 2d Session (Washington, D.C.: Gales & Seaton, 1851), 6:579.

22. *The Papers of James Madison* (David Mattern, ed.) (Charlottesville: University Press of Virginia, 1991), 17:152, T. Jefferson to J. Madison, 14 June 1798.

23. Smelser, *Congress Founds the Navy,* 169, observes that the bill may have been committed by the Republicans to fix definitely the interest rate of the stock and to limit the gun ratings of the ships. See *Annals,* 6:578–79.

24. The Senate passed the bill on 14 June, at which time the Philadelphia subscription was over $70,000, Newburyport's was completed, and New York had raised $25,000. By the time the bill was printed in New York (the *Commercial Advertiser* printed it on 19 June), Baltimore had subscribed $76,100.

25. Charles C. Bassett, "The Career of the Frigate Essex," *Essex Institute Historical Collections* 87 (1951): 17, cites receipts from the Essex papers as to the costs of labor in building the Salem subscription ship.

26. *The Spectator,* 27 June 1798.

27. For profiles of Stoddert, see Michael A. Palmer, *Stoddert's War: Naval Operations During the Quasi-War With France, 1798–1801* (Columbia: University of South Carolina Press, 1987), 10–13; White, *The Federalists,* 162–63; Elkins and McKitrick, *The Age of Federalism,* 634–35. Mrs. Adams's comments are in Massachusetts Historical Society, Boston, Massachusetts, Adams Family Papers, roll 389, A. Adams to G. Cabot, 17 June 1798. Stoddert's report is in Dudley W. Knox, ed., *Naval Documents Related to the Quasi-War Between the United States and France,* 7 vols. (Washington, D.C.: Government Printing Office, 1935–38), 2:113–14, Enclosure "A" from B. Stoddert to J. Dayton, 24 Dec. 1798.

28. Fletcher Pratt, *The Navy: A History* (Garden City, N.Y.: Garden City Publishing Co., 1941), 90; [Baltimore] *Telegraphe and Daily Advertiser,* 2 June 1798.

29. Henry E. Gruppe, *The Frigates* (Alexandria, Va.: TimeLife Books, 1979), 27.

30. Eugene S. Ferguson, *Truxtun of the Constellation* (Annapolis, Md.: Naval Institute Press, 1982), x, 145.

31. Webster (1758–1843), the grammarian and dictionary writer, wrote widely and insightfully as an economic thinker, scientist, and political pamphleteer. Webster saw his newspaper's function as vindicating the policies of Washington and Adams, but Hamilton's feuding with Adams disheartened Webster, causing him to abandon political journalism and sell his newspapers. Harlow Giles Unger, *Noah Webster: The Life and Times of an American Patriot* (New York: John Wiley & Sons, Inc., 1998); *Dictionary of American Biography,* (hereafter referred to as *DAB*) 10:594–97.

32. *Commercial Advertiser,* 30 June 1798.

33. Albert Gallatin (1761–1849) was Republican floor leader in the House (1795–1801). Later, he served as treasury secretary to Jefferson and Madison, and

as peace commissioner at Ghent to end the War of 1812. See Raymond Walters, Jr., *Albert Gallatin: Jeffersonian Financier and Diplomat* (New York: Macmillan Co., 1957).

34. P. Smith, *John Adams*, 2:967, cites A. Adams to Tufts, 8 June 1798.

35. *Annals*, 7:2033–34.

36. *Annals*, 7:2034, speech of 23 June 1798.

37. *Annals*, 6:590–92, 28 June 1798.

38. The Act had five sections. Sections four and five dealt with the manning and officering of the vessels. Section three provided that the president might accept any number of vessels donated to the navy. Section two detailed how many ships of each gun rate the president might accept in exchange for stock: four of at least thirty-two guns; three might mount twenty to twenty-four guns; and five were to have no more than eighteen guns. (These numbers are not actually in the Act itself, but are the correct figures when read in tandem with an earlier act). Section one authorized the president to accept "the proposals of any persons who shall offer and undertake to complete, provide and deliver, to the use, and upon the credit of the United States, . . . any vessel or vessels . . . of a model and size which he shall approve, and armed and equipped, or suitable to be armed for the public service."
Two provisos to section one limited the loan certificates to a 6 percent interest rate and the number of subscription ships to twelve. Act of 30 June 1798, chp. sixty-four, 1 Stat. 575 (1845)

39. Adams Family Papers, roll 389, A. Adams to J. Q. Adams, 12 June 1798; P. Smith, *John Adams*, 2:967 and Brown, *Presidency of John Adams*, 73–74.

Chapter 3. The Newburyport Example

1. Morison, *Maritime History*, 101, 151–54, quoting Timothy Dwight, *Travels in New England* (London: 1823), 1:400–407; E. Vale Smith, *History of Newburyport* (Newburyport: 1854), 147 (listing vessels owned in 1790); Robert K. Cheney, *Maritime History of the Merrimac* (Newburyport: Newburyport Press, Inc., 1964); Labaree, *Partisans and Patriots*, 97–98; *Federal Gazette & Baltimore Daily Advertiser*, 15 Oct. 1800 (in August 1800, Newburyport had 2,819 white males, 3,053 white females, and 65 "people of color").

2. E. Smith, *History of Newburyport*, 152–53; Morison, *Maritime History*, 151; Labaree, *Patriots and Partisans*, 98–99. On the early history of American corporations, see Adolf A. Berle, Jr., and Gardiner C. Means, *The Modern Corporation and Private Property* (Buffalo, N.Y.: William S. Hein & Co., 1982 [orig. pub. 1932]), 128–34. The use of the corporate form is thought to be one of the major factors of the extraordinary American economic development of that time. Cochran, *Frontiers of Change*, 21.

3. On American privateering, see Edgar Stanton Maclay, *A History of American Privateers* (New York: D. Appleton & Co., 1899), 7–9.

4. Labaree, *Patriots and Partisans*, 207–18; Gardner Weld Allen, *Massachusetts Privateers of the Revolution* (Boston: Massachusetts Historical Society, 1927) (listing data on owners and commanders of privateers); Smith, *History of Newburyport*, 349–51 (on Bartlet), 369–70 (on Farris); Cheney, *Maritime History of the Merrimac* (lists vessels built or owned by each man); Massachusetts Historical Society, Boston, Adams Family Papers, reel 119, J. Adams to J. McHenry, 24 Aug. 1798 (enclosing Stocker's

letter); John J. Waters, Jr., *The Otis Family in Provincial and Revolutionary Massachusetts* (New York: W. W. Norton & Co., 1968), 207.

5. Knox, *Naval Documents...Quasi-War,* 1:214–15, B. Stoddert to J. Sheafe, 16 July 1798.

6. Peabody Essex Museum, Salem, Mass., Hackett Family Papers, Box 1, Folder 5, E. Stocker to W. Hackett, 4 June 1798.

7. Philip Chadwick Foster Smith, *The Frigate Essex Papers: Building the Salem Frigate 1798–1799* (Salem: Peabody Museum, 1974) 43–46, 51; *Works of John Adams,* 10:25, J. Adams to J. Varnum, 5 Jan. 1813 (conversation with Thevenard); Foster Rhea Dulles, *The Old China Trade* (Boston: Houghton Mifflin Co., 1930), 32–38 (providing the *Massachusetts*'s dimensions and Prince's quote); K. Jack Bauer, *A Maritime History of the United States: The Role of America's Seas and Waterways* (Columbia: University of South Carolina Press, 1988), 59 (on the decay of the *Massachusetts*); Chapelle, *American Sailing Navy,* 68; Chapelle, *American Sailing Ships,* 59.

8. *Newburyport Herald and Country Gazette,* 8 June 1798; *Porcupine's Gazette,* 9 June 1798 (noting a Boston report of 4 June that the contracts were let); Knox, *Naval Documents...Quasi-War,* 3:53, W. Winder to W. Bartlet, 15 April 1799; ibid., 2:113–15, B. Stoddert to J. Dayton, 24 Dec. 1798 (enclosure "A").

9. Currier, *History of Newburyport,* 112–13; Morison, *Maritime History,* 151 (on the shallow water of Newburyport).

10. *Columbian Centinel,* 11 July 1798; Cheney, 11 (location of yard).

11. *Newburyport Herald and Country Gazette,* 6 July 1798.

12. E. Smith, *History of Newburyport,* 352–56; Edgar Stanton Maclay, *Moses Brown, Captain U.S.N.* (New York: Baker & Taylor Co., 1904); Russell Leigh Jackson, "The Seafaring Browns," *Essex Institute Historical Collections* 80 (1944): 55–68.

13. Knox, *Naval Documents...Quasi-War,* 1:214, B. Stoddert to W. Bartlet, 16 July 1798; ibid., 1:367–68, B. Stoddert to J. Adams, 1 Sept. 1798; ibid., 1:490–91, B. Stoddert to M. Brown, 4 Oct. 1798; ibid., 1:513–14, B. Stoddert to W. Burrows, 9 Oct. 1798 (passing along Bartlet's marine officer recommendation to commandant); ibid., 2:8, W. Bartlet to B. Stoddert, 6 Nov. 1798 (Bartlet's recommendations for last three warrant officers); ibid., 2:60, B. Stoddert to M. Brown, 3 Dec. 1798 (enclosing commissions and warrants); ibid., 1:542–43, B. Stoddert to J. Adams, 17 Oct. 1798.

14. *Federal Gazette & Baltimore Daily Advertiser,* 18 Sept. 1798, reprinting article dated Boston, 5 Sept. 1798.

15. *Newburyport Herald and Country Gazette,* 11 Sept. 1798.

16. *Newburyport Herald and Country Gazette,* 12 Oct. 1798.

17. James M. Barriskill, "The Newburyport Theatre in the 18th Century," *Essex Institute Historical Collections* 91 (1955): 345–48; Labaree, *Patriots and Partisans,* 117.

18. Knox, *Naval Documents...Quasi-War,* 1:490–91, B. Stoddert to M. Brown, 4 Oct. 1798; ibid., 1:513, B. Stoddert to W. Burrows, 9 Oct. 1798.

19. Knox, *Naval Documents...Quasi-War,* 2:138, M. Brown to N. Johnson, 30 Dec. 1798.

20. Knox, *Naval Documents...Quasi-War,* 2:60, B. Stoddert to M. Brown, 3 Dec. 1798; ibid., 2:61–62, B. Stoddert to S. Higginson, 3 Dec. 1798; ibid., 2:70–72, B. Stoddert to J. Barry, 7 Dec. 1798.

21. Currier, *History of Newburyport*, 114, citing *Newburyport Herald and Country Gazette*, 14 Dec. 1798; Knox, *Naval Documents...Quasi-War*, 2:8, W. Bartlet to B. Stoddert, 6 Nov. 1798 (noting that "by the Spring Tides on the approaching full Moon [the *Merrimack*] will be ready & can pass our Bar").

22. Knox, *Naval Documents...Quasi-War*, 2:211, C. Coley to N. Johnson, 4 Jan. 1799; National Archives, Washington, D.C., Record Group 45, entry 392, "Journal Kept on Board the U.S.S. *Merrimack*" (hereafter referred to as *Merrimack* Journal) by Midshipman Joseph Brown, 3 Jan. 1799.

23. Maclay, *Moses Brown*, 141–47; *Merrimack* Journal, 7 Jan. 1799. Sever's command, the *Congress*, lost all three masts in a storm on 11 to 12 January 1800. Midshipman Henry Wadsworth described the ship looking like Noah's ark "beating and boxing about without sail or spars . . . totally dismasted, rolling and straining about. Now she's down almost on her beam-ends. Now she rights again and plunges her bows into the foaming wave . . ." Christopher McKee, *Edward Preble: A Naval Biography 1761–1807* (Annapolis, Md.: Naval Institute Press, 1996 [orig. pub. 1972]), 78–79.

24. *Merrimack* Journal, 9–10, 16–18 Jan. 1799.

25. *Merrimack* Journal, 19–27 Jan. 1799; Maclay, *Moses Brown*, 150–53.

26. Maclay, *Moses Brown*, 156; Knox, *Naval Documents...Quasi-War*, 3:49–51, B. Stoddert to T. Truxtun, 15 April 1799. For contemporary British convoy theory and organization, see Brian Lavery, *Nelson's Navy: The Ships, Men and Organisation 1793–1815* (Annapolis, Md.: Naval Institute Press, 1997 [orig. pub. 1989]), 305–10.

27. *Merrimack* Journal, 31 Jan. – 14 Feb. 1799; Knox, *Naval Documents...Quasi-War*, 2:361–62, M. Brown to J. Barry, 16 Feb. 1799.

28. *Merrimack* Journal, 15–18 Feb. 1799.

29. *Merrimack* Journal, 19 Feb. 1799; Maclay, *Moses Brown*, 157–59.

30. *Merrimack* Journal, 20 Feb. 1799; Maclay, *Moses Brown*, 159.

31. *Merrimack* Journal, 21–28 Feb. 1799; Maclay, *Moses Brown*, 160.

32. *Merrimack* Journal, 11–30 March 1799; Maclay, *Moses Brown*, 163–64; Knox, *Naval Documents...Quasi-War*, 4:574, B. Stoddert to M. Brown, 28 Dec. 1799 (referring to Brown's mistake in paying half of the $2,625.18 to the navy agent in Boston, since the United States was not entitled to salvage).

33. *Merrimack* Journal, 1 April – 15 May 1799; Knox, *Naval Documents...Quasi-War*, 3:49–51, B. Stoddert to T. Truxtun, 15 April 1799; ibid., 3:168, B. Stoddert to S. Higginson, 11 May 1799.

34. Knox, *Naval Documents...Quasi-War*, 3:200, B. Stoddert to M. Brown, 17 May 1799 (enclosing ibid., 3:199–200, B. Stoddert to T. Truxtun, 17 May 1799); ibid., 3:234–35, B. Stoddert to J. Adams, 23 May 1799; ibid., 3:248–49, B. Stoddert to M. Brown, 24 May 1799.

35. Knox, *Naval Documents...Quasi-War*, 3:285, J. Adams to B. Stoddert, 31 May 1799; Adams Family Papers, reel 119, J. Adams to Boston Marine Society, 7 Sept. 1798; Knox, *Naval Documents...Quasi-War*, 3:280, J. Adams to M. Brown, 30 May 1799; *Merrimack* Journal, 7 June 1799; Knox, *Naval Documents...Quasi-War*, 3:314–15, B. Stoddert to S. Higginson, 7 June 1799.

36. *Merrimack* Journal, 10–28 June 1799; Knox, *Naval Documents...Quasi-War*, 3:540, T. Tingey to A. McElroy, 25 July 1799 (appointing McElroy to command the *Retali-*

ation and ordering him to convoy duty); ibid., 3:543–45, T. Tingey to B. Stoddert, 26 July 1799 (noting that the *Magicienne* had thrown eight guns overboard "according to their custom" before being taken); ibid., 4:71, B. Stoddert to J. Adams, 14 Aug. 1799 (noting arrival); ibid., 3:424, advertisement for sale. As to the history of the *Retaliation,* ex-*Magicienne,* ex-*Retaliation,* ex-*Croyable,* see Palmer, *Stoddert's War,* 30–31, 68–71, 116. Both Palmer (116) and Knox, *Naval Documents...Quasi-War* (3:iii), refer to the *Magicienne* as a privateer. She was, in fact, as Midshipman Brown put it, a "French National Schooner" (i.e., a French navy ship). *Merrimack* Journal, 28 June 1799. Since this was the case, the *Merrimack* was entitled to head and gun money, as Stoddert informed Brown. Knox, *Naval Documents...Quasi-War,* 4:574, B. Stoddert to M. Brown, 28 Dec. 1799. As to head money and gun money in the British navy, see Dudley Pope, *Life in Nelson's Navy* (London: Unwin Hyman Ltd., 1987 [orig. pub. 1981]), 232. It is not clear why the *Merrimack* did not receive prize money from the purchase of the *Magicienne* into the navy.

37. Knox, *Naval Documents...Quasi-War,* 3:543–45, T. Tingey to B. Stoddert, 26 July 1799; ibid., 4:92–97, T. Tingey to B. Stoddert, 19 Aug. 1799; *Merrimack* Journal, 15 July and 7 Aug. 1799; *Federal Gazette & Baltimore Daily Advertiser,* 14 Sept. 1799 (reprinting extract of Brown's letter of 10 Aug. 1799 to Stoddert, regarding the capture of the *Buonaparte*).

38. Knox, *Naval Documents...Quasi-War,* 5:91–92, B. Stoddert to M. Brown, 17 Jan. 1800 (referring to Tingey's claim). For the protracted correspondence related to the Swedish cargo, see ibid., 4:432, R. Soderstrom to B. Stoddert, 20 Nov. 1799; ibid., 4:434–35, B. Stoddert to R. Soderstrom, 21 Nov. 1799; ibid., 4:441, R. Soderstrom to T. Pickering, 22 Nov. 1799; ibid., 5:71, R. Soderstrom to B. Stoddert, 13 Jan. 1800; ibid., 5:74, B. Stoddert to R. Soderstrom, 14 Jan. 1800; ibid., 5:84, B. Stoddert to M. Brown, 15 Jan. 1800; ibid., 5:86–87, R. Soderstrom to B. Stoddert, 16 Jan. 1800; ibid., 5:106, B. Stoddert to M. Brown, 20 Jan. 1800; and ibid., 5:106–7, B. Stoddert to S. Higginson & Co., 20 Jan. 1800.

39. Knox, *Naval Documents...Quasi-War,* 5:106, B. Stoddert to M. Brown, 20 Jan. 1800.

40. Knox, *Naval Documents...Quasi-War,* 3:472–73, reprinting Protest of Capt. Lufkin, 11 Sept. 1799, ibid., 4:92–97, T. Tingey to B. Stoddert, 19 Aug. 1799; *Merrimack* Journal, 16 Aug. 1799. Despite her pint size, the *John* had sailed from Gloucester in June bound for Surinam. The three American captors later split one-fifth of the value of the *John* ($250) as salvage.

41. *Merrimack* Journal, 19 Aug. – 23 Aug. 1799.

42. Knox, *Naval Documents...Quasi-War,* 4:52, B. Stoddert to T. Tingey, 9 Aug. 1799; ibid., 4:201–2, T. Tingey to M. Brown, 18 Sept. 1799 (enclosing extracts of Stoddert's letter).

43. *Merrimack* Journal, 20–22 Sept. 1799.

44. *Merrimack* Journal, 24–25 Sept. 1799. The *Charming Nancy* missed New York, however, and sailed into Newport, Rhode Island. Gibbs & Channing, the navy agents at Newport, filed a libel in the U.S. district court to determine the salvage value to which the *Merrimack* was entitled; the *Charming Nancy* carried 40 puncheons of rum, 8 barrels of sugar, and 255 bushels of salt. Knox, *Naval Documents...Quasi-War,* 4:312–13, Gibbs & Channing to B. Stoddert, 23 Oct. 1799, and 4:335, Gibbs & Channing to B. Stoddert, 28 Oct. 1799. The appraisers valued the schooner at

$500; the rum at 75¢ per gallon; the sugar at $12 per hundred[weight]; and the salt at 67¢ per bushel. The libel, decree, appraisal report, interrogatories, a letter from Moses Brown, and the 5 September 1799 clearance from St. Kitts (listing her tonnage, master, cargo, and destination) all can be found in National Archives–New England Region, Waltham, Mass., Record Group 21, Records of the United States District Courts, United States District Court for the District of Rhode Island, *Brown v. The Schooner Charming Nancy*, November term 1799.

45. *Merrimack* Journal, 25 Sept. 1799. No records exist as to what happened to the *Elizabeth*.

46. *Merrimack* Journal, 28 Sept. – 19 Oct. 1799.

47. *Merrimack* Journal, 5, 10 Oct. 1799.

48. *Merrimack* Journal, 20–23 Oct. 1799.

49. *Merrimack* Journal, 24–25 Oct. 1799.

50. *Merrimack* Journal, 25 Oct. – 21 Nov. 1799. Whether Captain Brown enjoyed fishing himself, encouraged fishing to supplement his crew's diet, or fished to encourage competition between watches, is not clear. The fishing episodes are recorded in Midshipman Brown's *Journal* for 30 October and 10 November.

51. *Merrimack* Journal, 24 Nov. – 8 Dec. 1799; Knox, *Naval Documents...Quasi-War,* 4:439–40, B. Stoddert to M. Brown, 22 Nov. 1799; ibid., 4:518–19, D. Stickney to W. Burrows, 10 Dec. 1799 (reporting to the commandant the *Merrimack*'s arrival in Boston).

52. Knox, *Naval Documents...Quasi-War,* 4:574, B. Stoddert to M. Brown, 28 Dec. 1799; ibid., 4:524–25, S. Higginson to N. Johnson, 11 Dec. 1799 (requesting a half-dozen Newburyport caulkers to take the stage to Boston to redo the "Decks & upper works" of the *Merrimack* in Hartt's yard); ibid., 5:105, B. Stoddert to M. Brown, 20 Jan. 1800 (referring to resignations).

53. Knox, *Naval Documents...Quasi-War,* 5:145–46, B. Stoddert to M. Brown, 28 Jan. 1800; ibid., 6:137–38, B. Stoddert to J. Adams, 12 July 1800 (listing the *Merrimack* as due to return no later than 9 February 1801).

54. Knox, *Naval Documents...Quasi-War,* 5:403–4, letter from *Merrimack* officer to friend, 4 April 1800, reprinted from *Claypoole's American Daily Advertiser* [Philadelphia], 7 June 1800; Knox, *Naval Documents...Quasi-War,* 5:392, list of vessels under *Merrimack*'s convoy, reprinted from *Claypoole's American Daily Advertiser,* 7 April 1800; Knox, *Naval Documents...Quasi-War,* 5:572–73, B. Stoddert to D. Clarkson, 29 May 1800 (informing St. Kitts navy agent of the *Anna*'s appropriate salvage value).

55. Knox, *Naval Documents...Quasi-War,* 5:432-33, extract from log of *Union,* reprinted from *Claypoole's American Daily Advertiser,* 16 May 1800; Knox, *Naval Documents...Quasi-War,* 6:5, statement of Capt. Ebenezer Cheney, reprinted from *Connecticut Courant* [Hartford], 7 July 1800.

56. Knox, *Naval Documents...Quasi-War,* 5:532, extract of a letter from Capt. Joseph Woodman, reprinted from *Connecticut Journal* [New Haven], 9 July 1800; Ulane Bonnel, *La France, les Etates-Unis et la Guerre de Course (1797–1815)* (Paris: Nouvelles Editions Latines, 1961), 326 (listing the *Ceres*'s capture). No record exists of the *Ceres*'s salvage valuation.

57. *Federal Gazette & Baltimore Daily Advertiser,* 20 Aug. 1800, reprinting extract of H. Geddes's letter dated 30 July 1800; ibid., 23 Aug. 1800, reprinting extract from a

letter from Curaçao dated 2 Aug. 1800; Knox, *Naval Documents…Quasi-War,* 6:218–19, B. Phillips to sec. of state, 2 Aug. 1800. As to the navy's inactivity, see Palmer, *Stoddert's War,* 196.

58. It is extraordinarily difficult to determine the tonnage of these ships. According to the navy, the *Merrimack* was 530 tons and the *Patapsco* was 380 tons. Knox, *Naval Documents…Quasi-War,* 7:368–69. These numbers are almost certainly wrong. Admittedly, Stoddert listed the *Merrimack* at 530 tons in a statement to Congress on 24 December 1798. Charles W. Goldsborough, *The United States Naval Chronicle* (Washington, D.C.: privately printed, 1824), 99. Currier, *History of Newburyport,* 111, and E. Smith, *History of Newburyport,* 156, both list the *Merrimack* at 355 tons. On the other hand, by carpenters' measurement, the *Patapsco* measured 418 tons. National Archives, Washington, D.C., Record Group 36, French Spoliation Claims (Philadelphia District), Proof of Ownership of Registered Vessels, 9 Oct. 1801 – 1 Oct. 1802, Proof No. 38, 3 April 1802.

59. Palmer, *Stoddert's War,* 196–200; Knox, *Naval Documents…Quasi-War,* 6:337–41, W. Robinson to B. Stoddert, 19 Dec. 1800; ibid., 6:341–42, letter of a New York merchant, reprinted from *New Hampshire Gazette* [Portsmouth], 25 Nov. 1800.

60. Knox, *Naval Documents…Quasi-War,* 6:423-24, T. Truxtun to B. Stoddert, 2/27 Oct. 1800.

61. Knox, *Naval Documents…Quasi-War,* 6:489, bill of sale of the *Phénix;* ibid., 6:525, log of the *President,* 9 Nov. 1800 (spoken to by schooner with information of the *Merrimack's* prize); Goldsborough, *U.S. Naval Chronicle,* 183, lists the *Phénix* with 14 guns and 128 men. Benjamin Whitmore, a midshipman, recalled in 1846 that the *Merrimack* captured the *Brilliant* as she sailed from Curaçao. Maclay, *Moses Brown,* 187. From the documentary evidence, it seems likely that Whitmore confused the *Phénix* for the *Brilliant.*

62. Knox, *Naval Documents…Quasi-War,* 6:423–24, T. Truxtun to B. Stoddert, 2/27 Oct. 1800; ibid., 6:509–10, T. Truxtun to M. Brown, 28 Oct. 1800.

63. Knox, *Naval Documents…Quasi-War,* 7:5, T. Truxtun to M. Brown, 3 Dec. 1800; ibid., 7:86–90, T. Truxtun to B. Stoddert, 15 Jan. 1801; ibid., 7:114–15, Prize Court decree (3 Feb. 1801) and statement of sale of the *Brilliant* (14 Feb. 1801).

64. Knox, *Naval Documents…Quasi-War,* 7:5, T. Truxtun to M. Brown, 3 Dec. 1800; ibid., 7:69, T. Truxtun to M. Brown, 4 Jan. 1801.

65. Knox, *Naval Documents…Quasi-War,* 7:106, B. Stoddert to M. Brown, 27 Jan. 1801.

66. Knox, *Naval Documents…Quasi-War,* 7:126, S. Smith to S. Brown, 1 April 1801.

67. Knox, *Naval Documents…Quasi-War,* 7:307, Statement of Sales of Public Vessels; Currier, *History of Newburyport,* 114.

68. Knox, *Naval Documents…Quasi-War,* 7:176, S. Smith to M. Brown, 3 April 1801.

69. Maclay, *Moses Brown,* 192–95; E. Smith, *History of Newburyport,* 355.

Chapter 4. The *Philadelphia*'s Story

1. *Moreau de St. Méry's American Journey 1793–1798* (translated by Kenneth Roberts and Anna M. Roberts) (Garden City, N.Y.: Doubleday & Co., 1947), 257–363; "D.M. Erskine: Letters from America 1798–99," *William & Mary Quarterly* 6, third series (1949), 265–68.

2. Erskine's Letters, 276–77; Marion V. Brewington, "Maritime Philadelphia 1609–1837," *Pennsylvania Magazine of History and Biography*, 63 (1939), 93–117; Rhys Richards, "United States Trade With China 1784–1814," *American Neptune* 54 (1994), 10–22; Charles Lyon Chandler, *Early Shipbuilding in Pennsylvania 1683–1812* (Philadelphia: Franklin Institute, 1932), 36–37. As to Philadelphia's syndications, see Cochran, *Frontiers of Change*, 29, 35, 46.

3. The City Tavern, on Second near Walnut, functioned as an exchange. Merchants gathered there each afternoon to find out about prices, ship movements, and news. A messenger was dispatched daily to New Castle, Delaware, to discover the homeward-bound ships. The merchants assessed themselves a fee for these services and, of course, could eat and drink. *Moreau*, 354.

4. *Porcupine's Gazette*, 11 June 1798; *Federal Gazette & Baltimore Daily Advertiser*, 15 June 1798.

5. Joseph Anthony (1738–98) was a merchant, formerly a shipmaster, from Newport, Rhode Island, who settled in Philadelphia in 1782. See Harold E. Gillingham, "Old Business Cards of Philadelphia," *Pennsylvania Magazine of History and Biography* 53 (1929), 208–11. Anthony, a Federalist, described as "an old and eminent merchant; of irreproachable manners, great experience, and firm principles" (*Federal Gazette & Baltimore Daily Advertiser*, 9 Aug. 1798), died the next month, probably of yellow fever. Ibid., 4 Oct. 1798.

6. David Hayfield Conyngham (1750–1834) had emigrated as a boy from Ireland to Philadelphia. He became a prominent merchant whose firm after 1783 was called Conyngham, Nesbit & Co. His cousin, Gustavus Congngham, was a navy captain in the Revolutionary War. See Townsend Ward, "The Germantown Road and Its Associations," *Pennsylvania Magazine of History and Biography* 6 (1882), 18–19.

7. Daniel Smith, originally from Cape May, New Jersey, was in 1798 a junior member of the merchant firm Gurney & Smith. See Townsend Ward, "South Second Street and Its Associations," *Pennsylvania Magazine of History and Biography* 4 (1880), 49.

8. Joseph Smith was a Philadelphia merchant, also in the iron business, who was a cousin of Robert Fulton, the inventor. See Joseph S. Harris, letter reply to article "Nationality of Robert Fulton," *Pennsylvania Magazine of History and Biography* 3 (1879), 475.

9. *The Spectator* [New York], 16 June 1798; *Federal Gazette & Baltimore Daily Advertiser*, 16 June 1798; *Porcupine's Gazette*, 14 June 1798.

10. Apparently, FitzSimons has no biographer. See *DAB*, 3:444–45; Henry Flanders, "Thomas Fitzsimmons," *Pennsylvania Magazine of History and Biography* 2 (1878), 306–14; James A. Farrell, "Thomas FitzSimons, Catholic Signer of the American Constitution," *American Catholic Historical Society Record* 39 (1928), 175–224; and Robert K. Wright, Jr. and Morris J. MacGregor, Jr., *Soldier-Statesmen of the Constitution* (Washington, D.C.: U.S. Army Center of Military History, 1987), 88–90.

11. *DAB*, 10:302–3.

12. *DAB*, 5:205; Edward K. Eckert, "William Jones: Mr. Madison's Secretary of the Navy," *Pennsylvania Magazine of History and Biography* 96 (1972), 167–82.

13. The other members of the committee were Crawford, Daniel Smith, Joseph Sims, and James Yard. *Columbia Centinel* [Boston], 23 June 1798. All were merchants.

14. *Federal Gazette & Baltimore Daily Advertiser,* 18 June 1798; *The Spectator,* 27 June 1798. The complete list of Philadelphia subscribers is in the Appendix. Perhaps it is not surprising that building a ship to fight France did not attract a "loan" from Stephen Girard, the wealthiest merchant of all.

15. *Federal Gazette & Baltimore Daily Advertiser,* 16 July 1798; Davis Rich Dewey, *Financial History of the United States* (New York: Longmans, Green and Co., 1903), 110 (summarizing receipts); *Porcupine's Gazette,* 14 June 1798 ("none but men of family attached to the Federal Government ought to earn a shilling in the building or equipping [of] these vessels . . ."

16. *Porcupine's Gazette,* 16 July 1798; *Aurora & General Advertiser,* 17 July 1798; Chapelle, *American Sailing Navy,* 161; Knox, *Naval Documents…Quasi-War,* 1:265, B. Stoddert to J. Fox, 1 Aug. 1798.

17. Merle T. Westlake, Jr., "Josiah Fox, Gentleman, Quaker, Shipbuilder," *Pennsylvania Magazine of History and Biography* 88 (1964), 316–327.

18. Chandler, *Early Shipbuilding in Pennsylvania,* 23–25; Chapelle, *American Sailing Navy,* 119–20; Chapelle, *American Sailing Ships,* 85–86; Ferguson, *Truxtun of the Constellation,* 109–112; Smelser, *Congress Founds the Navy,* 72–73; Pratt, *The Navy,* 83–85.

19. Pratt, *The Navy,* 85; C. S. Forester, *The Age of Fighting Sail* (Garden City, N.Y.: Doubleday & Co., 1956), 43–45; Maury Baker, "Cost Overrun, An Early Naval Precedent: Building the First U.S. Warships, 1794–98," *Maryland Historical Magazine* 72 (1977), 361–72.

20. Chapelle, *American Sailing Navy,* 163–64.

21. Knox, *Naval Documents…Quasi-War,* 1:184, B. Stoddert to J. McHenry, 10 July 1798.

22. Historical Society of Pennsylvania, Philadelphia, Pa., Joshua Humphreys Letterbook 1797–1800, J. Humpheys to B. Stoddert, 20 July 1798.

23. Knox, *Naval Documents…Quasi-War,* 1:317, B. Stoddert to J. Humphreys, 17 Aug. 1798. Humphreys found that, although the *Ganges* had been built in the spring of 1795, her white-oak timbers already had decayed throughout the ship. Humphreys Letterbook, J. Humphreys to B. Stoddert, 26 Aug. 1798.

24. The first extant Humphreys drawing of a 74-gun ship bears the date of 20 March 1799. Richard Eddy, "'Defended by an Adequate Power': Joshua Humphreys and the 74-Gun Ships of 1799," *American Neptune* 51 (1991), 179.

25. Knox, *Naval Documents…Quasi-War,* 1:143, B. Stoddert to T. FitzSimons, 26 June 1798; ibid., 1:160, B. Stoddert to S. Sewall, 2 July 1798; ibid., 1:173, B. Stoddert to J. Yellott, 6 July 1798.

26. Humphreys Letterbook, J. Humphreys to O. Wolcott, 24 May 1798.

27. Chapelle, *American Sailing Navy,* 122; Fletcher Pratt, *Preble's Boys: Commodore Preble and the Birth of American Sea Power* (New York: William Sloane Associates, 1950), 74–75. There has been considerable historiographical debate as to the relative roles played by Humphreys and Fox in drawing the plans of these ships, kindled first by descendants of Fox and of Humphreys, and then by Chapelle, who tended to depreciate Humphreys in light of "Fox's superior training" which "evidently permitted him to achieve ascendancy in technical matters." More recent scholarship grants Humphreys the decisive role. William P. Bass, "Who Did Design the First U.S. Frigates?" *Naval History* 5 (1991), 49–54.

28. Chapelle, *American Sailing Navy*, 161–64. As to diagonal riders generally, see Eddy, "'Defended by an Adequate Power,'"185–87, and Tyrone G. Martin and John C. Roach, "Humphreys's Real Innovation," *Naval History* 8 (1994), 32–37. According to Martin and Roach, 37, Fox "is known to have disagreed with Humphreys on this [diagonal riders] and many other design features" and "undoubtedly left them out" of the *Chesapeake*, a Fox design. Whatever the truth about the *Chesapeake*, diagonal riders were designed for and almost certainly were installed in the *Philadelphia*. First, eight diagonal riders were contracted for in the live-oak timber contract. Knox, *Naval Documents…Quasi-War*, 1:215–16, (17 July 1798 contract between T. FitzSimons and J. Morgan). Second, Nathaniel Hutton later informed Joshua Humphreys that he would ship the live-oak diagonal riders in Philadelphia to New York and install white-oak diagonal riders into the *Philadelphia* instead. Humphreys Letterbook, N. Hutton to J. Humphreys, 28 Sept. 1798. As to the use of red cedar, see National Archives, Washington, D.C., Record Group 45, Subject File 1775–1910, Box 14, Folder 18, contains Accountant of the Navy Thomas Turner's "Dissection of the Accounting of Thomas FitzSimons Esquire for Cost & Equipment of Frigate Philadelphia" (hereafter, "Dissection of the Accounting . . ."), which lists payments for thousands of feet of red cedar.

29. *Porcupine's Gazette*, 16 July 1798.

30. Humphreys Letterbook, J. Humphreys to B. Stoddert, 28 Sept. 1798; ibid., [June 1798], "Quantity of each class of Live Oak Timber suitable for a large 44 Gun Frigate now on hand in the Following Places . . ." (indicating that Philadelphia had, for example, sufficient "floor raising timbers," 103 of 146 "first futtocks," 63 of 146 "second futtocks," 85 of 146 "third futtocks," 139 of 146 "Top timbers," and 13 of 180 "Half timbers").

31. Tench Coxe (1755–1824), who apparently had Loyalist sympathies during the Revolution, was an early and effective advocate of the Federal Constitution. Coxe served as Hamilton's assistant secretary of the treasury in 1789 and became commissioner of the revenue in 1792. Adams dismissed him in December 1797, and Coxe became a Republican and office holder under Jefferson and Madison. *DAB*, 2:488–89.

32. Chandler, 31, *Early Shipbuilding in Pennsylvania*, quoting Tench Coxe, *A View of the United States of America* (Philadelphia: 1794).

33. National Archives, Washington, D.C., Record Group 45, Subject File 1775–1910, Box 14, Folder 18, Samuel Humphreys' indent. As to live oak, see Virginia Steele Wood, *Live Oaking: Southern Timber for Tall Ships* (Annapolis, Md.: Naval Institute Press, 1995 [orig. pub. 1981]), 3–6, 24–25.

34. Wood, *Live Oaking*, 25–32; Knox, *Naval Documents…Quasi-War*, 1:215–16 (July 1798 contract); National Archives, "Dissection of the Accounting . . ."

35. See Palmer, *Stoddert's War*, 34; Knox, *Naval Documents…Quasi-War*, 2:129–34, B. Stoddert to J. Parker, 29 Dec. 1798.

36. Eddy, "'Defended by an Adequate Power,'"176, citing W. B. Clark, *Gallant John Barry, 1745–1803: The Story of a Naval Hero* (New York: Macmillan Co., 1938), 395–97. Bursting cannon were a recurring problem. See Knox, *Naval Documents…Quasi-War*, 2:21, T. Pickering to S. Talbot, 14 Nov. 1798 (responding to Talbot's "disappointments on account of the bursting & deficiencies of the nine pounders cast by Mr. Brown [at the Hope Furnace] for the Ship *George Washington*").

37. Maurer Maurer, "Coppered Bottoms for the United States Navy, 1794–1803," U.S. Naval Institute *Proceedings* 17 (1945), 693–94; Renee Lynn Ernay, "The Revere Furnace, 1787–1800," University of Delaware unpublished M.A. thesis (1989); Humphreys Letterbook, J. Humphreys to G. Cottringer, 27 Dec. 1798 (reporting on copper requirements for a 136-foot-keel, 1,145-ton frigate).

38. National Archives, "Dissection of the Accounting . . ." and loose documents related to the overseas financing. As to the rejection of some of the domestically supplied copper, see Historical Society of Pennsylvania, Philadelphia, Pa., Maitland Family Papers, Folder F-14, FitzSimons's reconciliation of accounts notes. Knox, *Naval Documents. . . Quasi-War,* 3:372, B. Stoddert to S. Decatur, 20 June 1799 ("The Guns and Military Stores, I presume, will be intirely furnished by the public"). Spencer Tucker, *Arming the Fleet: U.S. Navy Ordnance in the Muzzle-Loading Era* (Annapolis, Md.: Naval Institute Press, 1989), 58–62 (describing cannon manufacturing 1798–1800). As to the British statute, see *Federal Gazette & Baltimore Daily Advertiser,* 18 May 1799 and Palmer, *Stoddert's War,* 141.

39. National Archives, "Dissection of the Accounting . . ."; *Federal Gazette & Baltimore Daily Advertiser,* 9 Nov. 1799.

40. On shipyard consumption of alcohol, see Wood, *Live Oaking,* 94–96. The committee's purchases are detailed in National Archives, Washington, D.C., Record Group 45, Subject File 1775–1910, Box 14, Folder 18, "John W[h]arton for the Committee of Merchts" indent.

41. Knox, *Naval Documents. . . Quasi-War,* 4:457–58, reprinting *Claypoole's American Daily Advertiser* [Philadelphia], 29 Nov. 1799; *Federal Gazette & Baltimore Daily Advertiser,* 2 Dec. 1799.

42. See National Archives, "Dissection of the Accounting . . ."; National Archives, Washington, D.C., Record Group 45, Subject File 1775–1910, Box 14, Folder 18, "Statement of the Account of Thomas FitzSimons," October 1806; ibid., "Reconciling Statement with the Navy Department," 30 June 1808; Farrell, "Thomas FitzSimons, Catholic Signer," 205–7.

43. *DAB,* 3:186–87; Knox, *Naval Documents. . . Quasi-War,* 1:116, J. McHenry to S. Decatur, 15 June 1798.

44. Knox, *Naval Documents. . . Quasi-War,* 1:141–42, B. Stoddert to S. Decatur, 26 June 1798 (ordering the *Delaware* to sea); ibid., 1:175, T. Pickering to R. King, 9 July 1798; ibid., 1:175–76, reprinting *Columbian Centinel,* 14 July 1798 and 8 Aug. 1798 (the capture of the *Croyable*); ibid., 2:77–78, B. Stoddert to S. Decatur, 10 Dec. 1798 (ordering the *Delaware* to Havana); ibid., 2:220, S. Decatur to B. Stoddert, 7 Jan. 1799 (reporting on the safe arrival of a 15-ship convoy); ibid., 3:144, Address of Havana merchants, 6 May 1799; ibid., 3:216, B. Stoddert to S. Decatur, 20 May 1799 ("You have had a hard Service, & have performed it well . . ."); ibid., 3:372, B. Stoddert to S. Decatur, 20 June 1799 (appointing him captain of the *Philadelphia*).

45. *Works of John Adams,* 9:12, J. Adams to B. Stoddert, 8 Aug. 1799.

46. See, e.g., Knox, *Naval Documents. . . Quasi-War,* 5:239, A. Thomas to R. Gill, 21 Feb. 1800 (instructing navy storekeeper to deliver to Decatur and William Lane on account the quantities of saltpeter he required to manufacture gunpowder for the navy).

47. I have not been able to locate a muster roll of the *Philadelphia.* Its officers can be pieced together from Knox, *Naval Documents. . . Quasi-War,* 7:315–58. The midship-

men referenced were Clement Biddle, Jr., James Penrose, and Joseph B. Wharton. Another midshipman warranted was Archibald McCall, namesake of a leading Philadelphia merchant who had subscribed $1,500 to building the *Philadelphia* and who served on the first board of electors of the Insurance Company of the State of Pennsylvania, along with FitzSimons, Willing, and Gurney. See J. Thomas Scharf and Thompson Westcott, *History of Philadelphia 1609–1884* (Philadelphia: L.H. Everts & Co., 1884), 3:2115.

48. Historical Society of Pennsylvania, Philadelphia, Pennsylvania, Maitland Family Papers, Folder F-14, has a list of costs that resembles a modern-day "punchlist," the last entry of which bears the date 17 April 1800, the date on or about which the *Philadelphia* was placed in commission.

49. Knox, *Naval Documents...Quasi-War*, 5:246, B. Stoddert to S. Decatur, 26 Feb. 1800 (recruiting instructions); ibid., 5:319, B. Stoddert to J. Cassin, 17 March 1800 (recalling New York recruiting officer); ibid., 5:342, B. Stoddert to W. Burrows, 22 March 1800 (detaching fifty marines and two officers).

50. Knox, *Naval Documents...Quasi-War*, 4:516, B. Stoddert to Murray & Mumford, 10 Dec. 1799; ibid., 4:564–65, B. Stoddert to J. Watson, 24 Dec. 1799.

51. Knox, *Naval Documents...Quasi-War*, 5:377–79, B. Stoddert to S. Decatur, 3 April 1800.

52. Gerard H. Clarfield, *Timothy Pickering and the American Republic* (Pittsburgh: University of Pittsburgh Press, 1980), 211; Beinecke Library, Yale University, New Haven, Conn., Griswold Family Papers, Box 2, Folder 34, R. Griswold to F. Griswold, 27 March 1800.

53. Knox, *Naval Documents...Quasi-War*, 5:438, S. Decatur to T. Pickering, 23 April 1800; Gerard H. Clarfield, *Timothy Pickering and American Diplomacy 1795–1800* (Columbia: University of Missouri Press, 1969), 213 (noting Pickering's dismissal in the second week of May 1800, after months of bitter relations).

54. Knox, *Naval Documents...Quasi-War*, 5:529–31, Protest of George Hastie, master of the *Betsey*, 25 June 1800; ibid., 6:155, extract from Lt. Thomas Wilkey Journal, 15 July 1800. The unlikely named *Chou-Chou* was sent under a master's mate and four hands for prize proceedings to Philadelphia, arriving on 22 August. The U.S. Attorney, Jared Ingersoll, libeled the ship on 2 September, and Judge Richard Peters entered the decree condemning the *Chou-Chou* at the end of the month. The *Chou-Chou* and her cargo brought $8,393.50 to be split between the *Philadelphia* and *Connecticut* and the United States after the subtraction of fees. See National Archives – Mid-Atlantic Region, Philadelphia, Pa., Record Group 21, Records of the U.S. District Courts, M992, Information Case Files 1789–1843 . . . for the U.S. District Court for the Eastern District of Pennsylvania, *United States v. The Armed French Vessel Chou-Chou*, Bill of Costs, 7 April 1801.

55. Knox, *Naval Documents...Quasi-War*, 6:185, extract from Lt. Thomas Wilkey Journal, 26 July 1800; ibid., 6:216, J. McKnight to W. Burrows, 1 Aug. 1800; *Federal Gazette & Baltimore Daily Advertiser*, 7 May 1800; Knox, *Naval Documents...Quasi-War*, 6:354, reprinting anonymous letter in *Poulson's Daily Advertiser*, 29 Oct. 1800.

56. Knox, *Naval Documents...Quasi-War*, 6:201, B. Stoddert to S. Decatur, 30 July 1800; ibid., 6:440–41, T. Truxtun to S. Decatur, 5 Oct. 1800; ibid., 6:554, 6:556, 7:8, 7:47, 7:49, 7:50–51 (Lt. Thomas Wilkey Journal extracts from 26 Nov., 27 Nov., 3 Dec.

25 Dec., 26 Dec., 27 Dec., 29 Dec. 1800); ibid., 7:166, B. Stoddert to S. Decatur, 31 March 1801.

57. Dudley W. Knox, ed., *Naval Documents Related to the United States Wars with the Barbary Powers* (Washington, D.C.: U.S. Government Printing Office, 1939–44), 1:427, S. Smith to J. Humphreys, 3 April 1801; ibid., 1:428, A. Thomas to S. Decatur, 9 April 1801; ibid., 1:434, S. Smith to S. Decatur, 15 April 1801 (retaining officers); ibid., 1:437, S. Smith to S. Decatur, 21 April 1801; ibid., 1:437, S. Smith to S. Barron, 22 April 1801 ("A Letter is this Moment received from Capt. Decatur requesting permission to decline going on the present Expedition . . ."); ibid., 1:441, S. Smith to S. Decatur, 30 April 1801 (noting receipt of Decatur's letter of 25 April, the acting secretary noted it would not "revoke" orders given as a result of Decatur's earlier request). Decatur served as a judge on the court martial of Captain Little in Boston (see Chapter Six) and was dismissed from the service in October 1801. Knox, *Naval Documents...Quasi-War*, 7:292, R. Smith to S. Decatur, 22 Oct. 1801.

58. Knox, *Naval Documents...Barbary Powers*, 1:497–99, R. Dale to R. Smith, 2 July 1801 (reporting on arrival at Gibraltar and leaving the *Philadelphia* to blockade Tripolitan ships); ibid., 2:122, R. Smith to commanding officer, 16 April 1802; ibid., 2:201, R. Smith to commanding officer, 13 July 1802 (putting the *Philadelphia* in ordinary); ibid., 2:412, R. Smith to W. Bainbridge, 21 May 1803; ibid., 2:420, R. Smith to D. Bedinger, 24 May 1803 (the *Philadelphia* returned to commission and to be readied for sea).

59. Knox, *Naval Documents...Barbary Powers*, 3:171–73, W. Bainbridge to R. Smith, 1 Nov. 1803; ibid., 3:173, W. Bainbridge to E. Preble, 6 Nov. 1803 (reporting that 40 hours after he surrendered the frigate, "a strong Westerly wind . . . raised the Sea so as to enable them to get her off," an event that "still adds to our calamity"); ibid., 3:173–74, W. Bainbridge to E. Preble, 12 Nov. 1803; ibid., 3:175, Preble diary extract, 24 Nov. 1803. An intriguing account of the "what might have beens" had Bainbridge put up a stronger resistance can be found in David F. Long, *Ready to Hazard: A Biography of Commodore William Bainbridge, 1774–1833* (Hanover, N.H.: University Press of New England, 1981), 67–77.

60. Knox, *Naval Documents...Barbary Powers*, 3:414–15, S. Decatur, Jr. to E. Preble, 17 Feb. 1804. The dramatic burning of the *Philadelphia* is the subject of vast literature. Excellent renditions can be found in Charles Morris, *The Autobiography of Commodore Charles Morris* (Boston: A. Williams & Co., 1880), 25–31; Glenn Tucker, *Dawn Like Thunder: The Barbary Wars and the Birth of the U.S. Navy* (Indianapolis: Bobbs-Merrill Co., 1963), 269–280; Leonard F. Guttridge and Jay D. Smith, *The Commodores* (Annapolis, Md.: Naval Institute Press, 1986 [orig. pub. 1969]), 86–91.

Chapter 5. Baltimore's "Charming Little Ships"

1. *Federal Gazette & Baltimore Daily Advertiser,* 4 June 1799.

2. *Federal Gazette & Baltimore Daily Advertiser,* 20 June 1799.

3. Louis-Philippe, *Diaries of My Travels in America,* trans. Stephen Becker (New York: Delacorte Press, 1977), 16, 19; *Moreau,* 76–78; Norman Ruckert, *The Fells Point Story* (Baltimore: Bodine & Associates, Inc., 1976), 27.

4. John Mullin, *The Baltimore Directory, for 1799, Containing the Names, Occupations, and Places of Abode of the Citizens, Arranged in Alphabetical Order* (Baltimore: Warner & Hanna, 1799), 126.

5. Palmer, *Stoddert's War,* 6–7; Maryland Historical Society, Baltimore, Md., MS 626.1, Robert Oliver Record Books, Box 3, Letterbook 1796–1800, 206–209, R. Oliver to J. Kirwan, 10 March 1798 and R. Oliver to W. Lowrey, 10 March 1798.

6. *Federal Gazette & Baltimore Daily Advertiser,* 10 May 1798; [Baltimore] *Telegraphe and Daily Advertiser,* 21 June 1798; Maryland Historical Society, MS. 680, Pringle Letterbook, 1:1796–98, 387, M. Pringle to J. Miller, 18 May 1798; Robert Oliver Letterbook, 219, R. Oliver to Lance & Boone, 10 April 1798.

7. *Federal Gazette & Baltimore Daily Advertiser,* 2, 9, 13, and 15 June 1798.

8. Ibid., 15 June 1798.

9. Thorowgood Smith (1743–1810) ran a mercantile partnership with his brother Isaac from Bowleys Wharf. Mullin, *Baltimore Directory,* 62. An organizer of the Bank of Maryland in 1790, Smith owned a half-dozen ships and was a magistrate of the city before his property losses from French and British captures threw him into bankruptcy. He nevertheless was elected the mayor of Baltimore (1804–1808).

10. *Federal Gazette & Baltimore Daily Advertiser,* 16 June 1798. All five men were merchants. Robert Oliver, born in Ireland in 1757, emigrated to Baltimore in 1783. A Federalist, he would later become an original director of the Baltimore & Ohio Railroad. Stuart Weems Bruchey, *Robert Oliver: Merchant of Baltimore, 1783–1819* (Baltimore: Johns Hopkins University Press, 1956). David Stewart was on the boards of the Bank of Baltimore and the marine insurance office. John Stricker (1758–1825) had been a junior officer in Smallwood's regiment of the Maryland line during the Revolution. In the 1790s he owned a mill on the Jones Falls and was a colonel in the militia; at the Battle of North Point in 1814, he would command a brigade against the British regulars. He was a Republican, and the Jefferson administration appointed him the navy agent at Baltimore in 1801. James Barry owned a wharf and vessels based at Fells Point.

11. *Federal Gazette & Baltimore Daily Advertiser,* 19, 20, 22, and 23 June 1798; Robert Oliver Letterbook, 250–51, R. Oliver to B. Stoddert, 24 July 1798 (noting that the subscription then exceeded $100,000).

12. Jeremiah Yellott (d. 1805), known as "Captain Yellott" for his commands of three privateers in the Revolution, emigrated from Yorkshire in 1774. A spectacularly successful trader and a Federalist, by the early 1780s he owned his own wharf, a warehouse, and had investments in fourteen vessels. He was a leading proponent of the pilot-boat schooner and was the navy agent at Baltimore from 1798 to 1800. John Bosley Yellott, Jr., "Jeremiah Yellott—Revolutionary War Privateersman and Baltimore Philanthropist," *Maryland Historical Magazine* 86 (1991), 176–89.

13. Robert Gilmor (1748–1822) emigrated from Scotland at nineteen. Mercantile partner to Robert Morris and William Bingham of Philadelphia, Gilmor helped begin American trade with the East Indies. An original director of the Bank of Maryland (1790), he established the first joint-stock insurance company, the Maryland Insurance Company, in 1795, and built a gunpowder mill on the Gwynns Falls. A Federalist, he served on the First Branch of the Baltimore City Council and as its presi-

dent. Robert Gilmor, Jr., *Memoir, or Sketch of the History of Robert Gilmor of Baltimore* (unpublished Maryland Historical Society manuscript, 1840).

14. William Patterson (1752–1835), born in Donegal, emigrated to Philadelphia at fourteen to work in the countinghouse of a local merchant. In 1775 he risked all his property to buy gunpowder in France to supply Washington's army at a critical time. For two years he was a purchasing agent for the Continental Congress on St. Eustatius and Martinique. Original president of the Bank of Maryland, he was related by marriage to Gen. Samuel Smith. His daughter, Elisabeth, caused a national sensation by marrying Napoleon's brother, Jerome, in 1803. In later years Patterson gave land for a city park which bears his name and was one of the incorporators and first directors of the B&O Railroad. S. Mitchell, *A Family Lawsuit: The Story of Elisabeth Patterson and Jerome Bonaparte* (New York: Farrar, Straus and Cudahy, 1958), 7–9.

15. Thomas Cole, a merchant, was an officer aboard one of Yellott's privateers in the Revolution.

16. Archibald Campbell, a merchant, was a Federalist and member of the boards of the Bank of Maryland and marine insurance office. When Yellott resigned as navy agent, the Adams administration appointed Campbell to the position.

17. Mark Pringle (1751–1819), a merchant and a Federalist, was a director of the marine insurance office.

18. The list is found in the National Archives, Washington, D.C., Records of the Bureau of the Public Debt, Record Group 53, entry 263, 948:100–103.

19. William McCreary (spelled in the list "MacCreery") (1750–1814), a merchant and a Republican, became a three-term congressman from Baltimore (1803–1809) and later served in the Maryland state senate.

20. Moore Falls (spelled "Moor" in one entry and without the "s" in his last name in the other), a physician (Mullin, *Baltimore Directory*, 24) was an investor in shipping, having an interest in the merchant ship *Dolphin*, which traded with the East Indies. Robert Oliver Letterbook, 238, R. Oliver to J. McHenry, 29 May 1798.

21. Margaret Sprigg may have been the widow of Republican Congressman Richard Sprigg (of Anne Arundel County) who died in November 1798 "at his seat on the West River." *Federal Gazette & Baltimore Daily Advertiser,* 27 Nov. 1798. In the House, Sprigg voted against the establishment of a navy department, against suspending trade with France, and against emergency military spending. Ibid., 3 Oct. 1798.

22. Col. John Eager Howard (1752–1827) fought in the Maryland line from 1776 to the end of the Revolution. After the war, he was a delegate to the Continental Congress, governor of Maryland (1788–91), turned down President Washington's offer to be secretary of war, and served as a United States Senator (1795–1803). Howard was the vice presidential candidate in the Federalist party's last, unsuccessful campaign in 1816. *DAB*, 9:279.

23. John Swan (spelled in the list "Swann"), a merchant and a Federalist, was a director of the marine insurance office and brigadier general in command of the Baltimore militia. Frank A. Cassell, "The Structure of Baltimore's Politics in the Age of Jefferson, 1795–1812," in *Law, Society and Politics in Early Maryland*, eds. Audrey C. Land, Lois Green Carr and Edward C. Papenfuse (Baltimore: Johns Hopkins University Press, 1977), 291.

24. Benjamin Harwood (1751–1826) of Annapolis was state treasurer.

25. John O'Donnell (d. 1805), a Federalist and a merchant, owned the *Palas*, which sailed to the Orient in 1785 and brought to Baltimore the first cargo from China. Hamilton Owens, *Baltimore on the Chesapeake* (Garden City, N.Y.: Doubleday, Doran & Co., 1941), 155. A director of the Bank of Maryland, O'Donnell was also a lieutenant colonel of militia, in charge of the 6th Regiment.

26. *Federal Gazette & Baltimore Daily Advertiser,* 25 June 1798; ibid., 28 Sept. 1798 (public letter supporting Winchester). Despite Samuel Smith's status as a "merchant prince" of Baltimore, he was the city's Republican leader and cultivated the artisans and laborers of Baltimore through his command of the militia. William Bruce Wheeler, "The Baltimore Jeffersonians, 1788–1800: A Profile of Intra-Factional Conflict," *Maryland Historical Magazine* 66 (1971), 165.

27. John D. Kilbourne, "The Society of Cincinnati in Maryland: Its First One Hundred Years, 1793–1888," *Maryland Historical Magazine* 78 (1983), 169–85.

28. [New York] *Spectator,* 23 June 1798, reprinting letter from a Baltimore gentleman to his New York friend dated 17 June.

29. Knox, *Naval Documents…Quasi-War,* 1:145–46, B. Stoddert to J. Yellott, 27 June 1798; ibid., 1:170, B. Stoddert to D. Stewart, 6 July 1798; ibid., 1:170, B. Stoddert to J. Yellott, 6 July 1798.

30. Knox, *Naval Documents…Quasi-War,* 1:220, B. Stoddert to A. Campbell, 19 July 1798.

31. Geoffrey M. Footner, *Tidewater Triumph: The Development and Worldwide Success of the Chesapeake Bay Pilot Schooner* (Mystic, Conn.: Mystic Seaport Museum, 1998), 70–79 (as to Price's ships in the 1790s); Ralph J. Robinson, "Shipbuilding on the Patapsco; Part II: The Glorious Eighteenth Century," *Baltimore* 50 (1957), 48. As to Price owning slaves, see Charles G. Steffen, *The Merchants of Baltimore: Workers and Politics in the Age of Revolution 1763–1812* (Urbana: University of Illinois Press, 1984), 39–40.

32. Both men showed little activity in their own yards in 1795 to 1796, when other Fells Point shipyards were churning out vessels. It is possible that Price and de Rochbrune, with their laborers, helped Stodder's yard on the *Constellation,* the quid pro quo for which was the Baltimore merchants' promise that they would receive future navy contracts in Baltimore.

33. William J. Kelley, "Shipbuilding at Federal Hill Baltimore" (1964), typescript MS. at Maryland Historical Society; "Earle's Maryland Shipbuilding Collection 1680–1910," index at Maryland Historical Society, book I, sheet 31; Marion V. Brewington, comp., "Lists of Carpenters Certificates 1790–1831" (1957), typescript MS. at Maryland Historical Society. I am grateful to Mrs. Renee Barnett Webster and Mrs. Riggs Griffith for sharing information about their ancestor, Lewis de Rochbrune, with me.

34. Robert Oliver Letterbook, 250–51, 255–56, R. Oliver to B. Stoddert, 24 July 1798; Knox, *Naval Documents…Quasi-War,* 1:242–43, B. Stoddert to R. Oliver, 26 July 1798.

35. Maryland Historical Society, Baltimore, Md., MS.2543, Certificate of *Maryland* (RG 36, Certificates of Registry Issued at Baltimore, Maryland 1789–1801, roll 2, no. 242, from National Archives). The tonnage, called the carpenter's measure,

was obtained by multiplying the length of the ship's keel by the extreme breadth and multiplied again by the interior vertical dimension (called "depth of hold"), the whole divided by ninety-five. Thomas C. Gillmer, *Pride of Baltimore: The Story of the Baltimore Clippers 1800–1990* (Camden, Maine: International Marine, 1992), 189. Tonnage, therefore, was not a measure of weight.

36. National Archives, Washington, D.C., RG 36, French Spoilation Claims (Philadelphia District), Proof of Ownership of Registered Vessels, October 9, 1801–October 1, 1802, Proof No. 38, 3 April 1802.

37. Chapelle found two sloop-of-war plans that *might* reflect the design of the Baltimore ships. One was for a "spar-decked sloop of war," rated for twenty guns, but mounting twenty-four or twenty-six guns. That vessel would have measured 106 feet, 4 inches between perpendiculars, 29-foot moulded beam, a depth of hold of 13 feet, 6 inches—a rather "sharp-ended vessel." Chapelle, *American Sailing Navy*, 155. The other plan called for a ship of eighteen guns, with a length of 95 feet along the keel, a 32-foot beam, 116 feet between perpendiculars, and a 13-foot, 6-inch depth of hold. Chapelle calculated her tonnage at about 430 tons. Ibid., 160. The plan is marked "Copied by Sam Humphreys Phila. 1798" which, even assuming that the plan represents one of the Baltimore ships, does not shed light on who drew the plans originally, and Chapelle concedes the designer is unknown. Ibid., 159, 160. W. M. P. Dunne assumes that Josiah Fox designed both ships, but this is set forth by implication. W. M. P. Dunne, "An Inquiry into H. I. Chapelle's Research in Naval History," *American Neptune* 49 (1989), 54 n.70. That Fox or any Philadelphia-based naval architect was the designer seems doubtful given the secretary's ignorance of the designs, the arguably faulty design, and the sharpness of the design with its pilot-boat schooner attributes.

38. Knox, *Naval Documents...Quasi-War*, 1:262–63, B. Stoddert to J. Adams, 31 July 1798; Robert Oliver Letterbook, 262, R. Oliver to B. Stoddert, 28 Aug. 1798.

39. Robert Oliver Letterbook, 276, R. Oliver to B. Stoddert, 8 and 10 Oct. 1798; Knox, *Naval Documents...Quasi-War*, 2:55, B. Stoddert to R. Gilmor, 28 Nov. 1798; ibid., 3:100–01, B. Stoddert to J. Yellott, 27 April 1799 ("Cannon for one of the Vessels will be sent from hence—the other is provided—The Public has powder in the hands of Messrs. Gilmore [sic] & Co.'s Works"); *Documents Accompanying a Message from the President of the United States, with Sundry Statements Containing Detailed Accounts of the Expenditures of Public Monies, by Naval Agents; From 1st January, 1797 to 31st December 1801* (Washington, D.C.: William Duane & Son, 1803), 227, in Ralph R. Shaw and Richard H. Shoemaker, comp., *American Bibliography: A Preliminary Checklist for 1801–1819* (New York: Scarecrow Press, 1958–83).

40. Knox, *Naval Documents...Quasi-War*, 1:536, B. Stoddert to R. Oliver, 15 Oct. 1798 (noting that "Gen. Washington, Gen. Lee & other respectable men of Virginia" recommended Captain John Spotswood for one of the Baltimore vessels); John C. Fitzpatrick, ed., *The Writings of George Washington* (Washington, D.C.: Government Printing Office, 1941), 36:486–87, G. Washington to B. Stoddert, Oct. 9, 1798; Robert Oliver Letterbook, 250–51, 255–56, R. Oliver to B. Stoddert, 24 and 31 July 1798.

41. Charles Oscar Paullin, *Commodore John Rodgers: Captain, Commodore, and Senior Officer of the American Navy, 1773–1838* (Annapolis, Md.: Naval Institute Press, 1967

[orig. pub. 1910]); Knox, *Naval Documents...Quasi-War*, 3:335, B. Stoddert to J. Rodgers, 13 June 1798 (enclosing commission as captain and ordering him to take command of the ship).

42. Knox, *Naval Documents...Quasi-War*, 4:144, B. Stoddert to J. Adams, 2 Sept. 1799; Charles E. Claghorn, *Naval Officers of the American Revolution: A Concise Biographical Dictionary* (Metuchen, N.J.: Scarecrow Press, 1988), 119; Adams Family Papers, reel 120, J. Adams to B. Stoddert, 9 Sept. 1799; Knox, *Naval Documents...Quasi-War*, 4:222, B. Stoddert to H. Geddes, 24 Sept. 1799

43. Historical Society of Pennsylvania, Philadelphia, Pa., AMN 950, John Rodgers Papers, Copy Book 1799–1805, J. Rodgers to B. Stoddert, 7 Sept. 1799. As to opening recruiting, ibid., Rodgers to [?], 3 August 1799.

44. Knox, *Naval Documents...Quasi-War*, 1:563–64, T. Truxtun to J. Yellott, 8 Jan. 1799; ibid., 3:507–8, B. Stoddert to J. Yellott, 17 July 1799; ibid., 4:159–60, J. Buchanan to T. Pickering, 5 Sept. 1799. Chapelle, *American Sailing Navy*, 156, cites the Buchanan letter in a passage indicating that the Baltimore-built ships were "overgunned," especially in comparison with British warships of like size. As to this comparison, Dunne, "Chapelle's Research," 45–46, points out that the British ships' weight of armament was *not* what Chapelle believed and that the *Maryland* and *Patapsco* "carried the armament they had been designed for," which is correct. However, the armament for which they were designed might have been flawed in theory (especially given the extra men, shot, powder, and provisions necessitated by additional or heavier guns), and there is no gainsaying the fact that Rodgers, the *Maryland*'s captain, shared the opinion of the low gun deck. Buchanan, in his letter, went on to make the comparison to British sloops of war, which Chapelle took up.

45. Howard I. Chapelle, *The Baltimore Clipper: Its Origin and Development* (Hatboro, Pa.: Tradition Press, 1965 [orig. pub. 1930]), 3.

46. *Federal Gazette & Baltimore Daily Advertiser,* 22 August, 9 and 14 Sept. 1799 (the latter reprinting extract from Norfolk Herald, 5 Sept.).

47. John Rodgers Papers, Copy Book 1799–1805, J. Rodgers to B. Stoddert, 20 Sept. 1799.

48. Adams Family Papers, reel 120, J. Adams to B. Stoddert, 30 Aug. 1799.

49. Knox, *Naval Documents...Quasi-War*, 4:158, B. Stoddert to J. Rodgers, 5 Sept. 1799.

50. Ibid., 4:159–60, J. Buchanan to T. Pickering, Sept. 5, 1799.

51. For Truxtun's system on board the *Constellation* and its influence on Rodgers, see Ferguson, *Truxtun of the Constellation*, 139–41. For Rodgers's standing orders, see Paullin, *Commodore John Rodgers*, 55–60, and William L. Clements Library, University of Michigan, John Rodgers Papers.

52. *Federal Gazette & Baltimore Daily Advertiser,* 17 Dec. 1799 (reprinting extract from an officer about the *Maryland,* dated Surinam, 17 Oct.); John Rodgers Papers, Copy Book 1799–1805, J. Rodgers to D. McNeill, 22 Oct. 1799; Knox, *Naval Documents...Quasi-War*, 4:160–61, B. Stoddert to D. McNeill, 5 Sept. 1799.

53. John Rodgers Papers, Copy Book 1799–1805, J. Rodgers to B. Stoddert, 20 Nov. 1799.

54. *Federal Gazette & Baltimore Daily Advertiser,* 24 Dec. 1799 (reprinting extract from an officer on the *Maryland* to his friend in Baltimore, dated 21 Nov.); Knox, *Naval*

Documents…Quasi-War, 4:373–74, A. Murray to B. Stoddert, 9 Nov. 1799; ibid., 4:441–42, J. Neale to W. Burrows, 22 Nov. 1799.

55. Knox, *Naval Documents…Quasi-War*, 4:222, 265, 312, 357–58, B. Stoddert to H. Geddes, 24 Sept., 8 and 23 Oct., and 5 Nov. 1799.

56. *Federal Gazette & Baltimore Daily Advertiser*, 17 and 18 Sept. 1799.

57. Knox, *Naval Documents…Quasi-War*, 4:380, 392–93, B. Stoddert to H. Geddes, 11 and 14 Nov. 1799; *Federal Gazette & Baltimore Daily Advertiser*, 19 Nov. 1799. Despite the potential for confusion in naming both a sloop of war and a frigate the *Chesapeake*, the Baltimore-built ship continued to be called the *Chesapeake* in the newspapers. In official correspondence she was the *Patapsco* by the end of October.

58. Knox, *Naval Documents…Quasi-War*, 5:206.

59. Knox, *Naval Documents…Quasi-War*, 5:282, reprints extract of log of the USS *Warren*, 7 March 1800 (noting "Spoke the U.S. Ship *Petapsco* [sic] from Havanna Having under Convoy a fleet of Merchantmen"); *Federal Gazette & Baltimore Daily Advertiser*, 21 March 1800 (noting arrival of the brig *Dorsey*, Pierce, fifteen days from Havana, which had been under convoy of the *Patapsco* for four days from Havana until she separated from the convoy off of Florida); Knox, *Naval Documents…Quasi-War*, 5:327–28, B. Stoddert to H. Geddes, 19 March 1800; ibid., 5:47, B. Stoddert to H. Geddes, 14 April 1800.

60. John Rodgers Papers, Copy Book 1799–1805, J. Rodgers to T. Tufts, 26 Dec. 1799 and 16 Jan. 1800.

61. John Rodgers Papers, Copy Book 1799–1805, J. Rodgers to B. Stoddert, 20 Nov. 1799; *Federal Gazette & Baltimore Daily Advertiser*, 24 Dec. 1799; Knox, *Naval Documents…Quasi-War*, 5:181–82, T. Tufts to Secretary of State, 3 Feb. 1800; Palmer, *Stoddert's War*, 148.

62. After two of McNeill's men deserted, he sent an armed party ashore to seize them. The British governor protested and demanded an apology, which McNeill refused. The British then expelled the *Portsmouth* from Surinam, leaving Rodgers and the *Maryland* alone on the South American station. Palmer, *Stoddert's War*, 143, 194.

63. John Rodgers Papers, Copy Book 1799–1805, J. Rodgers to T. Tufts, 18, 27, and 31 Jan. 1800; Knox, *Naval Documents…Quasi-War*, 5:234, T. Tufts to commanders of American vessels, 20 Feb. 1800; ibid., 5:181–82, T. Tufts to Secretary of State, 3 Feb. 1800.

64. Knox, *Naval Documents…Quasi-War*, 4:373–74, A. Murray to B. Stoddert, 9 Nov. 1799; ibid., 6:364–65, J. Rodgers to B. Stoddert, 20 Sept. 1800.

65. Ibid., 6:366, J. Rodgers to B. Stoddert, 20 Sept. 1800; ibid., 6:436–39, Solicitor General of St. Kitts to Judge J. Garnett of Court of Admiralty, 3 Oct. 1800; ibid., 6:434–35, T. Truxtun to B. Stoddert, 4 Oct. 1800.

66. See Knox, *Naval Documents…Quasi-War*, 6:366; J. Rodgers to B. Stoddert, 20 Sept. 1800; John Rodgers Papers, Copy Book 1799–1805 (listing each vessel under convoy, its owner, port of origin, and cargo). As to the capture and trial of the *Aerial*, see Knox, *Naval Documents…Quasi-War*, 6:312, J. Rodgers to B. Stoddert, 2 Sept. 1800; John Rodgers Papers, Copy Book 1799–1805, J. Rodgers to L. Hollingsworth, 9 Oct. 1800; ibid., J. Rodgers to J. Lockhart, 22 Nov. 1800. The *Aerial* does not appear in the Navy Department's list of prizes taken in the war. Knox, *Naval Documents…Quasi-War*, 7:59, 311–12.

67. Paullin, *Commodore John Rodgers*, 367; Knox, *Naval Documents...Quasi-War*, 4:156, Circular to J. Rodgers, 6 Sept. 1799; ibid., 5:313–14; B. Stoddert to Secretary of Treasury, 17 March 1800; ibid., 6:367–68, J. Rodgers to B. Stoddert, 20 Sept. 1800; ibid., 6:420–21, B. Stoddert to J. Rodgers, 1 Oct. 1800.

68. Knox, *Naval Documents...Quasi-War*, 6:420–21, B. Stoddert to J. Rodgers, 1 Oct. 1800.

69. *Federal Gazette & Baltimore Daily Advertiser*, 25 July 1800.

70. Knox, *Naval Documents...Quasi-War*, 7:59, 311–12; National Archives—Mid-Atlantic Region, Philadelphia, Pa., Records of the District Courts of the United States, RG 21, Records of the U.S. District Court for the Eastern District of Pennsylvania, Records Relating to Forfeitures in Customs, Internal Revenue and Other Cases, Case Filed (Informations) 1789–1910, *United States v. The Armed French Vessel the Dorade*, Bill of Costs.

71. *Federal Gazette & Baltimore Daily Advertiser*, 20 Aug. 1800, extract of Geddes' letter of 30 July 1800. Palmer, *Stoddert's War*, 196, observes that "[a]t least two of the American commanders on the station were privy to the information, but if it found its way to Commodore Decatur, he chose to do nothing."

72. *Federal Gazette & Baltimore Daily Advertiser*, 20 and 23 Aug. 1800; Palmer, *Stoddert's War*, 196–99.

73. Palmer, *Stoddert's War*, 200; Knox, *Naval Documents...Quasi-War*, 6:337–41, W. Robinson to B. Stoddert, n.d.; ibid., 6:500–01, B. Phillips to Secretary of State, 25 Oct. 1800.

74. Knox, *Naval Documents...Quasi-War*, 6:337–41, W. Robinson to B. Stoddert, n.d.; ibid., 6:451–52, B. Phillips to U.S. squadron commander, 10 Oct. 1800.

75. *Federal Gazette & Baltimore Daily Advertiser*, 9 Dec. 1800.

76. Knox, *Naval Documents...Quasi-War*, 6:505–6, T. Truxtun to H. Geddes, 27 Oct. 1800.

77. Ibid., 7:3, reprints extract from Mullowny journal, 1–17 Dec. 1800; ibid., 7:24, B. Stoddert to G. Harrison, 12 Dec. 1800; ibid., 7:165, B. Stoddert to G. Harrison, 31 March 1801; National Archives, Washington, D.C., Records of Bureau of Customs, RG 36, Proof of Ownership of Registered Vessels (Philadelphia District) 9 October 1801–1 October 1802, Proof of Ownership No. 38, 3 April 1802.

78. Knox, *Naval Documents...Quasi-War*, 7:141, 147, 148, B. Stoddert to J. Rodgers, 7, 16, and 18 March 1801; *Federal Gazette & Baltimore Daily Advertiser*, 23 March 1801; John Rodgers Papers, Copy Book 1799–1805, J. Rodgers to Commandant, 9 May 1801; Paullin, *Commodore John Rodgers*, 69–71; Massachusetts Historical Society, Boston, Thomas Jefferson Papers, reel 6, A. Homberg to T. Jefferson, 7 July 1801.

79. Knox, *Naval Documents...Quasi-War*, 7:279, R. Smith to J. Rodgers, 31 Aug. 1801; ibid., 7:290, R. Smith to J. Stricker, 2 Oct. 1801; Maryland Historical Society, Records of Bureau of Customs, RG 36, Certificates of Registry Issued at Baltimore, Maryland 1789–1801, MS 2543, roll 2, Certificate of Registry No. 242, 9 Dec. 1801; Knox, *Naval Documents...Quasi-War*, 7:307, Statement of Sales of Public Vessels, 8 Dec. 1801; Carl C. Cutler, *Greyhounds of the Sea: The Story of the American Clipper Ship* (New York: Halcyon House, 1930), 399.

80. Knox, *Naval Documents...Quasi-War*, 7:11, T. Truxtun to B. Stoddert, 5 Dec. 1800; ibid., 7:292, R. Smith to J. Rodgers, 22 Oct. 1801; Guttridge and Smith, *The Commodores*, 104.

Chapter 6. The *Boston* and the Perils of Taking Prizes

1. *Columbian Centinel,* 22 May 1799; Knox, *Naval Documents...Quasi-War,* 3:223–24, reprinting *Massachusetts Mercury,* 21 May 1799; *Federal Gazette & Baltimore Daily Advertiser,* 27 May 1799.
2. *Columbian Centinel,* 26 May and 23 June 1798.
3. *Columbian Centinel,* 27 June 1798; [New York] *Spectator,* 4 July 1798.
4. *Massachusetts Mercury,* 29 June 1798; *Columbian Centinel,* 30 June 1798.
5. Phillips (1750–1827), a leading benefactor of Phillips Academy, Andover, later served twelve terms as lieutenant governor of Massachusetts and as president of Massachusetts General Hospital. *DAB,* 7:548.
6. Perkins (1764–1854) sailed to Canton as a supercargo in 1789, and sailed with grain ships to Bordeaux to relieve famine facing France in the throes of Revolution in 1794. With his brother James, T. H. Perkins established one of the major mercantile firms in Boston. A Federalist, he served in the state senate and left a lasting philanthropic legacy. See Thomas G. Cary, "Thomas Handasyd Perkins," in Freeman Hunt, ed., *Lives of American Merchants* (New York: Derby & Jackson, 1858), 1:33–102.
7. Quincy (1772–1864) was first elected to the House in 1804, and rose to be a Federalist leader. He resigned after the United States declared war in 1812. A zealous reform mayor of Boston (1823–28), and an effective Harvard president (1829–45), in his last days Quincy heartily supported Lincoln and the Union cause in the Civil War. *DAB,* 8:308–11.
8. See Appendix.
9. *Columbian Centinel,* 4 July 1798.
10. Thomas Davis, John Coffin Jones, Henry Jackson, William Parson, David Sears, Thomas Handasyd Perkins, and Gorman Parsons. *The Spectator,* 7 July 1798. Jones founded the Massachusetts Fire Insurance Co. (1785). Jackson was a former navy agent and land speculator with Henry Knox. David Sears was a merchant.
11. Knox, *Naval Documents...Quasi-War,* 1:170, B. Stoddert to D. Sears, 6 July 1798.
12. Knox, *Naval Documents...Quasi-War,* 1:262–63, B. Stoddert to J. Adams, 31 July 1798.
13. Chapelle, *American Sailing Navy,* 166. In the index, Chapelle lists the *Boston* at 700 tons. Ibid. at 533. In the account of the *Boston*'s launching in the *Columbian Centinel,* on 22 May 1799, the frigate was said to be "about 800 tons."
14. Ernay, "Revere Furnace," 41, quoting Massachusetts Historical Society, Revere Family Papers, Letterbook 1783–1800, P. Revere to J. Brown, 24 April 1797.
15. Jayne E. Triber, *A True Republican: The Life of Paul Revere* (Amherst: University of Massachusetts Press, 1998), 178, 185; Maurer, "Coppered Bottoms," 698; Ernay, "Revere Furnace," 27, 44, quoting Massachusetts Historical Society, Revere Family Papers, Letterbook 1783–1800, P. Revere to J. Sheaf, 4 Jan. 1799; ibid., 47, quoting Revere Letterbook 1783–1800, P. Revere to B. Stoddert, 31 Dec. 1798; ibid., 49–51.
16. Knox, *Naval Documents...Quasi-War,* 2:97, B. Stoddert to D. Sears, 18 Dec. 1798.
17. Knox, *Naval Documents...Quasi-War,* 1:328–29, S. Higginson to B. Stoddert, 23 Aug. 1798; Massachusetts Historical Society, Adams Family Papers, microfilm reel 119, J. Adams to B. Stoddert, 10 Sept. 1798 (enclosing signed commission for Captain Chapman); Knox, *Naval Documents...Quasi-War,* 2:249, B. Stoddert to J. Chapman, 17 Jan. 1799.

18. Massachusetts Historical Society, Miscellaneous Bound MSS, J. Jones to G. Little, 2 April 1799. President Adams endorsed the committee's decision and signed the commission for Little. Adams Family Papers, reel 119, J. Adams to B. Stoddert, 26 April 1799.

19. *DAB*, 6:298–99. As to the furious battle between the *Protector* and the *Admiral Duff*, see Miller, *Sea of Glory*, 425–26 (largely quoting account of Luther Little, George Little's brother). References to Little are in Isaac Bailey, compiler, *American Naval Biography* (Providence: H. Mann & Co., 1815), 16; *Works of John Adams*, 8:664–65, J. Adams to B. Stoddert, 8 July 1799.

20. George Henry Preble, "The Navy, and the Charlestown Navy Yard," Chapter 5 of *The Memorial History of Boston*, ed. Justin Windsor, vol. 4 (Boston: James R. Osgood & Co., 1881), 335 n.1 quotes *Columbia Centinel*, 29 May, 12 June 1799. Knox, *Naval Documents...Quasi-War*, 3:503, B. Stoddert to S. Higginson, 15 July 1799 ("I am exceedingly disappointed and mortified at the delay of the *Boston* which I expected would have been at Saint Domingo by the first of August . . ."); ibid., 4:168, J. Adams to B. Stoddert, 9 Sept. 1799.

21. Adams Family Papers, reel 119, J. Adams to G. Little, 25 June 1799 (regarding Knox); ibid., J. Adams to B. Stoddert, 16 Aug. 1799 (endorsing Dr. Winship's request for appointment); ibid., J. Adams to B. Stoddert, 8 June 1799 (reaction to Williston and Savage).

22. Knox, *Naval Documents...Quasi-War*, 3;452, B. Stoddert to G. Little, 2 July 1799; Non-Intercourse Act of 9 February 1799, U.S. Statutes 1:613–16; Massachusetts Historical Society, H. G. Otis Papers, Circular Letter from B. Stoddert, 12 March 1799. The Circular Letter noted in part:

> A proper discharge of the important duties enjoined on you, arising out of this act, will require the exercise of a sound and impartial judgment. You are not only to do all that in you lies to prevent all intercourse, whether direct or circuitous, between the ports of the United States and those of France and her dependencies, in cases where the vessels or cargoes are apparently, as well as really, American, and protected by American papers only; but you are to be vigilant that vessels or cargoes really American, but covered by Danish or other foreign papers, and bound to or from French ports, do not escape you.
>
> Whenever, on just suspicion, you send a vessel into port to be dealt with according to the aforementioned law, besides sending with her all her papers, send all the evidence you can obtain to support your suspicions, and effect her condemnation. . . .

23. Knox, *Naval Documents...Quasi-War*, 3:535–36, J. Church to W. Burrows, 24 July 1799.

24. Knox, *Naval Documents...Quasi-War*, 4:191–92, reprints extract of letter from G. Little to editor, *New Hampshire Gazette*, 6 Nov. 1799.

25. Knox, *Naval Documents...Quasi-War*, 4:349, Journal kept aboard *Constitution*, 1 Nov. 1799. After another "Fair Tryal at Sailing," Little reportedly was "now fully satisfyd of the *Constitution*'s Superiority." Ibid., 4:353, 3 Nov. 1799.

26. Knox, *Naval Documents...Quasi-War*, 4:284, G. Parsons to G. Little, 14 Oct. 1799.

27. Knox, *Naval Documents...Quasi-War*, 4:366–67, W. Bainbridge to unknown, 7 Nov. 1799; ibid., 5:190–93, court file, U.S. District Court; ibid., 5:235, B. Stoddert to J. Steele, 20 Feb. 1800; ibid., 5:237, B. Stoddert to J. & W. Forbes, 19 March 1800.

28. National Archives–New England Region, Waltham, Mass., Record Group 21, Records of the United States District Courts, United States District Court for the District of Massachusetts, *Little v. The Brigantine Flying Fish,* January term 1800 [hereafter, "*Little v. The Brigantine Flying Fish* Casefile"], Hinson's Answers to Interrogatories and his "Public Instrument of Protest."

29. *Little v. The Brigantine Flying Fish* Casefile, William Lacher James's Answers to Interrogatories.

30. *Little v. The Brigantine Flying Fish* Casefile, Hinson's "Public Instrument of Protest." The author has inserted the quotations in what appears to be Hinson's recounting of Little's actual words.

31. *Little v. The Brigantine Flying Fish* Casefile, Hinson's "Public Instrument of Protest." Beale is identified as the prizemaster in a paper he wrote in the casefile supporting a motion to unload the *Flying Fish*'s perishable cargo upon arrival at Boston.

32. Knox, *Naval Documents...Quasi-War,* 4:468, C. Perry to "a gentleman," 5 Dec. 1799.

33. Knox, *Naval Documents...Quasi-War,* 4;424, T. Burgess' Protest, 20 Dec. 1799; ibid., 6:73–74, list of the *Boston* prizes; ibid., 6:191–92, B. Stoddert to J. Carey, 28 July 1800; ibid., 6:213, B. Stoddert to S. Higginson, 31 July 1800.

34. Franklin Delano Roosevelt Library, Hyde Park, N.Y., George Little Papers [hereafter, "George Little Papers"], S. Higginson to G. Little, 11 Aug. 1800.

35. Hinson conceded that he had been master of ships that had called at New York and that, as a boy, he had sailed in an American vessel. *Little v. The Brigantine Flying Fish* Casefile, Hinson's Answers to Interrogatories.

36. *Little v. The Brigantine Flying Fish* Casefile, Needham's Answers to Interrogatories.

37. *Little v. The Brigantine Flying Fish* Casefile, Barreme's Answers to Interrogatories.

38. A certified copy of Goodman's 1798 British passport, as well as an affidavit submitted on his behalf by merchants in St. Thomas, are in the *Little v. The Brigantine Flying Fish* Casefile.

39. Knox, *Naval Documents...Quasi-War,* 4:467, G. Little to E. Stevens, 3 Dec. 1799.

40. Knox, *Naval Documents...Quasi-War,* 4:486–87, E. Stevens to G. Little, 4 Dec. 1799.

41. Knox, *Naval Documents...Quasi-War,* 4:486–87, E. Stevens to G. Little, 4 Dec. 1799; ibid., 4:458–59, N. Levy to G. Little, 29 Nov. 1799.

42. Knox, *Naval Documents...Quasi-War,* 4:468, C. Perry to "Gentleman," 5 Dec. 1799.

43. *Little v. The Brigantine Flying Fish* Casefile, Hinson's Answers to Interrogatories (emphasis in original).

44. *Little v. The Brigantine Flying Fish* Casefile, Haswell's testimony.

45. Knox, *Naval Documents...Quasi-War,* 4:486–87, E. Stevens to G. Little, 4 Dec. 1799.

46. *Little v. The Brigantine Flying Fish* Casefile, Hinson's Public Instrument of Protest.

47. See F. C. Leiner, "The Seizure of the *Flying Fish,*" *American Neptune* 56 (1996), 131–43; *Little v. Barreme,* 6 U.S. 170 (1804).

48. Knox, *Naval Documents...Quasi-War,* 4:561, S. Talbot to G. Little, 22 Dec. 1799. For the chasing of the American merchantmen, see ibid., 4:554, 18 Dec. 1799; ibid., 4:581, 29 Dec. 1799; ibid., 4:584, 30 Dec. 1799 (all Commodore Talbot's journal entries).

49. Mystic Seaport Museum, Mystic, Connecticut, G. W. Blunt-White Library, Silas Talbot Papers [hereafter, "Silas Talbot Papers"], S. Talbot to G. Talbot (with Statement), 6 Feb. 1800.

50. National Archives–New England Region, Waltham, Massachusetts, Record Group 21, United States Circuit Court for the District of Massachusetts, *Talbot v. Little* Casefile, October term 1800 [hereafter, "*Talbot v. Little* Casefile"], Deposition of C. R. Perry, 14 Aug. 1800.

51. Silas Talbot Papers, S. Talbot to C. Perry and S. Talbot to G. Little, 18 Jan. 1800.

52. Silas Talbot Papers, S. Talbot to J. Bayard, 21 Jan. 1802.

53. *Talbot v. Little* Casefile, Deposition of C. R. Perry, 14 Aug. 1800.

54. National Archives–New England Region, Waltham, Massachusetts, Record Group 21, United States District Court for the District of Massachusetts, *Little v. Les Deux Anges* Casefile, March term 1800; Silas Talbot Papers, S. Talbot to E. Stevens, 5 Feb. 1800.

55. F. C. Leiner, "Anatomy of a Prize Case: Dollars, Side-Deals, and *Les Deux Anges*," *American Journal of Legal History* 39 (1995), 214–32.

56. National Archives–New England Region, Waltham, Massachusetts, Record Group 21, Records of the United States District Court for the District of Massachusetts, *Davis v. The Brigantine L'Espoir*, September term 1800, Decree of Judge Lowell; Knox, *Naval Documents…Quasi-War*, 5:271, reprinting *Massachusetts Mercury*, 25 July 1800.

57. *Federal Gazette & Baltimore Daily Advertiser*, 26 Sept. 1799; Knox, *Naval Documents…Quasi-War*, 4:505, E. Stevens to B. Stoddert, 9 Dec. 1799; ibid., 4:437, reprinting New York *Daily Advertiser*, 17 Jan. 1800.

58. Knox, *Naval Documents…Quasi-War*, 5:325–26, G. Little to B. Stoddert, 19 March 1800; ibid., 5:271, reprinting *Massachusetts Mercury*, 25 July 1800 (printing the *Boston* logbook extracts).

59. George Little, Jr. (1781–1811), graduated with the A.B. degree from Harvard in 1800, although he had been suspended for four months for "irreverent behavior" and "frequent indecorum" in chapel. Harvard University Archives, Cambridge, Massachusetts, Faculty Records 7:47–48, 61; ibid., Class of 1800 Class Book. Edward Preble Little (1791–1875) would serve eight years in the Massachusetts legislature, as a Democrat in the U.S. House of Representatives (1852–53), and as collector of customs at Plymouth, Massachusetts. See *Biographical Directory of the United States Congress* (Washington, D.C.: Government Printing Office, 1989), 1377–78.

60. Stephen Clough kept a journal aboard the *Boston* in which he noted in sweeping cursive script "Nephew to the Commander of said Frigate." Henry Huntington Library, San Marino, California, frigate Boston log [*sic*] [hereafter, Clough Journal].

61. Robert Haswell had sent a letter to President Adams asking for an appointment for his brother John. The president looked over young Haswell and "was so much pleased & satisfied with his person and deportment" that he ordered Secretary Stoddert to issue him a midshipman's warrant. Adams Family Papers, reel 120, J. Adams to B. Stoddert, 6 Aug. 1800. See ibid., J. Adams to B. Stoddert, 9 Oct. 1800 (enclosing letter from Boston merchant Thomas Amory recommending William Haswell for a lieutenant). Robert Haswell married Mary Cordis in 1798; Joseph was her brother. Frederic William Howay, "Some Notes on Robert Haswell," Massachusetts Historical Society *Proceedings* 65 (1936), 599.

62. *Works of John Adams*, 9:70–71, J. Adams to B. Stoddert, 3 Aug. 1800.

63. On her first cruise, thirty midshipmen and boys learned navigation and naval science, which the president warmly supported. *Works of John Adams*, 9:65, J. Adams to S. Dexter, 25 July 1800.

64. Knox, *Naval Documents…Quasi-War*, 6:229, B. Stoddert to G. Little, 7 Aug. 1800.

65. See Howay, "Some Notes on Robert Haswell," 592–600; Frederic W. Howay, ed., *Voyages of the "Columbia" to the Northwest Coast 1787–1790 and 1790–1793* (Boston: Massachusetts Historical Society, 1941), viii and xviii; the Boston merchants' opinion of Haswell is in Adams Family Papers, reel 338, S. Higginson to unknown, 19 April 1798; Haswell's declining of the offers from Nicholson and McNeill is in National Archives, Washington, D.C., Record Group 45, Miscellaneous Letters Received by the Secretary of the Navy, R. Haswell to B. Stoddert, 16 Feb. 1801.

66. Knox, *Naval Documents…Quasi-War*, 6:229, B. Stoddert to G. Little, 7 Aug. 1800 (informing Little that the *Boston*'s next cruise would be to Guadeloupe).

67. Clough Journal, 16 Sept. 1800.

68. Massachusetts Historical Society, Log of the *Boston*.

69. Log of the *Boston*, 13 Oct. 1800. Interestingly, Lt. Clough used almost the identical words to describe the action. See Clough Journal, 13 Oct. 1800.

70. Log of the *Boston*, 14 Oct. 1800; *Federal Gazette & Baltimore Daily Advertiser*, 5 Dec. 1800, reprinting letter of G. Little to B. Stoddert, 15 Nov. 1800; Notes of Ellis Ames, Massachusetts Historical Society *Proceedings* 20 (1883), 269–74.

71. The French original is in the Archives Nationale, Paris, Fonds Marine BB4/149. Rather surprisingly, the full text of Clement's report was published (in French) in the New York *Le Moniteur*, 5 Jan. 1801, a copy of which is also in the French archives. I have used the translation of Edgar Stanton Maclay, *A History of the United States Navy From 1775 to 1898* (New York: D. Appleton & Co., rev. ed., 1898), 1:209–12.

72. Archives Nationale, Paris, Fonds Marine, MAR/BB4/149, ship file on corvette *Berceau*, Report to the First Consul, March 1801; *Federal Gazette & Baltimore Daily Advertiser*, 4 Dec. 1800, reprinting extract of letter dated 16 Nov. 1800; ibid., 5 Dec. 1800, reprinting letter of G. Little to B. Stoddert, 15 Nov. 1800; Log of the *Boston*, 14–19 Oct. 1800.

73. Log of the *Boston*, 14 Oct.–11 Nov. 1800.

74. *Message From the President of the United States, Transmitting Sundry Documents Respecting the French Corvette Berceau* (Washington, D.C.: A. & G. Way, 1802), 6, reprinting extract of letter from S. Higginson & Co. to B. Stoddert, 12 Dec. 1800. The Boston *Independent Chronicle* first printed a short report of the French-American peace accord in its issue for 6–10 November 1800; it reported the *Boston*'s arrival with the *Berceau* in its 13–17 November issue. For other Boston newspaper accounts, see *Columbian Centinel*, 19 Nov. and 10 Dec. 1800, and *Massachusetts Mercury*, 18 Nov. 1800.

75. Knox, *Naval Documents…Quasi-War*, 6:555, B. Stoddert to G. Little, 27 Nov. 1800.

76. *Message From the President*, 6, S. Higginson to B. Stoddert, 12 Dec. 1800; ibid., 7, B. Stoddert to S. Higginson, 19 Dec. 1800; National Archives–New England Region, Waltham, Massachusetts, Record Group 21, Records of the United States District Court for the District of Massachusetts, *Little v. The Ship Berceau*, Dec. 1800 term,

Libel; Answers to Interrogatories of Lts. Clement, Pouten, Mean, and Troquereau; Decree; Marshal's Auction Report; and Clerk's calculation of costs and charges.

77. See Oliver Warner, *The Battle of the Nile* (New York: Macmillan Co., 1960), 129, and Ira Dye, *The Fatal Cruise of the Argus* (Annapolis, Md.: Naval Institute Press, 1994), 89.

78. Archives Nationale, Paris, Marine BB4/149.

79. Knox, *Naval Documents…Quasi-War,* 6:458, B. Stoddert to G. Little, 30 Dec. 1800; *Independent Chronicle,* 22–26 Jan. 1801.

80. *Columbian Centinel,* 28 Jan. 1801; Knox, *Naval Documents…Quasi-War,* 6:458–60, declaration dated 10 Feb. 1801.

81. National Archives, Washington, D.C., Record Group 125, Records of General Courts Martial and Courts of Inquiry of the Navy Department, 1799–1867, Court of Inquiry into the Conduct of Captain George Little, 30 June–8 July 1801 (National Archives Microfilm Publication M273, roll 3).

82. Knox, *Naval Documents…Quasi-War,* 7:266, H. Dearborn to G. Little, 2 July 1801.

83. *The Papers of James Madison: Secretary of State Series,* vol. 1 (4 March – 31 July 1801) (Charlottesville: University Press of Virginia, 1986), 367–69, R. Livingston to J. Madison, 1 July 1801.

84. Nowhere in the record of Captain Little's court martial is his lawyer identified. The author surmises that Little retained Samuel Dexter, Jr., who had served in the House and Senate and then as President Adams's secretary of war and of the treasury. With the Federalist electoral defeat of 1800, Dexter, one of the ablest lawyers of his day, returned to private practice in Boston. In 1801, Dexter represented Little in the Supreme Court in *Little v. Barreme* (the appeal of the *Flying Fish* case).

85. National Archives, Washington, D.C., Record Group 125, Records of General Courts Martial and Courts of Inquiry of the Navy Department, 1799–1867, Court Martial of Captain George Little, 1–7 Sept. 1801 (National Archives Microfilm Publication M273, roll 3); George Little Papers, draft questions, n. d.

86. Knox, *Naval Documents…Quasi-War,* 6:461–66.

87. Knox, *Naval Documents…Quasi-War,* 6:467, 25 Sept. 1801.

88. Compare Knox, *Naval Documents…Quasi-War,* 7:292, R. Smith to H. Campbell, to J. Rodgers, and to S. Decatur, 22 Oct. 1801, with ibid., 7:293, R. Smith to G. Little, 22 Oct. 1801 (omitting only from the letter to Little the sentence "how very painful it is for me to make you this unpleasant Communication. . . .").

89. Before Robert Smith became the navy secretary, Henry Dearborn as acting secretary wrote that "Before any order is taken . . . in the Selection of Officers to be retained in the Service, or to be discharged of those belonging to the *Boston,* the result of the enquiry must be known at this Office." Knox, *Naval Documents…Quasi-War,* 7:255–56, H. Dearborn to G. Little, 19 June 1801.

90. George Little Papers, H. Dearborn to G. Little, 3 July 1801; Knox, *Naval Documents…Quasi-War,* 6:272, B. Stoddert to T. Turner (Accountant of the Navy), 21 Aug. 1800 ("As this person appears to have done the duty of Captains Clerk, as well as Schoolmaster, I suppose it is right he should receive pay for both").

91. George Little Papers, unknown to G. Little, 18 July 1801.

92. National Archives, Washington, D.C., Record Group 45, "Miscellaneous Letters Received by the Secretary of the Navy," R. Haswell to B. Stoddert, 1 April 1801; Howay, "Some Notes on Robert Haswell," 592–600.

93. George Little Papers, Howe Affidavit, 11 Sept. 1801.

94. *DAB*, 6:298–99.

95. French Ministere de la Defense, Service historique de la marine, Vincennes, France, class CC7, dossier 501. The author wishes to thank M. Pierre Waksman, conservateur en chef of the French navy archives, for supplying the Clement file.

96. *Message From the President*, 41–45, S. Brown to R. Smith, 31 Oct. 1801.

97. Archives Nationales, Paris, Centre d'accueil et de recherche [CARAN], Fonds marine, BB5 5, f. 35. The author wishes to thank M. Philippe Henrat for providing a narrative of the *Berceau*'s later services.

98. As to McNeill's 1802 activities commanding the *Boston*, see Christopher McKee, *A Gentlemanly and Honorable Profession: The Creation of the U.S. Naval Officer Corps, 1794–1815* (Annapolis, Md.: Naval Institute Press, 1991), 192–93; Gardner W. Allen, *Our Navy and the Barbary Corsairs* (Boston: Houghton Mifflin Co., 1905), 108–9. The *Boston*'s deterioration is recounted in Phillips Library, Peabody Essex Museum, Salem, Massachusetts, Josiah Fox Papers, Letterbook 3:320, Survey of U.S. Frigate Boston, 7 Feb. 1806.

99. A dramatic account of the burning of the Washington Navy Yard is in Walter Lord, *The Dawn's Early Light* (New York: W.W. Norton & Co., 1972), 161–62, 173–74.

Chapter 7. Politics of Procurement, Politics of Preferment

1. John Brown (1736–1803) was one of the early nation's great entrepreneurs. A leading supplier to the Continental Army in the Revolution, John Brown had an ownership interest for a half-century in the "Hope Furnace," which manufactured cannon for the army and navy. Along with his brothers Nicholas, Joseph, and Moses, Brown laid the foundation for Brown University. John Brown's activities included manufacturing spermaceti candles and pig iron and investing in far-flung maritime trade. His ship, the *General Washington*, was the first Providence vessel to Canton in 1787. He is described by a biographer as a "cold, calculating, practical" man, and a man of grand projects. He also served one term (1799–1801) in Congress as a Federalist. See James B. Hodges, *The Browns of Providence Plantations* (Cambridge: Harvard University Press, 1952, 1967), 14. His *DAB* entry notes that, in 1798, he "rode the wave of patriotic fervor to his own advantage." *DAB*, 2:128–29.

2. Knox, *Naval Documents…Quasi-War*, 1:220–21, B. Stoddert to J. Anthony, 19 July 1798; ibid., 1:277–78, B. Stoddert to J. Brown, 7 Aug. 1798.

3. Knox, *Naval Documents…Quasi-War*, 1:351–52, B. Stoddert to S. Talbot, 29 Aug. 1798 (ordering Talbot to examine the *George Washington*). As to Talbot's role, also see William M. Fowler, Jr., *Silas Talbot: Captain of Old Ironsides* (Mystic, Conn; Mystic Seaport Museum, 1995), 137–38. The references to Talbot are in *Works of John Adams*, 8:637, J. Adams to B. Stoddert, 27 April 1799, and in Knox, *Naval Documents…Quasi-War*, 2:516–17, T. Truxtun to B. Stoddert, 26 March 1799.

4. Knox, *Naval Documents…Quasi-War*, 1:428–29, B. Stoddert to S. Talbot, 20 Sept. 1798 (Stoddert concluded to buy the *George Washington*, and asked Talbot to "do the best he could" with Brown, who was to supply the guns, cannonballs, etc.); ibid., 1:423, B. Stoddert to J. Brown, 18 Sept. 1798 (acquiescing in the price terms, including the delay charge); Hodges, *Browns of Providence Plantation*, 2:72–73 (describing negotiations).

5. Knox, *Naval Documents...Quasi-War*, 2:59, B. Stoddert to P. Fletcher, 3 Dec. 1798 (ordering the *George Washington* to Windward Islands); ibid., 2:303, *Merrimack* Journal extract, 2 Feb. 1799 (escorting seven merchant ships with the *George Washington*); ibid., 2:486, *Pickering* log extract, 18 March 1799 (convoying thirty-six merchant ships with the *George Washington*); ibid., 3:190, *Pickering* log extract, 15 May 1799 (the *George Washington* convoying about sixty merchantmen); ibid., 3:215, B. Stoddert to T. Truxtun, 20 May 1799 (referring to the *George Washington* as "dull Sailer"); ibid., 3:340–41, B. Stoddert to P. Fletcher, 15 June 1799 (requesting opinion); ibid., 3:343–44, B. Stoddert to S. Higginson, 15 June 1799 (the *George Washington* "worse than useless"); ibid., 4:351, Gibbs & Channing to B. Stoddert, 3 Nov. 1799 (reporting Fletcher's view); ibid., 4:411, Gibbs & Channing to B. Stoddert, 17 Nov. 1799 (bad copper); ibid., 4:538, B. Stoddert to Gibbs & Channing, 14 Dec. 1799 ("it is best to sell her at once," expecting $40,000); ibid., 5:112, B. Stoddert to Gibbs & Channing, 21 Jan 1800 (suggesting auction if private sale unsuccessful); ibid., 5:230, Gibbs & Channing to B. Stoddert, 19 Feb. 1800 (Humphreys's survey); ibid., 5:255, B. Stoddert to Gibbs & Channing, 28 Feb. 1800 ("If you can get 30,000 Drs. . . . .take it"). As to the *George Washington* debacle, see Long, *Ready to Hazard*, 40–54; G. Tucker, *Dawn Like Thunder*, 19–25, and Allen, *Our Navy and the Barbary Corsairs*, 75–85.

6. P. C. F. Smith, *The Frigate Essex Papers*, 19–24. As to Stoddert's stock offer for a Charleston ship, see Knox, *Naval Documents...Quasi-War*, 1:230, B. Stoddert to J. Simons, 21 July 1798.

7. Knox, *Naval Documents...Quasi-War*, 1:339, B. Stoddert to G. Crowninshield & Sons, 25 Aug. 1798 (emphasis added); ibid., 2:294, B. Stoddert to J. Brown, 30 Jan. 1799; ibid., 1:369–70, G. Crowninshield & Sons to J. Adams, 1 Sept. 1798; P. C. F. Smith, *Frigate Essex Papers*, 22–26. Smith believes that the Crowninshields simply misunderstood the subscription-loan statute. While it is true that Stoddert informed the Crowninshields that the law enabled the navy to acquire new or building ships only, Stoddert's purchase of the *George Washington* with stock sheds some doubt as to how mistaken the Crowninshields were.

8. *The Norfolk Herald*, 25 June 1798.

9. The Petersburg committee consisted of James Campbell, Watson Stott, William Haxhall, Robert Colquhoun, and Christopher M'Connico. *Norfolk Herald*, 28 June 1798. On the Richmond committee were Robert Gamble, Bushrod Washington, William Mitchell, James Brown, and Cornelius Buck. [Philadelphia] *Aurora & General Advertiser*, 4 July 1798.

10. *Federal Gazette & Baltimore Daily Advertiser*, 30 June 1798. The Norfolk committee consisted of Robert Taylor, William Pennock, Moses Myers, Thomas Willock, and Warren Ashley. *Norfolk Herald*, 30 June 1798.

11. A superb biography of Marshall is J. E. Smith, *John Marshall*. As to Bushrod Washington, see Albert P. Blaustein and Roy M. Mersky, ""Bushrod Washington," in *The Justices of the Supreme Court 1789–1969*, eds. Leon Friedman and Fred L. Israel (New York: Chelsea House Publishers, 1969), 243–57.

12. Edward Carrington (1749–1810) served as the quartermaster general of the Continental Army of the South under Nathaniel Greene, and was considered an excellent soldier. A member of the Virginia House of Delegates (1784–85) and the Continental Congress (1785–86), Carrington was a friendly correspondent of

Jefferson's. President Washington appointed him U.S. marshal of Virginia in 1789 and the next year Carrington married John Marshall's sister-in-law. In 1807, Carrington served on the jury at Aaron Burr's trial for treason in Richmond. See Henry B. Carrington, *Battles of the American Revolution 1775–1781* (New York: Promontory Press, n.d. [orig. pub. 1877].), 530; Henry Lumpkin, *From Savannah to Yorktown: The American Revolution in the South* (New York: Paragon House, 1981), 178–80 (Carrington's role at Hobkirk Hill); *Papers of John Marshall*, ed. Herbert A. Johnson (Chapel Hill: University of North Carolina Press, 1974–), 1:217 n. (précis on Carrington). John Harvie (1742–1807) had introduced Jefferson's Bill for Establishing Religious Freedom in the Virginia House of Delegates as a member from Albemarle County in 1779, although the bill was not enacted until 1786. Harvie served as register of the Virginia Land Office (1780–91), and, after his death, his son married John Marshall's daughter. *DAB*, 5:20; *Papers of John Marshall*, 1:92n (précis on Harvie) and 2:321 n.5 (son's marriage).

13. There is no biography of Myers. The major source for his life is Malcolm H. Stern, "Moses Myers and the Early Jewish Community of Norfolk," *Journal of the Southern Jewish Historical Society* 1 (1958), 5–13. As to Myers's kindness to the French, see *Moreau*, 34, who also noted that in 1794, Myers owned the packet ship sailing from Norfolk to Baltimore (which cost a passenger a $8.50 fee). Ibid., 71. Truxtun referred to Myers's "more than friendly (brotherly) attention to me at Norfolk" as adding to "our very longstanding acquaintance." Knox, *Naval Documents...Quasi-War*, 6:507, T. Truxtun to M. Myers, 27 Oct. 1800. Samuel Myers (1754/5–1836), apparently no relation to Moses Myers, was the son of Myer Myers, the renown New York silversmith. Stern, "Moses Myers," 11 n.7. As to Moses Myers generally, and his motives for relocating to Norfolk, I am indebted to Joseph Mosier who is cataloging the Myers papers at the Chrysler Museum in Norfolk.

14. Stern, "Moses Myers," 11 n. 11.

15. National Archives, Washington, D.C., Records of the Bureau of Customs, Record Group 36, Proof of Ownership of Registered Vessels (Philadelphia District), registration of *Richmond*, 18 June 1801 (as to tonnage); Knox, *Naval Documents . . . Barbary Powers*, 6:330 (as to cost); Knox, *Naval Documents...Quasi-War*, 1:261, B. Stoddert to J. Campbell, 31 July 1798; ibid., 1:279, B. Stoddert to J. Nevison and J. Granbery, 7 Aug. 1798; ibid., 1:425, B. Stoddert to S. Barron, 19 Sept. 1798.

16. Knox, *Naval Documents...Quasi-War*, 3:331, B. Stoddert to W. Pennock, 12 June 1799 ("probable" that navy would buy Myers's ship); ibid., 3:344, B. Stoddert to W. Pennock, 15 June 1799 ("buy the Brig at a fair price"). Captain Truxtun inspected the *Augusta* before her purchase and said she was "nearly perfect." Ibid., 4:54, B. Stoddert to S. Higginson & Co., 9 Aug. 1799. Stoddert ordered Humphreys to inspect the *Augusta*, recognizing she was "slight" and would last only two or three years. Ibid., 4:125–26, B. Stoddert to J. Humphreys, 27 Aug. 1798. Humphreys's report is in Historical Society of Pennsylvania, Philadelphia, Joshua Humphreys Letterbook 1797–1800, J. Humphreys to B. Stoddert, 16 Sept. 1799. The comments about her sailing are in Knox, *Naval Documents...Quasi-War*, 5:367, letter of a captain, 31 March 1800, reprinted from *Norfolk Herald*, 26 April 1800.

17. There is no biography of Samuel Barron. His brother wrote a short notice of him, James Barron, "Commodore Samuel Barron," *Virginia Historical Register and Lit-*

erary Note Book 4 (1851), 198–204, and there are references to him in William Oliver Stevens, *An Affair of Honor: The Biography of Commodore James Barron, U.S.N.* (Chesapeake, Va.: Norfolk County Historical Society, in cooperation with Earl Gregg Swem Library, College of William & Mary, 1969), 11–14. For a reference to Barron's voyage in Myers's brig *Elizabeth Leamy* in 1796, see Earl Gregg Swem Library, College of William & Mary, Williamsburg, Va., Samuel Barron Papers, Box 1, account of Capt. S. Barron on account with Moses Myers. For the letter of recommendation of the mayor and alderman, see ibid., typescript copy dated 24 July 1798. The other letters are in National Archives, Washington, D.C., Record Group 45, Subject File 1775–1910, Box NN [applications for appointments]: M. Myers to H. Knox, 15 Nov. 1794, enclosed with G. Meade to H. Knox, 4 Dec. 1794; ibid., petition from twelve inhabitants of Norfolk to J. Adams, 23 July 1798; ibid., J. Parker to B. Stoddert, 24 July 1798; ibid., R. Gilmore to B. Stoddert, 1 Aug. 1798.

18. Knox, *Naval Documents…Quasi-War,* 1:425, B. Stoddert to S. Barron, 19 Sept. 1798 (Barron's choices, if seconded by Parker and the Norfolk navy agents, would be placed before President Adams and appointed by him). Ibid., 1:495–96, J. Parker to B. Stoddert, 5 Oct. 1798 (listing officers); ibid., 1:489, B. Stoddert to S. Barron, 4 Oct. 1798 (recruiting instructions).

19. Knox, *Naval Documents…Quasi-War,* 2:144–45, Truxtun Journal extract 31 Dec. 1798; ibid., 2:72, B. Stoddert to S. Barron, 7 Dec. 1798 (the *Richmond* placed under Truxtun); ibid., 2:73–74, B. Stoddert to T. Truxtun,, 8 Dec. 1798 (orders for squadron); ibid., 1:538–40, B. Stoddert to T. Pickering, 16 Oct. 1798 (disposition of ships). Stoddert had sent the *Montezuma, Norfolk,* and *Retaliation* to the West Indies where the *Retaliation* was captured by two French frigates, and the others barely escaped. Goldsborough, *U.S.Naval Chronicle,* 127–30; Gardner W. Allen, *Our Naval War with France* (Boston: Houghton Mifflin Co., 1909), 72–75.

20. Knox, *Naval Documents…Quasi-War,* 2:234, Truxtun Journal extract, 12 Jan. 1799; ibid., 2:266, T. Truxtun to S. Barron, 20 Jan. 1799; ibid., 2:269–70, T. Truxtun to J. Barry, 21 Jan. 1799.

21. Knox, *Naval Documents…Quasi-War,* 2:307–08, T. Truxtun to B. Stoddert, 4 Feb. 1799; ibid., 2:311–12, T. Truxtun to T. Williams, 5 Feb. 1799.

22. Knox, *Naval Documents…Quasi-War,* 3:388, T. Truxtun to B. Stoddert, 23 June 1799 ("none more deserving" than Samuel Barron, also noting the merchants of Norfolk "all seemed . . . to interest themselves in his Behalf"); ibid., 2:491–92, T. Truxtun to J. Barry, 20 March 1799 (proposing transfer). James Barron had saved the *United States* from destruction in a gale off Cape Hatteras. See W. M. P. Dunne, "Pistols and Honor: The James Barron–Stephen Decatur Conflict, 1798–1807," *American Neptune* 50 (1990), 249.

23. Knox, *Naval Documents…Quasi-War,* 1:128, B. Stoddert to J. Yellott, 22 June 1798 (merchants had approached Stoddert to make Speake a lieutenant, and Stoddert complied); ibid., 1:153, B. Stoddert to J. Yellott, 29 June 1798 (appointing Speake first lieutenant). As to the outrage perpetrated on the *Baltimore,* see Goldsborough, *U.S. Naval Chronicle,* 115–24; Palmer, *Stoddert's War,* 61–66; and Guttridge and Smith, *The Commodores,* 37–39. Guttridge and Smith assert that Speake and Stoddert were distant cousins; perhaps so, but in the initial letter to

Yellott cited above, Stoddert refers to him as "a Capt. Speake." Stoddert's orders to Speake are in Knox, *Naval Documents...Quasi-War,* 2:314, B. Stoddert to J. Speake, 6 Feb. 1799.

24. Knox, *Naval Documents...Quasi-War,* 2:513, T. Truxtun to J. Speake, 25 March 1799.

25. Knox, *Naval Documents...Quasi-War,* 3:31, T. Truxtun to J. Speake, 8 April 1799 (ordering the *Richmond* out for second cruise); ibid., 3:73, T. Truxtun to J. Speake, 20 April 1799 (ordering three ships to cruise again and to rendezvous at St. Kitts on 2 May 1799); ibid., 3:129–30, T. Truxtun to J. Speake, 3 May 1799 (admonishing Speake); ibid., 3:142–43, T. Truxtun to D. Clarkson, 6 May 1799 (asking the navy agent at St. Kitts to "dispose of" the prize, which Truxtun called the *Lewis,* and its cargo). Goldsborough, *U.S. Naval Chronicle,* 183, lists the ship as the *Louise,* but Knox, *Naval Documents...Quasi-War,* 7:372, lists her as the *Louis* and her date of capture as 26 April 1799.

26. Knox, *Naval Documents...Quasi-War,* 3:218–20, T. Tingey to B. Stoddert, 20 May 1799; ibid., 3:339, B. Stoddert to J. Adams, 15 June 1799; ibid., 4:65–66, B. Stoddert to S. Higginson & Co., 12 Aug. 1799. The two vessels are identified in ibid., 6:276, "List of Vessels Captured and Recaptured by the United States Brig Eagle and Others." Prize money was still due one year later for the *Mahitable.* Ibid., 6:563, B. Stoddert to C. Biddle, 29 Nov. 1800.

27. Knox, *Naval Documents...Quasi-War,* 3:326–27, T. Tingey to B. Stoddert, 11 June 1799.

28. Knox, *Naval Documents...Quasi-War,* 3:511 and 3:515, B. Stoddert to J. Speake, 18 and 19 July 1799; ibid., 4:23, H. Williams to W. Burrows, 2 Aug. 1799.

29. Fowler, *Silas Talbot,* 8, 72, 83–84, 107–08, 132–33; Silas Talbot Papers, C. Talbot to S. Talbot, 5 Sept. 1798 (Hobart's letter to Adams and Foster's introduction to President and Stoddert); ibid., C. Talbot to S. Talbot, 27 Oct. 1798 ("Voyages have been so unsuccessfull . . ." and Hobart, Morris, and Watson interested in his application); Knox, *Naval Documents...Quasi-War,* 3:252–53, B. Stoddert to J. Adams, 25 May 1799 (nominating Cyrus Talbot); ibid., 3:317, B. Stoddert to C. Talbot, 8 June 1799 (enclosing commission); ibid., 3:539, B. Stoddert to C. Talbot, 25 July 1799 (Cyrus Talbot had been sent to New York for the *Richmond,* although Speake had sailed on the 18th).

30. *Federal Gazette & Baltimore Daily Advertiser,* 14 Oct. 1799 (noting arrival of *Richmond* in Hampton Roads on 5 October and that she would go on a cruise "in a few days, under the command of lieutenant Talbot"); Knox, *Naval Documents...Quasi-War,* 4:86, B. Stoddert to C. Talbot, 16 Aug. 1799 (orders); ibid., 4:260, H. Williams to W. Burrows, 6 Oct. 1799 (72-day cruise); ibid., 4:512–14, muster roll of the *Richmond.*

31. *Federal Gazette & Baltimore Daily Advertiser,* 8 Nov. 1799 (noting the *Richmond*'s arrival in Charleston on 22 October, having lost her rudder); Silas Talbot Papers, C. Talbot to S. Talbot, 12 Jan. 1800; ibid., B. Stoddert to S. Talbot, 20 Jan. 1800; Knox, *Naval Documents...Quasi-War,* 5:179, B. Stoddert to C. Talbot, 1 Feb. 1800.

32. Adams Family Papers, reel 119, J. Adams to B. Stoddert, 30 Aug. 1798 (enclosing letter from Judge Law and Captain Hinman recommending the younger Law, and requesting Stoddert to put Law's name "on the list"); ibid., J. Adams to B. Stod-

dert, 3 Oct. 1798 (enclosing Ellsworth's letter which, Adams wrote, "deserves great respect"); National Archives, Washington, D.C., Record Group 59, Letters of Application and Recommendation during the Administration of John Adams, R. Law to J. Adams, 14 Feb. 1798. As to the *Trumbull*'s battle with the *Watt*, see Miller, *Sea of Glory*, 424–25. As to Judge Law, see *DAB*, 6:41–42.

33. Knox, *Naval Documents…Quasi-War*, 4:551, B. Stoddert to R. Law, 17 Dec. 1799 (enclosing commission); ibid., 4:589, B. Stoddert to R. Law, 31 Dec. 1799 (listing nine vacancies among commissioned and warrant officers); ibid., 4:552, B. Stoddert to J. & E. Watson, 18 Dec. 1799 (requesting New York navy agents to provide supplies for storeship); ibid., 5:51, B. Stoddert to R. Law, 8 Jan. 1800 (admonishing Law).

34. Knox, *Naval Documents…Quasi-War*, 5:104, B. Stoddert to R. Law, 20 Jan. 1800 (orders); ibid., 5:225, extract from Isaac Hull Journal, 17 Feb. 1800 (noting arrival of the *Richmond*). As to the underway replenishment, see Fowler, *Silas Talbot*, 161–62, and Tyrone G. Martin, "Underway Replenishment, 1799–1800," *American Neptune* 46 (1986), 162.

35. Silas Talbot Papers, S. Talbot to R. Law, 19 Feb. 1800 (orders); ibid., R. Law to S. Talbot, 10 April 1800; Knox, *Naval Documents…Quasi-War*, 6:58, N. Keene to W. Burrows, 18 June 1800 (reporting Law's comment which Keene hoped "will secure him the esteem of every Officer in the Corps").

36. The *Richmond* sailed in the Bite from no later than mid-March, Knox, *Naval Documents…Quasi-War*, 5:311–12, E. Stevens to T. Pickering, 16 March 1800, and was there three weeks later, ibid., 5:381–83, E. Stevens to T. Pickering, 4 April 1800. For Law's interpreting his orders widely, see Silas Talbot Papers, R. Law to S. Talbot, 10 April 1800. For a notice about the convoy and the *Pearl*, see *Federal Gazette & Baltimore Daily Advertiser*, 14 April 1800. About the recaptures, see ibid., 2 June 1800, reprinting letter of R. Law to B. Stoddert, 28 April 1800, and Knox, *Naval Documents…Quasi-War*, 6:27–29, reprinting *Connecticut Courant*, 28 July 1800, letter from officer aboard the *Connecticut*.

37. Silas Talbot Papers, S. Talbot to E. Stevens, 20 May 1800; ibid., S. Talbot to R. Law, 24 May 1800 (sending remonstrance to Parker); Knox, *Naval Documents…Quasi-War*, 6:65, S. Talbot to R. Law, 21 June 1800 (orders to Bite); ibid., 6:181, Hull's Journal, 25 July 1800 (noting departure of the *Constitution* and Murray assuming command of squadron); ibid., 6:287, A. Murray to R. Law, 31 July 1800 (orders); ibid., A. Murray to R. Law, 26 Aug. 1800 ("rather unfortunate" that Law did not receive Murray's earlier letter).

38. Knox, *Naval Documents…Quasi-War*, 6:314, A. Murray to B. Stoddert, 3 Sept. 1800 (noting the *Richmond*'s arrival and that she would be ordered to cruise off Cuba); ibid., 6:333–34, A. Murray to R. Law, 9 Sept. 1800 (orders); ibid., 6:469–70, R. Law to J. Sever, 12 Oct. 1800.

39. Knox, *Naval Documents…Quasi-War*, 7:133, B. Stoddert to J. & E. Watson, 3 March 1801 (just advised of the *Richmond*'s arrival, Stoddert ordered her crew paid off); ibid., 7:133–34, B. Stoddert to R. Law, 3 March 1801 (instructing Law to place brig "in a safe situation"); ibid., 6:314, A. Murray to B. Stoddert, 3 Sept. 1800 (Murray's opinion of Law); ibid., 7:174, S. Smith to R. Law, 2 April 1801 (dismissing Law). As to Cyrus Talbot's resignation, see Fowler, *Silas Talbot*, 182–83. As to

Speake's dismissal, see Knox, *Naval Documents...Quasi-War,* 7:187, S. Smith to J. Speake, 11 April 1801, and his reinstatement as sailing master on 6 June 1801 is in ibid., 7:351. Very little has been written on Samuel Barron. For his lackluster command of the Mediterranean squadron in the Barbary Wars, see G. Tucker, *Dawn Like Thunder.* After his disappointing performance in the Mediterranean, poor health and stigmatization as James Barron's brother left Samuel Barron unemployed and reduced to half-pay until 1810, when the navy assigned him command of the Norfolk Navy Yard. He died that year at age forty-five. See McKee, *Gentlemanly and Honorable Profession,* 337.

40. Knox, *Naval Documents...Quasi-War,* 7:126, B. Stoddert to J. Parker, 20 Feb. 1801 (Navy planned to sell the *Richmond,* hoping to receive $6,000); ibid., 7:172, S. Smith to D. Ludlow, 1 April 1801 (ordering the *Richmond's* military equipment to be stripped and the vessel to be sold after fifteen days notice); ibid., 7:307 (sale of the *Richmond*). Peter J. Wrike of Cobbs Creek, Virginia, provided his conclusions of the fate of the *Richmond* to the author from his review of consular records in the National Archives.

Chapter 8. Squandered Ship

1. *Papers of Alexander Hamilton,* 21:462, A. Hamilton to J. McHenry, 17 May 1798 and ibid., 21:463 n.4 citing *Greenleaf's New Daily Advertiser,* 16 May 1798.
2. *The Spectator,* 2 June 1798.
3. *Federal Gazette & Baltimore Daily Advertiser,* 16 June 1798.
4. *The Spectator,* 16 June 1798.
5. Murray (1737–1808), a leading merchant and one of the chief shipowners in America, was president of the New York Chamber of Commerce and was an original incorporator of the Bank of New York. The Murray Hill section of New York is named for his landholding. *DAB,* 7:359–60.
6. Alexander Hamilton wrote that Barnewall "has been bred a sailor is well acquainted with all that appertains to vessels—has done considerable business as a Merchant & is of very good reputation for integrity," although he had served as a British naval officer in the Revolution. *Papers of Alexander Hamilton,* 21:480–81, A. Hamilton to O. Wolcott, 2 June 1798.
7. Bayard (1761–1826) was a partner with Herman LeRoy in a prominent merchant firm and was president of the Bank of America..
8. *The Spectator,* 20 June 1798.
9. *The Spectator,* 23 June 1798; [New York] *Commercial Advertiser,* 27 June 1798; *The Spectator,* 4 July 1798.
10. Knox, *Naval Documents...Quasi-War,* 1:146–47, B. Stoddert to J. Murray, et al., 27 June 1798.
11. Ibid., 1:153–54, B. Stoddert to J. Murray, et al., 30 June 1798 (enclosing Joshua Humphrey's tabular dimensions).
12. Ibid., 1:262–63.
13. *The Spectator,* 11 Aug. 1798.
14. Chapelle, *American Sailing Navy,* 164; Historical Society of Pennsylvania, Philadelphia, Pa., Joshua Humphreys Letter Book 1797–1800, "Particular Dimensions of a 36 Gun Frigate building in New York for the Merchants . . ." 1 Jan. 1799.

15. Adams Family Papers, microfilm roll 389, North to J. Adams, 5 June 1798; Knox, *Naval Documents...Quasi-War,* 7:347.

16. The keel laying of the *Adams* was announced in *Porcupine's Gazette,* 1 Aug. 1798; the *President's* keel was laid on 6 August 1798, as reported in *The Spectator,* 11 Aug. 1798, the same issue noting that the keel of the merchants' frigate "will be laid in a few days."

17. John G. B. Hutchins, *The American Maritime Industries and Public Policy, 1789–1914* (Cambridge: Harvard University Press, 1941), 181. The lack of skilled carpenters had been foreseen by Stoddert but, with warships under construction in all the major ports, there was nothing he could do. Knox, *Naval Documents...Quasi-War,* 1:165, B. Stoddert to J. Watson, 5 July 1798.

18. *New York Commercial Advertiser,* 24 April 1800 (the *New York's* launching); *Federal Gazette & Baltimore Daily Advertiser,* 14 April 1800 (the *President's* launching).

19. Simon P. Newman, *Parades and the Politics of the Street: Festive Culture in the Early American Republic* (Philadelphia: University of Pennsylvania Press, 1997), 29–31, 104–9.

20. *Federal Gazette & Baltimore Daily Advertiser,* 30 April 1800; McKee, *A Gentlemanly and Honorable Profession,* 106, 108. McKee concludes that political affiliation played "very little" role in the selection of officers for the navy. Ibid. at 104.

21. *Federal Gazette & Baltimore Daily Advertiser,* 30 Sept. 1800.

22. Ibid., 13 Oct. 1800.

23. Knox, *Naval Documents...Quasi-War,* 4:32–33, B. Stoddert to Merchants Committee, 5 Aug. 1799; ibid., 4:79, B. Stoddert to J. Murray; ibid., 5:88, B. Stoddert to T. Robinson, 16 Jan. 1800 (enclosing his commission and continuing his superintendence of the *New York*); *Federal Gazette & Baltimore Daily Advertiser,* 22 July 1800 (noting that the *Adams* had returned the previous afternoon from a cruise of "almost 10 months"); Knox, *Naval Documents...Quasi-War,* 6:262, B. Stoddert to R. Morris, 18 Aug. 1800 (ordering him to assume command of the *New York*); ibid., 6:304, T. Robinson to B. Stoddert, 30 Aug. 1800 (outlining officer exchanges between the *New York* and *Adams*).

24. Knox, *Naval Documents...Quasi-War,* 6:450–51, B. Stoddert to T. FitzSimons, 18 Oct. 1800.

25. Ibid., 6:488, B. Stoddert to R. Morris, 20 Oct. 1800; ibid., 6:522–23, B. Stoddert to T. Truxtun, 6 Nov. 1800 (enclosing copy of letter by the *New York*).

26. New Hampshire Historical Society, Jonathan Sawyer Collection, Log of *President,* 6 Dec. 1800; Historical Society of Pennsylvania, Truxtun Collection, T. Truxtun to R. Morris, 7 Dec. 1800; Log of the *President,* 31 Dec. 1800; Knox, *Naval Documents...Quasi-War,* 7:86–90, T. Truxtun to B. Stoddert, 15 Jan. 1801.

27. Knox, *Naval Documents...Quasi-War,* 7:216–17, S. Smith to R. Morris, 3 May 1801.

28. Knox, *Naval Documents...Quasi-War,* 7:134–38, sets forth Peace Establishment Act. See McKee, *Gentlemanly and Honorable Profession,* 106; G. Tucker, *Dawn Like Thunder,* 153.

29. Knox, *Naval Documents...Quasi-War,* 7:216–17, S. Smith to R. Morris, 3 May 1801 (ordering him to relinquish command to his first lieutenant, who was to "send the ship round to this place"); ibid., 7:265, T. Tingey to S. Smith, 1 July 1801 (reporting on unmooring the *New York* to allow the "side which has ben most expos'd to the Sun — a little respite . . ."); Knox, *Naval Documents...Barbary Wars,* 2:233, R.

Smith to J. Barron, 13 Aug. 1802 (ordering him to command the *New York* and to ready her "with the utmost dispatch for sea"); ibid., 2:270, W. Osborn to W. Burrows, 8 Sept. 1802 (describing accident); ibid., 2:270–71, Survey of Topmasts, 10 Sept. 1802; ibid., 2:323, Survey, 25 Nov. 1802; ibid., 2:325, Survey, 27 Nov. 1802.

30. J. Worth Estes, "A Naval Surgeon in the Barbary Wars: Dr. Peter St. Medard on *New York* 1802–3," *New Aspects of Naval History* (Baltimore: Nautical & Aviation Publishing Co., 1985), 81–92; Allen, *Our Navy and the Barbary Corsairs,* 125–28; G. Tucker, *Dawn Like Thunder,* 164–77; Guttridge and Smith, *The Commodores,* 66–70.

31. Dye, *The Fatal Cruise of the Argus,* 32; William Plumer, *Memorandum of the Proceedings in the United States Senate 1803–1807,* ed. Everett Somerville Brown (New York: Macmillan Co., 1923), 240; Josiah Fox Papers, Peabody Essex Museum, Salem, Massachusetts, LetterBook 4:437, Report of 19 May 1809; Brina J. Agrinat, "Thorough and Efficient Repair: Rebuilding in the American Sailing Navy," unpublished M.A. Thesis at East Carolina University (1993), 114–19; William S. Dudley, ed., *The Naval War of 1812* (Washington, D.C.: Naval Historical Center, 1985), 1:593, C. Gordon to P. Hamilton, 17 Nov. 1812; *American State Papers: Naval Affairs 1789–1836* (Washington, D.C.: Gales and Seaton, 1834–64), 23:305, U.S. Senate, "Condition of the Navy, and the Progress Made in Providing Materials and Building Ships," 13th Cong., 2nd sess., 18 March 1813; Linda M. Maloney, *The Captain From Connecticut: The Life and Naval Times of Isaac Hull* (Boston: Northeastern University Press, 1986), 423.

Chapter 9. Charleston's "Two-Sided" Frigate

1. [Charleston] *City Gazette & Daily Advertiser,* 16 and 30 June, 12 and 18 July, 1798.

2. Knox, *Naval Documents…Quasi-War,* 1:230, B. Stoddert to J. Simons, 21 July 1798; ibid., 1:248–49, B. Stoddert to H. Desaussure, 28 July 1798.

3. *City Gazette & Daily Advertiser,* 30 July 1798. These men were leading Charleston merchants; in February 1800, Gilchrist, Tunno, and Hazlehurst were elected directors of the United States Bank's branch in Charleston. *Federal Gazette & Baltimore Daily Advertiser,* 10 March 1800.

4. Knox, *Naval Documents…Quasi-War,* 1:330–31, B. Stoddert to W. Crafts, 23 Aug. 1798; ibid., 1:401–2, B. Stoddert to T. Morris, 13 Sept. 1798.

5. *City Gazette & Daily Advertiser,* 4 Aug. 1798. William Washington (1752–1810), George Washington's cousin, commanded the American light cavalry in the southern campaigns of the Revolutionary War and was wounded and captured at Eutaw Springs. A South Carolina state legislator and Federalist elector in 1796 and 1800, Col. Washington had hosted his kinsman at Sandy Hill Plantation on President Washington's 1791 Southern tour. "George Washington Tours the South: His Journey Through South Carolina," S.C. Department of Archives and History (1991). Thomas Pinckney (1750–1828), a Middle Temple–trained lawyer, served as an aide to Count d'Estaing in the Revolution, and was wounded and captured at Camden. Pinckney served as governor of South Carolina, presided over the state's Constitutional Convention in 1788, and served in Washington's administration as minister to Britain and then to Spain. In 1796, as a Federalist, he received votes for vice president; from 1797 to 1801, he represented the state in Congress. *DAB,* 7:617–19. Ladson, a friend of Pinckney's, was also a Middle Tem-

ple lawyer and former Revolutionary War officer. Henry Laurens, a merchant, who was selected for, but did not attend the Constitutional Convention in Philadelphia in 1788, ran unsuccessfully for governor in 1796 as a Federalist, and was notable for his advocacy of emancipation of slaves. George C. Rogers, Jr., *Charleston in the Age of the Pinckneys* (Columbia: University of South Carolina Press, 1980), 128, 142. Deas had been Pinckney's secretary in London. Russell was a leading shipowner and merchant.

6. *City Gazette & Daily Advertiser,* 11, 14 Aug. 1798.

7. P. C. Coker III, *Charleston's Maritime Heritage 1670–1865* (Charleston: Coker Craft Press, 1987), 139.

8. *City Gazette & Daily Advertiser,* 2 Aug. 1798.

9. Knox, *Naval Documents...Quasi-War,* 2:289, B. Stoddert to T. Morris, 28 Jan. 1799.

10. J. McNeil, *Charleston's Navy Yard* (Charleston: Naval Civilian Administrators Association, 1985), 20.

11. *South Carolina Gazette & Timothy's Daily Advertiser,* 19 Nov. 1798.

12. Knox, *Naval Documents...Quasi-War,* 1:105–6, G. Cross to R. Harper, 4 June 1798; Adams Family Papers, reel 119, J. Adams to B. Stoddert, 18 Aug. 1798 (noting the "recommendations from a great number of respectable Inhabitants of Charleston in favour of George Cross to be a Captain . . ."); Knox, *Naval Documents...Quasi-War,* 1:342–43, B. Stoddert to J. Adams, 27 Aug. 1798 (referring to Cross as "the Gentleman so strongly recommended by the Merchants of Charleston, through Mr. Rutledge . . ."); Historical Society of Pennsylvania, Philadelphia, Pa., Jones & Clarke Papers, G. Cross to W. Jones, 23 Aug. 1798 (asking "as a particular favor" of William Jones, a Philadelphia merchant, "to use your interest" with Stoddert); Adams Family Papers, reel 119, J. Adams to J. Rutledge, 3 Sept. 1798 (noting that the president had signed Cross's commission that day).

13. Knox, *Naval Documents...Quasi-War,* 3:307-8, J. Marsh to J. Robertson, May 1820.

14. Knox, *Naval Documents...Quasi-War,* 3:307-8, J. Marsh to J. Robertson, May 1820; Coker, *Charleston's Maritime Heritage,* 142.

15. P. A. Pinckney, *American Figureheads and Their Carvers* (New York: W.W. Norton & Company, 1940), 82.

16. Coker, *Charleston's Maritime Heritage,* 140; Pratt, *The Navy,* 145; Peabody Essex Museum, Salem, Mass., Josiah Fox Papers, Letter Book 4, 432–35, report dated 17 May 1809.

17. *City Gazette & Daily Advertiser,* 4 June 1799.

18. *South Carolina Gazette & Timothy's Daily Advertiser,* 6 June 1799.

19. McNeil, *Charleston's Navy Yard,* 21.

20. Knox, *Naval Documents...Quasi-War,* 2:484, B. Stoddert to W. Crafts, 18 March 1799.

21. *South Carolina Gazette & Timothy's Daily Advertiser,* 17 July 1799.

22. *South Carolina Gazette & Timothy's Daily Advertiser,* 17 July 1799.

23. Knox, *Naval Documents...Quasi-War,* 4:21, B. Stoddert to W. Crafts, 2 Aug. 1799.

24. *South Carolina Gazette & Timothy's Daily Advertiser,* 24 Oct. 1799.

25. McNeil, *Charleston's Navy Yard,* 21; *South Carolina Gazette & Timothy's Daily Advertiser,* 1 Nov. 1799.

26. *South Carolina Gazette & Timothy's Daily Advertiser,* 14 Nov. 1799.

27. Coker, *Charleston's Maritime Heritage,* 143.

28. Knox, *Naval Documents...Quasi-War,* 1:336, B. Stoddert to J. Adams, 25 Aug. 1798.

29. Knox, *Naval Documents...Quasi-War,* 4:243, B. Stoddert to G. Cross, 1 Oct. 1799.

30. Knox, *Naval Documents...Quasi-War,* 4:565. The officers—the *John Adams*'s second lieutenant, purser, lieutenant of marines, and a midshipman—were released after a personal remonstrance to the governor.

31. Knox, *Naval Documents...Quasi-War,* 5:247–48, Decree of U.S. District Court, 26 Feb. 1800.

32. Coker, *Charleston's Maritime Heritage,* 144.

33. Knox, *Naval Documents...Quasi-War,* 5:341, G. Cross to R. Morris, 16 April 1800; ibid., 5:565, Account of Sales of French Schooner Jason. Captain Cross's personal stake in the proceeds was about $508; Coker, *Charleston's Maritime Heritage,* 144.

34. Knox, *Naval Documents...Quasi-War,* 5:341, G. Cross to R. Morris, 16 April 1800.

35. Knox, *Naval Documents...Quasi-War,* 6:45, G. Cross to B. Stoddert, 24 June 1800 (as reported in *Federal Gazette & Baltimore Daily Advertiser,* 29 July 1800); ibid., 6:46, Survey of *La Decade,* 22 June 1800; ibid., 7:170 Account of Sales of French Schooner *Decade,* 1 April 1801.

36. Knox, *Naval Documents...Quasi-War,* 6:337–41, W. Robinson to B. Stoddert, 10 Sept. 1800.

37. Knox, *Naval Documents...Quasi-War,* 6:449, T. Truxtun to G. Cross, 10 Oct. 1800.

38. Knox, *Naval Documents...Quasi-War,* 6:540, T. Truxtun to G. Cross, 20 Nov. 1800.

39. Knox, *Naval Documents...Quasi-War,* 7:58, B. Stoddert to G. Cross, 31 Dec. 1800; ibid., 7:97–98, G. Cross to B. Stoddert, 18 Jan. 1801; ibid., 6:292, B. Stoddert to W. Crafts, 27 Aug. 1800.

40. *South Carolina Gazette & Timothy's Daily Advertiser,* 17 Dec. 1800.

41. Knox, *Naval Documents...Quasi-War,* 7:191, S. Smith to W. Burrows, 14 April 1801; ibid., 7:232, S. Smith to T. Tingey, 23 May 1801, Henry Adams, *History of the United States of America* (New York: Charles Scribner's Sons, 1889), 1:223, T. Jefferson to S. Smith, 17 April 1801.

42. Mystic Seaport Museum, Mystic, Conn., G.W. Blunt-White Library, Log No. 227, unidentified author aboard the USS *John Adams.*

43. Allen, *Our Navy and the Barbary Corsairs,* 125–26 and 129–31; Goldsborough, *U.S. Naval Chronicle,* 207–09, reprinting J. Rodgers to B. Stoddert, 4 Dec. 1803.

44. Beinecke Library, Yale University, New Haven, Conn., John Rodgers Papers; National Archives, Washington, D.C., Record Group 45, M441, Letters Sent by the Secretary of the Navy to Commandants and Navy Agents, 1808–1865, R. Smith to T. Tingey, 8 Jan. 1809 (ordering the *John Adams* to be "equipped and prepared for actual service").

45. Beinecke Library, Yale University, New Haven, Conn., John Rodgers Papers.

46. Harold D. Langley, "Respect for Civilian Authority," *American Neptune* 40 (1980), 29–31.

47. Beinecke Library, Yale University, New Haven, Conn., John Rodgers Papers; Mystic Seaport Museum, G. W. Blunt-White Library, Log No. 10, Journal kept aboard the *John Adams* by J. L. Cummings; *American State Papers* (class six) *Naval Affairs,* eds. W. Lourie and W. S. Franklin (Washington, D.C.: Gales and Seaton, 1834), 3:348–402, 753–87, Annual Reports of Secretary of Navy, 8 Dec. 1829 and 7 Dec.

1830; National Archives, Washington, D.C., Record Group 45, Bureau of Construction & Repair Drawing No. 85740.

48. Nimitz Library, U.S. Naval Academy, Annapolis, Md., Special Manuscript No. 33, Journal kept aboard the *John Adams* by Cdr. T. W. Wyman; J. Fenimore Cooper, *History of the Navy* (New York: Stringer & Townsend, 1856 [orig. pub. 1839]), 492; K. J. Bauer, *Surfboats and Horse Marines: U.S. Naval Operations in the Mexican War, 1846–48* (Annapolis, Md.: Naval Institute Press, 1969), 37, 41, 78, 99.

49. Tyrone G. Martin, *A Most Fortunate Ship: A Narrative History of "Old Ironsides"* (Chester, Conn.: Globe Pequot Press, 1980), 272.

50. E. K. Rawson and R. H. Woods, eds., *Official Records of the Union and Confederate Navies in the War of Rebellion* (Washington, D.C.: Government Printing Office, 1903), ser. I, 16:496.

51. Ibid., 16:217.

52. Ibid., 16:332.

53. McNeil, *Charleston's Navy Yard*, 24.

54. *Dictionary of American Naval Fighting Ships* (Washington, D.C.: Government Printing Office, 1968), 3:523.

Chapter 10. The *Essex* in the East Indies

1. Knox, *Naval Documents…Quasi-War*, 1:414, B. Stoddert to J. Barry, 17 Sept. 1798; ibid., 2:256–57, B. Stoddert to J. Murray and J. Mumford, 18 Jan. 1799; ibid., 3:85–86, B. Stoddert to B. Goodhue, 22 April 1799; ibid., 3:161–62, B. Stoddert to S. Sewall, 10 May 1799.

2. Knox, *Naval Documents…Quasi-War*, 3:161, B. Stoddert to J. Adams, 10 May 1799 (proposing sweep); *Works of John Adams*, 8:650–51, J. Adams to B. Stoddert, 19 May 1799 (approving and sending on Stoddert's letter to Sewall and endorsing sweep along French coast); Palmer, *Stoddert's War*, 122–24 (concept of sweep); Adams Family Papers, reel 119, J. Adams to B. Stoddert, 1 July 1799 ("much pleased" and suggests adding the *Boston*); Palmer, *Stoddert's War*, 134–35 (cancelled); Bailey, *American Naval Biography*, 56–57 (noting that, with the exception of two French navy corvettes blockaded temporarily by the *Insurgent* at Cadiz, Murray "never obtained sight of the enemy").

3. There is an enormous literature on the beginnings of American trade with the Orient. See, e.g, Robert G. Albion, William A. Baker, and Benjamin W. Labaree, *New England and the Sea* (Mystic, Conn.: Mystic Seaport Museum, Inc., 1972), 56–60; Morison, *Maritime History;* P. C. F. Smith, *Frigate Essex Papers*, 10 (by 1800, ninety Salem captains had rounded the Cape of Good Hope); Dulles, *Old China Trade*, 1–55; James Morton Callahan, *American Relations in the Pacific and the Far East 1784–1900* (Baltimore: Johns Hopkins University Press, 1901), 10–16.

4. Dulles, *Old China Trade*, 35–37 (perils of navigation); Richards, *"U.S. Trade with China"* (listing American vessels, including the *Experiment*). As to the invention of the chronometer, see Dava Sobel, *Longitude* (New York: Walker and Co., 1995).

5. North, *Economic Growth*, 46–54, after noting that the economic development of the United States from 1793 to 1808 was "tied to international trade and shipping," concludes that the "increased productivity of shipping, the rise in freight rates, and the favorable terms of trade combined to produce an era of unequaled affluence."

North also notes, ibid. at 42, that while the new trading routes to China and the East Indies employed only a small percentage of American vessels engaged in overseas trade, earnings from these voyages were disproportionately higher.

6. E. H. Derby (1739–1799), one of America's first millionaires, had interests in dozens of privateers during the Revolution, "invariably subscribing for such shares [in privateering syndicates] as might not be taken by his fellow townsmen." Ralph D. Paine, *The Old Merchant Marine* (New Haven: Yale University Press, 1919), 52–53. Emerging from the war as one of New England's wealthiest merchants, he pursued maritime trade aggressively in new markets. His ship *Light Horse* was the first American vessel to the Baltic (1784); his *Grand Turk* was the third American vessel to reach Canton (1786); and his ships were the first to carry Bombay cotton to America. Derby died just weeks before the *Essex*'s launch. P. C. F. Smith, *Frigate Essex Papers*, 7; Charles Oscar Paullin, *American Voyages to the Orient 1690–1865* (Annapolis, Md.: Naval Institute Press, 1971 [orig. pub. 1910–11]), 11; *DAB*, 3:249–50.

7. William Gray (1750–1825) owned a large fleet of vessels (Morrison, *Maritime History*, 96, states that before 1815, Gray owned 113 vessels) and was the leading merchant rival of Derby. He was a founder and first president of the Essex Bank (1792) and in 1803, organized and was the first president of the Essex Fire and Marine Insurance Company. Elected to the state senate as a Federalist, he broke with the party over the Embargo and, as a Jeffersonian Republican, was elected lieutenant governor of Massachusetts. See references to him in James Duncan Phillips, *Salem and the Indies* (Boston: Houghton Mifflin Co., 1947) and Edward Gray, *William Gray of Lynn, Massachusetts and Some of His Descendents* (Salem: Essex Institute, 1916).

8. *Diary of William Bentley, D.D.* (Gloucester, Mass.: Peter Smith, 1962 [orig. pub. 1907]), 2:266, 1 May 1798 (mustering of militia); ibid., 2:274, 4 July 1798 ("This Town has as yet taken no part . . ."); ibid., 2:277, 26 July 1798 (subscription "does not proceed with that energy discovered in many towns"); Knox, *Naval Documents...Quasi-War*, 1:366–67, B. Goodhue to T. Pickering, 1 Sept. 1798; *Diary of William Bentley*, 2:282, 10 Sept. 1798 (Gray to subscribe nine-tenths of Derby).

9. *Diary of William Bentley*, 2:284, 1 Oct. 1798 ("Subscription slowly") and 2 Oct. 1798 ("A Subscription carried round to all the inhabitants . . ."); ibid., 2:285, 17 Oct. 1798 (Salem had not reached Newburyport's level, and some to pay in labor); Salem *Gazette*, 14 Sept. 1798 (printing A SHOREMAN's letter). P. C. F. Smith, *Frigate Essex Papers*, 30, calls the letter "a half-witted epistle," but the letter was in the style of the heavily ironical humor of the era, and mocked the $16,000 raised. The letter was reprinted widely, see, e.g., *Federal Gazette & Baltimore Daily Advertiser*, 21 Sept. 1798, suggesting it was regarded as farcical. The Appendix reprints the subscribers from P. C. F. Smith, *Frigate Essex Papers*, 32–35. Other lists exist. See Bassett, "Frigate *Essex*," 9–40. For comments on the occupation of each subscriber from a person who knew them, see David Augustus Neal, "Salem Men in the Early Nineteenth Century," *Essex Institute Historical Collections* 75 (Jan. 1939), 1–14.

10. P. C. F. Smith, *Frigate Essex Papers*, 37–43; Paine, *Old Merchant Marine*, 104–5.

11. Chapelle, *American Sailing Ships*, 94 ("like a Continental frigate"); P. C. F. Smith, *Frigate Essex Papers*, 53–55; Chapelle, *American Sailing Navy*, 165–66.

12. P. C. F. Smith, *Frigate Essex Papers,* handles the contracting and building of the *Essex* masterfully and in great detail. A brief account is Bassett, "Frigate Essex," 15–17. The procession with the cable is mentioned in *Diary of William Bentley,* 2:318, 21 Sept. 1799, and Benjamin F. Browne, "Youthful Recollections of Salem," *Essex Institute Historical Collections* 49 (1913), 207–8. As to the *Essex*'s cannon, see Knox, *Naval Documents...Quasi-War,* 3:368–69, B. Stoddert to R. Gill, 19 June 1799 (enclosing order to the two foundries for 18 twelve-pounders); ibid., 3:369, B.Stoddert to S. Higginson & Co., 19 June 1799 (12 six-pounders part of shipment from London).

13. P. C. F. Smith, *Frigate Essex Papers,* 145–51; *Diary of William Bentley,* 2:319, 30 Sept. 1799.

14. P. C. F. Smith, *Frigate Essex Papers,* 161–63; Knox, *Naval Documents...Quasi-War,* 2:405–6, C. Goldsborough to R. Derby, 26 Feb. 1799.

15. Knox, *Naval Documents...Quasi-War,* 1:106–7, S. Higginson to T. Pickering [?], 6 June 1798; ibid., 2:207, B. Stoddert to E. Preble, 4 Jan. 1799 (to command the *Pickering*); ibid., 3:248, B. Stoddert to S. Higginson, 24 May 1799 ("make a figure"); ibid., 3:252–53, B. Stoddert to J. Adams, 25 May 1799 ("ought to have been a Captain'); ibid., 3:315, B. Stoddert to E. Preble, 7 June 1799 (promotion); Pratt, *Preble's Boys,* 13–24; McKee, *Edward Preble.*

16. P. C. F. Smith, *Frigate Essex Papers,* 164–86 (details frigate's preparations for sea); Knox, *Naval Documents...Quasi-War,* 4:364, E. Preble to B. Stoddert, 7 Nov. 1799 (announcing arrival and state of frigate); ibid., 4:397–98, B. Stoddert to E. Preble, 15 Nov. 1799 (orders the *Essex* to Newport by 15 December to take East Indies convoy "certain distance"); ibid, 4:435–36, E. Preble to B. Stoddert, 21 Nov. 1799 (recruiting); ibid., 4:494–95, E. Preble to B. Stoddert, 6 Dec. 1799 (reasons for delay).

17. Knox, *Naval Documents...Quasi-War,* 4:579, E. Preble to J. Waters, 29 Dec. 1799; *Essex Institute Historical Collections* 57 (1921), 176, J. Waters to W. Hackett, 3 Jan. 1800; P. C. F. Smith, *Frigate Essex Papers,* 188; Phillips, *Salem and the Indies,* 140.

18. Knox, *Naval Documents...Quasi-War,* 4:408, B. Stoddert to W. Gray, 16 Nov. 1799 (convoy trade "as far as the Line" and requesting Gray to inform other Salem merchants); ibid., 4:474, B. Stoddert to E. Preble, 3 Dec. 1799 (president determined two frigates to sail to Batavia); ibid., 4:408–9, B. Stoddert to J. and E. Watson (New York), to Gibbs & Channing (Newport), to A. Campbell (Baltimore), to W. Montgomery (Philadelphia) (giving notice to merchants); ibid., 4:475–76, B. Stoddert to S. Higginson & Co., 3 Dec. 1799 (notice to Boston merchants and noting it was "unfortunate this voyage had not been earlier determined on, that arrangements for its might have been earlier made"); ibid., 4:494–95, E. Preble to B. Stoddert, 6 Dec. 1799 (Salem merchants disdain convoy); Robert Oliver Letterbook 1796–1800, 448–49, R. Oliver to J. Kirwan & Sons, 6 Dec. 1799.

19. Knox, *Naval Documents...Quasi-War,* 5:47–48, E. Preble to B. Stoddert, 6 Jan. 1800; McKee, *Edward Preble,* 69–70, quotes J. Sever to E. Preble, 6 Jan. 1800, and return letter; Knox, *Naval Documents...Quasi-War,* 5:53, extract from Sailing Master Low's journal, 9 Jan. 1800; ibid., 5:299–300, E. Preble to B. Stoddert, 13 March 1800.

20. Knox, *Naval Documents...Quasi-War,* 5:62–63, J. Sever to B. Stoddert, 14 Jan. 1800 (reporting disaster in storm); ibid., 5:65–66, J. Cordis to B. Stoddert, 2 April 1800

(first lieutenant of the *Congress* contended Sever could have set the rigging to prevent the loss of the masts but Sever refused lieutenants' suggestions); ibid., 5:451–56, court of inquiry on dismasting of the *Congress* (exonerating Sever).

21. McKee, *Edward Preble*, 70; Knox, *Naval Documents...Quasi-War*, 5:70, Preble journal, 12 Jan. 1800; Peabody Essex Museum, Salem, Massachusetts, Richard Beale Journal, 12–13 Jan. 1800 (wearing ship to reset rigging, and frigate shipping water); Knox, *Naval Documents...Quasi-War*, Low journal, 13 Jan. 1800; Beale journal, 15–16 Jan. 1800 (noting heavy squalls, the *Essex* "laboring" in high seas and taking on water, but "People Employed Repairing the Rigging") and 24–26 Jan. 1800 (mainmast sprung but fished and "woulded" despite gale and "large hollow sea"); Knox, *Naval Documents...Quasi-War*, 5:299–300, E. Preble to B. Stoddert, 13 March 1800 (bad rigging).

22. Beale journal, 11 March 1800 (anchoring among British ships); McKee, *Edward Preble*, 71 (detailing social whirl of Preble's visit); P. C. F. Smith, *Frigate Essex Papers*, 189 (quoting *Essex* purser Mumford to J. Waters); Knox, *Naval Documents...Quasi-War*, 5:299–300, E. Preble to B. Stoddert, 13 March 1800 (intelligence learned and the *Essex* would not wait); ibid., 4:523, B. Stoddert to E. Preble, 11 Dec. 1799 (on French "Privateering system" and sending single frigate on if "unforeseen event" prevented other).

23. Beale journal, 28 March 1800 (departure), 4 May 1800 (resetting rigging) and 10 May 1800 (Osborne comment); P. C. F. Smith, *Frigate Essex Papers*, 189 (quotes W. Mumford to J. Waters, n.d.); Knox, *Naval Documents...Quasi-War*, 5:498, E. Preble to B. Stoddert, 10 May 1800.

24. Beale journal, 5 May 1800 ("saw the Island of Java"), 6 May 1800 (stopping of ex-*Friends*), 7 May 1800 (relinquished interest in the *Friends*); McKee, *Edward Preble*, 72–75.

25. Beale journal, 18 Jan. 1800 (confining James Cox for mutinous expressions), 11 May 1800 (Ash mutiny), 18 July 1800 (return of five "mutinous" sailors); McKee, *Gentlemanly and Honorable Profession*, 255–56 (referring to the "*Hermione* Phobia" and Ash); Christopher McKee, "Edward Preble and the 'Boys': The Officer Corps of 1812 Revisited," in James C. Bradford, ed., *Command Under Sail: Makers of the American Naval Tradition 1775–1850* (Annapolis, Md.: Naval Institute Press, 1985), 76 (Preble was "one of the Navy's harshest disciplinarians"). On the other hand, the historian of the *Hermione* mutiny suggests that "Frequent cases of 'insolence' and 'neglect of duty' are, curiously enough, usually more indicative of an unhappy ship than odd cases of 'mutinous behaviour.'" Pope, *The Black Ship*, 43. The two phenomena are not, unfortunately, mutually exclusive.

26. Beale journal, 14 May 1800 (saw shipping at Batavia), 15 May 1800 (anchored), 17–18 and 20 May 1800 (reprovisioning and departing Batavia), 22 May 1800 (spoke to the *Exchange*), 23–24 May 1800 (encountered five American merchant ships); Knox, *Naval Documents...Quasi-War*, 5:534, E. Preble to masters of American merchant ships, 19 May 1800; ibid., 6:224–26, E. Preble to B. Stoddert, 6 Aug. 1800 (boarded thirteen American merchantmen, "the whole of which" would have been taken); Beale journal, 27–28 May 1800 (watering), 10 June 1800 (the *Essex* loading "very bad Quality" food), 19 June 1800 (unmoored ship and made sail with twelve merchant vessels).

27. McKee, *Edward Preble*, 76–77; Beale journal, 21 June 1800; Knox, *Naval Documents…Quasi-War*, 6:224–26, E. Preble to B. Stoddert, 6 Aug. 1800.

28. One of the few English language sources on Surcouf is Donald Macintyre, *The Privateers* (London: Paul Elek Ltd., 1975), 112–28.

29. McKee, *Edward Preble*, 77; Beale journal, 22–23 June 1800; Knox, *Naval Documents…Quasi-War*, 6:224–26, E. Preble to B. Stoddert, 6 Aug. 1800.

30. Knox, *Naval Documents…Quasi-War*, 6:50, E. Preble to Governor General, 30 June 1800 (uncovering spy in Dutch proa working for Surcouf); ibid., 6:224–26, E. Preble to B. Stoddert, 6 Aug. 1800 (second chase of the *Confiance*); Beale journal, 24–25 June 1800; Macintyre, *Privateers*, 121–23.

31. Pratt, *Preble's Boys*, 25.

32. Harold D. Langley, *A History of Medicine in the Early U.S. Navy* (Baltimore: Johns Hopkins University Press, 1995), 63–64 and 370 n. 34 (remarking that only one death was "clearly associated with illness").

33. Palmer, *Stoddert's War*, 208.

34. Beale journal lists the dead as follows: 14 Feb. 1800 (John Wells and Daniel Woodman, who fell overboard while skylarking); 27 Feb. 1800 (William English, apoplectic fit); 15 April 1800 (Daniel Ahunifson [?]); 31 May 1800 (Midshipman William H. Williams); 4 July 1800 (Simon F. Williams); 11 July 1800 (John Law "after a sickness of 5 months"); 9 Aug. 1800 (Ezra Plum "died of a fever"); 14 Aug. 1800 (John Gardner and Charles Bailey, who both shipped at Batavia, "died after a long illness"); 11 Sept. 1800 (James Woodbury "died of the scurvy"); 12 Oct. 1800 (Charles Liveed, dysentary); 17 Oct. 1800 (Jason Howard, schoolmaster, "of a Natural decline"); 21 Oct. 1800 (Benjamin McDonald, "after a long illness"). In addition, Peter Anderson died on 5 August 1800. Gardner W. Allen, *Our Naval War with France* (Boston: Houghton Mifflin Co., 1909), 160, citing *Essex* log. Preble resigned command of the *Essex* in April 1801 because of health. Preble's illness began on the return from Java, and he was racked by illness for the rest of his life (he died in April 1807). Palmer, *Stoddert's War*, 208. Preble's biographer surmises that Preble had developed ulcers—which also might explain his choleric disposition. McKee, *Edward Preble*, 81, 88.

35. Beale journal, 4 July 1800 – 13 Aug. 1800.

36. Beale journal, 15 Aug. – 28 Nov. 1800; Allen, *Our Naval War with France*, 160–61.

37. Knox, *Naval Documents…Quasi-War*, 6:224–26, E. Preble to B. Stoddert, 6 Aug. 1800; ibid., 6:553, B. Stoddert to J. Mullowny, 26 Nov. 1800 (ordering the *Ganges* to Straits). Charles Goldsborough, a former chief clerk of the Navy Department, wrote that the *Ganges* and *Connecticut* were held in readiness to sail "but their sailing was suspended, in consequence of the treaty with France, being then before the Senate. . . . In this state of suspense, these ships continued, until the treaty being ratified, it was judged inexpedient to send them on the proposed service." Goldsborough, *U.S. Naval Chronicle*, 175. As to the Jefferson administration's initial thinking to deploy two frigates in the Indian Ocean, see *The Works of Thomas Jefferson*, ed. Paul Leicester Ford (New York: G. P. Putnam's Sons, 1905), 1:365, "Anas" entry dated 9 March 1801.

38. As to the *Essex*'s sailing characteristics being "spoiled," see Chapelle, *American Sailing Navy*, 166; Morison, *Maritime History*, 100, noting her sluggish progress on her

Pacific cruise, called the *Essex* "an uncommonly slow sailer." For accounts of the Pacific cruise, see Guttridge and Smith, *The Commodores*, 205, 237–45; Frank Donovan, *The Odyssey of the Essex* (New York: David McKay Co., 1969); Forester, *Age of Fighting Sail*, 203–12; David F. Long, "David Porter: Pacific Ocean Gadfly," in Bradford, *Command Under Sail*, 173–198. For the sorry weeks the *Essex* served in the Royal Navy, and her long, desultory demise, see P. C. F. Smith, *Frigate Essex Papers*, 201–03.

Conclusion

1. Chapelle, *American Sailing Navy*, 153.
2. Nobel E. Cunningham, ed., *Circular Letters of Congressmen to Their Constituents 1789–1829*, 3 vols. (Chapel Hill: University of North Carolina Press, 1978), 163–64, Robert G. Harper to constituents, 20 March 1799.
3. P. C. F. Smith, *Frigate Essex Papers*, 22.
4. *Annals*, 7:2034, speech 23 June 1798.
5. Knox, *Naval Documents...Quasi-War*, 4:32–33, B. Stoddert to Murray et al., 5 Aug. 1799; *Aurora & General Advertiser*, 18 July 1798.
6. Adams Family Papers, microfilm roll 395, O. Wolcott to J. Adams, 13 June 1799. The profitable rate of return varied depending on the investment options available in June and July 1798 compared to the inflation rate; the riskiness of other investments against United States stock guaranteed by the Fifth Amendment; and other items in the merchant's investment portfolio.
7. In May 1798, Stephen Girard's vessels sailing from Philadelphia to Havana were insured at 15 percent, although 5 percent would be refunded if there was no loss and if the vessel sailed with naval escort. Harold E. Gillingham, *Marine Insurance in Philadelphia 1721–1800* (Philadelphia: privately printed, 1933), 101. New England shipping to the West Indies was reportedly charged 30 percent for insurance. Albion, Baker, and Labaree, *New England and the Sea*, 73.
8. *Porcupine's Gazette*, 12 June 1798.
9. *The City Gazette and Daily Advertiser*, 2 Aug. 1798. These comments lend support to the argument that subscribers were losing money—were they profiting, obviously no one would "shrink from the service."
10. Knox, *Naval Documents...Quasi-War*, 1:277–78, B. Stoddert to Brown, 7 Aug. 1798.
11. National Archives, Washington, D.C., Records of the Bureau of Public Debt, Record Group 53, entry 263, 948:100. John Eager Howard, Federalist Senator from Maryland, together with John Swan, contributed $4,700. Swan was the brigadier general in charge of the Baltimore militia. Their contribution is noted "Society of Cincinnati." On the other hand, the original list of the Society of Cincinnati does not seem to be coincident with the Baltimore committee. Kilbourne, "Society of Cincinnati," 169–85.
12. *Federal Gazette & Baltimore Daily Advertiser*, 14 June 1798.
13. [Charleston] *City Gazette and Daily Advertiser*, 2 Aug. 1798.
14. Knox, *Naval Documents...Quasi-War*, 6:81, S. Higginson to G. Little, 25 June 1800, and ibid., 6:108–09, B. Stoddert to S. Higginson, 3 July 1800.
15. [New York] *Commercial Advertiser*, 30 June 1798.
16. Cunningham, *Circular Letters of Congressmen*, 1:284, John Stratton to constituents, 22 April 1802; Dewey, *Financial History of the United States*, 112.

17. Dewey, *Financial History of the United States,* 111, the expenditures for 1798.
18. *Letters of William Vans Murray to John Quincy Adams, 1797–1803,* ed. Ford Worthington Chauncey (Washington, D.C.: 1914 [orig. pub. 1912 in Annual Report of the American Historical Association at pp. 341–715]), 456–57, W. Murray to J. Q. Adams, 17 Aug. 1798; *Works of John Adams,* 9:125–26, statement to House of Representatives, 23 Nov. 1797.
19. Chapelle, *American Sailing Navy,* 154.
20. Chapelle, *American Sailing Navy,* 549, 547, 533, 539, 544.
21. *The Spectator,* 11 Aug. 1798. The frigate *Adams* (not to be confused with the *John Adams*) was also built in New York in 1799. Chapelle, *American Sailing Navy,* 144–45.
22. Hutchins, *American Maritime Industries,* 181.
23. Maclay, *Moses Brown,* 136, tries to prove that the *Merrimack* was the cheapest sloop of war built of the 1798 ships. While the conclusion may be true, Maclay compares the *Merrimack* to sloops of war *bought* by the navy from the merchant marine, not ships built as warships.
24. Alexander S. Balinky, "Albert Gallatin, Naval Foe," *Pennsylvania Magazine of History and Biography* 53 (1958), 293 (quoting Jefferson's Second Message to Congress, 15 Dec. 1802), 300. As to the stock redemption, see Rafael A. Bayley, *National Loans of the United States from July 4, 1776 to June 30, 1880* (Washington, D.C.: Government Printing Office, 1882), 119, and William F. DeKnight, *History of the Currency of the Country and of the Loans of the United States* (Washington, D.C.: Government Printing Office, 1897), 41. Curiously, one hundred years after the subscription, $100 remained outstanding.
25. *Works of John Adams,* 9:145, speech of 22 Nov. 1800.

Appendix

1. Massachusetts Historical Society, Boston, Massachusetts, S.A. Green Papers. A partial list of the Boston subscribers appeared in the 18 July 1798 *Porcupine's Gazette.* While twenty-three of the twenty-five names in the newspaper appear in the list of the Massachusetts Historical Society, one of the exceptions, "B. Lincoln," is troubling. Benjamin Lincoln (1733–1810), one of the American army's major generals in the Revolution, and a former lieutenant governor of Massachusetts, was, in 1798, the U.S. collector of customs in Boston. *DAB,* 6:259–61. It is hard to conceive how he could be listed in the newspaper but "missed" by a complete list.
2. National Archives, Washington, D.C., Navy Department Records, Record Group 45, Subject File 1775–1910, box 14, folder 18.
3. National Archives, Washington, D.C., Records of the Bureau of Public Debt, Record Group 53, entry 308, vol. 1149, "Journal of 8 per cent Stocks & Navy Loan."
4. Various partial lists exist. A complete list is in P. C. F. Smith, *Frigate Essex Papers,* 32–35.
5. See Chapter 5.
6. Bayley, *National Loans of the United States,* 42–43; DeKnight, *History of the Currency,* 41.
7. Noted as "returned."
8. The original document totals the sum of the subscriptions as $100,922.90. I am unable to reconcile the difference ($500).

Bibliography

Document Collections and Original Manuscripts

Published Papers

Adams, John. *The Life and Works of John Adams*. Ed. Charles Francis Adams. 10 vols. Boston: Little, Brown & Co., 1849–56.

Hamilton, Alexander. *The Papers of Alexander Hamilton*. Ed. Harold G. Syrett. 27 vols. New York: Columbia University Press, 1961–87.

Hamilton, Alexander, James Madison, and John Jay. *The Federalist Papers*. Ed. Clinton Rossiter. New York: New American Library, Inc., 1961.

Jefferson, Thomas. *The Works of Thomas Jefferson*. Ed. Paul Leicester Ford. 12 vols. New York: G.P. Putnam's Sons, 1905.

———. *The Writings of Thomas Jefferson*. Eds. Andrew A. Lipscomb and Albert Ellery Bergh. 20 vols. Washington, D.C.: Thomas Jefferson Memorial Association, 1903.

Madison, James. *The Papers of James Madison*. Eds. Robert J. Brugger and others. Charlottesville: University Press of Virginia, 1986– .

Marshall, John. *The Papers of John Marshall*. Eds. Herbert A. Johnson and Charles T. Cullen. Chapel Hill: University of North Carolina Press, 1974– .

Murray, William Vans. *Letters of William Vans Murray to John Quincy Adams, 1797–1803*. Ed. Ford Worthington Chauncey. Washington, D.C.: 1914 [orig. pub. 1912 in *Annual Report of the American Historical Association*, pp. 341–715].

Washington, George. *The Writings of George Washington*. Ed. John C. Fitzpatrick. Vol. 36. Washington, D.C.: Government Printing Office, 1941.

Collected Documents

American State Papers (class six) Naval Affairs 1789–1836. Washington, D.C.: Gales and Seaton, 1834–64.

Annals of Congress (5th Congress: 2d session). Washington, D.C.: Gales & Seaton, 1851.

Cunningham, Nobel E., Jr., ed. Circular Letters of Congressmen to Their Constituents 1789–1829. 3 vols. Chapel Hill: University of North Carolina Press, 1978.

Documents Accompanying a Message From the President of the United States, with Sundry Statements Containing Detailed Accounts of the Expenditures of Public Monies, by Naval Agents; From 1st January, 1797 to 31st December 1801. Washington, D.C.: William Duane & Son, 1803 [reprinted in Shaw, Ralph R., and Richard H. Shoemaker, compilers. American Bibliography: A Preliminary Checklist for 1801–1819. New York: Scarecrow Press, 1958–83].

Dudley, William S., ed. The Naval War of 1812. 2 vols. to date. Washington, D.C.: Naval Historical Center, 1985– .

Essex Institute Historical Collections 57 (1921), 176, letter from J. Waters to W. Hackett, 3 Jan. 1800.

Knox, Dudley. W., ed. Naval Documents Related to the Quasi-War Between the United States and France. 7 vols. Washington, D.C.: Government Printing Office, 1935–38.

———. Naval Documents Related to the United States Wars with the Barbary Powers. 6 vols. Washington, D.C.: Government Printing Office, 1939–44.

Library of Congress, Washington, D.C. Photo-Duplication Service. Fifth Congress 1797–99. Senate Bills (microfilm). 1966.

Message From the President of the United States, Transmitting Sundry Documents Respecting the French Corvette Berceau. Washington, D.C.: A.& G. Way, 1802. [reprinted in Shaw, Ralph R., and Richard H. Shoemaker, compilers. American Bibliography: A Preliminary Checklist for 1801–1819. New York: Scarecrow Press, 1958–83].

Rawson, E. K. and R. H. Woods, eds. Official Records of the Union and Confederate Navies in the War of Rebellion. Series I, vol. 16. Washington, D.C.: Government Printing Office, 1903.

Statutes at Large of England and of Great Britain. London: Eyre and Strahan, 1811.

United States Statutes.

United States Supreme Court Reports.

Manuscripts and Original Sources

Archives Nationale, Paris (France). Report of Louie-Marie Clement to Ministry of Marine and report of Ministry to First Consul (Fonds Marine B4/149).

———. Data on the corvette Berceau (Fonds Marine BB5/f.35).

Beinecke Library, Yale University, New Haven, Conn. John Rodgers Papers.

———. Roger Griswold Papers.

Earl Greg Swem Library, College of William and Mary, Williamsburg, Va. Samuel Barron Papers.

Franklin Delano Roosevelt Library, Hyde Park, N.Y. George Little Papers.

G. W. Blunt-White Library, Mystic Seaport Museum, Mystic, Conn. Silas Talbot Papers.

———. The John Adams log (Log 227).

———. Journal kept aboard the John Adams by J. L. Cummings (Log 10).

Harvard University Archives, Cambridge, Mass. Faculty Records.

———. Class of 1800 Class Book.

Henry Huntington Library, San Marino, Calif. Journal of Lt. Stephen Clough [identified as "Frigate Boston log"].

Historical Society of Pennsylvania, Philadelphia, Pa. John Rodgers Copy Book 1799–1805 in John Rodgers Papers.

———. Joshua Humphreys Letterbook 1797–1800.

———. Thomas Truxtun Collection.

———. Maitland Family Papers [items relating to Thomas FitzSimons].

———. Jones & Clarke Papers.

Maryland Historical Society, Baltimore, Md. Robert Oliver Letterbook 1796–1800 (MS. 626.1).

———. Mark Pringle Letterbook 1796–98 (MS. 680).

———. Robert Gilmor, Jr., *Memoir, or Sketch, of the History of Robert Gilmor of Baltimore* (original manuscript, 1840).

———. William J. Kelley "Shipbuilding at Federal Hill Baltimore" (typescript manuscript, 1964).

———. "Earle's Maryland Shipbuilding Collection 1680–1910" [index].

———. Marion V. Brewington, compiler, "List of Carpenters Certificates 1790–1831" (unpublished manuscript 1957).

———. "Certificates of Registry Issued at Baltimore, Maryland 1789–1801," (MS. 2543) [microfilm copy from National Archives, Record Group 36].

Massachusetts Historical Society, Boston, Mass. Thomas Jefferson Papers.

———. Adams Family Papers.

———. Harrison Gray Otis Papers.

———. S. A. Green Papers.

———. Frigate *Boston* log.

———. Miscellaneous Bound manuscripts.

National Archives—Mid-Atlantic Region, Philadelphia, Pa. Records of the United States District Courts, Record Group 21, Information Case Files 1789–1843 . . . for the U.S. District Court for the Eastern District of Pennsylvania, *United States v. The Armed French Vessel Chou-Chou* and *United States v. The Armed French Vessel the Dorade.*

National Archives—New England Region, Waltham, Mass. Records of the United States District Courts, Record Group 21, Case Files of the U.S. District Court for the District of Massachusetts. *Little v. The Brigantine Flying Fish* (January term 1800).

———. ———. *Little v. Les Deux Anges* (March term 1800).

———. ———. *Davis v. The brigantine L'Espoir* (September term 1800).

———. ———. *Little v. The Ship Berceau* (December term 1800).

———. Case Files of the U.S. District Court for the District of Rhode Island. *Brown v. the Schooner Charming Nancy* (November term 1799).

———. Records of the United States Circuit Court for the District of Massachusetts, Record Group 21. *Talbot v. Little* (October term 1800).

National Archives, Washington, D.C. Records of the Bureau of Public Debt, Record Group 53. Entry 263, vol. 948 (for Maryland).

———. ———. Entry 308, vol. 1149, "Journal of 8 per cent Stocks & Navy Loan" (for Virginia).

————. ————. Entry 162, vols. 475–76, journal and ledger of "Accounts for the Navy 6% Stock of 1798" (for Rhode Island).

————. Records of the Bureau of Customs, Record Group 36. French Spoliation Claims and Proofs of Ownership of Registered Vessels.

————. Miscellaneous Letters Received by the Secretary of the Navy, Record Group 45.

————. Records of General Courts Martial and Courts of Inquiry of the Navy Department, 1799–1867, Record Group 125.

————. Letters Sent by the Secretary of the Navy to Commandants and Navy Agents 1808–1865, Record Group 45, M441.

————. Letters of Application and Recommendation during the Administration of John Adams, Record Group 59.

————. Records of the Bureau of Construction and Repair, Record Group 45, Drawing No. 85740.

————. Subject File 1775–1910, Record Group 45, Box 14, Folder 18 [financial data related to the *Philadelphia*].

————. Subject File 1775–1910, Record Group 45, Box NN [applications for appointments].

————. Journal of Midshipman Joseph Brown, Record Group 45, entry 392.

New Hampshire Historical Society, Concord, N.H. Jonathan Sawyer Collection (log of the *President*).

Nimitz Library, U.S. Naval Academy, Annapolis, Md. Journal of Cdr. T. W. Wyman (MSS No. 33).

Peabody Essex Museum, Salem, Mass. Josiah Fox Papers.

————. Hackett Family Papers.

————. Journal kept by Lt. Richard C. Beale aboard the *Essex*.

Service historique de la marine, Ministry of Defence, Vincennes (France). Personnel file on Louis-Marie Clement (class cc7, dossier 501).

Virginia State Archives, Richmond, Va. *United States v. The French Armed Vessel The Brilliant*, decree of United States District Court for Virginia, 3 Feb. 1801.

William L. Clements Library, University of Michigan, Ann Arbor, Mich. John Rodgers Papers.

Secondary Sources

Books, Articles in Periodicals, and Unpublished Sources

Adams, Henry. *History of the United States of America*. Vol. 1. New York: Charles Scribner's Sons, 1889.

Agrinat, Brina. "Thorough and Efficient Repair: Rebuilding in the American Sailing Navy." Unpublished M.A. thesis, East Carolina University, 1993.

Albion, Robert G., William A. Baker, and Benjamin W. Labaree. *New England and the Sea*. Mystic, Conn.: Mystic Seaport Museum, 1972.

Allen, Gardner W. *Our Naval War With France*. Boston: Houghton Mifflin Co., 1909.

————. *Our Navy and the Barbary Corsairs*. Boston: Houghton Mifflin Co., 1905.

————. *Massachusetts Privateers of the Revolution*. Boston: Massachusetts Historical Society, 1927.

Ames, Ellis. Notes, Massachusetts Historical Society *Proceedings* 20 (1883): 269–74.

Anderson, William G. "John Adams, the Navy, and the Quasi-War with France." *American Neptune* 30 (1970): 117–32.

Bailey, Isaac, compiler. *American Naval Biography*. Providence: H. Mann & Co., 1815.

Baker, Maury. "Cost Overrun, An Early Naval Precedent: Building the First U.S. Warships, 1794–98." *Maryland Historical Magazine* 72 (1977): 361–72.

Balinky, Alexander S. "Albert Gallatin, Naval Foe." *Pennsylvania Magazine of History and Biography* 82 (1958): 293–304.

Barriskill, James M. "The Newburyport Theatre in the 18th Century." *Essex Institute Historical Collections* 91 (1955): 345–48.

Barron, James. "Commodore Samuel Barron." *Virginia Historical Register and Literary Note Book* 4 (1851): 198–204.

Bass, William P. "Who Did Design the First U.S. Frigates?" *Naval History* 5 (1991): 49–54.

Bassett, Charles C. "The Career of the Frigate Essex." *Essex Institute Historical Collections* 87 (1951): 9–40.

Bassett, John Spencer. *The Federalist System 1789–1801*. New York: Greenwood Press, 1969 [orig. pub. 1906].

Bauer, K. Jack. *A Maritime History of the United States: The Role of America's Seas and Waterways*. Columbia: University of South Carolina Press, 1988.

———. *Surfboats and Horse Marines: U.S. Naval Operations in the Mexican War, 1846–48*. Annapolis, Md.: Naval Institute Press, 1969.

Bayley, Rafael A. *National Loans of the United States from July 4, 1776 to June 30, 1880*. Washington, D.C.: Government Printing Office, 1882.

Bentley, William. *Diary of William Bentley, D.D.* Gloucester, Mass.: Peter Smith, 1962 [orig. pub. 1907].

Berle, Adolf A., and Gardiner C. Means. *The Modern Corporation and Private Property*. Buffalo: William S. Hein & Co., 1982 [orig. pub. 1932].

Biographical Directory of the United States Congress 1774–1989. Washington, D.C.: Government Printing Office, 1989.

Blaustein, Albert P., and Roy M. Mersky. "Bushrod Washington." In *The Justices of the Supreme Court 1789–1969*. Eds. Leon Friedman and Fred L. Israel. New York: Chelsea House Publishers, 1969.

Bonnel, Ulane. *La France, les Etats-Unis et la Guerre de Course (1797–1815)*. Paris: Nouvelles Editions Latines, 1961.

Brewington, Marion V. "Maritime Philadelphia 1609–1837." *Pennsylvania Magazine of History and Biography* 63 (1939): 93–117.

Brown, Ralph Adams. *The Presidency of John Adams*. Lawrence: University Press of Kansas, 1975.

Browne, Benjamin F. "Youthful Recollections of Salem." *Essex Institute Historical Collections* 49 (1913): 193–209. [reprinted from Salem *Gazette* 1869].

Bruchey, Stuart Weems. *Robert Oliver: Merchant of Baltimore, 1783–1819*. Baltimore: Johns Hopkins University Press, 1956.

Bryant, Arthur. *The Years of Endurance 1793–1802*. London: Collins, 1944.

Callahan, James Morton. *American Relations in the Pacific and the Far East 1784–1900*. Baltimore: Johns Hopkins University Press, 1901.

Carrington, Henry B. *Battles of the American Revolution 1775–1781.* New York: Promontory Press, n.d. [orig. pub. 1877].

Cary, Thomas G. "Thomas Handasyd Perkins." In *Lives of American Merchants.* Ed. Freeman Hunt. New York: Derby & Jackson, 1858.

Cassell, Frank A. *Merchant Congressman in the Young Republic: Samuel Smith of Maryland, 1752–1839.* Madison: University of Wisconsin Press, 1971.

———. "The Structure of Baltimore's Politics in the Age of Jefferson, 1795–1812." In *Law, Society and Politics in Early Maryland.* Eds. Audrey C. Land, Lois Green Carr and Edward C. Papenfuse. Baltimore: Johns Hopkins University Press, 1977.

Chandler, Charles Lyon. *Early Shipbuilding in Pennsylvania 1683–1812.* Philadelphia: Franklin Institute, 1932.

Chapelle, Howard I. *The Baltimore Clipper: Its Origin and Development.* Hatboro, Pa.: Tradition Press, 1965 [orig. pub. 1930].

———. *The History of American Sailing Ships.* New York: Bonanza Books, 1935.

———. *The History of the American Sailing Navy.* New York: Bonanza Books, 1949.

Cheney, Robert K. *Maritime History of the Merrimac.* Newburyport, Ma.: Newburyport Press, Inc., 1964.

Claghorn, Charles E. *Naval Officers of the American Revolution: A Concise Biographical Dictionary.* Metuchen, N.J.: Scarecrow Press, 1988.

Clarfield, Gerard H. *Timothy Pickering and American Diplomacy 1795–1800.* Columbia: University of Missouri Press, 1969.

———. *Timothy Pickering and the American Republic.* Pittsburgh: University of Pittsburgh Press, 1980.

Clark, Mary Elizabeth. "Peter Porcupine in America: The Career of William Cobbett, 1792–1800." Ph.D. dissertation, University of Pennsylvania, 1939.

Coase, Ronald H. "The Lighthouse in Economics." *Journal of Law and Economics* 17 (1974): 357–76.

Cochran, Thomas C. *Frontiers of Change: Early Industrialism in America.* New York: Oxford University Press, 1981.

Coker, P. C., III. *Charleston's Maritime Heritage 1670–1865.* Charleston, S.C.: Coker Craft Press, 1987.

Cooper, J. Fennimore. *History of the Navy.* New York: Stringer & Townsend, 1856 [orig. pub. 1839].

Currier, John J. *History of Newburyport, Mass. 1764–1905.* Newburyport: privately printed, 1906.

Cutler, Carl C. *Greyhounds of the Sea: The Story of the American Clipper Ship.* New York: Halcyon House, 1930.

Dauer, Manning J. *The Adams Federalists.* Baltimore: Johns Hopkins Press, 1953.

DeConde, Alexander. *The Quasi-War: The Politics and Diplomacy of the Undeclared War with France, 1797–1801.* New York: Charles Scribner's Sons, 1966.

DeKnight, William F. *History of the Currency of the Country and of the Loans of the United States.* Washington, D.C.: Government Printing Office, 1897.

Dewey, Davis Rich. *Financial History of the United States.* New York: Longmans, Green and Co., 1903.

Dictionary of American Biography. 10 vols. New York: Charles Scribner's Sons, 1964 [orig. pub. 1927–36].

Dictionary of the American Congress 1774–1971. Washington, D.C.: U.S. Government Printing Office, 1971.

Dictionary of American Naval Fighting Ships. 4 vols. Washington, D.C.: Government Printing Office, 1968.

"D.M. Erskine: Letters From America, 1798–99." *William & Mary Quarterly* 6, 3rd series (1949): 251–84.

Donahue, John D. *The Privatization Decision.* New York: Basic Books, 1989.

Donovan, Frank. *The Odyssey of the Essex.* New York: David McKay Co., 1969.

Dulles, Foster Rhea. *The Old China Trade.* Boston: Houghton Mifflin Co., 1930.

Dunne, W. M. P. "An Inquiry into H. I. Chapelle's Research in Naval History." *American Neptune* 49 (1989): 39–55.

———. "Pistols and Honor: The James Barron-Stephen Decatur Conflict, 1798–1807." *American Neptune* 50 (1990): 245–59.

Dye, Ira. *The Fatal Cruise of the Argus.* Annapolis, Md.: Naval Institute Press, 1994.

Eckert, Edward K. "William Jones: Mr. Madison's Secretary of the Navy." *Pennsylvania Magazine of History and Biography* 96 (1972): 167–82.

Eddy, Richard. "'Defended by an Adequate Power': Joshua Humphreys and the 74-Gun Ships of 1799." *American Neptune* 51 (1991): 173–94.

Elkins, Stanley, and Eric McKitrick. *The Age of Federalism: The Early American Republic, 1788–1800.* New York: Oxford University Press, 1993.

Ernay, Renee Lynn. "The Revere Furnace, 1787–1800." M.A. thesis, University of Delaware, 1989.

Estes, J. Worth. "A Naval Surgeon in the Barbary Wars: Dr. Peter St. Medard on *New York*, 1802–3." In *New Aspects of Naval History.* Baltimore: Nautical & Aviation Publishing Co., 1985.

Farrell, James A.. "Thomas FitzSimons, Catholic Signer of the American Constitution." *American Catholic Historical Society Record* 39 (1928): 175–224.

Ferguson, Eugene S. *Truxtun of the Constellation.* Annapolis, Md.: Naval Institute Press, 1982 [orig. pub. 1956].

Flanders, Henry. "Thomas Fitzsimmons." *Pennsylvania Magazine of History and Biography* 2 (1878): 306–14.

Footner, Geoffrey M. *Tidewater Triumph: The Development and Worldwide Success of the Chesapeake Bay Pilot Schooner.* Mystic, Conn.: Mystic Seaport Museum, 1998.

Forester, C. S. *The Age of Fighting Sail.* Garden City, N.Y.: Doubleday & Co., 1956.

Fowler, William M., Jr. *Jack Tars and Commodores: The American Navy 1783–1815.* Boston: Houghton Mifflin Co., 1984.

———. *Silas Talbot: Captain of Old Ironsides.* Mystic, Conn.: Mystic Seaport Museum, 1995.

"George Washington Tours the South: His Journey Through South Carolina." South Carolina Department of Archives and History, 1991.

Gillingham, Harold E. *Marine Insurance in Philadelphia 1721–1800.* Philadelphia: privately printed, 1933.

———. "Old Business Cards of Philadelphia." *Pennsylvania Magazine of History and Biography* 53 (1929): 208–11.

Gillmer, Thomas C. *Pride of Baltimore: The Story of the Baltimore Clippers 1800–1990.* Camden, Me: International Marine, 1992.

Goldsborough, Charles W. *The United States Naval Chronicle.* Washington, D.C.: privately printed, 1824.

Gray, Edward. *William Gray of Lynn, Massachusetts and Some of His Descendants.* Salem, Mass.: Essex Institute, 1916.

Gruppe, Henry E. *The Frigates.* Alexandria, Va.: Time-Life Books, 1979.

Guttridge, Leonard F., and Jay D. Smith. *The Commodores.* Annapolis, Md.: Naval Institute Press, 1986 [orig. pub. 1969].

Harris, Joseph S. Letter reply to article, "Nationality of Robert Fulton." *Pennsylvania Magazine of History and Biography* 3 (1879): 475.

Hodges, James B. *The Browns of Providence Plantations.* 2 vols. Cambridge: Harvard University Press, 1952, 1967.

Howay, Frederic W., ed. *Voyages of the "Columbia" to the Northwest Coast 1787–1790 and 1790–1793.* Boston: Massachusetts Historical Society, 1941.

———. "Some Notes on Robert Haswell." Massachusetts Historical Society *Proceedings* 65 (1936): 592–600.

Hutchins, John B. *The American Maritime Industries and Public Policy, 1789–1914.* Cambridge: Harvard University Press, 1941.

Jackson, Russell Leigh. "The Seafaring Browns." *Essex Institute Historical Collections* 80 (1944): 55–68.

Jenkins, E. H. *A History of the French Navy.* London: Macdonald and Co., 1973.

Kennedy, Roger G. *Orders From France: The Americans and the French in a Revolutionary World, 1780–1820.* New York: Alfred A. Knopf, 1989.

Kilbourne, John D. "The Society of Cincinnati in Maryland: Its First One Hundred Years, 1793–1888." *Maryland Historical Magazine* 78 (1983): 169–85.

Kohn, Richard H. *Eagle and Sword: The Federalists and the Creation of the Military Establishment in America, 1783–1802.* New York: Free Press, 1975.

Kurtz, Stephen G. *The Presidency of John Adams: The Collapse of Federalism 1795–1800.* Philadelphia: University of Pennsylvania Press, 1957.

Labaree, Benjamin W. *Patriots and Partisans: The Merchants of Newburyport 1764–1815.* Cambridge: Harvard University Press, 1962.

Langley, Harold D. *A History of Medicine in the Early U.S. Navy.* Baltimore: Johns Hopkins University Press, 1995.

———. "Respect for Civilian Authority." *American Neptune* 40 (1980): 23–37.

Lavery, Brian. *Nelson's Navy: The Ships, Men and Organisation 1793–1815.* Annapolis, Md.: Naval Institute Press, 1997 [orig. pub. 1989].

Leiner, Frederick C. "Anatomy of a Prize Case: Dollars, Side-Deals, and *Les Deux Anges.*" *American Journal of Legal History* 39 (1995): 214–32.

———. "The Seizure of the *Flying Fish.*" *American Neptune* 56 (1996): 131–43.

———. "The 'Whimsical Phylosophic President' and His Gunboats." *American Neptune* 43 (1983): 245–66.

Long, David F. "David Porter: Pacific Ocean Gadfly." In *Command Under Sail: Makers of the American Naval Tradition 1775–1850.* Ed. James C. Bradford. Annapolis, Md.: Naval Institute Press, 1985.

———. *Ready to Hazard: A Biography of Commodore William Bainbridge, 1774–1833.* Hanover, N.H.: University Press of New England, 1981.

Lord, Walter. *The Dawn's Early Light.* New York: W.W. Norton & Co., 1972.

Louis-Philippe. *Diaries of My Travels in America.* Trans. Stephen Becker. New York: Delacorte Press, 1977.

Lumpkin, Henry. *From Savannah to Yorktown: The American Revolution in the South.* New York: Paragon House, 1981.

Macintyre, Donald. *The Privateers.* London: Paul Elek Ltd., 1975.

Maclay, Edgar Stanton. *A History of American Privateers.* New York: D. Appleton & Co., 1899.

———. *A History of the United States Navy From 1775 to 1898.* New York: D. Appleton & Co., 1898.

———. *Moses Brown, Captain U.S.N.* New York: Baker & Taylor Co., 1904.

Maloney, Linda M. *The Captain From Connecticut: The Life and Naval Times of Isaac Hull.* Boston: Northeastern University Press, 1986.

Martin, Tyrone G. *A Most Fortunate Ship: A Narrative History of "Old Ironsides."* Chester, Conn.: Globe Pequot Press, 1980.

———. "Underway Replenishment, 1799–1800." *American Neptune* 46 (1986): 159–64.

Martin, Tyrone G., and John C. Roach. "Humphrey's Real Innovation." *Naval History* 8 (1994): 32–37.

Maurer, Maurer. "Coppered Bottoms for the United States Navy, 1794–1803." U.S. Naval Institute *Proceedings* 17 (1945): 692–99.

McDonald, Forrest. *Alexander Hamilton: A Biography.* New York: W.W. Norton & Co., 1979.

McKee, Christopher. "Edward Preble and the 'Boys': The Officer Corps of 1812 Revisited." In *Command Under Sail: Makers of the American Naval Tradition 1775–1850.* Ed. James Bradford. Annapolis, Md.: Naval Institute Press, 1985.

———. *Edward Preble: A Naval Biography 1761–1807.* Annapolis, Md.: Naval Institute Press, 1996 [orig. pub. 1972].

———. *A Gentlemanly and Honorable Profession: The Creation of the U.S. Naval Officer Corps, 1794–1815.* Annapolis, Md.: Naval Institute Press, 1991.

McNeil, J. *Charleston's Navy Yard.* Charleston, S.C.: Naval Civilian Administrators Association, 1985.

Miller, John C. *The Federalist Era 1789–1801.* New York: Harper & Bros., 1960.

Miller, Nathan. *Sea of Glory: A Naval History of the American Revolution.* Annapolis, Md.: Naval Institute Press, 1992 [orig. pub. 1974].

Mitchell, S. *A Family Lawsuit: The Story of Elisabeth Patterson and Jerome Bonaparte.* New York: Farrar, Straus and Cudahy, 1958.

Moreau de St. Méry's American Journey 1793–1798. Trans. Kenneth M. Roberts and Anna M. Roberts. Garden City, N.Y.: Doubleday & Co., 1947.

Morison, Elting E. *From Know-How to Nowhere: The Development of Technology.* New York: New American Library, 1977 [orig. pub. 1974].

Morison, Samuel Eliot. *The Maritime History of Massachusetts 1783–1860.* Boston: Houghton Mifflin Co., 1941 [orig. pub. 1921].

Morris, Charles. *The Autobiography of Commodore Charles Morris.* Boston: A. Williams & Co., 1880.

Mullin, John. *The Baltimore Directory, for 1799, Containing the Names, Occupations, and Places of Abode of the Citizens, Arranged in Alphabetical Order.* Baltimore: Warner & Hanna, 1799.

Neal, David Augustus. "Salem Men in the Early Nineteenth Century." *Essex Institute Historical Collections* 75 (1939): 1–14.

Newman, Simon P. *Parades and the Politics of the Street: Festive Culture in the Early American Republic.* Philadelphia: University of Pennsylvania Press, 1997.

North, Douglass C. *The Economic Growth of the United States 1790–1860.* New York: W.W. Norton & Co., 1966 [orig. pub. 1961].

Owens, Hamilton. *Baltimore on the Chesapeake.* Garden City, N.Y.: Doubleday, Doran & Co., 1941.

Paine, Ralph D. *The Old Merchant Marine.* New Haven, Conn.: Yale University Press, 1919.

Palmer, Michael A. *Stoddert's War: Naval Operations During the Quasi-War with France, 1798–1801.* Columbia: University of South Carolina Press, 1987.

Paullin, Charles Oscar. *American Voyages to the Orient 1690–1865.* Annapolis, Md.: Naval Institute Press, 1971 [orig. pub. 1910–11].

———. *Commodore John Rodgers: Captain, Commodore, and Senior Officer of the American Navy, 1773–1838.* Annapolis, Md.: Naval Institute Press, 1967 [orig. pub. 1910].

Phillips, James Duncan. *Salem and the Indies.* Boston: Houghton Mifflin Co., 1947.

Pinckney, P. A. *American Figureheads and their Carvers.* New York: W.W. Norton & Co., 1940.

Plumer, William. *Memorandum of the Proceedings in the United States Senate 1803–1807.* Ed. Edward S. Brown. New York: Macmillan Co., 1923.

Pope, Dudley. *The Black Ship.* New York: Henry Holt and Co., 1998 [orig. pub. 1963].

———. *Life in Nelson's Navy.* London: Unwin Hyman Ltd., 1987 [orig. pub. 1981].

Pratt, Fletcher. *The Navy: A History.* Garden City, N.Y.: Garden City Publishing Co., 1941.

———. *Preble's Boys: Commodore Preble and the Birth of American Sea Power.* New York: William Sloane Associates, 1950.

Preble, George Henry. "The Navy, and the Charlestown Navy Yard." Chapter 5 in *The Memorial History of Boston.* Ed. Justin Windsor. Boston: James R. Osgood & Co., 1881.

Richards, Rhys. "United States Trade With China 1784–1814." *American Neptune* 54 (1994): 5–76.

Robinson, Ralph J. "Shipbuilding on the Patapsco; Part II: The Glorious Eighteenth Century." *Baltimore* 50 (1957): 32–51.

Rogers, George C., Jr. *Charleston in the Age of the Pinckneys.* Columbia: University of South Carolina Press, 1980.

Ruckert, Norman. *The Fells Point Story.* Baltimore: Bodine & Associates, Inc., 1976.

Samuelson, Paul A. *Economics.* 10th ed. New York: McGraw-Hill Book Co., 1976.

Scharf, J. Thomas, and Thompson Westcott. *History of Philadelphia 1609–1884.* Vol. 3. Philadelphia: L.H. Everts & Co., 1884.

Schom, Alan. *Napoleon Bonaparte.* New York: HarperCollins, 1997.

Shaw, Peter. *The Character of John Adams.* New York: W.W. Norton & Co., 1977.

Smelser, Marshall. *The Congress Founds the Navy 1787–1798.* Notre Dame: University of Notre Dame Press, 1959.

———. "The Jacobin Phrenzy: Federalism and the Menace of Liberty, Equality, and Fraternity." *Review of Politics* 13 (1951): 457–82.

Smith, E. Vale. *History of Newburyport.* Newburyport: privately printed, 1854.

Smith, Jean Edward. *John Marshall: Definer of a Nation.* New York: Henry Holt and Co., 1996.

Smith, Page. *John Adams.* 2 vols. Garden City, N.Y.: Doubleday & Co., 1962.

Smith, Philip Chadwick Foster. *The Frigate Essex Papers: Building the Salem Frigate 1798–1799.* Salem: Peabody Museum, 1974.

Sobel, Dava. *Longitude.* New York: Walker & Co., 1995.

Steffen, Charles G. *The Merchants of Baltimore: Workers and Politics in the Age of Revolution 1763–1812.* Urbana: University of Illinois Press, 1984.

Stern, Malcolm H. "Moses Myers and the Early Jewish Community of Norfolk." *Journal of the Southern Jewish Historical Society* 1 (1958): 5–13.

Stevens, William Oliver. *An Affair of Honor: The Biography of Commodore James Barron, U.S.N.* Chesapeake, Va.: Norfolk County Historical Society, 1969.

Stinchcombe, William. *The XYZ Affair.* Westport, Conn.: Greenwood Press, 1980.

Triber, Jayne E. *A True Republican: The Life of Paul Revere.* Amherst: University of Massachusetts Press, 1998.

Tucker, Glenn. *Dawn Like Thunder: The Barbary Wars and the Birth of the U.S. Navy.* Indianapolis: Bobbs-Merrill Co., 1963.

Tucker, Spencer. *Arming the Fleet: U.S. Navy Ordnance in the Muzzle-Loading Era.* Annapolis, Md.: Naval Institute Press, 1989.

———. *The Jeffersonian Gunboat Navy.* Columbia: University of South Carolina Press, 1993.

Unger, Harlow Giles. *Noah Webster: The Life and Times of an American Patriot.* New York: John Wiley & Sons, Inc., 1998.

Walters, Raymond, Jr. *Albert Gallatin: Jeffersonian Financier and Diplomat.* New York: Macmillan Co., 1957.

Ward, Townsend. "The Germantown Road and Its Associations." *Pennsylvania Magazine of History and Biography* 6 (1882): 18–19.

———. "South Second Street and Its Associations." *Pennsylvania Magazine of History and Biography* 4 (1880): 49.

Warner, Oliver. *The Battle of the Nile.* New York: Macmillan Co., 1960.

Waters, John J., Jr. *The Otis Family in Provincial and Revolutionary Massachusetts.* New York: W.W. Norton & Co., 1968.

Westlake, Merle T., Jr. "Josiah Fox, Gentleman, Quaker, Shipbuilder." *Pennsylvania Magazine of History and Biography* 88 (1964): 316–27.

Wheeler, William Bruce. "The Baltimore Jeffersonians, 1788–1800: A Profile of Intra-Factional Conflict." *Maryland Historical Magazine* 66 (1971): 153–68.

White, Leonard D. *The Federalists: A Study in Administrative History.* New York: Macmillan Co., 1948.

Whitney, William T. "The Crowninshields of Salem, 1800–1808." *Essex Institute Historical Collections* 94 (1958): 1–7.

Williams, Frances Leigh. *A Founding Family: The Pinckneys of South Carolina.* New York: Harcourt Brace Jovanovich, 1978.

Windsor, Justin, ed. *The Memorial History of Boston.* Vol. 4. Boston: James R. Osgood & Co., 1881.

Wood, Virginia Steele. *Live Oaking: Southern Timber for Tall Ships.* Annapolis, Md.: Naval Institute Press, 1995 [orig. pub. 1981].

Wright, Robert K., Jr., and Morris J. MacGregor, Jr. *Soldier-Statesmen of the Constitution.* Washington, D.C.: U.S. Army Center of Military History, 1987.

Yellott, John Bosley, Jr. "Jeremiah Yellott—Revolutionary War Privateersman and Baltimore Philanthropist." *Maryland Historical Magazine* 86 (1991): 176–89.

Newspapers

Aurora & General Advertiser (Philadelphia)
The City Gazette and Daily Advertiser (Charleston)
Columbian Centinel (Boston)
Federal Gazette & Baltimore Daily Advertiser
Gazette (Salem)
Independent Chronicle (Boston)
Newburyport Herald and Country Gazette
New York Commercial Advertiser
Norfolk Herald
Massachusetts Mercury (Boston)
Porcupine's Gazette (Philadelphia)
South Carolina Gazette & Timothy's Daily Advertiser
The Spectator (New York)
Telegraphe and Daily Advertiser (Baltimore)

Index

About the Author

Frederick C. Leiner is a partner in the law firm of Tydings & Rosenberg, LLP in Baltimore. A graduate of the University of Pennsylvania, he earned an M.Phil. in international relations from Cambridge as a Thouron Scholar and later received a law degree from the University of Virginia. The author of a dozen articles on maritime and legal history published in *American Neptune,* the Mystic Seaport *Log,* the *American Journal of Legal History,* and other journals, he was awarded the 1993–94 Vice Admiral Edwin P. Hooper Prize by the Naval Historical Center to support his research. He is married and has two sons. This is his first book.

The Naval Institute Press is the book-publishing arm of the U.S. Naval Institute, a private, nonprofit, membership society for sea service professionals and others who share an interest in naval and maritime affairs. Established in 1873 at the U.S. Naval Academy in Annapolis, Maryland, where its offices remain today, the Naval Institute has members worldwide.

Members of the Naval Institute support the education programs of the society and receive the influential monthly magazine *Proceedings* and discounts on fine nautical prints and on ship and aircraft photos. They also have access to the transcripts of the Institute's Oral History Program and get discounted admission to any of the Institute-sponsored seminars offered around the country.

The Naval Institute also publishes *Naval History* magazine. This colorful bimonthly is filled with entertaining and thought-provoking articles, first-person reminiscences, and dramatic art and photography. Members receive a discount on *Naval History* subscriptions.

The Naval Institute's book-publishing program, begun in 1898 with basic guides to naval practices, has broadened its scope in recent years to include books of more general interest. Now the Naval Institute Press publishes about one hundred titles each year, ranging from how-to books on boating and navigation to battle histories, biographies, ship and aircraft guides, and novels. Institute members receive discounts of 20 to 50 percent on the Press's more than eight hundred books in print.

Full-time students are eligible for special half-price membership rates. Life memberships are also available.

For a free catalog describing Naval Institute Press books currently available, and for further information about subscribing to *Naval History* magazine or about joining the U.S. Naval Institute, please write to:

Membership Department
U.S. Naval Institute
291 Wood Road
Annapolis, MD 21402-5034
Telephone: (800) 233-8764
Fax: (410) 269-7940
Web address: www.usni.org